The Evolution of Inquiry

Controlled, Guided, Modeled, and Free

Daniel Callison

**LIBRARIES
UNLIMITED**™

An Imprint of ABC-CLIO, LLC
Santa Barbara, California • Denver, Colorado

Library of Congress Cataloging-in-Publication Data

Callison, Daniel, 1948-
   The evolution of inquiry : controlled, guided, modeled, and free / Daniel Callison.
      pages cm.
   Includes bibliographical references and index.
   ISBN 978-1-61069-386-8 (paperback) — ISBN 978-1-61069-387-5 (ebook)   1. Information literacy—Study and teaching.   2. School librarian participation in curriculum planning.   3. Inquiry-based learning.   I. Title.
   ZA3075.C343   2015
   028.7071–dc23   2015002526

ISBN: 978-1-61069-386-8
EISBN: 978-1-61069-387-5

19 18 17 16 15   1 2 3 4 5

This book is also available on the World Wide Web as an eBook.
Visit www.abc-clio.com for details.

Libraries Unlimited
An Imprint of ABC-CLIO, LLC

ABC-CLIO, LLC
130 Cremona Drive, P.O. Box 1911
Santa Barbara, California 93116-1911

This book is printed on acid-free paper ∞
Manufactured in the United States of America

Contents

Section IV: Additional Research Reviews

Preface

THE INQUIRY PROGRESSION

Driven by advances in information technologies and greater understanding of educational theories that support student-centered learning, inquiry has progressed across curricular standards to become a powerful educational culture. This book provides an extensive overview of the past five decades and the progression toward inquiry in science, history, and language arts education and in information literacy studies. In many ways it is an exploration of the evolution *toward* inquiry as well as the evolution *of* inquiry learning.

Each of the four stages of inquiry provides a scaffold that builds a support for the independent, mature learner who is free to explore the expanding information age with the tools and skills gained through controlled exercises, guided investigations, and modeled or mentored independent research projects. Student learning is centered on projects of depth, relevance, and personal interest as well as meeting the need for a rigorous experience. Authentic learning through inquiry is most likely found where personal, future professional, and current academic requirements meet in a confluence that motivates a desire for discovery.

DEFINING LEVELS OF INQUIRY

In 2004 Annette Lamb, Leslie Preddy, and I organized a cadre of teachers and school librarians to present at the American Library Association annual conference. This group introduced many of the principles defining levels of inquiry learning (Callison 2003). These included the following:

- Directed inquiry: meets standards and is manageable—a good place to start and practice.
  - Assigned questions are drawn from standards that match a student's grade level.
  - Questions can be addressed from the information sources that are locally organized and accessible.
  - Questions are of general interest to the student and to most of the class.
  - The assignment is challenging and demands use of multiple resources.
  - The primary goal is for students to learn through practicing a process.
- Guided inquiry: is challenging and exciting—maturation in application of inquiry.
  - The student, with guidance from the librarian and other teachers, selects inquiry questions of high personal interest.
  - Topics are examined through brainstorming, content mapping, and question extension.
  - Questions are often based on previous inquiry experiences.
  - Topics are developed with depth and meaning that will require consideration of multiple conclusions based on extensive reading and original data collection.
  - Results and recommendations can be presented in conjunction with peer presentations, allowing for comparison of experiences.
  - Collaborative groups can continue investigations as new questions are raised.

o **Modeled**—As a cognitive apprentice, the maturing inquirer works closely with a mentor who models higher level research techniques by completing projects with the learner.

- **Free inquiry** will often extend beyond the classroom, and the student takes on more independent responsibilities.

  o Questions are drawn from the independent student's personal curiosity and successful inquiry practice and are documented in a portfolio of previous inquiry projects.

  o The questions are so exciting to the student that the student dedicates a great deal of time beyond school hours to the investigation.

  o Original data are collected through appropriate methods, including interviews, observations, surveys, and/or experiments.

  o Presentation of results is as important as the process because it will engage peers, parents, and others from the learning community in critical defense of the findings.

  o The student's self-reflection attempts to identify those resources, techniques, and support groups that are most important and worthwhile in order to provide a framework for even more demanding inquiry in higher education and in a future career.

INQUIRY AND NATIONAL STANDARDS

Inquiry has progressed to the extent it influences all national learning standards and serves as the framework for the information curriculum of the twenty-first century, including guidelines from the American Association of School Librarians (AASL). Across the chapters of this book are elaborations on information inquiry that tie five key elements to each of the popular information process models (see figure 1). Questioning and exploration interact to open new venues of study. Assimilation and inference interact to develop critical thinking skills, generation of data, and selective acquisition of documentation—primary or secondary. Reflection on an individual piece of information, method, or extensive project helps both the learner and the teacher mature in their abilities to place value on information.

This text is constructed on research from academic leaders in science education, instructional technology, and communication, as well as reviewers of school library media management. It provides one of the most extensive and recent reviews of research on the Internet searching and electronic resource selection and application behaviors of young people. While information search processes are important, learner maturation in selection of credible information to answer information needs is critical.

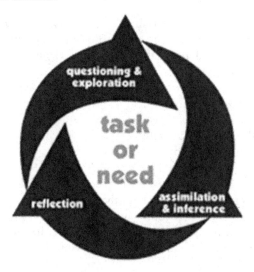

**Figure 1. Callison's Recursive Cycle of Information Inquiry
and Interactive Elements** (Callison 2003)

YOUNG LEARNERS AND CREDIBLE INFORMATION NEEDS

A meta-analysis of three hundred studies recently compiled through the Berkman Center for Internet & Society at Harvard University (Gasser et al. 2012) identified several behaviors by adolescents in selection and nonselection of credible information from the Internet, the medium that now dominates the information pool for teens:

- When searching through Web sites, younger users pay much attention to visual elements, including the quality of the graphics and multimedia.
- According to multiple studies, the termination of the search process depends not only on the finding of satisfactory information, but also on factors such as motivation, boredom, time limit, and information overload.
- Perhaps the most important cue for youth—in the search context as well as with respect to the evaluation of sites—is that of visual and interactive elements, as a number of studies indicate. Importantly, there is also some evidence that youth do see graphics and multimedia not just as indicators of overall quality, but as information objects that are open to quality judgments.
- Research shows that youth may acquire a number of skills as they create and disseminate content on the Internet. Broadly speaking, such practices allow youth to develop better skills in navigating the information environment and making judgments about the quality of information (9–10).

In addition, we also know that the more personally important the information is to young searchers (much like adults), the more likely it is that they will employ systematic evaluation of the information if they have learned and practiced such a methodical approach (Gross 2006). Competent adult mentors, including parents, classroom teachers, and school librarians, can greatly influence the motivation for engaging adolescents in complex information searching and credible information judgment if they model successful techniques on topics of high relevance to young learners.

TEACHERS SEE A NEED TO TEACH SELECTION OF CREDIBLE INFORMATION

Another national review from the Pew Research Center (Purcell et al. 2012) has reported growth in the use of Internet resources by high school students in advanced placement courses. Among the more positive impacts are the following:

- The best students access a greater depth and breadth of information on topics that *interest them.*
- Students can take advantage of the availability of educational material in engaging multimedia formats.
- Many students become more self-reliant researchers. (2012, 2)

However, most of the teachers surveyed also expressed concern that students rely too heavily on search engines, and a vast majority say a top priority in today's classrooms should be teaching students how to judge the quality of online information. These teachers also reported a shift away from doing research as a relatively slow process of intellectual curiosity and discovery to a fast-paced, short-term exercise aimed at simply locating just enough information to complete an assignment (Purcell et al. 2012).

COLLABORATION AND SPACE NEEDED FOR EFFECTIVE INQUIRY

Also reviewed in this book are the most current thoughts on collaboration among teachers and library media specialists, as well as future facility design concepts suited to stimulate meaningful inquiry. Spaces for the information learning laboratory are envisioned. In what new spaces can we provide students the opportunity to experiment with data, determine their value, and make revisions in order to support convincing arguments?

On a practical basis, this book reviews inquiry methods now adopted by leading educators in science education, historical inquiry, and language arts. Methods are introduced that draw on the new Common Core State Standards (CCSS) to suggest workable means to explore and exchange ideas. This book provides a review of leading inquiry models that have resulted in the following applications:

- Help educators gain an understanding of the historical development of inquiry learning in formal and informal settings.
- Showcase ways in which inquiry principles can be learned and applied across the K–12 curriculum.
- Equip professional library media specialists with an understanding of collaboration that supports a leadership role in curriculum development.
- Illustrate the expectations for inquiry learning based on critical thinking and the ability to make a clear argument with supporting, relevant evidence selected using logical reasoning.

STUDENT INFORMATION SCIENTISTS, GRAPHIC INQUIRY, AND THE ARGUMENT CURRICULUM

Based on an analogy of the "student as information scientist," an inquiry framework for students as critical evaluators of information is outlined in this book. Within our ever-expanding visual information world, the principles of information literacy are expanded to fully embrace "graphic inquiry" for teaching and learning through shared illustrations (see principles given in Table P.1. The most critical method yet to be introduced for determining the value of information, student debate of evidence in the "argument curriculum," is also described. Each of these approaches parallels selected standards in the 2014 CCSS, and they demonstrate an evolution beyond basic fact-finding activities.

RELATIONSHIP TO THE COMMON CORE

Evolution toward information inquiry is reflected in the Common Core State Standards Initiative "Key Shifts in English Language Arts" (2014):

Though the standards still expect narrative writing throughout the grades, they also expect a command of sequence and detail that are essential for effective argumentative and informative writing. The standards' focus on evidence-based writing along with the ability to inform and persuade is a significant shift from current practice.

The maturation of the student inquirer is measured by the abilities to select and use the best possible information available within his or her needs rather than settling for the most convenient information that simply meets initial satisfaction or finishes the assignment quickly. In the information age, powered by the Internet, students must employ inquiry methods that help them manage persistent information evaluation that leads to acceptance or rejection of new information while controlling for unfounded bias and incorrect interpretations.

A TIME LINE OF THE EVOLUTION

This text provides an extensive historical perspective on information literacy and inquiry learning. It shows the evolution to a greater understanding and acceptance of student-centered learning. Founded on this history, the future of inquiry-based learning K–12 is reflected in the chapters that follow.

Table P.1. Basic Reporting Steps Evolving Across Elements of Information Inquiry and Graphic Inquiry

Basic Descriptive Reporting	Information Inquiry for Support of Science and Argument	Graphic Inquiry to Clarify and Enhance Persuasive Evidence
What are the facts to record concerning who, what, where, and when?	**Questioning:** What questions focus on how and why, and which are most meaningful?	What visuals help to present data clearly and eventually derive new data leading to new questions?
Limited to a single event and a few immediately related events.	**Exploration:** A broad continuation of reading, listening, and viewing is done that gives a wider context for all associated happenings.	Viewing and producing various media help to determine the most effective manner to understand and to present information visually.
Do the facts fit together for a story?	**Assimilation:** Base knowledge is confirmed, clarified, revised, or rejected in order to see the value of new evidence. The most credible information is sought.	Insights are gained from visual patterns resulting in acceptance, modification, or rejection in order to edit the visuals in support of arguments.
Given what is known from this one incident, what might be suggested or elaborated?	**Inference:** Conclusions are reached based on evidence and are tested through argument, debates, and proposals for action.	Charts, tables, and other illustrations serve to strengthen arguments and clarify plans for change.
This is one single incident, and much more needs to be explored before adequate conclusions can be drawn.	**Reflection:** In what manner was the gathering and analysis of information unbiased, relevant, authoritative, and meaningful in addressing early questions and raising new questions? Has this inquiry provided lessons leading to more effective and efficient future investigations?	To what degree did visuals convey the messages essential to persuade the intended audience? Do the visuals not distort or in some manner lead to false conclusions? Do the visuals broaden the audience who will understand conclusions and recommendations?
Sample Relevant Common Core Standards:	Develop claims and counterclaims fairly and thoroughly, supplying the most relevant data and evidence for each while pointing out the strengths and limitations of both claims and counterclaims in a discipline-appropriate form that anticipates the audience's knowledge level, concerns, values, and possible biases.	Introduce a topic and organize complex ideas, concepts, and information so that each new element builds on that which precedes it to create a unified whole; include formatting (e.g., headings), graphics (e.g., figures, tables), and multimedia when useful to aiding comprehension.

This publication is a guide for those teachers and media specialists who wish to leave simple fact-only activities behind, and collaborate to explore the greater potential of well-managed inquiry. Such rich learning environments are yet to be fully realized, but they are waiting for those who have the abilities to experiment and lead. This is not a map of completed lessons ready to cut and paste. This is a collection of notions from over the past half century to help educators look forward to the next progressions of information inquiry.

For those who want to work from inquiry learning and teaching concepts proposed and practiced over the past fifty years, extensive resources are provided for dozens of ideas to test and expand. Those who are beginners in teaching the inquiry process may find useful entry level examples at http://www.schoollibrarymonthly.com/CCSS resources.pdf. Nearly all of these items can be accessed in full text through EBSCO and by searching the rich collection of materials from *School Library Monthly*. This book, therefore, is an important tool for educators to expand their thinking and practice of inquiry and to expand its evolution over the next fifty years. These pages provide the links to hundreds of proven activities.

FUTURE NEED: MEASURING INFORMATION INQUIRY

On the immediate horizon in the continued evolution of inquiry is the development of methods to measure the value of inquiry practices. How do we know the student has gained the valuable abilities described in various models for inquiry learning? Callison and Baker (2014) have identified the following as important questions yet to be answered in the continued evolution to measure information inquiry:

- How do students identify conflicting information, document its differences, and resolve use of that information which seems most credible?
- How can they document the value of primary and secondary sources, and select the bbest, not just those that are4 mediocre and simply satisfactory?
- How can they document how they deal with personal bias as well as bias found in the text?
- How do students deal with encountering new information that can shift the inquiry dramatically?
- How can students practice original data gathering and analysis in a mode that fits their cognitive level?
- How can students demonstrate growth in their sophistication to produce their own graphics to suit various audience expectations?
- In what manner can students reflect on their inquiry experience so that they demonstrate effective understanding of how to locate the most credible information possible?
- How can students document what they have learned from their peers and mentors?
- In what manner can students build a portfolio that is a record of inquiry achievements throughout their academic careers?
- How can the number of teachers and librarians who model inquiry and practice research skills increase so that more students can work closely with a mentor who is competent and motivates for success?

The more learners respect the competence of their mentors, understand various values of different sources, and are encouraged to test information through argument, debate and graphic representation, the stronger will be their inquiry skills in the Information Age.

REFERENCES

Callison, D. 2003. *Key Words, Concepts and Methods for Information Age Instruction*. Baltimore, MD: LMS Associates.

Callison, D., et al. 2004. "Information Inquiry: Key Words, Concepts, and Assessments for Literacy K–College." Paper presented at the American Library Association National Conference, Orlando, Florida.

Callison, D., and K. Baker. 2014. "The Elements of Information Inquiry, Evolution of Models, and Measured Reflection." *Knowledge Quest* 43, no. 2: 18–24.

Common Core State Standards (CCSS) Initiative. 2014. "Key Shifts in English Language Arts." http://www.corestandards.org/other-resources/key-shifts-in-english-language-arts/ (accessed September 25, 2014).

Gasser, U., et al. 2012. "Youth and Digital Media: From Credibility to Information Quality." Research Publication 2012-1, Berkman Center for Internet & Society at Harvard University.

Gross, M. 2006. *Studying Children's Questions*. Lanham, MD: Scarecrow.

Purcell, K., et al. 2012. *How Teens Do Research in the Digital World*. Washington, DC: Pew Research Center.

Acknowledgments

This book is dedicated to Patty because of her love, support, and encouragement over the past forty-five years.

I also express my thanks to several educators who have worked with me to determine the key elements of information inquiry. They include Annette Lamb, senior lecturer at Indiana University in Indianapolis; Paula Montgomery, founding editor of *School Library Media Activities Monthly*; Nancy Everhart, past president of AASL and chair of the top-ranked graduate school library media program at Florida State*; Leslie Preddy, president-elect of AASL and my coauthor on *The Blue Book*; Kym Kramer, director of graduate school library media programs at IUPUI; Julia Robinson, school library innovator in Indiana and New Mexico; Katie Baker, computer technology teacher at Sycamore School in Indianapolis; Deborah Levitov, managing editor of *School Library Monthly*; and Sharon Coatney, acquisition editor for Libraries Unlimited. My highest appreciation goes to recently promoted and tenured Carol L. Tilley at the University of Illinois, the top-ranked graduate program in services for children and young adults.*

*Based on the most recent rankings from *U.S. News and World Report*, March 26, 2013.

Section I

Inquiry Controlled, Guided, Modeled, and Free

Chapter 1

Key Artifacts Reflecting Progression and Evolution Toward Inquiry

Artifacts are items created by humans that provide information about the culture and values of those who first created them. In the case of the evolution of inquiry within the information literacy movement of the past forty years, the following artifacts taken from the school library media literature provide a quick description of the goals for learning and teaching through inquiry.

The progression to student-centered, inquiry-based learning through school library programs was clearly underway more than forty years ago. The full evolution, however, has yet to fully emerge.

1972: CREATIVE INQUIRY AND INSTRUCTIONAL MEDIA VIEWED AS EDUCATIONAL DOMAINS FOR MEDIA CENTERS

Taylor, Kenneth I. "Creative Inquiry and Instructional Media: A Revision of a Theory Underlying the Continuing Development of the School Instructional Media Center and Its Program." *School Media Quarterly* (Fall 1972): 18–26.

- "Because there is no set sequence of steps in creative inquiry, a student should be able to move from one condition to another with ease, working in one momentarily and in another at greater length. His ultimate goal is the pleasurable discovery of what are, at least to him, new ideas and, eventually, the development of original media in which he/she conveys his/her ideas to others" (20).
- "It is conceivable that the training of all students to create a variety of media for purposes of creative inquiry may become the most rapidly growing service of future media centers" (23).
- The learner is at the center of instructional interests, and learning is the central outcome (22).
- "When students have the opportunity to relate their own pasts of, say[,] twelve or fourteen years, to the pasts of others, they are in a position to develop personal ideas, personal procedures, and personal communications which are uniquely their own" (21).

1983: INFORMATION SKILLS ARE NEEDED ACROSS THE CURRICULUM

Marland, Michael. "Information Skills and the Whole-School Curriculum." Paper Presented to the British Library Conference, London, October 1983. Referenced by Betty Cleaver in "Thinking about Information: Skills for Lifelong Learning," *School Library Media Quarterly* (Fall 1987): 29–31.

- Michael Marland, a British educator and curriculum specialist, has been concerned that schools are not teaching students to be effective library and information *users*. Few schools have a whole-school curriculum policy that introduces, practices, and contextualizes the range of information handling skills.
- Marland's proposed curriculum would emphasize such concepts as selection, rejection, evaluation, organization, topic definition, and question definition. The student who masters these would be prepared to examine information critically, look for relationships, and put bits of information together in new ways that could result in new insights or knowledge. From Michael Marland, *Information Skills in the Secondary Curriculum*. London: Methuen Educational, 1981.

1984: SOCIAL STUDIES INFORMATION CREDIBILITY SKILLS IN THE INFORMATION MANAGEMENT CURRICULUM

National Council for Social Studies. Task Force on Scope and Sequence. "In Search of a Scope and Sequence for Social Studies." *Social Education* 48, no. 4 (April 1984): 260–261. Referenced in Jacqueline C. Mancall, Shirley L. Aaron, and Sue A. Walker, "Teaching Students to Think: The Role of the School Library Media Program," *School Library Media Quarterly* (Fall 1986): 18–27.

- Evaluate sources of information–print, visual, electronic.
- Use picture clues and picture captions to aid comprehension.
- Use a computer catalog service.
- Compare and contrast credibility of differing accounts of the same event.
- Combine critical concepts into a statement of conclusions based on information.
- Propose a new plan of operation, create a new system, or devise a futuristic scheme based on available information.
- Estimate the adequacy of information.

1985: SKILLS FOR CRITICAL THINKING USING ANALYSIS AND EVALUATION

Beyer, Barry K. "Critical Thinking: What Is It?" *Social Education* 49, no.4 (April 1985): 270–276. Referenced in Jacqueline C. Mancall, Shirley L. Aaron, and Sue A. Walker, "Teaching Students to Think: The Role of the School Library Media Program," *School Library Media Quarterly* (Fall 1986): 18–27.

Beyer has emphasized that critical thinking is not the same as problem solving per se. He sees agreement among specialists that critical thinking is the ability to assess the authenticity, accuracy, and/or worth of knowledge claims and arguments. He perceives this as a collection of discrete skills or operations, each of which to some degree or other combines analysis and evaluation.

In setting up a core group of competencies related to the acquisition of the ability to think critically, Beyer focuses on those areas school library media specialists have consistently identified as central to their instructional programs. The ten skills that represent a consensus of scholarly reflection, as well as learning research and classroom experience, are:

- distinguishing between verifiable facts and value claims;
- determining the reliability of a source;
- determining the factual accuracy of a statement;
- distinguishing relevant from irrelevant information, claims, or reasons;
- detecting bias;
- identifying unstated assumptions;
- identifying ambiguous or equivocal claims or arguments;
- recognizing logical inconsistencies or fallacies in a line of reasoning;
- distinguishing between warranted or unwarranted claims; and
- determining the strength of an argument.

1985: ERRORS EDUCATORS MAKE IN DESIGNING ACTIVITIES INTENDED TO TEACH CRITICAL THINKING

Sternberg, Robert J. "Teaching Critical Thinking, Part 1: Are We Making Critical Mistakes?" *Phi Delta Kappan* 67, no. 3 (November 1985): 194–198. Referenced in Jacqueline C. Mancall, Shirley L. Aaron, and Sue A. Walker, "Teaching Students to Think: The Role of the School Library Media Program," *School Library Media Quarterly* (Fall 1986): 18–27.

- Educators define problems for students to solve, while in the everyday world the first and often most difficult step is recognition that a problem exists.
- Educators pose well-structured problems, while life poses ill-structured ones.
- Educators provide along with the problem much of the information to solve it, while in everyday problem solving it is not obvious what information is needed or where it can be found.
- Educators pose problems in isolation, while solutions to everyday problems depend on context and interaction.
- Educators endorse a "best" solution, while everyday problems generally have no one right solution and no obvious criteria for a best solution.
- Educators pose problems based on formal knowledge, while solutions to everyday problems require as much informal as formal knowledge.
- Educators design problems to be solved on an individual basis, while everyday problem solving often occurs in groups.

1985: LEARNERS ARE AT RISK WITHOUT MEDIA SPECIALIST MEDIATION IN THE EMERGING INFORMATION WORLD

Liesener, James W. "Learning at Risk: School Library Media Programs in an Information World." *School Library Media Quarterly* (Fall 1985): 11–20.

- "The development of higher level intellectual and problem solving skills can only be developed in an environment where they can be repeatedly applied and tested throughout the learner's school experience. The cumulative effect of many of these kinds of experiences is what leads to the development of a self-directed learner able and motivated for life-long learning.

  This kind of information learning laboratory requires a level of sophistication and responsiveness far beyond the current service level of "materials availability" combined with the possibility of some limited assistance" (13).
- "The independence of mind that comes with a personal, free, and independent interaction with ideas also kindles the kinds of appreciations and understandings that permit the enjoyment of the subtleties of life and the aesthetic aspects of our world.

  The primary function performed by the school library media specialist or program can be viewed as a mediation function. From this perspective, the specialist plays the role of an intermediary between the incredibly complex and rapidly expanding information world and the client.

  In this sense, the library media specialist is no different than a librarian or information specialist in any other environment. It is the particular environment and the particular needs of the clients served that provide the special focus. Obviously, the environment in this case is the school and the clients are the students, teachers, school staff and, at times, parents" (14).
- "It is high time that this profession . . . redesign library media instruction and services in the light of our primitive but growing understanding of information seeking behavior as well as the impact of more sophisticated technology" (19).

1986: FROM 1950 TO 1984, THE PROFESSIONAL STANDARDS SUPPORTED THE EMERGING INSTRUCTIONAL ROLE

Craver, Kathleen W. "The Changing Instructional Role of the High School Library Media Specialist: 1950–84; A Survey of Professional Literature, Standards, and Research Studies. *School Library Media Quarterly* 14, no. 4 (Summer 1986): 183–191.

- "It is evident from an analysis of two data sources that an evolution in the instructional role of the library media specialist did occur from 1950 to 1984. A clear pattern of progressive development of the instructional role has persisted in the standards and the literature. The changes in the library media specialist's role from study hall monitor to curriculum designer can certainly be termed substantive. An analysis of research studies, however, indicates a possible time lag between the practiced instructional role of the library media specialist and the one espoused in the literature. In a profession that has undergone such a tremendous amount of change in such a short period of time, this gap is not surprising. Library media specialists should be congratulated that their professional organizations and publications have responded so quickly and positively to the need for change and that they have continued to successfully expand their instructional role with the school of the 1980s" (190).

1986: BEYOND LOCATION—TEACHING AND PRACTICING METACOGNITIVE SKILLS, BEHAVIORS, AND IDEAS

Mancall, Jacqueline C., Shirley L. Aaron, and Sue A. Walker. "Teaching Students to Think: The Role of the School Library Media Program." *School Library Media Quarterly* (Fall 1986): 18–27.

- "Library media specialists have traditionally described their raison d'etre as one of promoting access to a broad range of information and ideas, in order to assist students in acquiring the knowledge, skills, and attitudes necessary to function effectively in an information society.
  Library media specialists . . . realize that a major part of their time must be spent helping students develop the thinking skills that will equip them to not only locate, but also evaluate and use information effectively and thereby become information literate" (19).
- "If such [critical thinking and information use] instruction is to be effective, two conditions must be met: first, the student must be developmentally ready to learn the skill; and second, the student must realize that use of the skill will be effective in solving a personal cognitive problem" (22).
- "Information management skills instruction . . . must be broad and more process oriented. Focus must go beyond locational skills and 'correct answers' and move to strategies that will help students to develop insight and facility in structuring successful approaches to solving their information needs" (23).

1986: SCHOOL LIBRARY MEDIA SPECIALISTS AND OTHER TEACHERS CAN MODEL METACOGNITIVE BEHAVIORS

Bertland, Linda H. "An Overview of Research in Metacognition: Implications for Information Skills Instruction." *School Library Media Quarterly* (Winter 1986): 96–99.

Teachers should act as models of metacognitive behavior. As such, they should do the following:

- "Think out loud about the processes in which they engage, in terms of planning their approach to a problem, monitoring their comprehension, developing strategies, and performing self-evaluation. Such an approach is easily translated to techniques for teach[ing] students how to approach a research paper" (96).

- "Engage students in activities that force them to think about their own thinking. Help them to take a hard and clear look at what they know about a problem they are trying to solve; assist them in clearly spelling out what tasks are essential in solving the problem and in identifying the strategies they will use to perform the tasks" (96).
- "Allow students to teach each other by working in small groups. Have them keep records of their goals, the strategies used for reaching them, and evaluations of ongoing efforts" (97).
- "Provide opportunities for training in strategies that will help students monitor their own comprehension and planning activities" (97).
- "Help students develop the ability to ask the right question" (97).
- "Provide actual hands-on experience" (97).
- "Work with teachers on precise explanations of the exact nature of assignments so students are aware of the task parameters involved and the possible difficulties they may encounter along the way" (97).

1986: FREE INQUIRY CAN OPEN COLLABORATIVE OPPORTUNITIES FOR MEDIA SPECIALISTS AS TEACHERS

Callison, Daniel. "School Library Media Programs & Free Inquiry Learning." *School Library Journal* (February 1986): 20–24.

- "The media specialist as teacher must not only be concerned with demonstrating expertise as an instructor, but must resist the traditional classroom routines which prevent free inquiry learning from taking place" (22).
- "A team approach is the strongest method in the free inquiry exercise. Group work can lead to positive interactions and valuable peer reflections" (23).
- "Students are often placed in the position of submitting their work to one judge–the classroom teacher. Free inquiry should encourage a sharing of student findings with other students, teachers, and above all, parents" (23).
- "The key to measuring the success of free inquiry learning through the media program is observation of students who formulate their own questions. They extract [data] and summarize the issues and show us they not only can raise questions themselves, but know where and how to pursue the answer. We may not be able to measure satisfaction or enjoyment in the student, but media specialists should record the occasions when the active process of free inquiry takes place. Those happenings are the result of the teacher and media specialist successfully implementing the media program as a learning laboratory" (23).

1987: INQUIRY CAN BE MOST EFFECTIVE WHEN APPLIED TO LOCAL ISSUES OF INTEREST TO STUDENTS

Sheingold, Karen. "Keeping Children's Knowledge Alive through Inquiry." *School Library Media Quarterly* 15, no. 2 (Winter 1987): 80–85.

- "Inquiry is a complex process that includes formulating a problem or question, searching through and/or collecting information to address the problem or questions, making sense of that information, and developing an understanding of, point of view about, or 'answer' to the questions. Three elements of inquiry are particularly important–how inquiry can be motivated, the centrality of questions as part of inquiry, and the executive or metacognitive aspects of inquiry" (82).
- "Inquiry should be motivated by questions whose purpose, meaning, or relation to the real world is apparent to the child. If teachers, librarians, media specialists, and researchers . . . are successful in making inquiry part of children's education. . . . [w]e will see children working together on projects that come out of questions they have generated" (83–84).

1987: HIGHER-ORDER THINKING SKILLS CAN BE PRESENTED THROUGH MEDIA

Smith, Jane Bandy. "Higher-Order Thinking Skills and Nonprint Media." *School Library Media Quarterly* (Fall 1987): 38–41.

- "Thinking is a difficult task: it is not a natural phenomenon. Barriers to good thinking include our tendency to settle for the first solution, having biases that affect our decisions, and accepting evidence as factual without questioning it. Too many of us are addicted to being told what to think and do. Even in professional education sessions, people become irate if they are not given models to follow. They are antagonistic or frustrated if asked to develop their own patterns" (38).
- "When thinking skills are imbedded in course content, they should be introduced within content that students already know since it is difficult for them to perfect a skill and learn the content and ignore the thinking skills. Once students have a clear understanding of the purpose and procedure involved in a thinking process, they should be provided ample opportunity to practice using the skill. Students should also be given opportunities to apply reasoning skills to everyday situations so that they will see that thinking is part of everyday life" (39).
- "Mass media provide a bountiful source for materials that are useful in thinking-skill activities. Video recordings of political speeches or advertisements are opportunities to analyze information in order to detect evidence of propaganda techniques such as the bandwagon effect, glitteration, equivocation, and oversimplification. Watching different news reports of the same event can give students an opportunity to compare different treatments, various methods of organization, focuses, and points of view. . . . Visual literacy permeates thinking skill development. Students . . . should have to address the same multifaceted dilemmas that exist in the real world" (40–41).

1987: LIBRARY INFORMATION INSTRUCTION IS FOCUSED ON LEARNING, NOT SIMPLY SOURCES AND TOOLS

Kuhlthau, Carol C. "An Emerging Theory of Library Instruction." *School Library Media Quarterly* (Fall 1987): 23–28.

- "The broader view of library skills goes beyond location of materials to the use of information. It centers on thinking about the ideas in the library collection rather than merely locating the sources in the collection. It emphasizes seeking evidence to shape a topic rather than to answer a specific question. It considers the process of a search for information as well as the product of the library research" (23).
- "The main disadvantage of the source approach is the lack of transfer to other situations of information seeking. The knowledge of the tool rather than the application of the tool becomes the objective in different information need situations. Teaching sources in isolation does not promote understanding of the connections between sources or of the view of the library as an interconnected source of information" (24).
- "We are moving into a new era of school library media services where library instruction is fully integrated into classroom learning; where the information in the library media center is essential for meeting the instructional objectives of the school; where the library media program is critical to the thinking and learning taking place throughout the school. The emerging theoretical base for library instruction combining learning theory, research in information seeking behavior, and a broader view of library skills provides a framework for assessing existing instruction and developing new programs. Theory-based library instruction prepares children for learning in an information society" (27).

1987: THE SCHOOL LIBRARY MEDIA SPECIALIST MUST BE AN ACTIVE FORCE IN CURRICULUM DEVELOPMENT

Breivik, Patricia Senn. "The Role of Libraries in the Search for Educational Excellence." *School Library Media Quarterly* (Fall 1987): 45–46.

- "There also needs to be a reconsideration of how professional librarians and, in some cases, library support staff allocate their time. I would argue that time spent on curriculum and study committees are among the best uses of personnel time. I say that with the caveat that the librarians must function as full committee participants, not merely as watchdogs for library concerns. One hopes that when a librarian is on a curriculum committee, the librarian is contributing as much or more information than any other member both for personal experience and from appropriate information that can be retrieved from libraries" (46).

Chapter 2

Evolution of Controlled Inquiry

In 1999 Daniel Callison offered definitions for four levels of inquiry. In recent years Guided Inquiry (Kuhlthau 2010) has rightfully gained new and expanded attention. A reasonable, educated guess is that at least 90 percent of the multiple resource exercises now offered under the concept of inquiry are controlled or guided. Several studies have shown how difficult it is to move most students to levels of high self-regulation (Pitts 1995; Wolf 2007), or free inquiry. At controlled and guided levels, greater emphasis is given to meeting student interests and encouraging reasonable, age-appropriate, learner-centered roles. Such a shift forward in itself is a progression worth noting.

In the past two decades instructional interventions for teachers and library media specialists have been developed and implemented to not only increase the potential for student success in the inquiry experience, but also allow inquiry to be moved more and more in the direction of free, open, or independent inquiry driven by more responsible roles for the learner. The ultimate goal for promoting inquiry-based learning is for more and more students to reach the level of independent learner for college and career, and ultimately for life. These levels help us understand how we can establish situations in which students may demonstrate signs of mature inquiry abilities before leaving school.

Any given student may benefit more or less from different degrees of freedom in the inquiry process. A student who enters an inquiry project with a mature or sophisticated content level may move into mentored or even free inquiry, unlike a content novice who is the same age. The mature inquirer, however, may find the need to start with more controlled inquiry experiences if he or she is faced with a new content topic. Experiences gained in learning the inquiry process may move that learner forward at a faster pace than if he or she had not experienced inquiry before. Thus, experience with the process and being able to visualize the inquiry process through one of the models now available can result in efficient management of a complex set of tasks built on successful experiences (Wolf and Brush 2003).

FOUR INQUIRY LEVELS

Callison's four levels are presented again in this chapter and the next, with the basic definitions offered fifteen years ago. Additional notes that summarize new perspectives are provided in the coming pages. These inquiry levels have been used in revision of science education inquiry methods, reading education, and even application of inquiry principles to professional development (Dana et al. 2011).

They remain fluid, however, as inquiry-based learning continues to evolve and expand primarily because of the continued growing access to information through the Internet. Once found almost exclusively in science education, inquiry has become an expanding teaching culture in history, language arts, reading education, sociology, and art. Inquiry has a firm foundation in the American Association of School Librarians' *Standards for the 21st Century Learner in Action* (2009) as well as the new Common Core State Standards.

CONTROLLED OR STRUCTURED INQUIRY

Then (Callison 1999): Controlled inquiry involves practice of many skills, such as raising questions, seeking factual information from a variety of sources, and conducting an interview. The topics for inquiry are usually identified by the teacher, with assurance from the library media specialist that enough resources are on hand to support all students involved.

Now: Controlled inquiry should not be looked on as a simple process, but rather, when implemented as a collaborative learning engagement to build a solid foundation for more advanced inquiry possibilities that might follow, as a very important part of the scaffold building toward greater independent learning. If the outcome of the inquiry project can easily be predicted or is secondary to learning the initial procedures for the project, then the experience is likely a controlled inquiry process.

Virginia Rankin (1999) has documented some of the most beneficial steps that students learn through repeated practice until they can apply these skills effectively. These techniques include presearch, vocabulary building, forming questions, and abstracting or synthesizing information. Rankin often conducted such sessions with groups of students so they could learn by hearing ideas from each other. Her teaching approach has been learner focused, not resource focused. She has taught students to think and plan ahead, not just locate. Her students were well prepared to advance to the next levels of Guided Inquiry.

NUDGING TOWARD INQUIRY

In recent years Kristin Fontichiaro (2014) of Michigan University has written and coordinated a regular column in *School Library Monthly* (many practicing school librarians also contribute ideas). Fontichiaro shares specific examples of lesson plans revised from static, boring drills or worksheets into activities that engage students in intriguing situations.

These revisions center on student thinking, problem solving, and development of new understandings drawn from information found leading to new ideas students generate themselves. The movement is away from just sources toward situations that are relevant, challenging, interesting, and enjoyable for students. Fontichiaro nudges inquiry forward at each stage of Stripling's Inquiry Model (Stripling 2003), demonstrating that controlled inquiry can move into more meaningful Guided Inquiry levels, even within the same lesson. Stripling's stages of inquiry apply neatly across grade levels and academic disciplines as a basis for a modern interdisciplinary, inquiry-based curriculum.

Inquiry Enhancements

Enhanced lessons with more inquiry flavoring can be powerful if copresented by teachers and school librarians who follow these three principles:

1. They are not presented in isolation, but in conjunction with meaningful academic content, and are therefore purposeful.

2. They are presented at point of need and therefore are more likely to be understood, appreciated, and used.
3. They engage students with choice in active participation in their own learning and therefore are more likely to be valued.

CONTROL OF CRITICAL ISSUES TO FOCUS INQUIRY

Other examples of controlled inquiry can be found in the excellent issues-based resources and argument curriculum developed by ABC-CLIO (http://www.abc-clio.com/). Specifically, the "Inquiry into History" lessons identify a set of issues and foundational literature to introduce students to the practice of critical inquiry.

Different materials are provided for two distinctive learner audiences, elementary and secondary. Introductory exercises are "controlled," in that students at the same level review the same materials and explore the same issues. Often students are expected to take a stand on issues, thus practicing first-level argumentative inquiry, in which learning the application of evidence to support a claim is fundamental.

TEXT SETS MANAGE RESOURCES

Text sets have gained popularity. They have been gathered commercially and by individual classroom teachers, sometimes in collaboration with school librarians. The general intention is to provide the elementary classroom with an initial pool of print and nonprint resources, especially nonfiction, that will serve to immerse students in stories and visuals relevant to the larger topic the class will explore. Text sets work as an introduction to topics, events, names, and background information. They can set the stage for questions and stories.

These resources can spark conversations as children and teachers share what they find and begin to make visual displays and question lists that describe the paths the class inquiry will take (Donham 2013). This controlled set of resources, in the hands of a talented teacher and resourceful librarian, can generate inquiry projects that move students to the next guided levels. They move ahead with a rich sharing of common literature, hopefully resulting in a common vocabulary and common set of new issues they have identified to explore in a deeper manner through their school library media center (Ebbers 2002).

CONTROLLED INQUIRY TO FOCUS ON METHODS

Other options for controlled inquiry can be practiced in various modes or techniques of information gathering and presentation. The focus can be on "how to conduct an interview" or "how to keep notes on observations in a field journal" or "how oral histories are recorded and edited." In such cases, the students learn and practice techniques that will be used later in comprehensive inquiry experiences. These experiences can be foundational for students to gain understanding of how social scientists generate new information through authentic inquiry methods.

In recent practices in science education, confirmation or verification inquiry has been associated with the descriptions of controlled inquiry (Banchi and Bell 2008). Confirmation inquiry is useful when the teacher's goal is to reinforce a previously introduced idea. Thus students may replicate a standard experiment or data-collection exercise that will confirm a principle. No new knowledge results. Confirmation through a background literature review may serve to establish what is commonly understood on a given issue before the student is eventually guided into a more specific focus for new exploration. The student is learning information-gathering methods at this point, not new disciplinary content.

COMPUTER-ASSISTED CONTROLLED INQUIRY

I have coined the phrase "computer-assisted controlled inquiry" (CACI) to describe the growing number of software programs designed to present students with problems that require use of multiple resources and peer interactions to resolve. These programs are also called "technology-enhanced support" (Kali and Linn 2008) and "multimedia support" (Saye and Brush 2002), among other terms that describe simulations presented for student interaction, usually in groups, through computerized software.

Situations in science that involve large sets of data, perhaps risky or even dangerous experimentation and expensive resources, and are aimed at reinforcing a known phenomenon, are good candidates for computer-based learning scenarios. History, sociology, and geography also seem to be good candidates for computer-simulated controlled inquiry situations.

Computer-assisted controlled inquiry can provide a structure for students to examine some major questions and to do so while accessing information fairly efficiently because documents have been preselected. Outcomes or solutions to problems may be new to the students, but for the most part they are predictable. If new insights beyond those predicted by the software do not emerge, the program is controlled, and this is a very useful method to help establish a beginning feel and understanding of inquiry. Students experience fundamentals in how information can be used to support and counter arguments. Active examples of producers of interactive multimedia software for controlled inquiry include the following:

- The Center for Education Technologies (http://www.cet.edu/?) at the Wheeling Jesuit University. The center's goal is to improve learning and teaching of science and technology through professional outreach and development. Its software has included a reference librarian role for guiding teachers, including a librarian avatar. Reference librarian support has become important for its advanced distance education program. A pedagogical software agent, ADELE (Agent for Distance Education Environments), has been operational in providing hints and rationale to guide student inquiry. This agent or reference librarian avatar can suggest topics for projects that match student-centered preferences; help access high-quality collections of information; extract content from dynamically mined material and traditional library resources; guide student researchers who want to keep abreast of the latest developments; answer typical questions; and help construct annotated bibliographies, reviews, and proposals.
- NASA Education (http://www.nasa.gov/offices/education/about/index.html). In support of the National Science Education Standards, this service helps students who wish to engage in full or partial inquiry. Students may develop abilities or gain more understanding of selected aspects of inquiry methods. According to the NASA Education Web site, students might describe how they would design an investigation, develop explanations based on scientific information and evidence provided through a classroom activity, or recognize and analyze several alternative explanations for a natural phenomenon presented in a teacher-led demonstration. NASA employs a 5E model:
  o Engage to pique student interest. Video programs help students connect past and potential future projects.
  o Explore to get the student involved and build foundational understanding. Often students work in teams with the teacher providing background materials.
  o Explain: Students voice to others what they have learned and may use visual supports to help detail their presentations.
  o Extend: Students expand on the concepts they have learned, make connections to other related concepts, and apply their understandings to the world around them.
  o Evaluate: Students and teachers determine how much has been learned.
- Center for Implementing Technology in Education (http://www.cited.org/index.aspx) and its pages "Learning History with Multimedia Materials" (http://www.cited.org/index.aspx?page_id =145) link to several successful controlled inquiry exercises that can serve as excellent introductions,

discussions, methods, and ideas for inquiry that broaden the information base and will eventually serve to engage teachers and librarians in guiding a larger and student-centered process. Most of these are sites dealing with American history:

o Civil War Timeline
o Picturing the Thirties
o We're Writing the Constitution
o Analyzing Primary Sources
o Picturing Modern America
o Oral Histories

MULTIMEDIA HISTORY PROGRAMS

History especially can become greatly enhanced when students are confronted with an issue that resulted in massive conflict and destruction. Such events are impossible to capture in standard textbooks. Primary resources can serve to enlighten students about the compromises or concessions that led to the conflict or in-depth background that could have led to a resolution. Computer-stored, -organized, and -accessed portions of primary documents provide a rich information base for students to explore without worrying about document deterioration, damage, or loss.

As students learn to search for documents through such programs, retrieval of relevant documents is nearly always possible, and documents are nearly always relevant. This is not so in the real world of inquiry information searching. Real inquiry soon poses problems in selection among massive numbers of documents. Controlled inquiry programs not only provide a preselected set, they often fail to provide documents that could provide a clear contrast in document value based on authority, relevance, and accuracy. But the objective for controlled inquiry is not to explore literature and form new insights; it is to deal with the evidence presented and to apply logic and reason to address problems based on the information provided by the software authors.

NEED FOR A HUMAN MEDIATOR

Programs meeting the many options that evolve from multimedia-supported learning environments that present ill-structured problems and require students to engage in critical thinking have had mixed success. As Saye and Brush (2002) report, professional, human expertise in the form of a guiding teacher has value in reaching full implementation of inquiry interactions:

> Our findings suggest that expert guidance may be embedded into the learning environment to give students conceptual and strategic road maps that assist them in understanding the process of disciplined inquiry. However, our results also emphasize the difficulties in managing the cognitive challenges posed by ill-structured social problems and suggest limits to the embedded support that can be provided for complex thinking. Complex conceptual tasks may require spontaneous support that can only be provided by a skilled teacher. (77)

CONTROLLED, GUIDED, MODELED, AND FREE INQUIRY

The summarizing, contextualizing, inferring, monitoring, and corroborating (SCIM-C) strategy is a multimedia approach to help students compare evidence derived from primary historical sources (Hicks et al. 2004). This method focuses on those five broad phases. When students examine an individual source, they move through the first three phases and attempt to address questions such as those listed below.

- Summarizing: Students examine the documentary aspects of the text to find any information or evidence that is explicitly available from the source.
  - What type of document is the source?
  - What specific information, details, and/or perspectives does the source provide?
  - What is the subject and/or purpose of the source?
  - Who was the author and/or audience of the source"
- Contextualizing: Students attempt to place the source within its time and space and determine how this may affect the language of the source.
  - When and where was the source produced?
  - Why was the source produced?
  - What was happening within the immediate and broader context of the time when the source was produced?
  - What summarizing information can place the source in time and place?
- Inferring: Students revisit initial facts to begin to read subtexts and make inferences based on a developing understanding of the context.
  - What is suggested by the source?
  - What interpretations may be drawn from the source?
  - What perspectives or points of view are indicated by the source?
  - What inferences may be drawn from absences or omissions in the source?

By monitoring for reflection (the fourth phase) and analyzing several individual sources, students (guided by teachers) compare the sources collectively in the fifth phase, corroborating. This difficult process is more likely to be successful when effectively modeled by teachers (and librarians) and when students have enough time to practice and reflect on the decision-making processes. This support scaffolding also works best if students build from the more obvious to the more complex set of documents and issues. Logical arguments usually gain the most backing when they are understood by and within the cognitive abilities of the participating students. As a structured inquiry process, these exercises prepare the students for investigations that will range across the additional collaborative stages found in guided and mentored inquiry.

Brush and Saye updated their research on the effects of multimedia-supported problem-based inquiry in 2008. They found that the additional attention students were encouraged to give documents designed to facilitate their overall understanding of historical events greatly enhanced the process of students seeing issues and viewpoints. Providing more primary sources and a strategy to examine those sources along with information about the dilemmas faced by the historic figures resulted in what the researchers claimed was an authentic context for encountering historical content. The additional scaffolding provided by these text guides resulted in more advanced epistemological beliefs about history.

The Brush and Saye findings likely serve to reinforce the premise that history textbooks provide a useful structure for mapping out the timelines and association of events, but primary documents provide the depth for discussion and understanding of issues often missing from those textbooks. Students gained sufficient background from these controlled inquiry experiences to move forward to consider inquiry topics of greater personal interest.

COMPUTER-ASSISTED INFORMATION LITERACY INSTRUCTION

Advances have been made over the past decade in computer-assisted programs that introduce concepts of information literacy. Information problems are addressed, search strategies are experienced, and more and more students in these programs are expected to address issues of information authority and validity (Newell 2006). In a K–12 environment more and more instructional software takes into account standards calling for critical thinking and making judgments about the value of data or other information gathered for solving a problem.

Human library instruction programs that remain at the lower levels of controlled inquiry may encounter difficulty in justifying such activities if computer-assisted programs can provide the basic, introductory experiences required, and do so efficiently. School librarians need to direct information literacy assignment levels to those inquiry projects that are complex and that require human interaction to be successful, not only for more learning, but for their own survival.

The principles that guide development of technology-enhanced strategies for inquiry learning do not differ greatly from higher order inquiry teaching strategies in human learning environments (Kali and Linn 2008). The degree of clarity for implementation and thoroughness of human interactions make the major differences. Be mindful of human approaches as you read through these selected principles in computer-assisted program design that support inquiry:

- Connect to personally relevant examples (find student interest).
- Make thinking visible (or talk aloud).
- Provide students with templates to organize ideas (concept maps).
- Provide knowledge representation tools.
- Enable three-dimensional manipulation.
- Help and encourage learners to learn from each other (peer discussion online and off).
- Promote autonomous, lifelong learning (use free or open inquiry as a goal).
- Enable manipulation of factors in models and simulations.
- Encourage reflection (expressed both in writing and orally). (Kali and Linn 2008, 145)

REFERENCES

ABC-CLIO. http://www.abc-clio.com/ (accessed February 1, 2014).

American Association of School Librarians. 2009. *Standards for the 21st Century Learner in Action.* Chicago: American Library Association.

Banchi, H., and R. Bell. 2008. "The Many Levels of Inquiry." *Science and Children* 46, no. 2 (October): 26–29.

Brush, T., and J. Saye. 2008. "The Effects of Multimedia-Supported Problem-based Inquiry on Student Engagement, Empathy, and Assumptions about History." *Interdisciplinary Journal of Problem-based Learning* 2, no. 1. http://docs.lib.purdue.edu/cgi/viewcontent.cgi?article=1052&context=ijpbl (accessed March 15, 2014).

Callison, D. 1999. "Inquiry." *School Library Activities Monthly* 15, no. 6 (February): 38–42.

Dana, N. F., et al. 2011. *Inquiry: A Districtwide Approach to Staff and Student Learning.* Thousand Oaks, CA: Corwin.

Donham, J. 2013. "Text Sets, Deep Learning, and the Common Core." *School Library Monthly* 29, no. 6 (March): 5–7.

Ebbers, M. 2002. "Science Text Sets: Using Various Genres to Promote Literacy and Inquiry." *Language Arts* 80, no. 1 (September): 40–50.

Fontichiaro, K. 2014. "Evolution, Not Revolution: The Nudging toward Inquiry Approach." In *Inquiry and the Common Core*, edited by V. H. Harada and S. C. Coatney, 109–132. Santa Barbara, CA: Libraries Unlimited.

Hicks, D., et al. 2004. "The SCIM-C Strategy: Expert Historians, Historical Inquiry, and Multimedia." *Social Education* 68, no. 3 (April): 221–226.

Kali, Y., and M. C. Linn. 2008. "Technology-Enhanced Support Strategies for Inquiry Learning." In *Handbook of Research on Educational Communications and Technology*, 3rd ed., edited by J. M. Spector et al., 145–161. New York: Lawrence Erlbaum Associates,

Kuhlthau, C. C. 2010. "Guided Inquiry: School libraries in the 21st Century." *School Libraries Worldwide* 16, no. 1 (January): 17–28.

Newell, T. S. 2006. "Rethinking Information Literacy Learning Environments: A Study to Examine the Effectiveness of Two Learning Approaches." PhD diss., University of Wisconsin, Madison.

Pitts, J. 1995. "The 1993–1994 AASL Highsmith Research Award Study: Mental Models of Information." *School Library Media Annual* 13: 187–200.

Rankin, V. 1999. *The Thoughtful Researcher: Teaching the Research Process to Middle School Students.* Englewood, CO: Libraries Unlimited.

Saye, J. W., and T. Brush. 2002. "Scaffolding Critical Reasoning about History and Social Issues in Multimedia-Supported Learning Environments." *ETR&D* 50, no. 3: 77–96.

Stripling, B. K. 2003. "Inquiry-Based Learning." In *Curriculum Connections through the Library*, edited by B. K. Stripling and S. Hughes-Hassell, 3–39. Westport, CT: Libraries Unlimited.

Wolf, S. 2007. "Information Literacy and Self-regulation: A Convergence of Disciplines." *School Library Media Research* 10. http://www.ala.org/aasl/aaslpubsandjournals/slmrb/slmrcontents/volume10/wolf_informationliteracy (accessed January 31, 2014).

Wolf, S., and T. Brush. 2003. "The Big Six Information Skills as a Metacognitive Scaffold." *School Library Research* 6. http://www.ala.org/aasl/aaslpubsandjournals/slmrb/slmrcontents/volume62003/bigsix information (accessed March 19, 2014).

Chapter 3

Guided, Modeled, and Mentored Inquiry Enhanced by Cognitive Apprenticeship

GUIDED INQUIRY

Then (Callison 1999): Guided Inquiry combines research skills into a more natural flow of question raising and information seeking. Students often work in small groups, and the topic for exploration is common across the class, as all students are generally expected to deal with the same amount of information and eventually make a similar presentation. Final reports will be of similar length and content and will be assessed on the same rubric.

Now: Today's access to extensive resources, especially through the Internet, serves to update the earlier definition. While it is not unusual for a class of senior high school students to work under the same general framework for their inquiry topic selection, often each class member works on a subtopic or related topic from a more general set of issues selected to meet the school's curriculum. The extensive information pool now available (the Internet and much more) allows students to become more specialized and focused. The frequency of group engagements is also growing. Planning and reflection phases provide the opportunity to work in teams in which students openly share and analyze peer inquiry explorations. Frequent critical peer reviews and sharing of evidence are more manageable because of social technologies.

ENHANCING THE INFORMATION SEARCH PROCESS WITH GUIDED INQUIRY

Based on over twenty-five years of observational research as well as frequent implementation of Guided Inquiry techniques in senior high schools, Carol Kuhlthau (2010) and her colleagues have established a much wider base for the roles of teachers and school librarians in implementing Guided Inquiry intervention methods. Kuhlthau documented through her information search process (ISP) studies that "students need considerable guidance and intervention throughout the [inquiry] process to enable a depth of learning and personal understanding." "Guided Inquiry," she has concluded "is planned, targeted, supervised intervention throughout the inquiry process" (2010, 20).

INTERVENTIONS FOR INSTRUCTIONAL USE

Daniel Callison at Indiana University, Joy McGregor at Texas Woman's University, and Ruth Small at Syracuse University collaborated in the development and organization of the Sixth

Treasure Mountain Research Retreat (TM6), held near Portland, Oregon, in 1997. Papers were published the following year (Callison, McGregor, and Small 1998). Kuhlthau (1998) was invited to present the opening keynote presentation, in which she alluded, perhaps for the first time in a formal presentation, to Guided Inquiry.

Kuhlthau opened the retreat, setting the stage for applying sound educational notions for instructional interventions. "A constructivist theory of learning centers on the student in the active process of moving from uncertainty to understanding rather than [just] the transmission of facts centering on sources and texts. A constructivist theory is the basis of authentic learning approaches that are emerging as one of the most promising findings in the research to restructure schools for the Information Age. Authentic learning, . . . involves constructing knowledge through guided inquiry that has value beyond the school" (1998, 15).

With this, Kuhlthau established two important characteristics of Guided Inquiry. While student inquiry projects may have similar structures for purposes of content, resource, and time management, much more important is the guidance of inquiry so the student gains new understanding, shares these findings, and applies new learning while immersed in a topic that is significant and meaningful.

A decade later Kuhlthau, Maniotes, and Caspari (2007) authored *Guided Inquiry: Learning in the 21st Century*, in which they offered these additional insights:

> Inquiry is an approach to learning whereby students find and use a variety of sources of information and ideas to increase their understanding of a problem, topic, or issue. It requires more of them than simply answering questions or getting a right answer. It espouses investigation, exploration, search, quest, research, pursuit, and study. Inquiry does not stand alone; it engages, interests, and challenges students to connect their world with the curriculum. Although it is often thought of as an individual pursuit, it is enhanced by involvement with a community of learners, each learning from the other in social interaction. However, without some guidance it can be daunting. (2)

TM6 PAPERS ON MOTIVATED, MODELED, AND MENTORED INQUIRY

Several papers presented at TM6 in 1997 (Callison, McGregor, and Small 1998) were seeds for later expansion as interventions to guide students toward positive results at higher levels of inquiry. Among these futuristic ideas were the following:

- The role of the library media specialist is important in provision of motivational guidance as well as resource guidance (Small 1998).
- Teacher and librarian modeling of reading and writing processes are steps beyond guidance to levels of mentorship centered on the inquiry-based I-Search process. Focus is directly on the learning needs and preferences of the student (Tallman 1998).
- There is very likely a higher level in the inquiry process that enhances adolescent information use when reached through mentored or cognitive apprenticeship practices (Tilley and Callison 1998).

MOTIVATION

Small based her notion of and the need for addressing motivation on "one widely accepted goal of education: to develop intrinsically motivated, life-long learners who want to learn, who enjoy the learning experience while it is occurring, and who continue learning after the instruction has formally ended" (1998, 220). She constructed her techniques on four essential components of motivating instruction previously identified by Keller (1983):

- Attention: The instructor uses strategies for arousing and sustaining curiosity and interest.
- Relevance: The instructor links the instruction to important needs, interests, and motives.
- Confidence: The instructor helps students develop a positive expectation for successful achievement of a learning task.
- Satisfaction: The instructor manages extrinsic and intrinsic reinforcement.

In the years following the presentation of her paper, Small and her research colleagues developed and tested methods to determine the best application of several information literacy models. Working as teams of academic and practicing educators (Small, Arnone, Stripling, and Berger 2012), these researchers explored what types of motivational strategies encourage on-task behaviors and even enjoyment of the research process. Small also related these techniques to the issues of the emerging digital information society (Small 2005).

MODELING

Tallman (1998) took the I-Search writing method (Macrorie 1988) into dozens of school settings. Teams of teachers and media specialists applied techniques that emphasized allowing the topic to find the student (rather than the other way around or simply being assigned a topic) and motivating creative writing through students gaining topic ownership. Topics from their personal lives were the most motivational and arose from their individual need to answer their unique concerns and self-generated questions. "Students who owned their topics became the experts in the subject and shared their results with enthusiasm" (Tallman 1998, 233).

Journaling has often been identified as one of the most important tools for the student inquirer. Tallman described the value of journals:

> One of the strengths in having students keep a journal with their notes and reflections along with the story of their search success was the opportunity for the teaching team to probe students for more depth in their responses. To question students about their findings and to guide them in the use of their findings, the teacher and media specialist used verbs that focused on higher order thinking. They challenged students to: analyze, recognize, examine, simplify, discern, compare, determine, assess, decide, judge, prioritize, diagnose, accept or reject, combine, and re-organize. (1998, 242)

"Throughout the I-Search unit," reported Tallman, "the teaching team demonstrated and explained research techniques and strategies and modeled the way they worked in collecting data and reflection on the results" (1998, 242). She also reflected on situations in which, as recommended by Macrorie (1984), teachers wrote with students and exchanged compositions and writing challenges through periods of reading aloud. Adults struggled with the same frustrations and anxieties as the students.

Modeling encouraged deeper examination of the value of double-entry journaling, for example, leading to modifications that increased effective communications between students and teachers. Such modeling has been linked to higher student achievement (Cole and Chan 1994). Tallman and Joyce (2006) have updated I-Search strategies to include adult learners. Just as for adolescents, peer support structures are needed to support adult learners, and modeling can serve to provide much of this guidance for the older learner.

MENTOR COACH COGNITIVE APPRENTICESHIPS

Cognitive apprenticeship is a method of teaching and learning based on traditional apprenticeship. In cognitive apprenticeship, the teacher has three tasks: model, coach, and fade.

Underlying these tasks are the assumptions that the teacher describes his or her metacognitive processes in performing a skill and provides the student with scaffolded practice in performing that skill; tasks grow more complex than those that preceded them. The social nature of learning is emphasized, as is the need for continuous assessment. The expectation is that the successful student will mature to the level that self-assessment replaces mentor assessment, and the goal is eventually a fully independent learner.

The assumption is also that the mentor teaches not just through guidance, but also by example. The teachers (or library media specialists) who take the role of mentor for inquiry are immersed in inquiry themselves. They may explore topics of interest or professional need, such as documenting successful efforts in application of various teaching strategies, or, for librarians, the management of the resource center (Callison 2007; Preddy 2007; Dana and Yendol-Hoppey 2008; Dana et al. 2011).

One of the key ideas underlying cognitive apprenticeship is the notion that learning occurs primarily through social interaction. Knowledge, strategies, and processes are learned after students have opportunities to talk about them, try them out, and repeat those steps until the task is mastered.

A second key idea underlying cognitive apprenticeship is the importance of placing learning in an authentic context with authentic activities. What authentic learning situations need most is an authentic model or coach, a mentor who has "been there and done that, and done it well." Inquiry is more than searching for information; it is raising questions, analyzing information need and content, assimilating the new information, and inferring conclusions.

MENTORS PROVIDE GUIDANCE FOR CRITICAL SKILLS

The information inquiry elements that Tilley and Callison (1998; Callison 1994) were beginning to define included those experiences for which students need mentoring beyond the information search process. Students are also in need of mentors who can

- illustrate how to control bias;
- determine the best information for a given situation, for a given audience;
- show how to generate original data and apply different methods to meet different needs;
- demonstrate how to value information and select that which is most authoritative and relevant;
- accept or reject information and provide justification for doing so;
- assimilate new information to modify the working hypothesis, topic, and questions;
- determine the most valuable information for the project at hand and that will serve as an initial pool of information for similar future inquiry projects; and
- self-assess their own work and that of others.

To be effective mentors, school librarians need established expertise in the full range of inquiry, not just the process for information searching and location. Master mentors are exceptionally efficient and effective in using the tools and finishing products of their trade. Reflections are made on the quality and value of special information sources discovered through the inquiry process.

Cognitive mentors model with their thoughts as well as actions and converse in detail with the apprentices. Such conversations serve as a mental scaffold that moves the mature learner to his or her independent status. To be accepted as a cognitive mentor, the library media specialist needs to have experienced research beyond information location. He or she needs to practice inquiry methods openly for others to see and appreciate and to document them in local presentations of projects to fellow teachers. Mentors can provide experienced examples of inquiry when conversing with students, not only of dealing with information, but also of the challenges and frustrations of inquiry.

"Since cognitive apprenticeship emphasizes the need for ongoing assessment," note Tilley and Callison, "[mentors as evaluators, and mature inquirers as independent learners] must look to see if students are more consistently providing support for conclusions, using analogies, evaluating evidence, planning a course of action, restructuring problems, seeking patterns, and incorporating anomalous data into a coherent framework. Additionally, [they] propose that improved information use should lead students to achieve a greater frequency and accuracy in identifying their information needs, a greater use of evidence in supporting arguments, and a more logical organization of arguments in both written and oral formats" (1998, 250). Many of these expectations are similar to learning goals that show as shifts in learning expectations in the 2014 Common Core State Standards (Levitov 2014, 32):

1. Balancing Information and Literacy Text: 50 percent–50 percent balancing of literacy and nonfiction texts.
2. Content Area Literacy: Building knowledge, deep analysis to make arguments from the texts read; students find their own meaning—create opportunities for students to experience learning for themselves.
3. Staircase of Complexity/Increased Complexity of Texts: Close reading for comprehension of complex text; scaffolding as needed.
4. Text-based Questions and Answers: Evidence-based conversation about text/writing to show comprehension of text (observable through student's work).
5. Writing from Sources: Deep analysis of the text; using evidence from the text to make an argument supported with evidence. This involves the student's response to text to show understanding.
6. Vocabulary: Academic language acquired through increasingly complex text. Vocabulary needed to understand and use complex texts.

Definitions of Key Terms from Instructional Design

Vanessa Paz Dennen (2004) from Florida State University has defined key terms associated with cognitive apprenticeship techniques:

Cognitive Apprenticeship: A cognitive apprenticeship is much like a trade apprenticeship, with learning that occurs as experts and novices interact socially while focused on completing a task; the focus, as implied in the name, is on developing cognitive skills through participating in authentic learning experiences. . . . Learning in a cognitive apprenticeship occurs through legitimate peripheral participation, a process in which newcomers enter on the periphery and gradually move toward full participation. (814)

Scaffolding: Directive scaffolding is part of a more teacher-centered approach, in which the instructor devises skills and strategies to teach specified content. Supportive scaffolding, in contrast, is learner-centered and occurs as the learner co-constructs knowledge with others. (815)

Modeling: Cognitive modeling [is arguably more complex than modeling of psychomotor skills that usually involve imitation]. For example, a teacher might model a decision-making process by talking aloud about the considerations taken and explaining the rationale for the end result. The learner in this case would not be engaged in direct imitation but, rather, use of similar strategies in a related context. (817)

Mentoring (often Coaching): A mentor, by its most basis definition, is one who mediates expert knowledge for novices, helping that which is tacit become more explicit. The two most common uses of the word mentoring are to describe (a) a professional development relationship in which a more experienced participant assists a less experienced one in developing a career, and (b) a guiding relationship between an adult and a youth focused on helping the youth realize his or her potential and perhaps overcome some barriers or challenges. In both cases it is the mentor who provides advice and support and may serve as a role model. Whereas these examples generally imply long-term relationships, mentoring can be used as an instructional strategy on a smaller scale. (817)

TECHNIQUES LEADING TO HIGH POTENTIAL FOR MODELING AND MENTORING

Then (Callison 1999) and now: Modeled inquiry moves the student to a higher level of investigation (responsibilities) as he or she comes under the guidance of someone who has engaged in a great deal of previous inquiry. Through a more independent process, the student is an apprentice in the research process, but has more freedom of choice in developing research questions and methods. Modeled inquiry tends to work best when teachers involved have been successful themselves in completing inquiry projects and will engage in research alongside the students (Macrorie 1984). As models or mentors, teachers should employ scaffolding mechanisms to help students move to higher levels of responsibility. Peer scaffolding should also be employed, as sometimes students have differing abilities and can help each other move to higher levels.

"Instructional scaffolding can be defined as support provided by a teacher/parent, peer, or a computer- or a paper-based tool that allows students to meaningfully participate in and gain skill at a task that they would be unable to complete unaided" (Belland 2014, 505). Belland further summarizes the mechanism for scaffolding (507):

> Scaffolding mechanisms include (a) enlisting student interest, (b) controlling frustration, (c) providing feedback, (d) indicating important task/problem elements to consider, modeling expert processes, and (f) questioning (van de Pol et al. 2010; Wood et al. 1976). Enlisting student interest and controlling student frustration highlight (a) the role of scaffolding in creating and sustaining student motivation, and (b) the central role of student motivation in deploying and improving higher order skills (Brody 1999). Providing feedback involves informing students of the adequacy of their performance. Indicating important task/problem elements to consider involves telling students what they should focus on during their investigations. Modeling expert processes refers to showing students how an expert would approach solving a similar problem. Questioning involves tutors prodding students to articulate answers that can move them toward completing the task.

The research (Hillocks 1986, 1995) on student composition provides some evidence that in situations where the student is expected to make critical judgments in the analysis of information in order to compile a successful argument through coherent strings of evidence, and to make logical and supported claims, a cognitive apprenticeship framework is beneficial.

Cognitive apprenticeship is also a useful model for supporting novices as they seek greater responsibilities within a community of writers. Successful accomplishments involving smaller tasks build to more responsibilities and eventually, for the persistent and skilled student, result in higher roles of group editorship, planning, and management of publications (Beaufort 2000).

Higher level responsibilities place students in demanding situations with the expectation that they will become leaders and active participants in groups that debate and compose extensively documented communication. As the student demonstrates mastery, the teacher fades from providing close guidance and remains in the roles of facilitating and counseling only when absolutely necessary (Tilley and Callison 1998).

RESIST BEHAVIORS THAT DENY EFFECTIVE MENTORING

Experienced writing mentors have discovered how quickly student discussion and the beginnings of student insights can be stopped if they enter into arguments and move away from the mentorship role into a dominating master role:

> When the levels of interaction are high, and the interaction is *among* students rather than between the teacher and students in recitation fashion, student ideas and opinions become the focus of attention and substantially control the direction of classroom talk. This interaction gives students the necessary stake in what is happening. They become the authorities through their ideas. The teacher's role is to coach and prompt, to ask questions that push at the edges of student ideas, and to sustain the interchange among students. If the teacher provides authoritative answers to the problems under discussion, the interaction among students ceases and learning is curtailed. . . . Students saw no point in pursuing the problem when they could see that the teacher would eventually provide the "right" answer. (Hillocks 1986, 65)

PRACTICAL APPLICATION OF GUIDED INQUIRY

Many practicing school librarians have adopted the philosophy, learning principles, and teaching techniques documented by Kuhlthau, Maniotes, and Caspari (2007, 2012). A clear case study and guide for high school implementation of Guided Inquiry has been authored by head librarian Randell Schmidt (2013), based on her collaboration with teachers at Gill St. Bernard's School at Gladstone, New Jersey. Lessons based on Kuhlthau's research are presented as welcoming, nonthreatening workshop sessions for students facing various inquiry projects.

Exercises can be managed in groups or individually and by the novice ninth grader up to the more advanced senior. The modules can be completed as a basis for independent study, although Schmidt's program has demonstrated the value of "research buddies" or peer support through research teams that serve to help verbalize goals, needs, and information gap issues together.

Inquiry is student-centered, and this is made clear in handouts, various syllabi, and even letters to parents: "For three or four weekly class meetings the student will meet in the library to research a topic of the student's own choosing that the student wishes to learn about. Yes, that is correct: The student asks the question. The teacher and librarian guide the student through the search. During the research project the student will learn not only about the chosen topic but also how to access information in different formats, how to determine whether that information is useful, how to combine different sources of information, how to organize what has been found, and how to present the borrowed information" (Schmidt 2013, 150). Parents are often invited to celebrations and presentations of student inquiry accomplishments.

Workshop modules include sessions on identifying bias; gaining an understanding of personal learning styles, needs, and behaviors; understanding that information exploration and browsing are valuable and encouraged; focusing topic choice for meaning; evaluating information; and presenting designs to meet different audiences. Objectives for each workshop lesson are grounded in the new Common Core State Standards Initiative. An overall syllabus for the project gives each student an immediate snapshot of the total expectations and a clear idea of the opportunities to explore content that is exciting to him or her personally.

Across the development of the projects, formative evaluation points take place as the teacher and librarian guide the process. This includes examining content notes taken by each student, but more important, the teacher and librarian mentor the process by surveying how students feel about their progress and frustrations. On a regular basis, students are asked to summarize their positive and negative experiences, allowing for self-reflection as well as guided reflection.

MEASURING THE IMPACT OF INQUIRY

Funded by the Institute for Museum and Library Services, a process to track and assess student learning outcomes resulting from their engagement in Guided Inquiry was developed at the Center for International Scholarship in School Libraries at Rutgers University (Todd, Kuhlthau, and Heinstrom 2005). The School Library Impact Measure (SLIM) "is a toolkit that consists of four instruments that elicit students' reflections on their learning at three points in their inquiry process. The toolkit will enable collaborating school librarian–teacher teams to chart changes in students' knowledge and experiences throughout the process" (5).

Ross Todd, Rutgers associate professor, has led the testing and development of the SLIM instruments. The handbook is available free through the CISSL Web site: http://cissl.rutgers.edu/ and http://cissl.rutgers.edu/images/stories/docs/slimtoolkit.pdf. Todd's conclusions support the educational value of Guided Inquiry when implemented by collaborative teams of educators, including school library media specialists. Through the research of Todd and his colleagues (2005), CISSL has documented the following findings:

- Students' initial knowledge underwent a significant conceptual change.
- Students learned topical content in deep ways, shown in complex and coherent knowledge structures.
- Students became more skillful and confident as information seekers.
- Students became increasingly engaged, interested, and reflective during their learning process and saw information seeking as a constructive process of building both deep knowledge and deep understanding.
- Students became more critically aware of the broad variety of sources and their different purposes.
- Students gained practical skills in independent information seeking, moving from fact finding to information analysis and synthesis.
- Students showed increasing awareness of the varied quality of information, as well as of information as problematic and often contradictory. (6)

The various avenues developed over the past decade through CISSL for implementation of Guided Inquiry have provided tangible evidence that teachers in collaboration with school librarians can be not only effective guides, but also mentors in learning through inquiry. Higher levels of engagement are possible, and open or free inquiry can be a goal of more advanced implementation of these guided processes.

REFERENCES

Beaufort, A. 2000. "Learning the Trade: A Social Apprenticeship Model for Gaining Writing Expertise." *Written Communication* 17, no. 2: 185–223.

Belland, B. R. 2014. "Scaffolding: Definition, Current Debates, and Future Directions." In *Handbook of Research on Educational Communications and Technology*, edited by J. M. Spector et al., 505–518. New York: Springer.

Brody, J. 1999. "Toward a Model of the Value Aspects of Motivation in Education: Developing Appreciation for Particular Learning Domains and Activities." *Educational Psychologist* 34, no. 2: 75–85.

Callison, D. 1994. "Expanding the Evaluation Role in the Critical-Thinking Curriculum" In *Assessment in the School Library Media Center*, edited by C. C. Kuhlthau, 43–58. Englewood, CO: Libraries Unlimited.

Callison, D. 1999. "Inquiry." *School Library Activities Monthly* 15, no. 6 (February): 38–42.

Callison, D. 2007. "Action Research." *School Library Monthly* 23, no. 10 (June): 40–43.

Callison, D., J. H. McGregor, and R. V. Small, eds. 1998. *Instructional Intervention for Information Use.* San Jose, CA: Hi Willow Research.

Callison, D., and C. L. Tilley. 1998. "Informaton and Media Literacies: Toward a Common Core." In *Instructional Intervention for Information Use,* edited by D. Callison, J. H. McGregor, and R. V. Small, 110–116. San Jose, CA: Hi Willow Research.

Cole, P., and L. Chan. 1994. *Teaching Principles and Practice.* New York: Prentice Hall.

Common Core State Standards Initiative. 2014 http://www.corestandards.org/ (accessed February 1, 2014).

Dana, N. F., et al. 2011. *Inquiry: A Districtwide Approach to Staff and Student Learning.* Thousand Oaks, CA: Corwin.

Dana, N. F., and D. Yendol-Hoppey. 2008. *The Reflective Educator's Guide to Professional Development: Coaching Inquiry-Oriented Learning Communities.* Thousand Oaks, CA: Corwin.

Dennen, V. P. 2004. "Cognitive Apprenticeship in Educational Practice: Research on Scaffolding, Modeling, Mentoring, and Coaching as Instructional Strategies." In *Handbook of Research on Educational Communications and Technology,* edited by D. H. Jonassen, 813–828. Mahwah, NJ: Lawrence Erlbaum.

Hillocks, G. 1986. *Research on Written Composition: New Directions for Teaching.* Urbana: National Center on Research in English, University of Illinois.

Hillocks, G. 1995. *Teaching Writing as Reflective Practice.* New York: Teachers College Press.

Keller, J. M. 1983. "Motivation Design of Instruction." In *Instructional Design Theories and Models,* edited by C. M. Reigelth, 386–433. Hillsdale, NJ: Erlbaum.

Kuhlthau, C. C. 1998. "Keynote: Constructivist Theory for School Library Media Programs." In *Instructional Intervention for Information Use,* edited by D. Callison, J. H. McGregor, and R. V. Small, 14–21. San Jose, CA: Hi Willow Research.

Kuhlthau, C. C. 2010. "Guided Inquiry: School Libraries in the 21st Century." *School Libraries Worldwide* 16, no. 1 (January): 17–28.

Kuhlthau, C. C., L. K. Maniotes, and A. K. Caspari. 2007. *Guided Inquiry: Learning in the 21st Century.* Westport, CT: Libraries Unlimited.

Kuhlthau, C. C., L. K. Maniotes, and A. K. Caspari. 2012. *Guided Inquiry Design: A Framework for Inquiry in Your School.* Santa Barbara, CA: Libraries Unlimited.

Levitov, D. D. 2014. "School Librarians and the CCSS: Knowing, Claiming, and Acting on Their Expertise." In *Inquiry and the Common Core,* edited by V. H. Harada and S. Coatney, 31–47. Santa Barbara, CA: Libraries Unlimited.

Macrorie, K. 1984. *Writing to Be Read.* Upper Montclair, NJ: Boynton/Cook.

Macrorie, K. 1988. *The I-Search Paper.* Portsmouth, NH: Heinemann.

Preddy, L. B. 2007. *SSR with Intervention: A School Library Action Research Project.* Westport, CT: Libraries Unlimited.

Schmidt, R. K. 2013. *A Guided Inquiry Approach to High School Research.* Santa Barbara, CA: Libraries Unlimited.

Small, R. V. 1998. "Motivational Aspects of Library and Information Skills Instruction: Role of the Library Media Specialist." In *Instructional Interventions for Information Use,* edited by D. Callison, J. H. McGregor, and R. V. Small, 220–231. San Jose, CA: Hi Willow Research.

Small, R. V. 2005. *Designing Digital Literacy Programs with IM-PACT: Information Motivation, Purpose, Audience, Content, Technique.* New York: Neal Schuman.

Small, R. V., M. P. Arnone, B. K. Stripling, and P. Berger. 2012. *Teaching Inquiry: Engaging the Learner Within.* New York: Neal Schuman.

Tallman, J. I. 1998. "Effective Teaching and Learning Strategies Modeled through the I-Search: An Inquiry-based, Student-centered Research Writing Process." In *Instructional Interventions for Information Use,* edited by D. Callison, J. H. McGregor, and R. V. Small, 232–244. San Jose, CA: Hi Willow Research.

Tallman, J. I., and M. Z. Joyce. 2006. *Making the Writing and Research Connection with the I-Search Process.* New York: Neal Schuman.

Tilley, C. L. 2006. "Cognitive Apprenticeship." In *The Blue Book on Information Age Inquiry, Instruction, and Literacy*, edited by D. Callison and L. Preddy, 318–321. Westport, CT: Libraries Unlimited.

Tilley, C. L., and D. Callison. 1998. "The Cognitive Apprenticeship Model and Adolescent Information Use." In *Instructional Interventions for Information Use*, edited by D. Callison, J. H. McGregor, and R. V. Small, 245–252. San Jose, CA: Hi Willow Research.

Todd, R. J., C. C. Kuhlthau, and J. E. Heinstrom. 2005. "School Library Impact Measure." Center for International Scholarship in School Libraries, Rutgers University. http://cissl.rutgers.edu/images/stories /docs/slimtoolkit.pdf (accessed March 23, 2014).

Van de Pol, J., et al. 2010. "Scaffolding in Teacher-Student Interactions: A Decade of Research." *Educational Psychology Review* 22: 271–296.

Wood, D., et al. 1976. "The Role of Tutoring in Problem-Solving." *Journal of Child Psychology and Psychiatry* 17: 89–100.

Chapter 4

Free Inquiry
and Student-Centered Learning

FREE OR OPEN INQUIRY

Then and Now (Callison 1999): Free inquiry is the highest level of independent investigation. The student has ownership of the process, from raising questions and identification of key issues to completion of the final report and justification of the presentation mode. Access to information, analysis of data, and synthesis for presentation are the responsibility of the student inquirer. The student has gained experience and practice in the inquiry process and has matured to the level that he or she knows how to build on those previous experiences, without help, to create a truly unique project.

Full inquiry experiences are not limited to the processes of the information search, but include the processes of question initiation, information selection and application, and self-assessment of both the process and product. Progression to this level is not possible without previous guidance and mentoring, as detailed in previous levels of inquiry (Callison 1994).

Obviously such a high level is not reached by most students within their K–12 academic careers, although advancements in the interventions for inquiry instruction, along with the new Common Core State Standards (Levitov 2014), may increase the population who reach for such advanced levels. At best, advancement in the opportunity to experience inquiry at all levels can increase the quality of preparation of the lifelong learner in our digital information age (Stripling 2014).

EXTENDING INQUIRY LEARNING FOR INSIGHT

The challenge remains to create learning environments that provide enough time, resources, and talented teachers who can actually facilitate inquiry. Independent inquiry requires individual learning options that allow for exploring difficult-to-answer questions; addressing authentic real-world problems; encouraging student time beyond the school structure for observation, reading, and exploration; fostering healthy skepticism that can generate healthy curiosity; and providing interdisciplinary environments that result in wide and extended applications of inquiry to personal needs as well as careers and college (Donham 2014).

To be free and meaningful, inquiry investigations need to last more than the currently typical two weeks and extend beyond the typically assigned three factual citations. Topics should involve deep learning, be student-centered, and require high levels of mature self-regulation of behavior.

Jean Donham and June Gross (Donham 2008, 259) have illustrated how five key concepts related to information literacy must move from simply gathering factual information to higher order thinking levels that generate insights—knowledge new to the student and perhaps to others as well:

- Inquiry moves from being teacher-centered to being student-centered.
- Conceptualization (of the questions and topic) moves from fact-oriented to issue/concept-oriented assignments.
- Integration of information moves from emphasis on the product to emphasis on the process.
- Presentation of findings moves from being given to just the teacher to having an authentic audience.
- Reflection and assessment moves from being isolated to being collaborative and (student) self-oriented.

Programs that can fully offer student-centered free inquiry options are those that have established an extensive foundation in previous levels of inquiry. Where these options do exist, students are most likely to take on individual investigations as independent study: a focused, advanced project sponsored by an appropriate academic mentor. The role of the school library media specialist may range from little or no involvement, to that of co-mentor who provides resource support and research method advisement. At a few institutions, the school library media specialist who is certified in the subject area relevant to the student's investigation may serve as the academic mentor. In all cases, school librarians should seek participation in such advanced projects to the extent that they become active inquiry curriculum developers who set goals for the institution's program.

Does movement toward free inquiry mean that adolescents complete projects that contribute original and new knowledge to the human record? Many adult scientists seldom, if ever, reach such a level. Movement along the continuum outlined above is, however, a realistic goal, even if it is not usually reached. When applied with meaningful scaffolding for students to move upward toward the goal of insight, beyond just factual knowledge, the most powerful learning experience is when students begin to recognize that there are inquiry processes that can take them to higher order learning, and they begin to fashion tangible behaviors that will get them to that level. They realize they can think and do so critically and frequently.

SOME BASIC THEMES FROM INFORMATION LITERACY

Michael Eisenberg, codeveloper of one of the most popular approaches to information problem solving (Eisenberg and Berkowitz 1990; Eisenberg 2008) and Michael Brown identified key themes concerning the instruction of information literacy skills in 1992. In general, their recommendations have been consistent as guiding principles through the past few decades and continue to influence many who develop curricular materials for information literacy:

- Instruction in library and information skills is a valuable and essential part of the school's education program.
- Essential library and information skills encompass more than just location of and access to sources. The skills curriculum should emphasize general information problem-solving and research processes and the specific skills within these general processes (e.g., selection, analysis, synthesis, and evaluation).
- Library and information skills should not be taught in isolation. The skills program must be fully integrated with the school's curriculum.
- The use of innovative instructional methods and technologies can enhance the teaching of library and information skills.

These themes also apply to inquiry-based instruction, as the strategies leading to successful implementation should be taught in conjunction with the school's curriculum. Independent inquiry, while not group oriented, is also not conducted in isolation. It can become the most advanced aspect of the curriculum, across multiple disciplines (science, history, literature, and more). Independent study can focus on content not specifically in the curriculum, but be oriented to the curriculum if the expectation is that the student will experience such a high level of investigation as a part of his or her academic experience.

Independent development and presentation, however, should evolve out of a clear supporting curriculum in which inquiry skills have been scaffold and supported by teachers and mentors in previous briefer controlled or guided research exercises. The potential for exceptional student learning, especially in demonstrating student performances that meet most state and national standards, can culminate in student inquiry experiences that are presented to various audiences in the school and the greater community. A senior project, for example, could engage some students in a full year, or more, of exploration.

PROGRESSION TOWARD GREATER STUDENT-CENTERED INSTRUCTION

Student-centered does not mean student-exclusive in the processes for determining goals, actions, and evaluations, but it means there will be growing student input and a stronger role role, dependent on the degree of maturity and self-regulation, resulting in greater focus on student needs and desires. The goal is to move the student from introverted to extroverted vision, from knowing self to learning also to know others. Mentors are available, but the self-regulating, independent students know when to consult experts and when to seek reflection from peers.

Student-centered learning seems obvious for those who wish to enhance learning environments in today's expanding information age. The goal is for more teachers and students to eventually become independent, or nearly independent, in managing their own learning. Guiding students and teachers through the inquiry maze has become, over the past four decades, a dominant method to move learners closer to this independence. An additional goal of a learner-centered practice is for learning and teaching institutions to create environments, including virtual spaces, that optimize students' opportunities to actively engage in authentic, meaningful, and useful learning (Doyle 2011).

TEACHING FACILITATION PRACTICES IN HIGHER EDUCATION

Maryellen Weimer is an award-winning professor at Penn State. Now retired, she continues to edit a newsletter and blog covering successful teaching techniques in higher education. In her latest book, *Learner-Centered Teaching* (2013), she describes several metaphors for the teacher's role as facilitator and emphasizes that carrying this role to its most effective engagements is hard work and a difficult challenge:

> Facilitative teachers have been compared to guides, and many useful insights derive from this metaphor. Guides show those who follow the way, but those who follow walk on their own. Guides point out the sights; they've traveled this way before. Guides offer advice, they warn of danger, and they do their best to prevent accidents. Likewise, learner-centered teachers climb with students. Together they ascend what for many students are new and high peaks. (60)

Weimer goes on to list the key principles that are foundational to facilitative teaching that is student-centered. While her implementation of these principles is drawn from undergraduate classrooms, these applications are also valid for other educational settings:

Teachers let students do more learning tasks—Teachers need to stop doing so many of the learning tasks for students. Teachers should not always be organizing the content, generating the examples, asking the questions, answering the questions, summarizing the discussion, solving the problems, and constructing the diagrams. The key word here is *always*. On occasion teachers need to do all of these things for students. The principle is about gradually doing them less, until the point is reached when doing them is the exception, not the rule. (2013, 72)

Weimer extends her principles through the following:

- "Teachers do less telling so that students can do more discovering" (76).
- "Teachers need to do instructional design work more carefully" (77).
- "[Teachers] more explicitly model how experts learn. When solving a problem, the teacher can say out loud what is going through [his or her] mind. Teachers can tell students how to confront a difficult and confusing problem" (79).
- "[Teachers] encourage students to learn from and with each other" (81).

LEARNER-CENTERED INQUIRY AND INFORMATION LITERACY

Marjorie Pappas and Ann Tepe were among the first to link inquiry methods to information skills and information literacy instruction. Their 2002 publication *Pathways to Knowledge and Inquiry Learning* contains several examples of how they visualized student-centered learning as a mode of operation for activities to engage students in application of information skills. Their menu for student-centered learning includes the following target indicators:

- Critical thinking: Analysis, evaluation, and synthesis are employed by students who can interpret, apply, and see various perspectives, leading to transformation of thinking.
- Depth of content knowledge: Learners are engaged in learning the big ideas through essential questioning.
- Assessment: Assessment of content is done through demonstration of new knowledge.
- Authentic context: Learning reflects a broad connection to the world we live in.
- Learner choice and engagement: Learners have meaningful choices. They engage in problem/ questions/issues and topic development and make decisions about strategies for resolution.
- Interactive knowledge construction: Interaction occurs within student groups with a common task or problem that requires the synergy of group members to complete.
- Inquiry as process: Students independently apply a process approach and demonstrate a proficient or exemplary level for the information literacy standards (95).

TRANSFORMING INSTRUCTION

A leader in development of information literacy instruction at UCLA, Joan Kaplowitz (2012) claims that learner-centered approaches have transformed her teaching philosophy over the past three decades.

She notes that the vocabulary of the traditional teacher is usually limited to *inform, deliver, facts, memorize, replicate,* and *compete*. Teachers who view instruction with a more learner-centered perspective use such terms as *investigate, explore, facilitate, interact, ideas, construct, cooperate,* and *collaborate*.

"Although incorporating active learning techniques is a big part of learning-centered teaching (LCT)," writes Kaplowitz, "it is not the whole picture. LCT cannot be described simply in terms of methods used. Rather, it is a teaching philosophy that permeates every aspect of instruction. The three principles of this philosophy are collaboration, participation, and shared responsibility for learning among all participants—teachers and learners alike" (2012, 5).

According to Kaplowitz, information literacy instructors become more learner-centered when they

- listen to learners both prior to working with them and also during the actual instructional interactions;
- engage learners by allowing them to interact with the content in meaningful, relevant, and useful ways; and
- inspire learners to become lifelong learners by sharing their passion for the content and by expressing their heartfelt and honest belief in the potential of each and every one of them to become self-reliant, capable, self-confident learners and ultimately successful members of society (17—18).

SELF-REGULATION AND INFORMATION LITERACY

Student-centered learning suggests that the interests of the students should be recognized and groomed in order to help motivate greater involvement and appreciation for the students' learning activities, especially by the students themselves. Students need to demonstrate a high level of self-regulation and be active, responsible participants. Self-regulation of learning involves more than detailed knowledge of a skill. It involves the self-awareness, self-motivation, and behavioral skill to implement that knowledge appropriately (Zimmerman 2002).

Self-regulation can be defined as regulating the cognitive processes within oneself. Sara Wolf (2007), associate professor at Auburn University, was the first to raise and document the notion that there is a great deal of convergence between the disciplines of information literacy and self-regulation. Through her literature review, Wolf reports on the characteristics of self-regulation, including high personal initiative, perseverance, and the student becoming the driving force behind his or her learning. Students who have mastered high levels of self-regulation are able to adapt to different and difficult learning situations, changing learning strategies when necessary. Specific goal setting with a purpose and a desire to finish the task once started are also among the valued traits of the self-regulated student.

Wolf separates the basic information literacy steps from the self-regulated students' goal setting, metacognitive awareness, and motivational characteristics. She does, however, see convergence in these skills:

- Acquire and develop skills over a long term that are essential to lifelong learning.
- Have the ability to select and apply strategies that are appropriate to learning situations.
- Examine goals and strategies in light of success and failure; adjust as needed to accommodate varying levels of success.
- Integrate new information into existing knowledge in order to adapt current understanding of domain-specific knowledge.

Clearly, the student needs to mature to the highest levels of self-regulation before he or she enters the more demanding stages of inquiry at the open and free levels, as those levels require independent thought and persistent self- management abilities.

EVOLUTION IN INFORMATION LITERACY INSTRUCTION AND STUDENT-CENTERED LEARNING

Since the early 1980s there has been a clear progression in the school library field from education through information sources held in the library to instructional design and delivery based on student-centered learning. Some of these pathways have evolved through practice to upgrade the school librarian's role in the information age. Others have come directly from instructional theory being applied to the teaching role. Student-based inquiry has gained new acceptance in recent years.

While a few of the instructional models for teaching information literacy have dominated the past three decades, numerous additional interpretations of the instructional methods that work best to engage students and teachers have emerged. In nearly all cases, they have moved toward the principles of constructivist learning and inquiry. These processes and models are reviewed here to show how the progression has influenced national standards for school library media programs and has changed the mind-set of those who now see the major role of school libraries as being an environment that supports, enhances, and expands student learning. This has been a major evolution over the past five decades.

MEETING DIFFERENT LEARNING NEEDS

One of the best sources to monitor the history and development of information literacy and information skills instruction has been created by professor Nancy Pickering Thomas at Emporia State University. Now in its third edition (2011) and recently coauthored with assistant professor Sherry R. Crow of the University of Nebraska, Kearney, and award-winning educator Lori L. Franklin, *Information Literacy and Information Skills Instruction* clearly shows an expanding number of threads that have incorporated inquiry and student-centered learning into established and emerging information literacy instructional models.

One of many important summaries provided by Thomas and her colleagues is a description of the need to differentiate research tasks in ways that make them more student-focused in order to reach different individual learning challenges:

> A useful way to accommodate the learning styles and capitalize on learning strengths that individuals bring to learning tasks within the context of the library-based information-seeking tasks is to reframe or have students reframe research questions based on their own preferences. Handling research assignments in this way ensures that students actually have to interact with and apply the information they find to resolve a specific issue and present a synthesis in their own words. (121)

Different learning styles can be addressed through strategies that are multidimensional and student-centered. Among those that Thomas and her colleagues recommend are the following:

- Environmental: Provide for formal and informal settings; provide quiet and noisy spaces.
- Cognitive: Explain tasks in advance and provide an overview; provide oral, visual, as well as written instructions; provide multisensory approaches to learning; provide activities that call for both analysis and synthesis; where appropriate, encourage collegiality over authority; provide choices of projects, resources, activities, and equipment.
- Emotional: Expect responsible behavior in the completion of tasks; make learning activities relevant to student interests and concerns; express confidence and provide positive feedback.
- Social/cultural: Plan for both individual and small group work; interact with students as they work on projects; be sensitive to stylistic differences in behavior; provide research topics that are racially and ethnically inclusive.
- Physical: Allow for activity as well as reflection; vary activities and include some break time (Thomas, Crow, and Franklin 2011, 123).

BEING SUPPORTIVE OF DIFFERENT CULTURES

Kafi Kumasi (2010) at Wright State University has introduced aspects of what she describes as cultural inquiry to strengthen at least two student-centered aspects often missing in traditional inquiry models. If students are to gain independent status as they mature in the inquiry process, they should experience truly critical issues in learning spaces where they can openly challenge and explore structural inequalities.

> Inquiry-based instruction teaches students *how* to think rather than *what* to think. . . . Critical educators, according to Darder (1991), are those who "perceive their primary purpose as a commitment to creating the conditions for students to learn skills, knowledge and modes of inquiry that will allow them to critically examine the role that society has played in their self-formation."
>
> One way this sort of critical education can be achieved by librarians is by providing learners with opportunities to read and discuss books that incorporate multiple perspectives on a variety of topics or themes (e.g. immigration) and allow participants to openly grapple with the complexities of race and the human experience. (2010, 4)

According to Kumasi, "the difference between traditional inquiry models and cultural inquiry is that the latter emphasizes helping learners develop questions stemming from their social and cultural environments. . . . Essentially, information inquiry and information literacy divorces information problems from their social context and sees knowledge construction as discrete or autonomous facts. By contrast, cultural inquiry is rooted in sociocultural notions of knowledge which recognize learning as a communal act that is deeply intertwined with social, historical, and political forces" (2010, 3–4).

Teachers of inquiry need to enhance learning environments to support a greater understanding of these cultural factors, as they will inform the formation of inquiry topics and eventually the level of independence the student can gain in his or her own self-guided research.

BUILDING MORE THAN A BETTER HIGH SCHOOL TERM PAPER

Two early processes for library skills instruction that emerged in the 1980s and have had substantial influence since then are the information search process (IPS), developed by Carol Collier Kuhlthau (1983) and REACTS, formulated by Barbara Stripling and Judy Pitts (1988). This is not to say that these two methods are the "best," but they have proven to be frequently practiced, as have the Big6 problem-solving skill sets promoted by Mike Eisenberg and Bob Berkowitz (1990). While many models have been successfully implemented, IPS and REACTS serve to illustrate the progression toward greater student-centered inquiry education grounded in information skills.

Both IPS and REACTS were initially developed to improve the effectiveness and efficiency of the typical senior high school term paper and to generate some variety in the typical library assignment. Kuhlthau (1985) was seeking methods that would improve library skills instruction beyond the traditional source-oriented method and would be centered on the information held in the library. She had established a workable set of activities for teaching library skills to elementary grade students (1981), and her dissertation took her into the observation of high school students who successfully navigated the term paper assignment (1983). Stripling and Pitts were seeking methods to enrich the school library as more than a study-centered environment. They envisioned higher levels for creative student work. They were all experimenting with new approaches prior to the computer revolution, specifically prior to the Internet.

In both models, their creators examined then current practices and both proposed interventions to build a better product. While both took into account the needs of students, neither referenced inquiry learning as a process for expanding opportunities for enhancing learning through student-driven discovery. Both were tied to given academic assignments in need of modification. They each delivered many options for meaningful change, however.

MEETING COGNITIVE AND EMOTIONAL NEEDS THROUGH KUHLTHAU'S ISP

Kuhlthau (1983) accomplished her modifications of teaching the high school research and writing processes through observation of and interviews with advanced-level students engaged in their term paper projects. She applied learning theory explored in her doctoral studies at Rutgers University, combined with the successful intervention experiences she developed as an elementary school library media specialist. Her interventions, designed to meet the cognitive and emotional demands faced by students, not only proved to be effective in a small group of gifted high school students, but also have proven effective across dozens of other learning environments—formal and informal, adolescent and adult—and durable during the resource explosion of the information age. With an understanding of the information search process (ISP) stages, students made better use of their time and better use of library resources.

Kuhlthau published her "emerging theory for library instruction" in 1987. While making reference to inquiry learning, she remained more narrowly focused on the examination of information-seeking behavior and the application of constructivist learning theory to the writing process. This focus was understandable, as the emerging national guidelines (AASL and AECT 1988) for school libraries concentrated on the power of information access, management, and use.

Perhaps of greatest value have been Kuhlthau's techniques for gaining insight into student emotional needs and frustrations. Knowledge of when and how to intervene is essential for the teacher and school media specialist who want to successfully establish a more student-centered learning environment. Gaining this depth of understanding of student behavior creates positive teacher assurance and supportive confidence so that they and their students are more likely to be comfortable in a learning environment. Clearly her early intervention descriptions were foundational for teachers to become facilitators and counselors for learning through inquiry.

KUHLTHAU'S EMERGING THEORY ON LIBRARY INSTRUCTION

In 1987 the American Association of School Librarians published Kuhlthau's foundational article on an emerging theory of library instruction. Based on her successful interventions with teaching library skills to elementary school students and her dissertation on information-processing behaviors of high school students, Kuhlthau outlined the case for moving away from teaching library tools (the catalog, reference books, and indexes) and library orientations that emphasized information location and access skills, to emphasis on teaching students the processes of selecting and applying information.

Successful students, she found, managed to work their way through several important stages that took them from topic initiation, through literature exploration, to a focus on final presentation. Most successful students cycled back through these stages when necessary to address information gaps. Even more successful were those students who displayed the self-initiative to deal with frustrations and anxieties. Kuhlthau's emerging theory went beyond breaking the narrow tool orientation practice to the heart of dealing with students' cognitive and emotional needs as they tackled information research projects that were often not only new to them, but a monumental endeavor.

Nancy Pickering Thomas of Emporia State University (Thomas, Crow, and Franklin 2011) compiled an insightful review and clarification of Kuhlthau's work. Among her reflections are the following:

Interestingly, Kuhlthau found that exploration was a difficult stage for many students. Indeed, impatience with having to do the reading necessary to obtain an overall understanding of the topic sometimes caused students to jump over both exploration and formulation stages entirely and immediately to begin collecting information. Taking time to reflect on information obtained through exploring a topic thoroughly prepares students to create a focus. Unfortunately, as Kuhlthau notes, most information-seeking sessions are not structured to include time for processing information in this way. (40)

In Kuhlthau's view, it is essential that school librarians learn to recognize student moods so that they can intercede if students sustain an invitational mood so long that they are unable to decide on a topic or end a search so early that they select a focus without the necessary reflection. An emphasis on location and access skills may also serve to encourage students to close down prematurely their information-seeking activities before exploring all their options. (41)

Publication of *Seeking Meaning* (1993) galvanized Kuhlthau's user-centered research and gave greater emphasis to the various advising and counseling roles for librarians in higher education as well as K–12. She found that in more complex information-seeking tasks, feelings of uncertainty commonly increased and resulted in difficulties for focus formulation and completing the later stages of the writing process. Guidance from an educator who understood and had mastered such anxiety could increase the likelihood of successful information search and reporting procedures for the student.

Kuhlthau (1993) defined the following roles for librarians as educators. They illustrate the progression in the levels of intervention, based on student need, and would also be determined by the level of inquiry the student is expected to perform:

- Organizer: no assistance.
- Lecturer: introduction to the library; reference assistance.
- Instructor: assistance in locating and using a variety of relevant resources.
- Tutor: identification and use of relevant resources in a sequence.
- Counselor: assistance in understanding the process, in the development of search strategies, in the formulation of a focus, and determining relevance of retrieved items.

KUHLTHAU'S RESEARCH RECORD

Among many research studies completed over the past three decades, the following publications, selected from many authored or coauthored by Kuhlthau, tested various principles for successful application of constructivist learning theory to information use instruction:

- 1988: "Meeting the Information Needs of Children and Young Adults: Basing Library Media Programs on Developmental Stages." *Journal of Youth Services in Libraries* 2, no. 1: 51–57. Connecting cognitive-developmental stages to learning in libraries.
- 1989: "The Information Search Process of High-, Middle-, and Low-Achieving High School Seniors." *School Library Media Quarterly* 17, no. 4: 224–228. A large-scale examination of the information search process with high school seniors.
- 1990: "Validating a Model of the Search Process: A Comparison of Academic, Public, and School Library Users." *Library and Information Science Research* 12, no. 1: 5–32. Confirmation of the ISP in various types of libraries.
- 1993: "Implementing a Process Approach to Information Skills: A Study Identifying Indicators of Success in Library Media Programs." *School Library Media Quarterly* 22, no. 1: 11–18. Identifies inhibitors and enablers of implementing the ISP in K–12 contexts.
- 1993: "A Principle of Uncertainty for Information Seeking." *Journal of Documentation* 49, no. 4: 339–355. Explanation of the impact of emotion on the ISP.

- 1994: "Students and the Information Search Process: Zones of Intervention for Librarians." In *Advances in Librarianship*, edited by I. Goodden, 57–72. Academic Press. Introduction to the critical moments at which students need assistance and guidance.
- 1999: "The Role of Experience in the Information Search Process of an Early Career Information Worker." *Journal of the American Society for Information Science (JASIS)* 50, no. 5: 388–412. Comparison of novice/expert use of ISP in the workplace.
- 2004: *Seeking Meaning.* 2nd ed. Libraries Unlimited. Uncovers the problem of seeking meaning from information and the various roles librarians play in guiding the information search process.

A more extensive listing of Kuhlthau's studies resulting in progression and development of her ISP can be found in Kuhlthau, Maniotes, and Caspari (2007). Proven intervention strategies are described in relation to student readiness and ability for best implementing guidance from a member of an inquiry teaching team in Kuhlthau, Manitoes, and Caspari (2012). (An enhanced revision from Libraries Unlimited is scheduled for 2015.) Strategies that have been successful include the following:

- Immerse the students in exploring information and ideas prior to engaging in topic selection.
- Explore interesting, meaningful and challenging potential topics and expect students to retell information that is of interest to them and others.
- Have students reflect (with instructors, peers, parents, and within themselves for self-reflection) as they move through the process and log their experiences, thoughts, and feelings.
- Provide opportunities in inquiry conferences for students to test their ideas and determine the value of their topics and the information that may be accessible to support their endeavor.
- Support students, regardless of grade level, in going beyond the facts in order to interpret and extend meaning in the information they consider.
- Provide the opportunity for students to share their findings as a motivation to complete the process.

KUHLTHAU'S INFLUENCE AND PROGRESSION TOWARD GUIDED INQUIRY

As evidenced above, no other researcher has had a greater impact on the development of methods to guide students in the information search and use processes. More than forty years of practice and research have produced not only dozens of books and articles by Kuhlthau, but also an extensive array of hundreds of articles and dissertations by other researchers who have tested and applied her ISP model. She remains one of the most cited researchers in the library and information science discipline. In 2008 Kuhlthau, Heinstrom, and Todd revisited Kuhlthau's research record, and many associated studies to that date, in order to project ISP usefulness for future educational applications. In summary, they concluded that among other applications:

The [ISP] model is a useful framework for teaching students information seeking. In recent years, the Center for International Scholarship in School Libraries has used it as a conceptual framework for developing a program of inquiry-based learning. It has employed the model as a mechanism for teachers and school librarians to recognize critical moments when instructional interventions are essential in students' information-to-knowledge experiences. Students are often driven by the end product without allowing themselves time for gathering and synthesizing information as part of the process (McGregor and Streitenberger 2004). Particularly focus formation is challenging (Broch 2000; Branch 2003), [although] concept mapping has been found to help students in focus formation (Gordon 2000). When the model is used as a framework for guiding inquiry, students move away from simply collecting and compiling information to please teachers; rather, they become involved in thinking processes that require extensive exploration of ideas and formulation of thoughts before developing their own deep understanding of their topics and presenting it. By allowing time for reflecting and formulating while they are exploring and collecting information, they avoid missing the critical stages of learning. This close connection between the ISP model and learning reveals how important it is for teachers and librarians to guide students through this process (Kuhlthau et al. 2007). The diagnostic value of the model seems even more crucial in today's digital age. Research evidence suggests that students appear to settle for the first related information found. Now accustomed to easy access to information, students tend to skip preliminary exploratory searching and focus formulation and proceed to information collection for their final product, without building background knowledge and formulating essential questions that drive and direct their information seeking.

To address these problematic behaviors, Kuhlthau refashioned the ISP model to an instructional intervention agenda tailored on the principles of guided inquiry (2010). She recommended formation of instructional teams, including the school library media specialist, to provide the guidance needed to best enable successful student performance and to raise the level of the inquiry experience across all grades.

At this stage in the progression toward more emphasis on inquiry methods and student-centered learning, the question remains: Will more school librarians move to a team-oriented (interventionist and constructivist) role to guide inquiry, or will they remain only in their resource support role? Are we finally moving past theory and into effective practice? What can emerge over the coming decade in more frequent student-directed free inquiry?

Since 2008 the processes and principles of Guided Inquiry have become Kuhlthau's professional focus. Based on the research studies conducted by Kuhlthau and her colleagues, the Center for International Scholarship in School Libraries (CISSL) has been established at Rutgers, The University of New Jersey. Ross Todd serves as the director. The work at this center displays the evolution of inquiry applied to information literacy instruction across the past four decades. The following principles for Guided Inquiry, all student-centered, are promoted:

- Students learn by being actively engaged and reflecting on that experience.
- Students learn by building on what they already know.
- Students develop higher order thinking through guidance at critical points in the learning process.
- Students' development occurs in a sequence of stages.
- Students have different ways of learning.
- Students learn through social interaction with others.

Today, the researchers, staff, and members of the advisory board for CISSL work to uphold several beliefs. These clearly show adoption of and support for inquiry and student-centered learning over the past decades. Among these beliefs are the following:

- Inquiry learning is at the heart of effective teaching.
- Inquiry learning shifts emphasis to student questioning, critical thinking, problem solving, engagement with diverse information sources, and development of deep knowledge and understanding.
- Carefully designed teaching and learning initiatives that guide and engage students in their inquiry enable students to transform information into knowledge.

STRIPLING EVOLVES FROM REACTS TO AN INQUIRY CYCLE

Barbara Stripling and Judy Pitts were educators in the Arkansas public schools in the 1980s. Professionally active as coeditors of the AASL research journal *School Library Media Quarterly*, they were close colleagues with David Loertscher during his time in Arkansas as a school media educator. Their association led to Loertscher's (1982) development of a taxonomy to describe levels of growth in the educational services of the school library media center.

Stripling and Pitts used a similar taxonomy to describe the progression in learning skills that can increase depth, creativity and critical information use in library-based assignments, especially in secondary schools. Following the various assignments, they detailed (similar to Bloom's 1956 learning levels) how teachers and librarians could work together to build better library-based projects. Such thinking was evolutionary and their book, *Brainstorms and Blueprints* (1988), gained national attention.

Stripling and Pitts's REACTS taxonomy represented six levels of learning:

- Recalling—reporting the main facts
- Explaining—summarizing and paraphrasing information
- Analyzing—breaking a subject into its component parts and showing information relationships that highlight causes, effects, problems, and solutions
- Challenging—making critical judgments
- Transforming—bringing information together for a conclusion
- Synthesizing—creating an original product and visualizing and verbalizing findings to various audiences, especially those in the community (1988, 9–10).

As experienced and practicing school media specialist supervisors, Stripling and Pitts used the assignments drawn from national educational standards to move the planning and implementation of teaching information skills into a systematic process. They tied the library to the classroom and demonstrated how the library could be a center for learning across the schools.

While a wide variety of learning activities was possible, the team did not incorporate inquiry learning as a model until they entered doctoral studies later in their respective careers. They were, however, early movers for involving teachers with media specialists as co-instructional designers. Stripling (2011) documented again in her dissertation that a school librarian's effectiveness is diminished if librarians limit their role to that of resource provider, resulting in no integration into classroom instruction.

Eventually both Pitts and Stripling entered doctoral studies. Pitts explored the mental model development of middle grade students in project-based learning situations (Pitts 1994). Stripling, several years later, completed her doctoral dissertation at Syracuse University, exploring the potential for historical inquiry exploration by students and teachers at the secondary school level (Stripling 2011).

In both studies, these two exceptional leaders in the school library instruction field found, from the vantage point of researcher, with greater observation and analysis, that moving students as well as their teachers toward grasping the principles of inquiry was an extremely formidable task. School library media specialists are not likely to accomplish that task without a deep understanding of inquiry as well as being accepted fully into a co-instructional role. This implies extensive education in inquiry principles and application for those who seek a position as an educator in a twenty-first-century learning environment.

THE LEARNING CYCLE AND LEARNER-CENTERED TEACHING

Both Pitts and Stripling embraced learner-centered education through the school library media center. The library program is to be centered on the learning needs of students and the instructional needs of teachers as the persistent top goals. They raised the bar high for successful inquiry programs. Referring to the 2007 AASL standards for information skills and student learning, Stripling noted: "Also necessary for inquiry are dispositions (attitudes toward learning), responsibilities, and self-assessment or reflection" (2008, 50).

Stripling (1995) published a collegial analysis of Pitts's dissertation one year after Pitts tragically passed away from cancer. She highlighted several findings that support learning-centered inquiry but indicate that greater teacher and library media specialist guidance is required to address issues:

- Educators will not succeed in changing students' limited or incorrect mental models unless the models themselves are addressed. Educators must help students identify what those mental models are and where additional information or experience is needed.
- Each learning experience probably involves two strands—one content and one process. These strands are inextricably interwoven throughout learning. Pitts's very important finding is that instruction in information seeking and use must be integrated with content for subject matter learning to occur.
- Whatever framework is used for learning (the scientific method, a problem-solving model, a research-process model, or something else), students and teachers must remember that learning is recursive. Students move backward and forward throughout the process as they encounter difficulties, reflect on their own progress, make decisions, and react to input from others.
- This whole thoughtful-learning-cycle structure is surrounded by an essential network of ongoing assessment involving both reflection and feedback. Peers, teachers, and the learners themselves should reflect on the content and process and provide feedback to the learner at all phases of the learning cycle.

Clearly a major goal of those who foster a student-centered approach is that learning environments must be fashioned to increase the engagement of students directly with resources, peers, and teachers who will facilitate meaningful inquiry. To facilitate does not mean stepping back from the process. It means creating support systems that will make student-centered learning work. It means that library media teachers should hold master's-level credentials in both instruction and information management. Figure 1, constructed by Callison for this book, illustrates the progression of inquiry instruction, student-centered learning, and the educational roles needed to support such maturation.

In 2003 Stripling published details of her inquiry model. Explaining how inquiry may vary in methods employed for various disciplines, she also emphasized that students need to gain independence in order to fully engage in inquiry. The Internet, for example, has moved students more and more into the role of the first selector of information, rather than dealing with the information preselected for them through their school library collections. In order for student-centered learning to be established, teaching inquiry and literacy skills must be present across the curriculum. This is essential "to help individuals become independent learners who take ownership and responsibility for their own learning" (2003, 29).

Controlled Inquiry ———► Guided Inquiry ———► Modeled/Mentored Apprentice Inquiry ———► Free Inquiry

Instructional Purpose: Introduction & Practice ➤ Guidance ➤ Mentoring —————————► Independence

Student from Novice —————————► Student as Engaged Learner —————► to Mature Lifelong Learner

Master Teacher & Information Specialist ➤ Counselor ➤ Facilitator ➤ Mentor Independent Partner

Figure 1. The Progression of Inquiry Learning and the Change in Roles of Teacher and Student

REFERENCES

American Association of School Librarians (AASL). 2007. "Standards for the 21st-Century Learner." http://www.ala.org/aasl/standards-guidelines/learning-standards (accessed March 24, 2014).

American Association of School Librarians (AASL) and the Association for Educational Communications and Technology (AECT). 1988. *Information Power: Guidelines for School Library Media Programs*. Chicago: American Library Association.

Bloom, B. 1956. *Taxonomy of Educational Objectives*. New York: Longmans & McKay.

Branch, J. L. 2003. "Instructional Intervention Is the Key: Supporting Adolescent Information Seeking." *School Libraries Worldwide* 9, no. 2: 47–61.

Broch, E. 2000. "Children's Search Engines from an Information Search Process Perspective." *School Library Media Research* 3. http://www.ala.org/aasl/aaslpubsandjournals/slmrb/slmrcontents/volume32000/childrens (accessed March 22, 2014).

Callison, D. 1994. "Expanding the Evaluation Role in the Critical-Thinking Curriculum" In *Assessment in the School Library Media Center*, edited by C. C. Kuhlthau, 43–58. Englewood, CO: Libraries Unlimited.

Callison, D. 1999. "Inquiry." *School Library Monthly* 15, no. 6 (February): 38–42.

Center for International Scholarship in School Libraries (CISSL). n.d. Rutgers, the State University of New Jersey. http://cissl.rutgers.edu/ (accessed December 4, 2013).

Darder, A. 1991. *Culture and Power in the Classroom: A Critical Foundation for Bicultural Education*. New York: Bergin Garvey.

Donham, J., et al. 2001. *Inquiry-Based Learning*. Worthington, OH: Linworth.

Donham, J. 2008. *Enhancing Teaching and Learning*. New York: Neal-Schuman.

Donham, J. 2014. "Inquiry." In *Inquiry and the Common Core*, edited by V. H. Harada and S. Coatney, 3–16. Santa Barbara, CA: Libraries Unlimited.

Doyle, T. 2011. *Learner-Centered Teaching: Putting the Research on Learning into Practice*. Sterling, VA: Stylus.

Eisenberg, M. B. 2008. "Information Literacy: Essential Skills for the Information Age." *Journal of Library & Information Technology* 28, no. 2 (March): 39–47.

Eisenberg, M. B., and R. B. Berkowitz. 1990. *Information Problem-Solving: The Big Six Skills Approach to Library and Information Skills Instruction*. Norwood, NJ: Ablex.

Eisenberg, M. B., and M. K. Brown. 1992. "Current Themes Regarding Library and Information Skills Instruction: Research Supporting and Research Lacking." *School Library Media Quarterly* 20, no. 2 (Winter). http://www.ala.org/aasl/aaslpubsandjournals/slmrb/editorschoiceb/infopower/selcteisenberg (accessed March 22, 2014).

Kaplowitz, J. R. 2012. *Transforming Information Literacy Instruction Using Learner-Centered Teaching*. New York: Neal-Schuman.

Kuhlthau, C. C. 1981. *School Librarian's Grade-by-Grade Activities Program: A Complete Sequential Skills Plan for Grade K–8*. West Nyack, NY Center for Applied Research.

Kuhlthau, C. C. 1983. "The Library Research Process: Case Studies and Interventions with High School Seniors in Advanced Placement English Classes Using Kelly's Theory of Constructs." EdD diss., Rutgers, The State University of New Jersey.

Kuhlthau, C. C. 1985. *Teaching the Library Research Process*. West Nyack, NY: Center for Applied Research in Education.

Kuhlthau, C. C. 1987. "An Emerging Theory of Library Instruction." *School Library Media Quarterly* 16, no. 1 (Fall): 23–28.

Kuhlthau, C. C. 1993. *Seeking Meaning*. Norwood, NJ: Ablex.

Kuhlthau, C. C. 2004. *Seeking Meaning*. 2nd ed. Westport, CT: Libraries Unlimited.

Kuhlthau, C. C. 2010. "Guided Inquiry: School Libraries in the 21st Century." *School Libraries Worldwide* 16, no. 1: 17–28.

Kuhlthau, C. C., J. Heinstrom, and R. J. Todd. 2008. "The Information Search Process Revisited: Is the Model Still Useful?" *Information Research* 13, no. 4 (December). http://www.informationr.net/ir/13-4/paper355.html (accessed March 25, 2014).

Kuhlthau, C. C., L. K. Maniotes, and A. K. Caspari. 2007. *Guided Inquiry.* Westport, CT: Libraries Unlimited.

Kuhlthau, C. C., L. K. Maniotes, and A. K. Caspari. 2012. *Guided Inquiry Design: A Framework for Inquiry in Your School.* Santa Barbara, CA: Libraries Unlimited.

Kumasi, K. D. 2010. *Cultural Inquiry: A Framework for Engaging Youth of Color in the Library.* Detroit, MI: Wayne State University School of Library and Information Science Faculty Research Publications.

Levitov, D. D. 2014. "School Librarians and the CCSS: Knowing, Claiming, and Acting on Their Expertise." In *Inquiry and the Common Core,* edited by V. H. Harada and S. Coatney, 31–47. Santa Barbara, CA: Libraries Unlimited.

Loertscher, D. V. 1982. "The Second Revolution: A Taxonomy for the 1980s." *Wilson Library Bulletin* 56, no. 6 (February): 417–421.

Loertscher, David V. 2000. *Taxonomies of the School Library Media Program.* San Jose, CA: Hi Willow.

McGregor, J., and D. Streitenberger. 2004. "Do Scribes Learn?" In *Copying and Information Use,* edited by M. K. Chelton and C. Cool, 95–118. Lanham, MD: Scarecrow.

Pappas, M. L., and A. E. Tepe. 2002. *Pathways to Knowledge and Inquiry Learning.* Greenwood Village, CO: Libraries Unlimited.

Pitts, J. M. 1994. "Personal Understandings and Mental Models of Information." PhD diss., Florida State University.

Stripling, B. K. 1995. "Learning-Centered Libraries: Implications from the Research." *School Library Media Quarterly* 23, no. 3 (Spring): 163–170.

Stripling, B. K. 2003. "Inquiry-Based Learning." In *Curriculum Connections through the Library,* edited by B. K. Stripling and S. Hughes-Hassell, 3–39. Westport, CT: Libraries Unlimited.

Stripling, B. K. 2008. "Inquiry: Inquiring Minds Want to Know." *School Library Monthly* 25, no. 1 (September): 50–52.

Stripling, B. K. 2011. "Teaching the Voices of History through Primary Sources and Historical Fiction." DPS diss., Syracuse University.

Stripling, B. K. 2014. "Inquiry in the Digital Age." In *Inquiry and the Common Core,* edited by V. H. Harada and S. Coatney, 93–108. Santa Barbara, CA: Libraries Unlimited.

Stripling, B. K., and J. M. Pitts. 1988. *Brainstorms and Blueprints: Teaching Library Research as a Thinking Process.* Littleton, CO: Libraries Unlimited.

Thomas, N. P., D. Vroegindewey, and C. Wellins. 1997. "Tailoring Research Assignments to Student Learning Styles." Paper presented at the annual conference of the American Association of School Librarians, Portland, OR.

Thomas, Nancy Pickering, Sherry R. Crow, and Lori L. Franklin. 2011. *Information Literacy and Information Skills Instruction.* 3rd ed. Santa Barbara, CA: Libraries Unlimited.

Weimer, Maryellen. 2013. *Learner-Centered Teaching: Five Key Changes to Practice.* San Francisco: Jossey-Bass.

Wolf, Sara. 2007. "Information Literacy and Self-regulation: A Convergence of Disciplines." *School Library Media Research* 10. http://www.ala.org/aasl/aaslpubsandjournals/slmrb/slmrcontents/volume10/wolf_informationliteracy (accessed March 22, 2014).

Zimmerman, B. J. 2002. "Becoming a Self-Regulated Learner." *Theory into Practice* 41, no. 2: 64–70.

Chapter 5

Various Models and Multiple Perceptions of Inquiry

Inquiry levels can be further clarified when placed in relation to different learning theories. Esther Grassian and Joan Kaplowitz (2009) provide a clear discussion, classification, and application of learning theories to various learner population needs that arise during information literacy instruction. They wisely conclude that the most successful instructor of information use will be the professional who understands how to combine principles from different learning theories to address varied learner styles in different learning situations.

Some of the information in table 1 has been drawn from their summaries (46–49). Additional content is added to show how the progression in learning theories matches the progression in inquiry from controlled, to guided, to modeled, to mentored, and finally, as a goal that is very difficult to reach, to free inquiry. A review of inquiry models and learning standards given in this chapter illustrates that inquiry is much, much more than teaching a library research process. It is a way of learning and knowing that you are learning.

NRC AND SCIENCE INQUIRY STANDARDS FOR LEARNERS

One of the early attempts to define inquiry and the need to change some curricular practices to allow inquiry to progress more widely into the classroom was made by the National Research Council in 1996. The recommendations listed in table 2 are designed to create more opportunities for teachers and students to explore open, complex, and demanding inquiry projects through science education. This dichotomy provides illumination of what inquiry is not but can be if time, talented teachers, technology, and other resources are devoted to its practice.

By 2000 inquiry was fully embraced as the center of science education. Scientific inquiry refers to the diverse ways in which scientists study the natural world and propose explanations based on the evidence derived from their work. Inquiry also refers to the activities of students in which they develop knowledge and understanding of scientific ideas, as well as an understanding of how scientists study the natural world. It focuses on a scientifically oriented question, problem, or phenomenon, beginning with what the learner knows and actively engaging him or her in the search for answers and explanations (National Research Council 2000). Inquiry in science education is based on the following principles:

- Understanding science is more than knowing facts.
- Students build new knowledge and understanding on what they already know and believe.

Table 1. Levels of Inquiry Categorized by Education Theories

Structured or Controlled Inquiry	Guided and Modeled Inquiry	Mentored and Free Inquiry
Behaviorism (Watson, Skinner, Thorndike)	Constructivism (Vygotsky, Piaget, Dewey)	Humanism (Maslow, Rogers, Knowles)
Operates on the principles of stimulus–response. Assumes the learner is essentially passive, responding to environmental stimuli. The learner starts off as a clean slate. Behavior is shaped through positive or negative behavior in the learner. The learner is usually viewed as a passive recipient of instruction. The learner should be fully informed of learning objectives, determined by the teacher. Formative and summative evaluations are controlled by the teacher.	Learning is an active, constructive process; people actively construct or create their own subjective representations of objective reality. Learning is an active, contextualized process of constructing knowledge. Knowledge is constructed based on personal experiences and hypotheses. Each person has a different interpretation and construction of the knowledge process. The learner is not a blank slate, but brings past experiences and cultural factors to a situation.	Learning is viewed as a personal act to fulfill one's potential. Learning is student centered and personalized. The goal is to develop self-actualized people in cooperative, supportive environments. It is necessary to study the learner as a whole, especially as an individual grows and develops over the life span. The student participates completely in the learning process and has control over its nature and direction. Self-evaluation is the principal method of assessing progress.
Sample Teaching Practices: Break material into small units. Test for mastery at each level. The learner does not proceed to next step until achieving mastery of present step. Use guided experience plus hands-on practice. Include active question and answer periods. Provide immediate feedback for all responses and exams. Praise learners for correct answers, proper study habits, and other desirable behavior through supportive verbal or written comments. Allow time for learners to think and respond.	**Sample Teaching Practices:** Emphasize the active role of the learner. Emphasize learning through self-discovery. Allow learners to try things out and see what will happen— pose questions and seek their own answers. Allow sharing of results. Promote the learner as a discoverer who becomes an expert and then shares his or her new knowledge with the rest of the group. Attend to learner's state of readiness for a particular learning task. Place as much emphasis on how people learn (processes) as on the content material they are studying.	**Sample Teaching Practices:** Create comfortable, safe, and encouraging learning environments. Act as facilitator or coach who advises learners on how to develop their full potential. Give learners a role in determining their own goals and objectives. Give learners options about how to approach and learn about new material. Allow learners to participate in evaluation of their own work. Encourage people to learn more about themselves and how they relate to their role in society. Ask learners to think for themselves and to make their own decisions.

Table 2. Changing Emphasis to Promote Inquiry

Less emphasis on	More emphasis on
Activities that demonstrate and verify science content.	Activities that investigate and analyze science questions.
Investigations confined to one class period.	Investigations over extended periods of time.
Process skills out of context.	Process skills in context.
Individual process skills as observation or inference.	Understanding multiple process skills: manipulation, cognitive, procedural.
Getting an answer.	Using evidence and strategies for developing or revising an explanation.
Science as exploration and experiment.	Science as argument and explanation.
Providing answers to questions about science content.	Communicating science exploration.
Individuals and groups analyzing and synthesizing data without defending a conclusion.	Groups of students often analyzing and synthesizing data and defending conclusions.
Doing few investigations in order to leave time to cover large amounts of content.	Doing more investigations in order to develop understanding, ability, values of inquiry, and knowledge of science content.
Concluding inquiries with the result of an experiment.	Applying the results of experiments to scientific arguments and explanations.
Management of materials and equipment.	Management of ideas and information.
Private communication of student ideas and conclusions to teacher.	Public communication of student ideas and work to classmates.

Source: National Research Council (1996, 113).

- Students formulate new knowledge by modifying and refining their current concepts and by adding new concepts to what they already know.
- Learning is mediated by the social environment in which learners interact with others.
- Effective learning requires that students take control of their own learning.
- The ability to apply knowledge to novel situations, that is, transfer of learning, is affected by the degree to which students learn with understanding.

Inquiry-based learning can be used to stimulate growth in student understanding and application of scientific research methods in student-centered, community-centered, knowledge-centered, and assessment-centered environments. When students practice inquiry, it helps them develop their critical thinking abilities and scientific reasoning, while developing a deeper understanding of science (National Research Council 2000).

The following additional points can be drawn from National Research Council's *Inquiry and the National Science Education Standards* (2000) to define inquiry in relationship to science education and the scientific method:

- Scientific inquiry reflects how scientists come to understand the natural world and is at the heart of how students learn.
- Students learn how to ask questions and use evidence to answer them. In the process of learning the strategies of scientific inquiry, students learn how to conduct an investigation and collect evidence from a variety of sources, develop an explanation from the data, and communicate and defend their conclusions.

- Teachers should implement approaches to teaching science that cause students to question and explore and to use those experiences to raise and answer questions about the natural world. The learning cycle approach is one of many effective strategies for bringing explorations and questioning into the classroom. Librarians can enhance this through resource support of science papers and fairs.

- There is no fixed sequence of steps that all scientific investigations follow. Different kinds of questions suggest different kinds of scientific investigations. Different sources may have more or less value in various situations, and students should make informed judgments in selecting the best documentation.

THE FIVE E's LEARNING CYCLE IN NATIONAL GEOGRAPHIC SCIENCE CLASSROOMS

Judith Lederman (2009), director of teacher education at the Illinois Institute of Technology, has introduced a set of inquiry techniques organized under the following levels:

- Exploration: During these activities, students are given the question and instructions about how to go about answering it. Exploration activities often create experiences that cause students to become more curious and ask more questions.
- Direct inquiry: The problem and procedure are given directly, but the students are left to reach their own conclusions. Students have the opportunity to examine the same data and come to different conclusions.
- Guided inquiry: The research problem or question is provided, but students are left to devise their own methods and solutions. They apply analytical skills to support their evidence-based conclusions.
- Open-ended inquiry: The goal is for students to take full responsibility for all aspects of the investigation. Students determine problems, questions, methods, evidence, and conclusions.

The model for this practical application of inquiry is based on the five Es of learning: engagement, exploration, explanation, elaboration, and evaluation.

STANDARDS OF AASL, AECT, AND EVOLUTION TO THE NEW COMMON CORE

In 1998 the American Association of School Librarians (AASL), in cooperation with the Association for Educational Communications and Technology (AECT), prepared the document *Information Literacy Standards for Student Learning*. This publication provided for the first time tangible examples of the levels of information literacy and inquiry across the curriculum. Many of the content area standards for this AASL/AECT guide were extracted from Kendall and Marzano's (1997) *Content Knowledge: A Compendium of Standards and Benchmarks for K–12 Education*. Information literacy skills were clearly integrated with the content curriculum for all grade levels and shown in a progression from basic to proficient to exemplary student performance measures. Following is one example summarized from many detailed progressions:

- The student who is information literate uses information accurately and creatively.
  - Indicator 1: Organizes information for practical application.
    - Basic: Describes several ways to organize information: for example, chronologically, topically, and hierarchically.
    - Proficient: Organizes information in different ways according to the information problem or question at hand.

- Exemplary: Organizes an information product that presents different types of information in different ways.
- Students organize information to make sense of it and to present it most effectively to others. They understand their intended audience, the demands of the presentation format, and the essential ideas in the topic or issue being presented.
- Students integrate new information into their current knowledge, drawing conclusions by developing new ideas based on information they gather and connecting new ideas with their prior knowledge.

Examples drawn from across the curriculum include the following:

- Arts, theater: Applies research from print and nonprint sources to script writing, acting, design, and directing choices.
- English language arts: Synthesizes information from multiple research studies to draw conclusions that go beyond those found in any of the individual studies.
- Geography: Transforms primary data into maps, graphs, and charts.
- Health: Knows how to locate and use community health data, products, and services that provide valid health information.
- History: Knows how to construct time lines ordering significant historical developments that mark at evenly spaced intervals the years, decades, or centuries.
- Life skills: Uses tables, charts, and graphs in constructing arguments.
- Mathematics: Represents problem situations in and translates among oral, written, concrete, pictorial, and graphical forms.
- Physical education: Uses information from fitness assessments to improve selected fitness components (e.g., cardiorespiratory endurance, muscular strength and endurance, flexibility, and body composition).
- Science: Designs and conducts scientific investigations by formulating testable hypotheses; identifying and clarifying the questions, method, controls, and variables; organizing and displaying data; revising methods and explanations; presenting the results; and receiving critical response from others.
- Technology: Knows the common features and uses of desktop publishing software (e.g., documents are created, designed, and formatted for publication).

In 2007 the American Association of School Librarians adopted new "Standards for the 21st-Century Learner." The document is available without charge to any student, parent, or educator. It can be downloaded from http://www.ala.org/aasl/standards-guidelines/learning-standards.

Jean Donham (2014), a leading educator in school library studies at Northern Iowa University, states how important and unique the AASL Standards are, and in her description she enhances the definition of true inquiry:

> These student behaviors define a process that goes well beyond assembly of information toward constructing new understandings and insights. Further, [they] delineate skills, dispositions, and responsibilities, and self-assessment strategies to be applied in the inquiry process. No other standards encompass all these dimensions of learning. Yet genuine inquiry clearly requires more than skills. It demands of students the dispositions of a learner, such as curiosity, open-mindedness, and perseverance. Beyond dispositions and skills, inquiry requires a sense of responsibility for ethical use of information. To be an independent person of inquiry, one must be meta-cognitive: able to self-assess and self-correct. (7)

Following are selected portions of the Standards that illustrate the progression of inquiry-based learning concepts and principles. The online document provides many additional statements that are relevant to inquiry methods. The following are key.

All learners (including teachers) use skills, resources, and tools to do the following:

- Inquire, think critically, and gain knowledge. Selected examples:
  - Follow an inquiry-based process in seeking knowledge in curricular subjects and make the real world connection for using this process in one's own life.
  - Use prior and background knowledge as context for new learning.
  - Develop and refine a range of questions to frame the search for new understanding.
  - Find, evaluate, and select appropriate sources to answer questions.
  - Evaluate information found in selected sources on the basis of accuracy, validity, and appropriateness for needs, importance, and social and cultural context.
  - Read, view, and listen to information presented in any format (e.g., textual, visual, media, digital) in order to make inferences and gather meaning.
  - Make sense of information gathered from diverse sources by identifying misconceptions, main and supporting ideas, conflicting information, and point of view or bias.
  - Monitor gathered information and assess it for gaps or weaknesses.
- Draw conclusions, make informed decisions, apply knowledge to new situations, and create new knowledge. Selected examples:
  - Continue an inquiry-based research process by applying critical thinking skills (analysis, synthesis, evaluation, organization) to information and knowledge in order to construct new understandings, draw conclusions, and create new knowledge.
  - Use the writing process, media and visual literacy, and technology skills to create products that express new understandings.
  - Demonstrate flexibility in the use of resources by adapting information strategies to each specific resource and by seeking additional resources when clear conclusions cannot be drawn.
  - Use both divergent and convergent thinking to formulate alternative conclusions and test them against the evidence.
  - Determine how to act on information (accept, reject, modify).
  - Develop directions for future investigations.

The 2014 Common Core State Standards (CCSS) Initiative (http://www.corestandards .org/) also contains many statements for student learning that reflect inquiry-based learning across the grade levels and academic disciplines. The American Association of School Librarians has developed a curricular crosswalk that matches inquiry performances and information learning standards from AASL to the CCSS Initiative (http://www.ala.org/aasl/standards-guidelines /crosswalk). A few standards that illustrate the CCSS relationship to inquiry are listed here, and many others are noted in other chapters of this book:

- Write arguments to support claims with clear reasons and relevant evidence.
- Write informative/explanatory texts to examine a topic and convey ideas, concepts, and information through the selection, organization, and analysis of relevant content.
- Conduct short research projects to answer a question, drawing on several sources and generating additional related, focused questions for further research and investigation.
- Gather relevant information from multiple print and digital sources, using search terms effectively; asses the credibility and accuracy of each source; and quote or paraphrase the data and conclusions of others while avoiding plagiarism and following a standard format for citation.

COLLEGE AND CAREER STANDARDS FROM OTHER STATES: THE INDIANA EXAMPLE

A few states have decided not to adopt the national Common Core standards. Their reasons seem to be based more on political arguments opposing the methods for review and implementation than on specific academic content. Individual states, such as Indiana, have adopted their own standards based on the premise that these are recommended guidelines for schools to provide the best learning environment to prepare students for college and careers. The Indiana Academic Standards include the expectation for teachers to understand and implement inquiry methods across all grade levels for the purpose of teaching and learning in science, mathematics, social studies, and language arts. Specific examples of skills associated with inquiry include the following:

- Argumentative Writing. Grades 11–12: Introduce precise, knowledgeable claims(s), establish the significance of the claim(s), distinguish the claim(s) for alternate or opposing claims, and create an organization that logically sequences claims, counterclaims, reasons, and evidence. Develop claim(s) and counterclaim(s) fairly and thoroughly, supplying the most relevant evidence for each while pointing out the strengths and limitations of both in a manner that anticipates the audience's knowledge level, concerns, values, and possible biases.
- The Research Process. Grades 9–10: Conduct short as well as more sustained research assignments and tasks to build knowledge about the research process and the topic under study. Formulate an inquiry question, and refine and narrow the focus as research evolves. Gather relevant information from multiple authoritative sources, using advanced searches effectively, and annotate sources. Assess the usefulness of each source in answering the research question.
- Discussion and Collaboration. Grades 9–10: Initiate and participate effectively in a range of collaborative discussions (one-on-one, in groups, and teacher-led) on grade-appropriate topics, texts, and issues, building on others' ideas and expressing personal ideas clearly and persuasively.
- Comprehension. Grades 9–10: Integrate multiple sources of information presented in diverse media and formats (e.g., visually, quantitatively, orally) evaluating the credibility and accuracy of each source. SL. 3.2: Evaluate a speaker's point of view, reasoning, and use of evidence and rhetoric, identifying any fallacious reasoning or exaggerated or distorted evidence.
- Presentation of Knowledge and Ideas. Grades 9–10: Present information, findings, and supporting evidence clearly, concisely, and logically such that listeners can follow the line of reasoning and the organization, development, substance, and style are appropriate to purpose, audience, and task.
- Media Literacy. Grades 9–10: Critically analyze information found in electronic, print, and mass media used to inform, persuade, entertain, and transmit culture.

COMMUNITY INQUIRY AT ILLINOIS

Working with local educators in Illinois, Bruce and Bishop (2008) have coordinated several interactive learning experiences that demonstrate how inquiry in and of itself is the experience of learning and knowing when meaningful learning has transpired. They provide the following definition:

Community inquiry research focuses on people participating with others, on the lived experiences of feeling, thinking, acting, and communicating. It sees literacy as part of living in the world, not simply as a skill to be acquired in the classroom. Inquiry is central, because as people live, they encounter challenges. Through inquiry, people recognize a problem, mobilize resources, engage actively to resolve it, collaborate, and reflect on the experience. Making sense of experience in this way, and doing so in concert with others in embodied, historical circumstances, is fundamental to learning. (699)

While warning that their inquiry cycle should not be interpreted as a linear or recursive cycle in which steps neatly follow and flow from one to the next, five aspects of their cycle clearly illustrate the processes that take place as humans (working together as much as possible) grapple with problems and options that may be or may not be solutions. These steps are to ask, investigate, create, discuss, and reflect.

Grounded in John Dewey's (1991) educational philosophy, participants in community inquiry face what Dewey identified as "indeterminate situations" (asking) and work in collaborative ways to test alternative solutions (investigating possible answers). In authentic contexts, teachers, students, and other community members become partners in inquiry, to deal with both personal and academic needs. They engage in hands-on learning to create possible new meanings from various roles as problem solvers.

Discussion is key to the process, as participants learn from listening to each other. Through discussion or dialogue, construction of knowledge becomes a social enterprise. Reflection brings out at least two aspects that are important: (1) action to be taken from the new meaning drawn from the process; and (2) recognizing additional, likely new or previously unseen, indeterminacies, leading to continuing inquiry (new questions and more discussion).

GRAPHIC INQUIRY: LAMB AND CALLISON

Graphic inquiry involves extracting information from and presenting information in visual formats such as political cartoons, diagrams, maps, photos, charts, tables, and multimedia. Graphics are visual representations created on paper, the computer screen, or other surfaces to communicate information. Although graphics may simply provide a visual illustration of a concept, they often include numbers, words, and other symbols. Graphics may also represent fiction or nonfiction content. For example, an artist may create a 3-D picture of a fantasy world using imaging software, while a geologist may draw and label a cross section of a mountain (Callison and Lamb 2007a).

Graphic Inquiry (Lamb and Callison 2012) presents activities for all grade levels, designed in support of the Common Core State Standards Initiative, that call for students to translate quantitative or technical information expressed in words in a text into visual form (e.g., a table or chart) and translate information expressed visually. Graphic inquiry covers a wide range of media skills in support of the expectation that students will integrate visual information with other information in print and digital texts. "Graphic Inquiry for All Learners" (Lamb and Callison 2011) is reprinted in section II of this book to help illustrate the learning and teaching aspects of graphic inquiry.

Children learn to read pictures before they read words. Unfortunately, we often stop teaching visually once children can read. In the information age, it's important to continue to help them interpret the visual world. From books and television to billboards and animation, children are bombarded with graphic images (Callison and Lamb 2007b). Lamb maintains an extensive interactive Web site, Get Graphic (http://www.eduscapes.com/sessions/graphic/graphic inquiry.htm), to which she adds new examples of learning activities. She has presented workshops in graphic inquiry across the country and links these activities to her graduate courses at Indiana University-Purdue University at Indianapolis.

INFORMATION INQUIRY: CALLISON AND LAMB

Daniel Callison has defined information inquiry in relationship to a debate or argument curriculum. The overriding task for the student is to determine the validity of evidence and to build arguments based on the most current, relevant, authoritative evidence possible. There are also roles for the student to play in discussions to question the validity of evidence presented by others. Thus the student engages in establishing claims and cross-examination of counterclaims. Annette Lamb maintains a Web site on virtual information inquiry and graphic inquiry (http://eduscapes.com/sessions/graphic/dynamic.htm) that provides examples of information inquiry at various student learning maturation levels.

Callison defined information inquiry in *The Blue Book for Information Age Inquiry, Instruction and Literacy* (Callison and Preddy 2006) as follows:

> Information inquiry is a teaching and learning process based on five information and media literacy elements of questioning, exploration, assimilation, inference, and reflection. These elements are common to most models for information search and use as well as information problem solving. These elements are represented in a cyclical process [see figure 1] necessary to address new questions that arise in an investigation. These elements interact and trigger each time the inquirer confronts new information. The five elements of information inquiry have been matched to the essential questions of the information curriculum [see table 3].
>
> Learning is often based on authentic projects, issues, and reflections that are interwoven among personal, academic, and workplace information needs.... Specifically related to information literacy, information inquiry involves those processes to determine the adequacy of the information needed, located and selected for use. Judgment of information adequacy will include reflection on the information in terms of age, authority, completeness, and relevance to information need, task, argument, and audience. [If the information held is not adequate, then students should use appropriate methods to generate original data. Therefore, information inquiry instruction may include introduction to basic data generating methods, and the student may take steps similar to the professional information scientist in gathering and analyzing new data.]
>
> Through Socratic Methods applied to dialogue, discussion, and debate, the ultimate task in information inquiry is to determine the dequacy of information as convincing evidence from which justification can be made to present meaningful arguments, conclusions, and actions. Reflection includes considering the ethical methods in obtaining information, the limitations of the information acquired, and the adjustments that should be made to increase efficiency and effectiveness in information access and use to meet further needs and tasks (81–82).

The measures of success in information literacy, therefore, include the student's ability not only to show the value of information through argument and comparison of information

Figure 1. Callison's Recursive Information Inquiry Cycle with Interactive Elements.

Table 3. Information Curriculum* and Portfolio Questions**

Five Elements of Information Inquiry	Information Skill Portfolio Question	The student should demonstrate the ability to:
Questioning Raising the information need	What do I need to do?	Analyze the information task. Analyze the audience's information need or demand. Describe a plan of operation. Select important or useful questions and narrow or define the focus or the assignment. Describe possible issues to be investigated.
Exploring Reading, viewing, listening	Where could I go?	Determine the best initial leads to relevant information. Determine possible immediate access to background information (gaining the larger picture). Consider information sources within and beyond the library.
	How do I get the information?	Identify relevant materials. Sense relationships between information items (supporting or countering each other; one leading to others based on sources cited). Determine which resources are most likely to be authoritative and reliable. Consider and state the advantages and disadvantages of bias. Consider discovered facts and search for counter facts. Consider opinions and look for counter opinions. Determine extent of need for historical perspective.
Assimilation Accepting, incorporating, rejecting	How shall I use the resources?	Determine if the information is pertinent to the topic. Estimate the adequacy of the information. Test validity of the information. Group data in appropriate categories according to appropriate criteria.
	Of what should I make a record?	Extract significant ideas and summarize supporting, illustrative details. Define a systematic method to gather, sort, and retrieve data. Combine critical concepts into a statement of conclusions. Restate major ideas of a complex topic in concise form. Separate a topic into major components according to appropriate criteria. Sequence information and data in order to emphasize specific arguments or issues.
Inference Application for solution and meaning	Do I have the information I need?	Recognize instances in which more than one interpretation of material is valid and necessary. Demonstrate that the information obtained is relevant to the issues of importance if necessary, state a hypothesis or theme, and match evidence to the focused goal of the paper or project. Reflect, edit, revise, and determine if previous information search and analysis steps should be repeated.

(*continued*)

Table 3. Information Curriculum* and Portfolio Questions** (*continued*)

	How should I present it?	Place data in tabular form using charts, graphs, or illustrations. Match illustrations and verbal descriptions for best impact. Note relationships between or among data, opinions, or other forms of information. Propose a new plan, create a new system, interpret historical events, and/or predict likely future happenings. Analyze the background and potential for reception of ideas and arguments by the intended audience. Communicate orally and in writing to teachers and peers.
Reflection Adjustment for additional questioning	What have I achieved?	Accept and give constructive criticism. Reflect and revise again, and again if necessary. Describe the most valuable sources of information. Estimate the adequacy of the information acquired and judge the need for additional resources. State future questions or themes for investigation. Seek feedback from a variety of audiences.

*Marland (1981).

**Callison (1993, 1994, 1998).

to determine that which is most credible, but also to demonstrate how he or she becomes more effective and efficient in information access and application with practice over time. Efficient students can identify key resources, search guides, and expert contacts. Success in new knowledge experiences makes them more likely to enter into future inquiry projects. They understand when various types of data may be most useful: primary, secondary, or tertiary; popular, professional, or academic; original, secondary, or standard.

Part of the students' reflection on their projects can be a review of sources used and determining which were most valuable and which were least relevant and least useful. Students experienced in information inquiry can move to more mature levels of framing new inquiry projects from the beginning and focus on the important phases, leading to the conclusion of their projects often in a more rapid manner because they are experienced in the inquiry method.

As an example, this book could be taken as a project that I, as an adult inquirer, could reflect on for purposes of identifying the best sources of information pertaining to inquiry methods and challenges in teaching students how to select valid information. Examples drawn from such an analysis could include the following as actions for future inquiry:

- Follow future reports on digital media and learning from the MIT Press sponsored by the John D. and Catherine T. MacArthur Foundation (e.g., Ito et al. 2010).
- Employ on a local basis the survey that Flanagin and Metzger (2010) developed for measuring a national student and parent population concerning their understanding and use of credible online sources.
- Follow closely the best practices of school library media specialists such as Frances Jacobson Harris at the University of Illinois Lab School and converse with them frequently on the issues they attempt to address in teaching inquiry and refined searching of the Internet.
- Read frequently the research compilations from fields such as instructional systems technology and from information literacy, in addition to the evolving standards from the American Association of School Librarians, in order to gain a wider perspective on successful teaching techniques that apply sophisticated technologies.

- Follow closely the research and publications of the Center for International Scholarship in School Libraries at Rutgers University, as well as the growing number of publications on information inquiry from such publishers as Libraries Unlimited and ALA.

This is a list of information inquiry content learned from the inquiry experience. It sets the stage for further investigation. Of course not all student researchers will summarize a future inquiry agenda in such an academic manner, but they will find value in reflecting on their best information sources. Such consideration can transform their future inquiry studies no matter how formal or informal.

MOVING BEYOND SATISFACTORY INFORMATION TO THE BEST INFORMATION

The more mature information inquirer is also a learner who does not settle for just satisfactory information to address the information need, but persists to identify and acquire the best and most credible information possible. This determination is a characteristic of the successful students expected to emerge from application of the new Common Core State Standards. The portrait of mature information inquirers (paraphrased from the introduction to "English Language Arts Standards"; CCSS Initiative n.d.) should include the following:

- Demonstration of moving toward independence (and eventually becoming free inquirers).
- Building strong content knowledge as well as an understanding of methods and processes for gathering information and engaging in effective communications.
- The ability to respond to varying demands of audience, task, purpose, and academic discipline.
- The ability to comprehend as well as offer critique.
- Valuing credible evidence (as they become aware of what problems invalid information can cause).
- Understanding and valuing other perspectives and cultures.

An important part of the reflections that mature information inquirers make is the identification of resources of value of which they were not aware prior to the inquiry experience. They may discover, therefore, not only subject content, but also specific journals, content experts, databases, publishers, and more. Such increased knowledge of credible information sources should be noted by students in their reflections and serve to demonstrate a growth in sophistication of resource selection over time and across inquiry projects. In other words, information inquiry is not just a process to complete an investigation or to solve an information need; it is a learning experience through which the student accumulates knowledge of the quality levels within the information world and becomes more discriminating in the selection of resources.

Products of information inquiry (papers, media presentations) should be candidates for portfolios that represent the students' progression in information literacy across their academic careers. Information inquiry can be the foundation for more extensive knowledge and skills compiled by teachers and students as they gain more sophistication in the management of technologies for instruction and information. In 2008 Zmuda and Harada observed:

> Daniel Callison (Callison and Preddy 2006) coined the term "information inquiry" to succinctly capture this relationship of inquiry with information and media fluency. He says that information inquiry ranges from 'posing personal questions to organized student research activities, to formal investigations and academic thesis experiences, to research based on standard and rigorous methodologies' (Callison and Preddy 2006, 6). Callison also indicates that information

fluency, which is the ability to move effectively across "a variety of information search strategies, information systems, databases, and communication techniques" and to "assimilate, manage, and apply" these technologies and information systems (Callison and Preddy 2006, 81). The "Standards for the 21st Century Learner" from the American Association of School Librarians (2007) targets the vision that Callison describes. These new standards pose both challenge and opportunity for library media specialists to provide students with meaningful experiences in applying foundational skills that deal with information in productive and ethical ways. (87)

Callison created one of the first graduate courses in library and information science that deals extensively with the application of information inquiry. He launched Information Inquiry for School Teachers at Indiana University in Bloomington in 1991 along with a graduate course in information user education. Since his retirement, Annette Lamb, Leslie Preddy, and Kym Kramer have frequently taught these courses and have written and published widely on inquiry methods.

Lamb maintains an interactive Web site that supports the concepts related to information age inquiry and virtual inquiry, now a part of Eduscapes (http://eduscapes.com/). Stories, courses, and various educational situations on this Web site illustrate the evolution of inquiry in our personal lives as we grow and mature in learning effective use of information. In 2004 Callison and Lamb published an extensive discussion of the various aspects of authentic learning that are necessary for inquiry to be applied to real-world situations. The following year Callison (2005a, 2005b) published a description of the student as an information scientist, using the metaphor to illustrate the application of information inquiry that engages students to act as scientists in gathering, organizing, and evaluating information sources. The *School Library Monthly* articles that describe this student information scientist role are reprinted in section II of this book.

KUMASI'S CRITICAL AND CULTURAL INQUIRY

While working on her doctorate at Indiana University, Kafi Kumasi developed her perspectives on information inquiry. She found that several aspects were lacking in the traditional models for inquiry and information literacy instruction (Kumasi-Johnson 2007; Kumasi 2010). First, students were not placed in roles in which they could be truly critical. Second, students, especially minority students, faced issues within a cultural context of white society. In order to explore issues critically within their own historical heritage, minority students need to consider social issues in relation to their own culture. In both cases, this meant time for reading and discussion of these perspectives in addition to the other processes normally experienced in inquiry-based projects.

"Critical inquiry is much more than simply asking questions. Rather it deals with an understanding of the meaning and significance of the questions asked in relation to larger social issues. . . . Consequently, critical inquiry is often articulated in complex ways. . . . This approach to inquiry is rooted in critical theory and calls upon library media specialists to become change agents who provides spaces for students to openly question, challenge, and investigate social and cultural issues" (Kumasi-Johnson 2007, 42).

"Although library scholars have developed over a dozen inquiry models in recent years, these models offer a more general approach to learning that may not be useful in reaching young learners from historically underrepresented backgrounds. . . . Yet by itself, social constructivist theory does not fully help librarians understand how to tap into students' social and cultural environments as a place for them to develop personal meaning and tackle larger structural issues affecting their communities. . . . cultural inquiry is rooted in sociocultural notions of knowledge which recognize learning as a communal act that is deeply intertwined with social, historical, and political forces" (Kumasi 2010, 3–4).

"The first question that should be asked [by school librarians] is, *Can the youth in my community benefit from learning how to ask and answer questions that have to do with creating social consciousness and social justice for marginalized people?* If you answer 'yes' to this question, you cannot absolve yourself from the responsibility of attempting to create a library learning environment or program where cultural inquiry is fostered" (Kumasi 2010, 6).

PREDDY'S STUDENT INQUIRY IN THE RESEARCH PROCESS

Leslie Preddy is an award-winning state and national leader in school library media management. She was selected as AASL president-elect in 2014 (http://www.ala.org/news/press -releases/2014/05/preddy-elected-2015-2016-aasl-president). Preddy is also an author of strategies for effective silent reading promotion (Preddy 2007; 2010). Like some other school librarians, she has used the various models for teaching information literacy and problem solving to develop her own approach, tailored to the experiences and needs of her own local middle school students and teachers. She has also drawn heavily from various articles in *School Library Monthly*, especially key words in instruction, and from the book *Key Words, Concepts and Methods for Information Age Instruction: A Guide to Teaching Information Inquiry* (Callison 2003).

Preddy was awarded grant funding through the Indiana Department of Public Instruction to support development and field testing of her "Student Inquiry in the Research Process" program. She found that strategies involving student research journals, interviewing human resources, and drawing on primary sources frequently fit the needs of her students. Her teaching materials are also detailed in *The Blue Book for Information Age Inquiry, Instruction and Literacy* (Callison and Preddy 2006) and have been reprinted in *21st Century Learning in School Libraries* (Fontichiaro 2009).

Preddy and Callison (2006) have described inquiry as a process whereby students are involved in their learning; formulate questions; investigate widely; and then build new understandings, meanings, and knowledge. That knowledge may be used to answer a question, to develop a solution, or to support a position or point of view. The knowledge is usually presented to others and may result in some sort of action. New questions come from the inquiry experience in a never-ending cycle.

Preddy's personal definition of inquiry moves from the practical to the ideal, founded in the standards for school library programs. Describing inquiry research basics, she notes:

Inquiry seems like such a small, unassuming word that it can be overlooked as inconsequential. It's not a word that is used often in casual conversation with friends or co-workers. It's not even fun to say—it is actually a little awkward when you think about it. But the meaning behind that one little word in relation to student research has far-reaching potential. When trying to make sense of the world around us, and helping students make sense of the world as well, inquiry is a powerful word with even more powerful tools. Inquiry is a method to employ that allows students, teachers, and library media specialists to work together toward becoming independent thinkers. *A Planning Guide for Information Power: Building Partnerships for Learning* (ALA/AASL 1999) defines inquiry as the process for formulating appropriate research questions, organizing the search for data, analyzing and evaluating the data found, and communicating the results in a coherent presentation. It gets to the heart of that which we, as library media specialists and educators, are concerned: valuing the process a researcher goes through as much, if not more, than the final product. Inquiry is a method for recognizing the need to teach ourselves and others to think things through as we question, read, analyze, investigate, reflect, internalize, hypothesize, and present our findings and theories in a way that is audience appropriate. It is a way to get away from just reporting the facts and move toward developing the skills necessary for students to become independent thinkers with a self-awareness and ability to problem solve throughout life. (Callison and Preddy 2006, 225)

PATHWAYS TO INQUIRY: PAPPAS AND TEPE

Marjorie Pappas and Ann Tepe, an innovative teaching team in Ohio higher education, designed for the Follette Software Company an illustration of the processes for learning through student engagement with multiple resources. This model was one of the first visual depictions of stages relevant to inquiry learning that expanded out across the tools and technologies to support discovery. Pappas and Tepe added specific elements of inquiry in their book *Pathways to Knowledge and Inquiry Learning* (2002).

Unique to their framework is the beginning and central phase, describing the appreciation students and teachers need to gain for literature. The cultural background of meaningful documents is essential to moving through the pathways extending into inquiry projects. Students and teachers need to have this appreciation in order to have a foundation for asking intelligent questions. Pappas and Tepe explain this important first step as follows:

> Individuals appreciate literature, the arts, nature, and information in the world around them through varied and multiple formats, including stories, film, paintings, natural settings, music, books, periodicals, the Web, video, etc. Appreciation often fosters curiosity and imagination, which can be a prelude to a discovery phase in an information seeking activity. As learners proceed through the stages of information seeking their appreciation grows and matures throughout the process. (2002, 107)

The appreciation stage is followed by a presearch stage:

> The Presearch stage enables searchers to make a connection between their topic and prior knowledge. They may begin by brainstorming a web or questions that focus on what they know about their topic and what they want to know. This process may require them to engage in exploratory searching through general sources to develop a broad overview of their topic and explore the relationships among subtopics. Presearch provides searchers with strategies to narrow their focus and develop specific question or define information needs. (2002, 107)

Four additional stages follow: search, interpretation, communication, and evaluation. Each stage expands outward to include a wide variety of processes, nearly all student-centered. Pappas and Tepe are careful to note that the illustration of the Pathways to Knowledge includes recursive paths, as students and teachers often need to move in nonlinear directions that clarify, repeat, and reinforce.

According to Pappas (2000), "Inquiry requires students to be active rather than passive learners, which means that teachers and library media specialists must engage them in a learning task that allows meaningful choices. There is a social context to inquiry learning in the sense that students need opportunities to discuss and share new ideas. Such discussions allow students to discover new ideas, see relationships between ideas, and build new knowledge in ways that might not be possible if students were left to learn on their own."

Although not the original graphic model designed by Pappas and Tepe (2002), table 4 is a representation of the creative aspects of their early inquiry learning process.

Table 4. Pathways to Knowledge

Five Elements of Information Inquiry	Stages	Tasks	Strategies
Questioning Raising the Information Need	<u>Appreciation and Enjoyment</u>	Sensing, viewing, listening, reading, curiosity, enjoyment	
	<u>PreSearch</u> establish a focus	Develop an overview	Brainstorm, formulate initial questions, build background, identify key words, relate to prior knowledge, explore general sources.
Exploring Reading, Viewing, Listening		Explore Relationships	Define questions, cluster, outline, webbing, listing, and narrowing and broadening Provides searchers with strategies to narrow their focus and develop specific questions or define information need Makes a connection between their topic and prior knowledge
	<u>Search</u> planning and implementing search strategy	Identify Information providers	Home and computer resources, museums, zoos, historical sites, libraries, etc.
		Select information Resources and Tools	Indexes, people, Internet, media, reference resources, etc.
		Seek Relevant Information	Skim and scan, interview, confirm information and sources, record information, determine relevancy of information, explore and browse widely
Assimilation Accepting, Incorporating, Rejecting	<u>Interpretation</u>	Interpret Information	Assessing usefulness of information and reflecting to develop personal meaning Compare and contrast, integrate concepts, determine patterns and themes, infer meaning, analyze, synthesize, classify, filter, organize, and classify
Inference Application for Solution and Meaning	<u>Communication</u> Construct and present new knowledge	Apply information	Choose appropriate communication format, solve a problem, answer a question, and respect intellectual property
		Share new knowledge	Compose, design, edit, revise, use most effective medium such as video, report, mural, portfolio, and animation
Reflection Adjustment for additional questioning	<u>Evaluation</u> Think about process and product	Evaluate	End product, effective communication, redefining new questions, use of resources, meeting personal information needs. Evaluation is ongoing in their nonlinear information process and should occur throughout each stage. Through this continuous evaluation and revision process that searchers develop the ability to become independent searchers.

*Follett Software Company; Pappas and Tepe (1995).

STRIPLING'S INQUIRY MODEL

Barbara Stripling has been a leader in library and information skills curriculum development since her days in media program supervision in Arkansas and her collaborative work there with Judy Pitts and David Loertscher. Stripling and Pitts offered one of the early models for applying information literacy to the high school term paper. Their REACTS model offered progressive stages that enhanced the research and writing experiences and eventually served to help the team visualize learning as a cycle; it was documented as a part of Pitts's doctoral work at Florida State University (1994).

Working through her own doctoral studies, Stripling moved much of her previous thinking into a framework for inquiry, beyond the application in the science classroom only and across the curriculum in all disciplines. Her approach has been adopted in major school districts of New York and in recent years in many other schools in the nation. Stripling's progression to inquiry is expressed in the following statements defining inquiry and applying her model representing a cycle for inquiry learning: "Inquiry is a process of learning that is driven by questioning, thoughtful investigating, making sense of information, and developing new understandings. It is cyclical in nature because the result of inquiry is not simple answers, but deep understanding that often leads to new questions and further pursuit of knowledge. The goal of inquiry is not the accumulation of information; it is the exploration of significant questions and deep learning" (Stripling 2008, 50).

In her extensive discussion of inquiry connections across the curriculum, Stripling (2003) offered these observations:

> Inquiry is not just for science class anymore. In schools across the country, educators are responding to the increased emphasis on high standards and to a strengthening body of research about learning and the brain by developing an in-depth, inquiry-based approach to curriculum, teaching, and learning (4). . . .
>
> But inquiry is much more than simply following a process. It is an essence of teaching and learning that places students at the heart of learning by empowering them to follow their sense of wonder into new discoveries and insights about the way the world works (5). . . .
>
> Inquiry is essentially, although subtly, different from an information problem-solving model of student research. Both inquiry and information problem solving are based on a process, a frame for learning. . . . [I]nquiry more closely matches the principles of constructivism: meaning is constructed by the learner; the curriculum is based on big concepts; assessment is founded on student work rather than on teacher generated tests; and the teacher's role is to interact and mediate the environment. . . . Both inquiry and information problem solving result in a research product, but inquiry may be more likely to engender long-lasting, in-depth learning by each individual (5–6). . . .
>
> Inquiry is not a collection of process skills and strategies; it is a relationship between thinking skills and content. Learners are, therefore, engaged in scientific inquiry, historical inquiry, social inquiry, literacy inquiry, aesthetic inquiry, and other types of inquiry. The overall framework of inquiry is essentially the same for every content area, but the embedded process skills are applied in discipline-specific ways (6).

Stripling's new inquiry model is constructed on learning phases, depicted in a linear fashion here, but in practice recursive and interactive (2003, 8):

- Connect
  - o Connect to self, previous knowledge
  - o Gain background knowledge to set context for new learning
  - o Observe, experience

- Wonder
  - o Develop questions
  - o Make predictions, hypotheses
- Investigate
  - o Find and evaluate information to answer questions, test hypotheses
  - o Think about the information to illuminate new questions and hypotheses
- Construct
  - o Construct new understandings connected to previous knowledge
  - o Draw conclusions about questions and hypotheses
- Express
  - o Express new ideas to share learning with others
  - o Apply understandings to a new context, new situation
- Reflect
  - o Reflect on own process of learning and on new understandings gained from inquiry
  - o Ask new questions

The five elements of information inquiry are shown as an organizing framework for the REACTS model in table 5, and the Stripling Inquiry Model is shown in table 6. A comparison in table 7 shows the evolution of the process, although the five elements function as a core for inquiry and information literacy models and have tended to not change.

GUIDED INQUIRY: KUHLTHAU, TODD, MANIOTES, AND CASPARI

Evolving from the extensive research studies conducted by Carol Collier Kuhlthau, Guided Inquiry brings processes for instructional intervention to bear on the challenges teachers and students face in making the information literacy curriculum a reality in our schools. Kuhlthau and her colleagues have tested methods that enhance inquiry and make the process not only doable, but meaningful across all age groups. While practical, Kuhlthau's work is established on sound educational constructivist theory associated with such respected names as Dewey, Kelly, Piaget, Ausubel, Bruner, and Vygotsky.

Kuhlthau intends for teachers, library media specialists, and others who have expertise and are in guidance positions to intervene at strategic points to move students along in the information search process (ISP), which will serve the students to apply information to meet learning needs. These strategies are carefully planned, closely supervised, and targeted at the most effective times possible. The goal is to move typical student research projects to higher levels, with students engaged in complex investigations that are challenging and meaningful to them, their peers, and teachers.

In *Guided Inquiry: Learning in the 21st Century*, Kuhlthau, Maniotes, and Caspari (2007) describe the progression of inquiry across information literacy concepts:

Guided Inquiry incorporates transferable information literacy concepts into the inquiry process. It does not teach isolated information skills that are difficult for students to recall and apply. Too much of the mechanics of searching and resources [reference tool content] at the beginning of research discourages students and distracts them from the interesting ideas and questions that motivate them to learn (Kuhlthau 1985). Rather than attempting to teach all there is to know about information seeking prior to the assignment, Guided Inquiry incorporates information location, evaluation, and use concepts throughout the research process. Lasting information literacy is developed in practice when both information concepts and search skills in the inquiry process can be recalled and applied as needed. (5)

Table 5. REACTS Research Process Model*

Five Elements of Information Inquiry	Cognitive Tasks	Skills	Reflection Points	
Questioning Raising the Information Need	<u>Recalling</u> Fact-finding; reporting on the information	Choose a broad topic.		Calls on students to do preliminary reading and information seeking in anticipation of narrowing the topic, creating a thesis, and writing research questions.
		Get an overview of the topic.		
Exploring Reading, Viewing, Listening	<u>Explaining</u> Asking and searching; posing who, what, when, where questions and finding the answers	Narrow the topic.	Is my topic a good one?	
		Develop a thesis or statement of purpose.	Does my thesis statement of purpose represent an effective, overall concept for my research?	
	<u>Analyzing</u> Examining and organizing; posing why and how problems and organizing information to fit the product	Formulate questions to guide research.	Do the questions provide a foundation for my research?	
		Plan for research and production.	Is the research/production plan workable?	
Assimilation Accepting, Incorporating, Rejecting	<u>Challenging</u> Evaluating and deliberating; judging information on the basis of authority, significance, bias, and other factors	Find, analyze, and evaluate resources.	Are my sources usable and adequate?	
		Evaluate evidence, take notes, compile bibliography.	Is my research complete?	
Inference Application for Solution and Meaning	<u>Transforming</u> Integrating and concluding; drawing conclusions and creating a personal perspective based on information obtained	Establish conclusions/organize information into an outline.	Are my conclusions based on researched evidence? Does my outline logically organize my conclusions and evidence?	
Reflection How Were Goals Accomplished?	<u>Synthesizing</u> Conceptualizing; creating original solutions to problems posed	Create and present final product.	Is my paper/project satisfactory?	

*Stripling and Pitts (1988).

Source: Reprinted from Callison and Preddy (2006, Table B.6, 590).

Table 6. Stripling's Inquiry Model*

Five Elements of Information Inquiry	Stages	Inquiry Skills and Strategies
Questioning Raising the Information Need	Connect	Connect to own experience. Connect to ideas of others. Connect to previous knowledge and verify its accuracy. Gain background and context. Establish preliminary contact with idea through observation or experience.
Exploring Reading, Viewing, Listening	Wonder	Develop wonder questions that will lead to new understandings about key ideas. Frame questions using prior knowledge, focus and framework of instructional unit, and different levels of thinking. Develop questions to lead to active investigation and decision making. Make predictions or hypotheses based on prior knowledge, background information, and preliminary observations.
Assimilation Accepting, Incorporating, Rejecting	Investigate	Plan investigation and develop search strategies to find relevant, high-quality information. Identify, evaluate, and use multiple sources of information. Find and evaluate information to answer questions. Take notes using a variety of formats. Use information and information technology responsibly, efficiently, and ethically. Think about the information to formulate new questions and hypotheses: identify gaps and conflicting information, consider alternative explanations and predictions, and consider new questions to extend the investigation into a new area.
	Construct	Organize information to detect relationships among ideas. Draw inferences justified by the evidence. Think about the information to test predictions and hypotheses: compare evidence to hypotheses, compare patterns in data with what is already known, use evidence. Recognize author's point of view and consider alternate perspectives. Construct clear and appropriate conclusions based on evidence, explanations, interpretations, and connections. Connect new understandings to previous knowledge.
Inference Application for Solution and Meaning	Express	Apply understandings to new context; create a product to demonstrate new understanding. Select format based on needs of topic and audience. Communicate clearly both main and supporting points in product. Use the writing process to develop product (pre-write, write, revise, edit). Evaluate and revise own product based on self-assessment and feedback from others. Express new ideas or take action to share learning with others.
Reflection Adjustment for Additional Questioning	Reflect	Set high and clear standards for own work. Reflect with others. Use criteria to assess own process and product throughout the learning; make revisions when necessary. Reflect on own learning to be clear about the change in understanding (change in mental model). Adapt own standards and process based on personal reflection and feedback from others. Ask new questions; set new goals for learning.

*Stripling (2003).

Table 7. Comparison of REACTS to Stripling's Inquiry Model

Five Elements of Information Inquiry	Cognitive Tasks	REACTS	Stages of the Inquiry Process	Inquiry Skills and Strategies
Questioning Raising the Information Need	Choose a broad topic. Get an overview of the topic.	Recalling	Connect	Connect to self, previous knowledge. Gain background knowledge to set context for new learning. Observe, experience.
Exploring Reading, Viewing, Listening	Narrow the topic. Develop a thesis or purpose statement.	Explaining	Wonder	Develop questions. Make predictions, hypothesize.
	Formulate questions to guide research. Plan for research and production. Find, analyze, and evaluate resources.	Analyzing	Investigate	Find and evaluate information to answer questions, test hypotheses. Think about the information to formulate new questions and hypotheses.
Assimilation Accepting, Incorporating, Rejecting	Evaluate evidence. Take notes. Compile bibliography.	Challenging	Construct	Construct new understandings connected to previous knowledge. Draw conclusions about questions and hypotheses.
Inference Application for Solution and Meaning	Establish conclusions. Organize information into an outline. Create and present final product.	Transforming / Synthesizing	Express	Express new ideas to share learning with others. Apply understanding to new context, new situation.
Reflection Adjustment for Additional Questioning			Reflect	Reflect on own process of learning and on new understandings gained from inquiry. Ask new questions.

The progression from ISP to Guided Inquiry is also documented in detail on Kuhlthau's Web site (https://comminfo.rutgers.edu/~kuhlthau/guided_inquiry_design.htm). This progression is also evident in Table 8, showing a comparison between ISP and Guided Inquiry, both processes based on Kuhlthau's extensive research and her team's application to information use and instructional design.

Recently the methods to support students in experiencing the Guided Inquiry processes have been published in *Guided Inquiry Design: A Framework for Inquiry in Your School* (Kuhlthau, Maniotes, and Caspari 2012; a revision is scheduled for publication in 2015). These methods include inquiry discussion groups, inquiry journals and logs, and inquiry charts to visualize, organize, and synthesize ideas. These are proven strategies that enhance student comprehension and allow for more depth in topic exploration and construction. Now retired, Kuhlthau continues to work in the promotion of Guided Inquiry through her colleagues and their collaborative workshops and publications, sponsored by the Center for International Scholarship in School Libraries (http://www.cissl.rutgers.edu), directed by Ross Todd.

There are eight stages in the Guided Inquiry design process (Kuhlthau, Maniotes, and Caspari 2012, 30):

- Open—invitation to inquiry, open minds, stimulate curiosity.
- Immerse—build background knowledge, connect to content, discover interesting ideas.
- Explore—explore interesting ideas, look around, dip in.
- Identify—pause and ponder, identify inquiry question, decide direction.
- Gather—gather important information, go broad, go deep.
- Create—reflect on learning, go beyond facts to make meaning, create to communicate.
- Share—learn from each other, share learning, tell your story.
- Evaluate—evaluate achievement of learning goals, reflect on content, reflect on process.

The five elements of information inquiry are shown as an organizing framework for Kuhlthau's original ISP model in table 9 and repeated for the newer Guided Inquiry design model in table 10. These five elements function as a consistent core for inquiry and information literacy models, while methods tend to evolve with more refined practice.

HISTORIC INQUIRY: AMERICAN AND AUSTRALIAN SIMILARITIES

Historic inquiry has progressed to levels of study that engage students in what historians do. The demands placed on the student historian can be great, but students often gain a greater respect for what artifacts and historic documents have to tell us in relation to modern-day issues that affect our lives daily. Curriculum professors Linda Levstik from Kentucky University and Keith Barton from Indiana University note in their popular text *Doing History* (2010, 18):

As every teacher knows, few students have the skills necessary to conduct inquiry on their own. Although inquiry is essential to education, simply assigning such tasks won't guarantee meaningful results. Most students need direct help to make the most of their experiences, and teachers' most important responsibility is to provide them with the structure they need to learn—a process called scaffolding.

Unfortunately children rarely have the chance to take part in sustained interaction at school. Most often, they are expected to listen while teachers transmit information to them. Participation is usually limited to the common initiation-response pattern. The teacher asks a question, a student responds, and the teacher tells her whether the answer was right. The purpose of the interaction is to assess students' retention of information, not to help them pursue questions or issues that interest them. Other times, students may be given independent assignments or expected to "do research," but they aren't taught how to go about the process of learning.

Table 8. Comparison of Information Search Process (ISP) to Guided Inquiry Design

Five Elements of Information Inquiry	What students are doing in ISP	Stage of ISP	Phase of Guided Inquiry	What the inquiry community is doing in Guided Inquiry
Questioning Raising the Information Need	Prepare for the decision of selecting a topic; recognize a need for information.	Initiation	Open	Invite inquiry. Open minds. Stimulate curiosity.
	Decide on topic for research; identify and select the general area or topic to be investigated.	Selection	Immerse	Build background knowledge. Connect to content. Discover interesting ideas.
Exploring Reading, Viewing, Listening	Investigate information with the intent of finding a focus and extending personal understanding.	Exploration	Explore	Explore interesting ideas. Look around. Dip in.
	Formulate a focus from the information encountered.	Formulation	Identify	Pause and ponder. Identify inquiry question. Decide direction.
Assimilation Accepting, Incorporating, Rejecting	Gather information that defines, extends, and supports the focus.	Collection	Gather	Gather important information. Go broad. Go deep.
Inference Application for Solution and Meaning	Conclude the search for information to prepare for presenting or writing.	Presentation	Create	Reflect on learning. Go beyond facts to make meaning. Create to communicate.
			Share	Learn from each other. Share learning. Tell your story.
Reflection Adjustment for Additional Questioning	Evaluate the research process.	Assessment	Evaluate	Evaluate achievement of learning goals. Reflect on content. Reflect on process.

Table 9. Information Search Process*

Five Elements of Information Inquiry	Stage	Student Task	Feelings	Thoughts	Strategies	Actions
	Initiation	To prepare for the decision of selecting a topic—recognize a need for information	Apprehension and uncertainty	Contemplate assignment, prior learning; consider options.	Brainstorming, discussing, contemplating possible topics.	Talking with others, browsing the library, writing out questions.
Questioning Raising the Information Need	Selection	To decide on topic for research—identify and select the general area or topic to be investigated	Confusion, anxiety, brief elation after selection, anticipation	Compare topic criteria to personal interests, information available, time allotted; predict outcome of possible choices.	Discussing possible topics, using general sources for overview of possible topics (prereading), reading widely.	Making preliminary search of library, using reference collection to seek background information in the general area of concern, reading for overview.
	Exploration	To investigate information with the intent of finding a focus and extending personal understanding	Confusion, doubt, uncertainty	Be unable to always express precise information needed; identify several focus possibilities.	Reading to learn about topic, intentionally seeking possible focuses or points of view, maintaining list of key words.	Locating relevant information; reading to learn more about the topic; listing facts, ideas, names, and events (recalling, summarizing, paraphrasing); making bibliographic citations of useful sources and potential leads.
Exploring Reading, Viewing, Listening	Formulation	To formulate a focus from the information encountered	Turning point where uncertainty diminishes and confidence increases	Predict outcome; consider again personal interest, requirements of the assignment, availability of materials and time.	Making a survey of notes, listing possible foci, choosing a particular focus while discarding others, combining several themes to form one focus.	Reading and organizing notes for themes.

(*continued*)

Table 9. Information Search Process* (*continued*)

Assimilation Accepting, Incorporating, Rejecting	Collection	To gather information that defines, extends, and supports the focus	Confidence in ability to complete task increases, increased interest	Define, extend, and elaborate on focus; select most pertinent information, organize information from notes.	Taking detailed notes with bibliographic citations relevant to focus and research questions.	Using key works to search out pertinent information, making comprehensive search of various types of materials (reference, periodicals, nonfiction, etc.), seeking guidance.
Inference Application for Solution and Meaning	Presentation	To conclude search for information to prepare for presenting or writing	Sense of relief, satisfaction/disappointment	Identify any additional information for specific gaps; also notice most of additional information is redundant and resource options are nearly exhausted.	Returning to library to make summary, identifying need for any additional information, and exhausting resources.	Rechecking sources for information initially overlooked, confirming information and bibliographic citations.
Reflection Adjustment for Additional Questioning	Assessment	To evaluate the research process	Sense of accomplishment; perhaps also some disappointment	Experience an increase in self-awareness; identify problems and successes; understand and plan research strategy for future assignments.	Evaluating evidence of meeting focus, use of time, use of resources, use of library and librarian.	Visualizing the process in time-line or flow chart; writing an evaluative summary statement; discussing the process with teacher and librarian.

*Kuhlthau (1985).

Source: Reprinted from Callison and Preddy (2006, Table B.3, 587).

Table 10. Guided Inquiry Design*

Five Elements of Information Inquiry	Phases	Inquiry Community Tasks	Learning Team Tasks	Student Tasks
Questioning Raising the Information Need	Open	Invite inquiry. Open minds. Stimulate curiosity.	Decide on the learning goals, create powerful opener that invites learners in, establish an inquiry stance, introduce general topic to engage the inquiry community.	Spark conversations about ideas and themes, pose questions and problems, and highlight concepts related to the subject.
	Immerse	Build background knowledge. Connect to content. Discover interesting ideas.	Design engaging ways for students to immerse in the overall content ideas.	Think about what they already know and what seems particularly interesting, curious, surprising, or troubling.
Exploring Reading, Viewing, Listening	Explore	Explore interesting ideas. Look around. Dip in.	Guide students to browse and scan a variety of sources and encourage them to keep an open mind as they explore and reflect on new information.	Survey (dip into) a wide range of sources, read when they find something interesting, reflect on questions that begin to shape their inquiry.
	Identify	Pause and ponder. Identify inquiry question. Decide direction.	Introduce strategies that enable each student to sort through information and ideas to clearly articulate a meaningful inquiry question that will frame the rest of the inquiry.	Construct an inquiry question from the interesting ideas, pressing problems, and emerging themes they have explored.
Assimilation Accepting, Incorporating, Rejecting	Gather	Gather important information. Go broad. Go deep.	Guide students in structured approach for managing their search: locating, evaluating, and using information that leads to deep learning.	"Go broad" to find a range of sources that are useful for understanding their inquiry question. "Go deep" and choose a core of the most useful sources to read closely as they find connections and construct personal understanding.

(continued)

Table 10. Guided Inquiry Design* (*continued*)

Inference Application for Solution and Meaning	Create	Reflect on learning. Go beyond facts to make meaning. Create to communicate.	Guide students to go beyond simple fact finding and reporting and to summarize, interpret, and extend meaning of what they have learned and create a meaningful, interesting, clearly articulated, well-documented presentation that tells the story of what they have learned in the inquiry process.	Reflect on all they have learned about their inquiry question, construct their own understandings, and decide what type of presentation will best represent their engaging ideas, controversies, and theories generated through the inquiry for a particular audience.
	Share	Learn from each other. Share learning. Tell your story.	Organize share sessions to provide the best conditions for students to learn substantial content from each other.	Share the products they have developed to communicate what they have learned in an interesting, informative way.
Reflection Adjustment for Additional Questioning	Evaluate	Evaluate achievement of learning goals. Reflect on content. Reflect on process.	Guide students in reflection for self-assessment of their content learning and progress through the inquiry process; evaluate students' achievement of the learning goals.	Reflect on their content learning and learning throughout the inquiry process.

*Kuhlthau, Maniotes, and Caspari (2012).

Scaffolding takes many forms. First, teachers have to encourage students' interest in accomplishing tasks. Although children are naturally inquisitive, they are more likely to follow through with their investigations when teachers help them develop and maintain interest. . . . [S]tudents learn more from inquiry when teachers give them experience developing questions, identifying resources, and planning presentations than when they are just sent to the library.

Additional aspects of historical inquiry can be drawn from these standards from the National Center for History in the Schools (http://www.nchs.ucla.edu/) and the Historical Inquiry Project (http://www.historicalinquiry.com/):

- Historical inquiry proceeds with the formulation of a problem or set of questions worth pursuing.
- Students should obtain historical data from a variety of sources, including library and museum collections, historic sites, historical photos, journals, diaries, eyewitness accounts, newspapers, documentary films, oral testimony, and other primary resources. A growing number of historical documents are available to students and teachers through the Internet and provide a pool unprecedented for extensive inquiry.
- Students learn to corroborate sources through triangulation of primary documents, secondary documents, and expert opinion, a growing amount of which is available through the Internet and social media.
- Students shift from a story well told in a textbook to an emphasis on sources well scrutinized in history and mass media.
- Students' investigative strategies include a continuous cycle through five phases: summarizing, contextualizing, inferring, monitoring, and corroborating.
- History is a way of organizing and explaining the past. One cannot come to know history by merely learning overviews.
- At advanced levels, students should be able to interrogate historical information by uncovering the social, political, and economic context in which it was created; testing the data source for its credibility, authority, authenticity, internal consistency, and completeness; and detecting and evaluating for bias, distortion, and propaganda.

The Australian curriculum has over the past decade adopted standards in historical inquiry for all grade levels. According to the Australian Department of Education (https://classroom-connections.eq.edu.au/topics/Pages/2012/july/inquiry.aspx): "Historical inquiry involves the retrieval, comprehension and interpretation of sources, and judgment, guided by principles that are intrinsic to the discipline. . . . [H]istorical inquiry is the process of investigation undertaken in order to understand the past. To inform decisions and create new knowledge students need to study evidence sources using more than simple comparisons." The historical inquiry process includes the following learning outcomes: students can

- define the boundaries of an investigation;
- identify key questions that are raised within the study;
- develop hypotheses based on limited initial information;
- organize a logical investigation sequence;
- distinguish between relevant and irrelevant elements;
- prioritize the aspects to be explored;
- find sources of information and evidence;
- distinguish between relevant and irrelevant, fact and opinion, substantiated and unsubstantiated;
- organize and classify evidence into primary and secondary categories; and
- critically evaluate evidence.

Skills for presentation and evaluation are also presented. Valuable online resources that support historical inquiry are linked from Planning Historical Inquiry (http://historyinquiry

.weebly.com/). Emphasis, of course, is on Australian and British history. Experimentation with new e-document developments for display of the analysis of historic documents is an emerging part of the Australian curriculum.

In 2013 Mandy Lupton, senior lecturer at Queensland University of Technology, recommended the merits of a continuum framework for constructing a progressive inquiry-based curriculum in which the student took a greater responsibility for learning as he or she matured in the process. Similar to the four stages detailed in this book, the recommended National Research Council (2000) model is a continuum across three stages of development: structured, guided, and open. As seen in several chapters of this book, an additional stage that involves deep student and teacher collaboration through a mentoring process is extremely important in successfully moving the student to the status of independent and mature self-learner. The teacher who models inquiry will most often find students understanding and adopting the processes for meaningful investigations and research.

LOCAL ORAL HISTORIES AND I-SEARCH

A personal inquiry process that has had notable success in situations in which students can interview relatives and other local community members about the history of their own region, and document special skills many have to preserve their heritage, is the Foxfire method (Wigginton 1972). Made famous in the 1970s, this method of recording, editing, and publishing oral history has been a successful form of historical inquiry for many decades. The I-Search process (Tallman and Joyce 2006), connected to the writing and research processes, also serves to help students learn interview techniques, take research journal notes, and follow the results of their inquiry in ways that help them identify new areas of exploration and interest. The resulting passion for research serves to help students find their way to new understandings.

Formally defined by the Institute for Oral History (2003) at Baylor University, the term *oral history* refers to

- a qualitative research process based on personal interviewing, suited to understanding meanings, interpretations, relationships, and subjective experiences, resulting in
- a product (written, audio, or video) that is an original historical document; a new primary source for further research.

Typical topics that can serve as foundational experiences for oral history include the following (Sitton 1983):

- Living history—Classroom interviews of community informants: Students locate community people with unique life experiences, special skills, and other valuable firsthand knowledge about the community past. The living history project is an exploration of local history through direct, face-to-face interaction with persons who lived it.
- An oral history of the home neighborhood: This could be a study of a complete neighborhood or of some segment of one, such as a block or street. The objective is to find out how the neighborhood has developed and changed across time, as perceived by long-term residents.
- A memory book: Students brainstorm the questions to include in a memory book with which to interview one or both of their grandparents. The idea is to come up with a series of good questions all students can ask their grandparents, then write down the answers, and eventually compare and contrast the responses. Such exercises may help students gain a better understanding of the variety of cultures among their classmates.
- Researching the origins of local place-names: Using a topographic map of the home county as a basic reference, students use the oral history exploration to discover the origins of local place-names and associate those names with history, which often links back to Europe. Names

can have recent history and pertain to people and events within the current living generation or may extend back hundreds of years. Streets, streams, hills, and valleys are all good places to begin.

- An oral history of the school: Based on review of old school newspapers and yearbooks, questions can be generated to ask former students, teachers, principals, secretaries, and custodians. Students will have special interests in championship athletic events, faculty and student dress, and student pastimes and social events of previous decades (Callison 2006; 2007).

NET.SAVVY: THE FIVE A FRAMEWORK FOR DIGITAL INQUIRY

The teaching and administrative team of Jukes, Dosaj, and Macdonald (2000) started their promotion of centering inquiry on digital searching and virtual documents in the 1990s. Since then they have established a process called "Net.savvy." The skills framework is based on five As: asking, accessing, analyzing, applying, and assessing. All student and teacher work is focused on the Internet and whatever additional electronic documentation students can explore. Their approach challenges the notion that all student inquiry must be guided through the school library media center and opens consideration of new digital environments for students not only through school, but at home and beyond.

NOTE

Tables for this chapter that illustrate the five elements of information inquiry compared against specific inquiry models were designed by Katie Baker, computer technology teacher/technology integration specialist, Sycamore School, Indianapolis, Indiana.

REFERENCES

American Association for School Librarians (AASL). 1999. *A Planning Guide for Information Power: Building Partnerships for Learning with School Library Media Program Assessment Rubric for the 21st Century.* Chicago: American Library Association.

American Association of School Librarians. 2007. "Standards for the 21st-Century Learner." Chicago: American Library Association. http://www.ala.org/aasl/sites/ala.org.aasl/files/content/guidelines andstandards/learningstandards/AASL_Learning_Standards_2007.pdf (accessed March 5, 2014).

American Association of School Librarians and the Association for Educational Communications and Technology. 1998. *Information Literacy Standards for Student Learning.* Chicago: American Library Association.

Bruce, B. C., and A. P. Bishop. 2008. "New Literacies and Community Inquiry." In *Handbook of Research on New Literacies,* edited by J. Coiro et al., 699–742. New York: Lawrence Erlbaum.

Callison, D. 1993. "The Potential for Portfolio Assessment." In *School Library Media Annual,* edited by C. C. Kuhlthau, 11:30–39. Englewood, CO: Libraries Unlimited, 1993. Reprinted in *Assessment and the School Library Media Center,* Libraries Unlimited, 1994, 121–130.

Callison, D. 1994. "Expanding the Evaluation Role in the Critical-Thinking Curriculum." In *Information for a New Age: Redefining the Librarian,* 153–176. Englewood, CO: Libraries Unlimited.

Callison, D. 1998. "Information Literacy Portfolio Questions." In *Information Literacy,* edited by K. L. Spitzer, 143. Syracuse, NY: ERIC Clearinghouse on Information & Technology.

Callison, D. 2003. *Key Words, Concepts and Methods for Information Age Instruction: A Guide to Teaching Information Inquiry.* Baltimore, MD: LMS Associates.

Callison, D. 2005a. "The Student Information Scientist: Part I." *School Library Monthly* 22, no. 2 (October): 39–44.

Callison, D. 2005b. "The Student Information Scientist: Part II." *School Library Monthly* 22, no. 3 (November): 39–44.

Callison, D. 2006. "Oral History." In *The Blue Book on Information Age Inquiry, Instruction and Literacy*, by D. Callison and L. Preddy, 450–455. Westport, CT: Libraries Unlimited.

Callison, D. 2007. "A Kid's Inquiry Almanac." *School Library Monthly* 24, no. 4 (December): 41–44.

Callison, D., and A. Lamb. 2004. "Authentic Learning." *School Library Monthly* 21, no. 4 (December): 34–39.

Callison, D., and A. Lamb. 2007a. "Graphic Inquiry: Standards and Resources, Part I." *School Library Monthly* 24, no. 1 (September): 39–42.

Callison, D., and A. Lamb. 2007b. "Graphic Inquiry: Skills and Strategies, Part II." *School Library Monthly* 24, no. 2 (October): 38–42.

Callison, D., and L. Preddy. 2006. *The Blue Book on Information Age Inquiry, Instruction and Literacy*. Westport, CT: Libraries Unlimited.

Common Core State Standards Initiative. 2014. "English Language Arts Standards: Introduction." http://www.corestandards.org/ELA-Literacy/introduction/students-who-are-college-and-career-ready-in-reading-writing-speaking-listening-language/ (accessed June 15, 2014).

Dewey, J. 1991. "Experience and Education." In *John Dewey: The Later Works, 1938–1953*, edited by J. A. Boydston, 1–62. Carbondale: Southern Illinois University Press.

Donham, J. 2014. "Inquiry." In *Inquiry and the Common Core*, edited by V. Harada and S. Coatney, 3–16. Santa Barbara, CA: Libraries Unlimited.

Flanagin, A. J., and M. J. Metzger. 2010. *Kids and Credibility*. Cambridge, MA: MIT Press.

Fontichiaro, K., ed. 2009. *21st Century Learning in School Libraries*. Santa Barbara, CA: Libraries Unlimited.

Grassian, E. S., and J. R. Kaplowitz. 2009. *Information Literacy Instruction: Theory and Practice*. 2nd ed. New York: Neal-Schuman.

Indiana Department of Education. 2011. "Indiana Academic Standards." http://www.doe.in.gov/standards (accessed June 11, 2014).

Institute for Oral History, Baylor University. 2003. http://www.baylor.edu/oralhistory/ (accessed March 30, 2014).

Ito, M., et al. 2010. *Hanging Out, Messing Around, and Geeking Out: Kids Living and Learning with New Media*. Cambridge, MA: MIT Press.

Jukes, I., A. Dosaj, and B. Macdonald. 2000. *NetSavvy: Building Information Literacy in the Classroom*. Thousand Oaks, CA: Corwin Press.

Kendall, J. S., and R. J. Marzano. 1997. *Content Knowledge: A Compendium of Standards and Benchmarks for K–12 Education*. Aurora, CO: Midcontinent Research and Evaluation Laboratory.

Kuhlthau, C. C. 1985. *Teaching the Library Research Process*. West Nyack, NY: The Center for Applied Research in Education.

Kuhlthau, C. C., L. K. Maniotes, and A. K. Caspari. 2007. *Guided Inquiry: Learning in the 21st Century*. Westport, CT: Libraries Unlimited.

Kuhlthau, C. C., L. K. Maniotes, and A. K. Caspari. 2012. *Guided Inquiry Design: A Framework for Inquiry in Your School*. Santa Barbara, CA: Libraries Unlimited.

Kumasi, K. 2010. "Cultural Inquiry: A Framework for Engaging Youth of Color in the Library." *Journal of Research on Libraries and Young Adults* 2. http://www.yalsa.ala.org/jrlya/2010/11/cultural-inquiry-a-framework-for-engaging-youth-of-color-in-the-library/ (accessed March 25, 2014).

Kumasi-Johnson, K. 2007. "Critical Inquiry: Library Media Specialists as Change Agents." *School Library Monthly* 23, no. 9 (May): 42–45.

Lamb, A., and D. Callison. 2011. "Graphic Inquiry for All Learners." *School Library Monthly* 28, no. 3 (December): 18–22.

Lamb, A., and D. Callison. 2012. *Graphic Inquiry*. Libraries Unlimited.

Lederman, J. S. 2009. "Levels of Inquiry and the 5 E's Learning Cycle Model." National Geographic. http://www.google.com/url?sa=t&rct=j&q=&esrc=s&source=web&cd=1&ved=0CCAQFjAA&url=http%3A%2F%2Fsmdepo.org%2Fdownload%2Fe19a3d4a59d25&ei=yRTlVLb5OMW7ggSgoIL4Ag&usg=AFQjCNGpG9n9jjl3dpUWB3MXkF4Rk7SmTw&bvm=bv.85970519,d.eXY.

Levstik, L. S., and K. C. Barton. 2010. *Doing History: Investigating with Children in Elementary and Middle Schools*. 4th ed. Mahwah, NJ: Taylor & Francis.

Lupton, M. 2013. "Inquiry Pedagogy and the Australian Curriculum." *Primary and Middle Years Educator* 11, no. 2: 23–29.

Marland, M., ed. 1981. *Information Skills in the Secondary Curriculum: Recommendations of a Working Group Sponsored by the British Library and the Schools Council.* London: Methuen Educational.

National Research Council (NRC). 1996. *National Science Education Standards.* Washington, DC: National Academy.

National Research Council (NRC). 2000. *Inquiry and the National Science Education Standards.* Washington, DC: National Academy.

Pappas, M. L. 2000. "Managing the Inquiry Learning Environment." *School Library Monthly* 16, no. 7 (March): 27–30, 36.

Pappas, M., and A. Tepe. 1995. *Follett Information Skills Model and Teaching Electronic Information Skills.* McHenry, IL: Follett Software.

Pappas, M. L., and A. E. Tepe. 2002. *Pathways to Knowledge and Inquiry Learning.* Libraries Unlimited.

Pitts, J. M. 1994. "Personal Understandings and Mental Models of Information." PhD diss., Florida State University.

Preddy, L. B. 2007. *SSR with Intervention: A School Library Action Research Project.* Libraries Unlimited.

Preddy, L. B. 2010. *Social Readers: Promoting Reading in the 21st Century.* Santa Barbara, CA: Libraries Unlimited.

Sitton, T. 1983. *Oral History: A Guide for Teachers.* Austin: University of Texas Press.

Stripling, B. 2003. "Inquiry-Based Learning." In *Curriculum Connections through the Library*, edited by B. K. Stripling and S. Hughes-Hassell, 3–39. Westport, CT: Libraries Unlimited.

Stripling, B. 2008. "Inquiry: Inquiring Minds What to Know." *School Library Monthly* 25, no. 1 (September): 50–52.

Stripling, B., and J. Pitts. 1988. *Brainstorms and Blueprints: Teaching Library Research as a Thinking Process.* Englewood, CO: Libraries Unlimited.

Tallman, J. I., and M. Z. Joyce. 2006. *Making the Writing and Research Connection with the I-Search Process.* New York: Neal-Schuman.

Wigginton, E. 1972. *The Foxfire Book.* Garden City, NY: Doubleday.

Zmuda, A., and V. H. Harada. 2008. *Librarians as Learning Specialists: Meeting the Learning Imperative of the 21st Century.* Westport, CT: Libraries Unlimited.

Section II

Information Inquiry
Learning Practices from
School Library Monthly

A complete listing of inquiry articles from *School Library Monthly*, March 1997-May/June 2014 can be found on the Student Resource site, found at http://www.schoollibrarymonthly.com/CCSSresources.pdf.

Authentic Learning

Daniel Callison and Annette Lamb

The term "authentic" refers to the genuine, real, and true. Authentic learning involves exploring the world around us, asking questions, identifying information resources, discovering connections, examining multiple perspectives, discussing ideas, and making informed decisions that have a real impact. An authentic learning environment is engaging for students because the content and context of learning are accepted by the student as relevant to his or her needs and deemed by the teacher as simulating life beyond the classroom.

Callison has suggested that information inquiry comes near authentic learning at the intersection of workplace information problems, personal information needs, and academic information problems or tasks.

State and national learning standards found today across disciplines often attempt to stress real world applications. Students are asked to make academic connections to ordinary life experiences. Rather than surface-level, fact-based tasks, learners are asked to question, interpret, and apply information and ideas that have value in a larger social context. Many students aren't aware of how reading, writing, and mathematics are part of their daily life, and one of the challenges for educators is to help students make such real-world associations. A specific challenge of the library media specialist is to partner with other teachers to design learning activities and develop assessments that resemble constructive experiences beyond the school. Partnering and simulating real-world situations are not easy tasks and usually fall short of any ideal implied in definitions of authentic learning. Examples and situations given here may help teams of educators to consider how to move closer to developing authentic learning environments. Moving away from heavy use of common worksheets and skill drills, multiple-choice exams, and a standard formula applied to all student research projects is an evolution toward authentic learning.

Teaching teams who engage in information inquiry are most likely to create authentic learning environments when they act as mentors or master-level teachers who model for their learning apprentices. They engage in inquiry with their students, not simply assign tasks. They raise questions, seek information, interpret findings and draw conclusions, and illustrate their inquiry practices as they work with students. They discuss openly for students to hear and see the inquiry process and results, and share both personal inquiry successes and failures. As Carol Tilley has written, cognitive apprenticeship becomes the center of the

"Authentic Learning," by Daniel Callison and Annette Lamb, was published in *School Library Media Activities Monthly* 21, no. 4 (December 2004): 34–39.

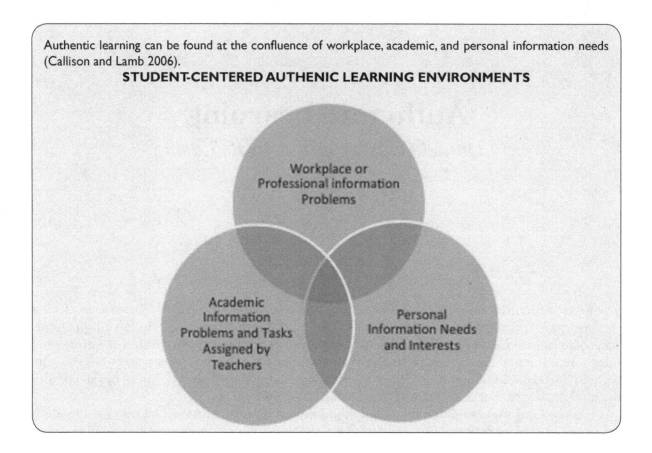

Authentic learning can be found at the confluence of workplace, academic, and personal information needs (Callison and Lamb 2006).

STUDENT-CENTERED AUTHENIC LEARNING ENVIRONMENTS

learning tasks when students grow intellectually and eventually move to a near independent learning level.

SIGNS OF AUTHENTIC LEARNING

Although this list probably is not exhaustive, the following are signs that teachers of information inquiry are reaching levels of learning that can be identified as authentic.

Learning Is Student-Centered. Not all of the questions for exploration are generated by the teacher, but most are raised, clarified, and become "owned" by the students working collaboratively to act more as problem-identifiers and not just problem-solvers.

Multiple Resources Accessed beyond the School. Questions are not answered to full satisfaction of the student, library media specialist, or other teachers by information provided in the school library media center alone. While some basic background information is accessible, the library media center is a clearinghouse for contacts to more in-depth resources and expertise in the community and beyond. Electronic documents and human experts are valued, monitored through master teacher guidance, and used extensively.

Student Acts as a Scientific Apprentice. As an "information scientist," the student is encouraged to be skeptical of the information located and seeks to corroborate facts and gain a variety of perspectives on issues and to determine credibility and authority of sources. The student learns from several systematic information exploration approaches that can be applied to meet a variety of current and future information problems. With the guidance of the master teacher, the student evaluates approaches to match to information needs and documents the results for future uses. Mapping the results of information gained from different sources becomes as important as gaining information content itself because this will help in becoming more efficient in future information seeking practices.

Student Moves toward Real Research. The opportunity for the student to gather original data through surveys, interviews, or experiments helps to enhance the project and places the student in the role of not just "library researcher," but closer to that of authentic researcher. The student moves beyond just location of documents and organized data to one who deals with analysis of findings and identification of additional information needs. The student learns how primary sources, artifacts, and observations of human behavior can all contribute to useful data. The student learns the value of documenting through a research journal their feelings and findings and to do so in a constructive manner that can be shared with others. The student learns how to analyze his or her audience in order to best communicate findings in order to inform, persuade, or engage others in their information problem-solving pursuits.

Lifelong Learning beyond the Assignment. The student finds information problems and questions to be interesting, exciting, challenging, and personally meaningful. They move toward the intersection of personal, academic, and potentially future workplace information needs. The agenda of questions continues to evolve beyond the school assignment and becomes an inquiry set that they follow outside of school as well as in future academic experiences. The agenda impacts the student's selection of reading, viewing, and discussion both for pleasure and for intellectual growth.

Process, Product, and Performance Assessment. Attempts are made by the guiding educators as well as the reflective student researcher to evaluate all aspects of inquiry. The process and product are both valued as artifacts of learning. Actions taken or performance of application of the inquiry become evidence of learning success. Has the student's thinking changed? Has the student changed the thinking of others? Has the student mastered inquiry to make a difference in some constructive manner?

Instructional Collaboration and Interchangeable Roles. Students are more likely to learn the value of inquiry and collaboration with others when they see it modeled by master teachers. Library media specialists and other teachers of inquiry demonstrate collaboration as a team to select and implement a suitable approach to information problem identification and solving. They perform as information literate educators and share with their students how they have determined quality information sources or conducted original information gathering. As a team, they freely share responsibilities for lesson planning, instructional presentation, and performance evaluation. Each member of the team is information resourceful and fluent in matching search strategies to meet information needs. Master teachers display their ideas and inquiry work along with their apprentice students. They may present findings in visuals, speeches, papers, or other media displayed for audience examination and critical discourse.

AUTHENTIC ACHIEVEMENT

Fred Newmann and Gary Wehlage from the University of Wisconsin-Madison stress that meaningful learning is critical to engage students and transfer learning to new situations. Their research focuses on the direct connection between authentic instruction and student achievement. In a recent study, they concluded that students in classrooms with high quality, authentic assignments scored higher on standardized achievement tests. Three criteria were used to define authentic achievement:

- Students construct meaning and produce knowledge;
- Students use disciplined inquiry to construct meaning; and
- Students aim their work toward production of discourse, products, and performances that have value or meaning beyond success in school. Newmann and Wehlage stress two problems that often result in conventional schooling not reaching authentic levels:
  o Often school work does not allow them to use their minds well.
  o The work has no intrinsic meaning or value to students beyond achieving success in school.

In their article "Five Standards of Authentic Instruction," Newmann and Whelage identified five continuous dimensional constructs that can be used to determine the authenticity of instruction. These are:

- Higher-order thinking,
- Depth of knowledge,
- Connectiveness to the world beyond the classroom,
- Substantive conversation, and
- Social support for student achievement.

There are many ways that students can demonstrate their understanding of academic content through authentic problems and projects. To demonstrate their skills in mathematics and social studies, students could develop a proposal regarding the use of a particular building or parcel of land in their city, create charts and graphs to speculate on whether racism or other factors impact local home sales, or demonstrate the distribution of wealth and population on different continents by using ratio and proportion.

AUTHENTIC ASSIGNMENTS

Authentic assignments are grounded in reality and require students to create meaning from their experiences. Students are involved with communicating through e-mail, writing letters, and keeping journals. They may collect oral histories, write about current events, or conduct and report on experiments.

Molly Nicaise, a faculty member in the School of Information Science and Learning Technologies at the University of Missouri, stresses that authentic learning is anchored in real-world activities. Students access the information and resources needed to address essential questions. Assessments of these activities are directly related to the task.

Authentic Context. Assignments should be rooted in a meaningful situation. Educators use simulations, scenarios, and problems to provide this context. The closer the context can be to a real-world situation, the more likely it is that students will see the connection between academic context and practical applications. Leo Vygotsky used the phrase "zone of proximal development" to describe how learners use context to understand and create knowledge. He found that cultural and historical factors impact how we learn and that learners are not always able to transfer learning to new situations.

An effective strategy is to ask students to connect local with national or international information. Students might conduct a poll in their building to collect information about whether people recycle paper, glass, or aluminum. They then could compare this to the national average. Comparisons also could be made by using local versus national population statistics or immigrant data. The same could be done by comparing the stories of local veterans with those from other countries.

Authentic Questions. Assignments begin with authentic questions generated from personally relevant concerns, issues, and topics. Questions are framed in a real context that build on personal experience and extend to the larger world.

Authentic Tasks. Learning tasks often are not explicit, requiring students to identify problems, develop strategies, make decisions, and be in charge of their own learning. Students often feel uncomfortable with these types of assignments because they require independent thinking and metacognitive skills. These types of assignments require careful guidance to help learning through the processes of problem identification. Scaffolding is a critical element of authentic learning environments. Students must connect new information to existing knowledge and experiences. Students need guidance in making these connections in inquiry-based projects. Authentic learning activities are not easy to manage.

Elliott Soloway, a professor at the University of Michigan, develops tools to provide the scaffolding needed for students to engage in authentic situations that require complicated subject matter. He stresses that teacher librarians must help learners evaluate digital content and use technology to access and use information. From handheld devices and science probes to software tools that help students with complex mathematics, he has worked with teachers to use technology to facilitate authentic learning. For example, middle school students have explored their own community environment through measuring the health of local rivers.

Tiffany Marra, the Program Manager for SmartGirl.org, asks the question, "Why should students learn how to solve problems about things that will never happen, when there is so much in their lives that already involves math, reading, writing, or any other subject matter?" Each year, SmartGirl.org along with the American Library Association conducts a reading survey to identify the interests of young women as part of Teen Read Week. Marra stresses that tasks can fall on a continuum of authenticity from reading books about art and going on virtual art museum visits to actually visiting an art gallery.

Authentic tasks often involve collaboration or competition with others. Many national writing contests, local media fairs, and science fairs provide opportunities to participate in a project that is shared beyond the school. Cyberfair (http:// www.globalschoolhouse.com) is a well-known Web-based authentic learning programs that focuses on youth research connecting knowledge to real-world applications in categories including local leaders, businesses, community organizations, historical landmarks, environment, music, art, and local specialties.

Authentic Activities. These activities are natural, not contrived. Rather than reading about city government in a textbook, students write questions and interview local government officials. By providing meaningful contexts for learning, authentic learning closely resembles actual situations where knowledge and skills will be used. Students read primary documents and original prose, create communications on meaningful topics for real audiences, and share work with real audiences. Students are asked to:

- Recall their prior knowledge and how it relates to a real situation;
- Articulate questions, problems, or a focus that are meaningful, relevant, and interesting; and
- Construct knowledge and discover connections in real-world contexts.

Authentic activities include working with the local chamber of commerce on promoting an annual event, natural resource, or historical building; providing nutrition and fitness information to seniors; or creating websites for local nonprofit agencies. Sometimes it is possible to become involved with large-scale projects such as identifying monarch butterflies, hummingbirds, or whooping cranes. In other cases, students might volunteer to participate in research being conducted by professionals at the United States Geological Survey or the National Park Service. For example, a middle school class in Idaho worked on a land survey at a local cemetery and a high school class in Washington assisted in identifying wildlife habitats.

AUTHENTIC RESOURCES

A wide variety of information resources, materials, tools, and technologies are used in authentic learning. Students increase their understanding of the world by examining primary resources, interacting with members of the community, and connecting with real-world issues. Authentic materials can be traced back to the original author or idea. Students can be involved with generating this information through e-mail interviews or original reporting of events and experiments. The library media specialist is essential in authentic learning environments. Students are expected to go beyond teacher-directed activities and textbooks.

The library media specialist can collaborate with the teacher to locate and organize authentic materials and resources from community or online experts to primary source documents or photographs. Partnerships also may be formed with the public library, community organizations, museums, natural areas, aquarium, botanical garden, zoo, or planetarium. Rather than simply reading the work of others, learners develop meaningful questions and gather information from many sources. They often generate new data and ideas by:

- Conducting oral histories with local senior citizens,
- Developing a plan to renovate a museum exhibit,
- Comparing local and national data on air and water pollution, or
- Interviewing a NOAA oceanographer through e-mail or video conferencing. Technology can provide a bridge to authentic environments.
- Use webcams to video conference with experts at remote locations.
- Go on virtual field trips to historical locations, museums, and natural places.
- Interact with experts on group discussion forums.
- Access primary sources and real-world data sources.
- Communicate with students from other cultures through e-mail.
- News broadcasts from other countries over the Web.
- Use a video camera to record oral histories.

AUTHENTIC COMMUNICATIONS AND AUDIENCES

Students need a real-world audience for their work. Authentic audiences might include the student government, local agencies, civic groups, and government offices. The oral history projects could be shared with local and national historical societies and organizations. Teachers should help students seek out stakeholders who have the authority to take action based on student recommendations. Students also should be prepared to witness the frustrations of democratic government in action, or nonaction, and be prepared to understand that not all recommendations succeed. Many voices may influence decisions in some situations while other decisions may be made unilaterally. The authentic experience, however, is one in which students are encouraged to find a voice and to participate as constructively as possible.

When examining the work of professionals across disciplines, Fred Newmann found that adults rely upon complex forms of communication to conduct their work and present their results. These tools involve verbal, symbolic, and visual communication to provide "qualifications, nuances, elaborations, details, and analogies woven into extended narratives, explanations, justifications, and dialogue."

Newmann states that "when adults write letters, news articles, organizational memos, or technical reports; when they speak a foreign language; when they design a house, negotiate an agreement, or devise a budget; when they create a painting or a piece of music—they try to communicate ideas that have an impact on others. In contrast, most school assignments, such as spelling quizzes, laboratory exercises, or typical final exams, have little value beyond school, because they are designed only to document the competence of the learner."

AUTHENTIC ASSESSMENT

Assessment is a critical component of authentic learning. Students learn by applying knowledge to solve problems that mirror the challenges of tasks found beyond the classroom. Authentic assessment asks students to determine whether they've met their goal.

Authentic assessment values both the processes and products involved in learning. For example, journals, logs, and concept maps may be developed as the project progresses. Final products might include a letter to the editor, online book review, or presentation to a local nonprofit group. Students are asked to demonstrate their knowledge and skills in meaningful ways. Rather than testing isolated skills, authentic assessments effectively measure student capabilities through accurately evaluating learning by examining a student's performance in a natural situation. A variety of tools can be used in authentic assessment including checklists, portfolios, and rubrics.

Authentic assessment is used to evaluate student work as well as provide feedback for improvement. Rather than comparing students with each other, authentic assessment focuses on individual strengths and weaknesses. In other words, authentic assessment is criterion-referenced rather than norm-referenced. This aspect may prove to have limits however, compared to many real-world situations that are driven by human competition.

Grant Wiggins, well-known for his work with authentic education, places emphasis on selecting engaging problems that require students to develop effective, creative performances and products. By having a real-life context for product development, assessment has more relevance. Students are aware of the criteria used for evaluation and have opportunities for self-checking. They also have a chance to see and judge the impact of their product in the real world.

AUTHENTIC LEARNING AND INFORMATION INQUIRY

Information inquiry is at the core of authentic learning. The ultimate value of an inquiry project lies in its authenticity. Rather than exploring superficial questions and problems, students are asked to explore essential questions that require deep thinking.

Carol Gordon while at the Educational Resources Library at Boston University conducted an action research study with high school English teachers and the library media specialist focusing on authentic research assignments. According to Gordon, most assignments ask students to report on the findings of others and draw conclusions based on readings. She stresses the importance of placing students in an active role as researcher by conducting interviews, administering questionnaires, and journaling observations. This data then are used to construct meaning. In other words, rather than asking students to simply be reporters, Gordon suggests that students become real researchers.

This idea has tremendous implications for teacher librarians. Rather than focusing on traditional information gathering approaches such as reading, taking notes, and summarizing, students become immersed in their research by using a variety of techniques to collect data, explore perspectives, and generate new ideas. Gordon notes that the ownership students feel for original work facilitates the construction process. Authentic inquiry may be an unreachable ideal, but the goal remains to raise the level educators should expect for student engagement and performance in meeting the information demands of their world both in and out of school.

Jinx Stapleton Watson from the University of Tennessee has written about higher expectations relevant to student inquiry in science fair projects:

> Most "research" projects assigned at the senior high school level do not provide an authentic application of scientific methods. Students who are limited to simple models that outline a linear research process will not experience the more meaningful aspects of research: personal selection of problems and research questions, application of proper methods, collection of original data, and reaching relevant conclusions. . . . [C]lean-cut exercises do not pretend to be about idea making or wondering, the essence of inquiry. Thus, teachers and school library media specialists who want students to pursue ideas that intrigue them enough to investigate

must communicate different expectations from the step-by-step procedures. They must communicate that wrong turns and mistakes in thinking may offer as much information as successful efforts. They must support the approach that such inquiry might not be pursued with a single course or class schedule, but rather, across disciplines, across the day, in flexible schedules of classroom and library [access] with significant adults ready to assist at wrong turns, mistakes, and plateau periods in the investigation. (2003)

FOR FURTHER READING

Brandt, Ron. "On Teaching for Understanding: A Conversation with Howard Gardner." *Educational Leadership* 50, no. 7 (April 1993): 4–7.

Brown, John Seely, A. Collins, and Paul Duguid. "Situated Cognition and the Culture of Learning." *Educational Researcher* 18, no. 1 (1989): 32–42.

Brown, John Seely, and Paul Duguid. "Organizational Learning and Communities of Practice: Towards a Unified View of Working, Learning, and Innovation." *Organization Science* 2, no. 1 (1991): 40–57.

Bruner, Jerome. *Actual Minds, Possible Worlds.* Cambridge, MA: Harvard University Press, 1986.

Callison, Daniel. "Authentic Assessment." *School Library Media Activities Monthly* 14, no. 5 (January 1998): 42–43, 50.

Collins, A., J. S. Brown, and S. E. Newman. "Cognitive Apprenticeship: Teaching the Craft of Reading, Writing, and Mathematics." In *Knowing, Learning and Instruction: Essays in Honor of Robert Glaser*, edited by L.B. Resnick. Hillsdale, NJ: Lawrence Erlbaum, 1988.

Duffy, Tom M., and David H. Jonassen. *Constructivism and the Technology of Instruction.* Hillsdale, NJ: Lawrence Erlbaum, 1992.

Gardner, Howard. *The Unschooled Mind: How Children Think and How Schools Should Teach.* New York: Basic Books, 1991.

Gordon, Carol. "Students as Authentic Researchers: A New Prescription for the High School Research Assignment." *School Library Media Research* 2, 1999. Available from the American Library Association website (http://www.ala.org/aasl/SLMR).

Kuhlthau, Carol C. "Learning in Digital Libraries: An Information Search Process Approach." *Library Trends* 45, no. 4 (1997): 575–806.

Lafer, Stephen. "Audience, Elegance, and Learning via the Internet." *Computers in the School* 13, nos. 1–2 (1997): 89–97.

Lebow, David G., and Walter Wager. "Authentic Activity as a Model for Appropriate Learning Activity: Implications for Emerging Instructional Technologies." *Canadian Journal of Educational Communication* 23 (Winter 1994): 231–244.

Marra, Tiffany. *Authentic Learning Environments.* 2004. Available from the University of Michigan website (http://www-personal.umich.edu/%7Etmarra/authenticity/authen.html).

Mims, Clif. "Authentic Learning: A Practical Introduction and Guide for Implementation." *Meridian: A Middle School Computer Technologies Journal* 6, no. 1 (Winter 2003). Available from the Meridian website (http://www.ncsu.edu/meridian/win2003/authentic_learning/).

Newman, Delia. "Alternative Assessment: Promises and Pitfalls." In *School Library Media Annual*, Vol. 11, edited by Carol Collier Kuhlthau, 13–20. Englewood, CO: Libraries Unlimited, 1993.

Newmann, Fred M., and Gary G. Wehlage. "Five Standards of Authentic Instruction." *Educational Leadership* 50, no. 7 (1993): 8–12.

Newmann, F. M., A. S. Bryk, and J. K. Nagaoka. *Authentic Intellectual Work and Standardized Tests: Conflict or Coexistence?* Consortium on Chicago School Research, 2001.

Nicaise, M. "Student Astronauts Blast Off in the Midwest: An Example of an Authentic Learning Environment." *Space Times: Magazine of the American Astronautical Society* 34, no. 5 (1995): 18–20.

Stripling, Barbara K. "Practicing Authentic Assessment in the School Library." In *School Library Media Annual*, Vol. 11, edited by Carol Collier Kuhlthau, 40–56. Englewood, CO: Libraries Unlimited, 1993.

Tilley, Carol. "Cognitive Apprenticeship." In *Key Words, Concepts and Methods for Information Age Instruction.* LMS Associates, 2003.

Vygotsky, L. S. *Mind in Society.* Cambridge, MA: Harvard University Press, 1930.

Watson, Jinx Stapleton. "Examining Perceptions of the Science Fair Project: Content or Process?" *School Library Media Research* 6 (2003). Available from the American Library Association website (http://www .ala.org/aasl/ SLMR).

Wiggins, Grant. "The Case for Authentic Assessment." *Practical Assessment, Research & Evaluation* 2, no. 2 (1990).

Wiggins, Grant. "Assessment: Authenticity, Context, and Validity." *Phi Delta Kappan* 75, no. 3 (1993): 200–214.

The Student Information Scientist, Part I

Daniel Callison

This article (Part I and Part II) is foundational to a presentation on "The Student as Information Scientist" at the 2005 National Conference of the American Association of School Librarians in Pittsburgh.

Information literacy standards for student learning, indicators for student performance, and hundreds of collaborative lesson plans around the country give us some indication of the skills students are expected to master as effective and efficient users of information. Hopefully the goal is that all involved in information literacy education become wiser consumers of information. In mastering the elements of information inquiry, teachers and school librarians acting as instructional specialists model, teach, and learn with their students the best ways to test and select information that is valid and relevant to solve information problems.

THE SCIENTIFIC METHOD AND INQUIRY

The basic definition of the Scientific Method includes these steps:

- observation and description of a phenomenon
- formulation of a hypothesis to explain the phenomena
- use of the hypothesis to predict existence of other phenomena
- performance of experimental tests of the prediction and inferring a conclusion
- some include a fifth step of presenting, debating and/or application of findings

The inquiry process gives heavy emphasis to development of questions at each step. What questions come from observation? What questions are relevant to the hypothesis? What questions formulate the prediction? What questions are answered from the test of the prediction and what questions, new and old, remain unanswered in part or in full? (See Figure 1)

The process of Information Inquiry involves application of the ancient Socratic Method of teaching through self-posed and mentor-posed questions in order to gain meaning in today's overwhelming Information Age. Further application of the Scientific Method gives a systematic structure to this process. It places students and teachers in the role of Information Scientists. This analogy will be explored as one that may open new paths for students and teachers to investigate not only phenomena identified from typical subjects of study, but to also test and predict the value, relevance and meaning of information itself. As "information scientists" should the learner be expected to journal, debate, compare, and present his or her observations on the

Observe	Watching carefully, taking notes, comparing and contrasting
Question	Asking questions about observations, asking questions that can lead to manageable investigations, evaluating and prioritizing questions
Hypothesize	Suggesting possible explanations consistent with available observations
Predict	Suggesting an event or result in the future based on analysis of observations
Investigate	Testing through gathering data and use of methods relevant to the questions
Communicate	Informing others through means of communication relevant to the conclusions and the audience addressed

Figure 1. What Scientists Do

value of the information encountered and the need for information that may not be available or possible to obtain?

THE PROFESSIONAL INFORMATION SCIENTIST

A case is not being made here to equate specific tasks of the professional information scientist with skills expected of the student information scientist. There are, however, some potential practices for the student that can be drawn from the business of adult information scientists. Gary Marchionini, a professor of information science at North Carolina University, has grouped his field of investigation into classification, use behavior, knowledge dissemination, social informatics, and human/computer interaction. These are defined in Figure 2.

WHAT STUDENT INFORMATION SCIENTISTS MIGHT INVESTIGATE

Information science is an emerging and complex discipline. Is application of information science to K-12 school settings meaningful? Yes, although student activities, processes and products will need to be scaled to meet student abilities, needs, and interests. Consider the value of the following experiences:

- **Key Terms and Strategies.** What have been the most effective search terms used to locate information on your topic? Answers might involve several combinations across different databases and different aspects of the information need. Illustrate or discuss these with other members of your class so that through comparison you may identify the best search strategies for various databases on various topics. What information would not have been available to you if you did not have access to online databases? The World Wide Web? Your school library? How would lack of access in each case have changed your report? How might you test this?
- **Journal the Research Experience.** As you encounter each new piece of information, describe how it helps or hinders your investigation. Write about how new information either confirms or counters what you have believed or have hypothesized. What information are you willing to accept that actually changes your mind, and why? What information do you reject, and why? In summary, along with your final report, do you believe you gave a fair and open mind to consider new information you encountered along the way? How might you involve others in judging your ability to fairly accept or reject new information?

Classification Theory	In what manner can knowledge or information be represented so that effective and efficient information retrieval can take place? In what manner should such representation change to meet different discourse, various disciplines, and changes in information format?
Information Use Behavior	In what manner do humans seek or not seek, and use or not use information? What information do they find useful and not useful, and why? How do diverse cultures and media formats affect these behaviors?
Knowledge Creation & Dissemination	In what manner can information be best communicated or transferred to meet the needs of different groups? How is knowledge communicated, validated, valued, and assimilated, and what patterns in these processes can be documented? What do these patterns tell us?
Social Informatics	What is the role(s) of information in the social and cultural milieu? Issues studied may involve information equity, information security, political or economic values of information, and intellectual property rights.
Interaction Studies	Also termed "information architecture" or "information design," this area draws from studies related to human-computer interaction. Software and website usability studies are common. Scientists seek to determine the processes that influence and are influenced by human use of information systems. Scientists strive to determine ways that interactive experiences can be well structured and properly positioned within the wider or global electronic information infrastructure.

Figure 3. A Question Exploration Ring.
Similar to Concept Maps, students can illustrate how an initial question expands and evolves as a new information source (book, website, human, video, etc.) is introduced. Each new ring represents a new set of questions derived from a new source and linked back to the initial question.

Figure 4. Extracting from Concept Maps or Question Explorations to Create a Central Focus.
Illustrating the critical and creative thinking processes for other students, teachers, parents, and administrators to see the complexities leading to an inquiry product. Information Maps, Evidence Linkages and Ratings, and Assessment Rubrics also help to illustrate that there is more involved than simply a "research paper."

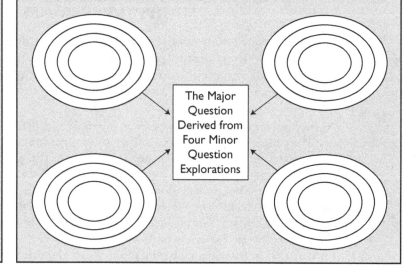

Figure 2. What Professional Information Scientists Do

- **Question Evolution.** How did your research questions evolve over the information search process? Document what you learned in each new source that may have influenced your questions and illustrate this inquiry evolution. How did your questions change after conversations with your teacher, or after presenting your idea to your classmates? Illustrate how the questions clustered into groups for various investigations. Show how the questions became more detailed, specific, or interesting as you explored more background information. At what point did you know you had the question you wanted to focus on for your inquiry project? Given your experience, what criteria are most important in determining a constructive inquiry project for you? Figures 3 and 4 provide a generic framework for students to illustrate question evolution through exploration of print, nonprint, and human resources.

- **Rating Resources.** What specific resources from various general formats (print, electronic, human) did you find most useful for your investigation, and why? What were the limitations? What are examples of leads to other relevant information you received from these formats? Consider "citations and references" in books, "links" from one authoritative website to another, and "recommendations" from people you interviewed for additional names, events, or resources to search. Illustrate how you have linked these information leads together.

- **Useful Patterns.** After each class member describes several of their best information resources and where these were accessed, what predictions can you make on the best locations for finding useful information on future questions similar to those addressed by members of your class? Do you see any patterns in specific indexes, online databases, library resources beyond your school?

- **Authority.** Of the websites explored by members of your class, which were considered the most authoritative and why? Do these observations provide any clues or give you any notions as to how to judge future websites? What criteria would you establish to help you determine the value of future websites? How do these criteria apply to other information sources?

- **Classics.** If your inquiry topic deals with a major historical event, biography, or controversial issue, consider what justifies a few of your sources as "classic" or the most respected sources on your topic. What evidence would you site to make the case that a source is so important that you could not have been able to complete your investigation without it? Is it a source that was referenced by many other sources? Is it a source that gave you a great deal of information that was relevant and meaningful to you? How might the most important resources on a given topic be determined, organized and disseminated for others to use?

- **Experts.** Is there an author who seems to be the most authoritative on your topic? What convinces you of that high authoritative status? In what future situations might you seek out this author again? Why is it important to learn the experts and key sources in a given field on a critical social issue?

- **Audience Analysis.** In what manner can your report or your group's report be best presented to the rest of the class? To parents? To students older than you? To students younger than you? To a local group of decision-makers who could take steps to make changes based on your report? What needs to be considered in terms of presentation format and content for each group who will hear your presentation? How can you determine if you have communicated the message you intend and that your audience has understood the conclusions you have drawn? How will you modify your presentation based on the feedback you get from your audience? How can you test and rehearse your various presentation approaches?

- **Linking Evidence.** In what manner can various pieces of relevant information be linked to provide evidence for a logical argument and the establishment of a reasonable conclusion? What information is lacking that would make the argument more convincing? How would you go about finding information or gathering data that will help you fill that information gap? Can you make predictions of places to seek information or steps to obtain information based on your previous experience?

- **Original Data.** How do you determine if you need to gather original data through personal observations, interviews or experiments? What specific questions will you try to answer? How will you select a method to gather this data? How will you go about a systematic and controlled way to guard against your own biases as you gather this data?

- **Future Applications.** You have completed your project and have received your evaluation. In what ways will you change your approach to a future similar project? In what ways would you keep your approach the same? What have proven to be your most valuable paths to information and gaining an understanding for the relevance and meaning of that information?

ABILITY LEVELS FOR SCIENCE AND INQUIRY

According to the National Academy of Sciences, students should be supported at very early grades to raise questions and discuss methods to address those questions. These abilities should transfer to similar situations in which students deal with information search and use problems and test methods to address those problems. Set within the framework of the Scientific Method, the Academy recognizes the following progression of abilities to deal with activities related to scientific inquiry:

By Grade 4

- Ask a question about objects, organisms, and events in the environment
- Plan and conduct a simple investigation
- Employ simple equipment and tools to gather data and extend the senses
- Use data to construct a reasonable explanation
- Communicate investigations and explanations

By Grades 5 to 8

- Identify questions that can be answered through scientific investigation
- Design and conduct a scientific investigation
- Use appropriate tools and techniques to gather, analyze, and interpret data
- Develop descriptions, explanations, predictions, and models using evidence
- Think critically and logically to make the relationships between evidence and explanations
- Recognize and analyze alternative explanations and predictions
- Communicate scientific procedures and explanations
- Use mathematics in all aspects of scientific inquiry

By Grades 9 to 12

- Identify questions and concepts that guide scientific investigations
- Design and conduct a series of scientific investigations
- Use technology and mathematics to improve investigations and communications
- Formulate and revise scientific explanations and models using logic and evidence
- Recognize and analyze alternative explanations and models
- Communicate and defend a scientific argument

Fundamental to these abilities are some basic understandings that students should be engaged in for discussion and application as early as elementary school:

- Scientific investigations involve asking and answering a question and comparing the answer with what scientists already know about the world.
- Scientists use different kinds of investigations depending on the questions they are trying to answer.
- Scientists develop explanations using observations (evidence) and what they already know about the world (scientific knowledge).

- Scientists make the results of their investigation public; they describe the investigation in ways that enable others to repeat the investigations.
- Scientists review and ask questions about the results of other scientists' work.

SIMILAR STANDARDS IN SOCIAL SCIENCE AND HUMANITIES

Similar standards for student performance are common in documents from state education agencies, local school corporations and national associations. Application of the Scientific Method and information inquiry as a student of information science are also found in the social science portions of curriculum outlines. Such is never an "add on" to the curriculum, but always a clear basic expectation that enriches the learning experience and takes both teaching and learning to levels that are beyond simply memorizing facts, names, and events. Mary Dalbotten's organization of student performance skills across the curriculum is a valuable tool to relate national learning standards to critical and creative thinking for inquiry. Examples that illustrate this are:

History and Social Sciences
- Historical thinking skills enable students to differentiate past, present, and future times; raise questions; seek and evaluate evidence; compare and analyze historical stories, illustrations, and records from the past; interpret the historical record; and construct historical narratives of their own.
- Real historical understanding requires that students have the opportunity to create historical narratives and arguments of their own. Such narratives and arguments may take many forms—essays, debates, and editorials, for instance. They can be initiated in a variety of ways. None, however, more powerfully initiates historical thinking than those issues, past and present, that challenge students to enter knowledgeably into the historical record and to bring sound historical perspectives to bear in the analysis of a problem.
- On contemporary issues across the full range of social science studies, students should practice skills that focus on relevant local and global issues in which they use information to identify, describe, explain, explain a position, take a position, and defend a position. An example is for the student to evaluate historical and contemporary political communications using such criteria as logical validity, factual accuracy, emotional appeal, distorted evidence, appeals to bias or prejudice and establishing criteria for judging information sources in light of such manipulation of communication. Another common example, this time relevant to simulating what political scientists do, is to evaluate, to take, and defend positions on the influence of the media on American political life.

Language Arts and Humanities
- Students present information, concepts, and ideas to an audience of listeners or readers on a variety of topics. Students adjust their use of spoken, written, and visual language to communicate effectively with a variety of audiences and for different purposes.
- Students read a wide range of print and nonprint texts to build an understanding of texts, of themselves, and of the cultures of the United States and the world; to acquire new information; to respond to the needs and demands of society and the workplace; and for personal fulfillment.
- Students apply a wide range of strategies to comprehend, interpret, evaluate, and appreciate texts. They draw on their prior experience, their interactions with other readers and writers, their knowledge of word meaning and of other texts, their word identification strategies, and their understanding of textual features, including graphics.
- Students conduct research on issues and interests by generating ideas and questions, and by posing problems. They gather, evaluate, and synthesize data from a variety of sources (print, nonprint, artifacts, people) to communicate their discoveries in ways that suit their purpose and audience.

- Students use a variety of technological and information resources (libraries, databases, computer networks, video, mass media, human experts) to gather and synthesize information and to create and communicate knowledge.
- Students participate as knowledgeable, reflective, creative, and critical members of a variety of literacy communities.

See figures 3 and 4 related to developing questions.

FOR FURTHER READING

Callison, Daniel. Bias. *School Library Media Activities Monthly.* 21:5. (January). 2005. 34–6.

Callison, Daniel. Inquiry, Literacy and the Learning Laboratory. In *New Millennium, New Horizons,* edited by Lyn Hay, Kylie Hanson and James Henri. Centre for Studies in Teacher Librarianship. Charles Sturt University. 2000. 55–64.

Callison, Daniel. Scaffolding. *School Library Media Activities Monthly.* 17:6. (February). 2001. 37–9.

Callison, Daniel and Annette Lamb. Audience Analysis. *School Library Media Activities Monthly.* 21:1. (September). 2004. 34–9.

Dalbotten, Mary S. *Inquiry in the National Content Standards. In Instructional Interventions for Information Use: Papers of Treasure Mountain VI* edited by Daniel Callison, Joy H. McGregor, and Ruth Small. Hi Willow Research. 1997. 246–304. Reprinted in *Information Literacy: Essential skills for the Information Age,* edited by Michael B. Eisenberg, Carrie A. Lowe and Kathleen L. Spitzer. Libraries Unlimited. 2004. 221–231.

Gordon, Carol A. Methods for Measuring the Influence of Concept Mapping on Student Information Literacy. *School Library Media Research.* Volume 5. 2002. www.ala.org/aasl/SLMR.

Guild, Sandy L. Modeling Recursion in Research Process Instruction. In *Curriculum Connections through the Library,* edited by Barbara K. Stripling and Sandra Hughes-Hassell. Libraries Unlimited. 2003. 141–155.

Harada, Violet H. Empowered Learning: Fostering Thinking across the Curriculum. In *Curriculum Connections through the Library,* edited by Barbara Stripling and Sandra Hughes-Hassell. Libraries Unlimited. 2003. 41–64.

Harada, Violet H. and Joan M. Yoshina. *Inquiry Learning through Librarian-Teacher Partnerships.* Linworth Publishing. 2004.

Harris, Frances Jacobson. There was a Great Collision in the Stock Market: Middle School Students, Online Primary Sources, and Historical Sense Making. *School Library Media Research.* Volume 5. 2002. www.ala .org/aasl/SLMR

Harvey, Stephanie and Anne Goudvis. *Think Nonfiction.* 30 minute video tape with study guide. Stenhouse Publishers. 2003.

Harvey, Stephanie and Anne Goudvis. *Strategies that Work: Teaching Comprehension to Enhance Understanding.* Stenhouse Publishers. 2000.

Inquiry and the National Science *Education Standards: A Guide for Teaching and Learning.* National Academy of Sciences, National Research Council, and the Center for Science, Mathematics, and Engineering Education. Washington, D.C. 2000.

Marchionini, Gary. Educating Responsible Citizens in the Information Society. *Educational Technology.* 39:2. 1999. 17–26.

Stripling, Barbara. Inquiry-Based Learning. In *Curriculum Connections through the Library,* edited by Barbara Stripling and Sandra Hughes-Hassell. Libraries Unlimited. 2003. 3–40.

The Student Information Scientist, Part II

Daniel Callison

This article (Parts I and II) is foundational to a presentation on "The Student as Information Scientist" given at the 2005 National Conference of the American Association of School Librarians in Pittsburgh.

Information literacy standards for student learning, indicators for student performance, and hundreds of collaborative lesson plans around the country give us some indication of the skills students are expected to master as effective and efficient users of information. Hopefully the goal is that all involved in information literacy education become wiser consumers of information. In mastering the elements of information inquiry, teachers and school librarians acting as instructional specialists model, teach, and learn with their students the best ways to test and select information that is valid and relevant to solve information problems.

SCAFFOLDS FOR INQUIRY SKILLS

Barbara Stripling has written one of the most comprehensive and convincing essays on the relationships among inquiry-based learning, information literacy, and K–12 curriculum. Among a rich list of curricular ties, she offers these examples that illustrate how teaching inquiry involves applications at different grade levels with the instructional media specialists working collaboratively to facilitate a progressive scaffolding of investigative experiences from elementary to secondary school (2003, page 26).

- Evaluation of sources is critical to inquiry in social studies because of the interpretative nature of the discipline. Students should assess the value of a source before they even look at the specific information within the source. If teachers and librarians have selected the source, then they should share their thinking process with students. The criteria that need to be emphasized (at age-appropriate times) are authoritativeness of the author/publisher; comprehensiveness of the information (students are seeking in-depth information, not collections of superficial facts); organization and clarity of the text (students need to be able to find and comprehend relevant information without getting lost in extraneous links or subtopics); and quality of the references (the sources of the cited evidence) [and further understand our quality citations can lead to additional relevant evidence]. Obviously, in the age of the Internet, responsibility for evaluation of sources has largely shifted from librarians to students. Careful instruction and guidance must accompany that shift.

"The Student Information Scientist, Part II" by Daniel Callison, was published in *School Library Media Activities Monthly* 22, no. 3 (November 2005): 37–41.

- Use of primary sources is an important component of inquiry in social studies. Students must be taught to observe and draw valid interpretations from artifacts, ephemera, images, maps, and personal accounts. Students must be taught to interpret the primary sources in light of its context (e.g., a soldier writing a letter about a recent skirmish may think it the bloodiest battle of the war because he was injured; a photographer shooting a peace march from a low angle may convey a huge crowd, while an overhead shot might show a small crowd with empty streets behind it). Because so many sources are being digitized, students have more access to primary sources than they have ever had before [and the amount available online will grow tremendously over the coming years]. Primary sources may be particularly exciting to elementary students who have limited background knowledge. They, therefore, need scaffolding to foster the validity of their interpretations. [Frances Jacobson Harris has demonstrated how challenging it is to manage visual and artifact interpretation skills of middle grade students.]
- Evaluation of specific information and evidence is also a key thinking strategy for inquiry in social studies. Librarians and classroom teachers probably want to emphasize discernment of fact versus opinion and help students understand how each can be used effectively. Students, particularly at the secondary level, must learn how to identify point of view and recognize its effect on the evidence. Their responsibility is to find enough evidence from different points of view that they [may consider] . . . a balanced perspective. Sources that present opposing viewpoints are helpful to provide that [attempted] balance of evidence. Secondary students must also be taught to detect degrees of bias (from slightly slanted point of view to heavily slanted propaganda).

MODELING INQUIRY WITH EARLY NONFICTION

Stephanie Harvey and Anne Goudvis have established themselves as purveyors of reading strategies that work in elementary school settings. They promote modeling by all teachers [and we will add all library instructional media specialists] of the processes for engaging themselves and their students in the understanding and use of nonfiction text. A few of their exercises for early readers of nonfiction are summarized below (2000, Appendix F). Each of these will lead to early practice to help guide and model inquiry and scientific mindedness. Children are naturally curious, but as humans they need help in organizing, making selections, prioritizing, and eventually gaining focus on what is meaningful to both themselves and their likely audiences. Students are invited to make initial choices and are guided by teachers who model and present options so that students are enabled to make logical revisions and extensions to what they bring to the nonfiction text.

For each of the examples from Harvey and Goudvis below, copies of text pages are made for students to feel free to mark and highlight. If original pages are used, teachers and students use sticky-notes. Sometimes different colors allow several students to contribute their ideas together to the same text pages and clearly show personal contributions. Notes can be moved from the text pages to large sheets of paper on which the sticky-notes can be organized to show patterns of observations. Charts and tables of combined ideas can be generated. These same methods can be used to produce individual or group thinking for concept maps through the use of software such as Inspiration.

- **Asking Questions throughout the Reading Process:** Readers ask questions before, during and after reading. Look at the cover [of the book] and read the title. Record any questions you might have before you start to read. While reading, highlight or mark a part of the text or picture where you have a question. When you finish reading, write down any remaining questions. Suggest possible answers to your questions.
- **Predicting:** While reading, highlight or mark a sentence or picture with P when you find yourself making a prediction. Write a sentence that had helped you think of the prediction. After you finish reading the complete text, note if your prediction was confirmed or contradicted.

- **Synthesizing Information:** While reading, highlight or mark a picture or part of the text with SZ for synthesize when you have a new idea. After completing the text, review your SZ notations and combine them into one or two major ideas you got from the entire text.
- **Determining Important Information:** Look for the any of the following text cues to important information—
  - Cause/Effect: since, because, due to, for this reason, therefore
  - Comparison/Contrast: likewise, as opposed to, however, but, nevertheless
  - Problem/Solution: one reason for that, a possible solution
  - Question/Answer: how, what, when, why, the best estimate, it could be that
  - Sequence: until, before, after, finally

PROBLEM IDENTIFIERS

Over recent years, Violet Harada, Professor of Library and Information Science at the University of Hawaii, has implemented several collaborative inquiry-based projects across K–12 learning environments. Harada has approached each project with problem-solving strategies modeled by the teacher and library media specialist team, but with the twist that before students can understand solutions they must be engaged to act as "Problem Identifiers." A typical sequence to foster problem awareness and solution options at the secondary school level follows.

- **Brainstorming:** Students work in small groups to brainstorm ideas generated by the driving question posed. Example—What does it mean to live healthier?
- **Webbing:** Each group creates a web with questions linked from the issue-driving question and each group shares their ideas with the rest of the class. Under teacher and library media specialist guidance, students create a total class web that reflects all key ideas. This can be the first of many information products from the students to be displayed for other teachers, students, and administrators to see the development of a critical thinking, problem-solving project.
- **Exploration of Sources:** Students focus on general information sources and gather ideas from each source to share with the class. Such background reading and viewing helps to formulate questions that make sense and helps students see which questions are also of greatest interest among classmates.
- **Individual Journaling:** Students begin to generate their own questions in a personal journal and expand this list as they engage in more reading, viewing, and small group discussions. Students apply guidance from the teacher and media specialist to select good questions.
- **Choosing a Research Focus:** Based on personal interest, relevance to the inquiry theme for the class, and availability of resources likely to support the investigation, students select questions for their extended investigation.
- **The Research Process:** Students step through the standard process of seeking information, selecting evidence, discussing what can be inferred from the evidence, need for additional sources, a summary of conclusions to address their questions, and methods of presenting results.

Along the way, many instructional problems arise. A brief list of these and how they are addressed illustrates collaborative roles that need to be played by the teachers and media specialist.

- Journal accounts revealed that students knew less about the general topic of nutrition than the teacher anticipated. The teacher added two more sessions for students to explore information resources, including more time to browse and report on resources in the library.
- Observations showed that students were fuzzy about keyword searching. The library media specialist spent another session on keyword search strategies.
- Observation revealed that students had limited prior knowledge about conducting surveys. The teacher added two sessions where she presented models for surveys.

- Students were able to gather survey data more quickly than anticipated. Time for the survey was reduced from two weeks to one.
- Observations indicated that students had different interpretations of data. The teacher used another session to guide students in consensus of interpretations.

Sandy Guild, a high school librarian in Pennsylvania, conducts research conferences with students as they work through the inquiry process. Two of her conversation guides are outlined below with the standard questions she raises.

Background Reading

- What best describes the kind of relationship you are investigating:
  o Cause and effect
  o Application of a concept
  o Influence
  o Comparison
  o Other
- What is the most exciting discovery you have made so far?
- On the back of this paper, draw a simple concept map using the results of your background reading. Include major people, places, concepts, and relationships that you have been able to identify.
- Using the concept map as a guide, briefly state what your thesis question is currently.
- What is confusing in the research you have conducted so far?
- [Adding to her list] What is reassuring in the research you have conducted so far?

Conferencing about Questions, Arguments, and Sources

- State the focus of your paper and list the topic areas that relate to it.
- On the back of this sheet, draw a simple concept map of your developing thesis. Be clear what kind of relationship(s) organize(s) your thesis.
- What new questions have you developed as a result of your research in supporting your thesis?
- What part of your argument is weakest?
- What resource so far has been the best for information? Why?
- What information are you looking for that you have not been able to find?

Barbara Stripling, Director of Library Programs at New Visions for Public Schools and former President of the American Association of School Librarians, has summarized the mentoring roles for instructional media specialists that are most likely to encourage inquiry-based learning. These roles are paraphrased as follows:

- Catalyst—when convinced of the power of inquiry and other investigative strategies based on the Scientific Method, take steps to change traditional curriculum so that student learning is centered on inquiry; take leadership.
- Connector—see the total curriculum, recognize the best teachers, support the best learning projects, acquire access to the most useful instructional materials and connect these whenever there is an opportunity; demonstrate the potential.
- Coach—model and reward the inquiry process by practicing it as a value process before students and other teachers, encourage and praise successful inquiry projects; assess practice and reward team efforts.
- Caregiver—independent learning is also encouraged and guided to meet special needs and interests supported by resources that meet specific levels; motivate each learner to achieve at his or her highest ability.

Added to this list is:

- [Communicator—demonstrate results of the process as well as products so that learners and teachers can visualize possibilities; display student efforts in critical and creative thinking.]

THE INFORMATION LEARNING LABORATORY

In the information inquiry learning laboratory, elementary and secondary, artifacts of the process as well as the products are displayed. Inquiry is illustrated on the wall as well as online for sharing, feedback, and modeling. Space is available for devising and testing information value, logic of arguments, and acceptance or rejection of evidence. The laboratory may include the library and classrooms—multiple spaces where student work can take place. Some of the tangible aspects of the laboratory are:

- Student journals have double entries with space devoted to reflections on the quality or limitations of information located and information still needed.
- Final reports include a section in which the student describes the value of the sources located, predicts best information for similar future projects, and describes the value of peers, parents, teachers, and librarians who may have helped to guide the inquiry.
- Large sections of wall space or bulletin boards are available for students to display the progress in their investigation by showing evolution of questions, expansion of concept maps, resources linked to generating new ideas, linkages from general information sources to more specific data and evidence, and rating of the quality of resources used.
- Space is provided for students to lay out evidence on large table tops and work in groups to assimilate the evidence, argue the merits of evidence, and to link evidence together to support and reject arguments.
- Video recording areas are provided for students to practice and critique oral presentation of arguments, practice debating issues, and organize multimedia presentations.
- Electronic discussion groups are maintained for the purpose of sharing ideas, arguments, and evidence. Software is used to support linking these items together to formulate a variety of ways to present findings and to express needs yet to be met before other conclusions can be determined.
- Portals are created so students may view and critique peer work at various draft stages.
- Connections are provided for access to databases and human resources beyond the school.
- A collection of previous student work is maintained, artifacts of both process and product, for future students to access and consider as they enter a level of inquiry new to them.
- Parents, students, teachers, and administrators may view examples of student inquiry work at special events sponsored through the library media center. Information Inquiry Fairs, similar to Science Fairs, may be based on themes and are advertised as celebrations of learning accomplishment. In addition to student poster presentations, illustrations are provided of the thought processes to focus on the most critical questions and the most valuable resources.
- The laboratory is always available for student information scientists who wish to return, often on an individual basis, to further their reading and investigations on problems that continue to interest them long after the academic assignment has been completed.

FOR FURTHER READING

Callison, Daniel. Bias. *School Library Media Activities Monthly*. 21:5. (January). 2005. 34–6.

Callison, Daniel. Inquiry, Literacy and the Learning Laboratory. In *New Millennium, New Horizons*, edited by Lyn Hay, Kylie Hanson and James Henri. Centre for Studies in Teacher Librarianship. Charles Sturt University. 2000. 55–64.

Callison, Daniel. Scaffolding. *School Library Media Activities Monthly*. 17:6. (February). 2001. 37–9.

98

The Evolution of Inquiry

Callison, Daniel and Annette Lamb. Audience Analysis. *School Library Media Activities Monthly.* 21:1. (September). 2004. 34–9.

Dalbotten, Mary S. Inquiry in the National Content Standards. In *Instructional Interventions for Information Use: Papers of Treasure Mountain VI* edited by Daniel Callison, Joy H. McGregor, and Ruth Small. Hi Willow Research. 1997. 246–304. Reprinted in *Information Literacy: Essential skills for the Information Age,* edited by Michael B. Eisenberg, Carrie A. Lowe, and Kathleen L. Spitzer. Libraries Unlimited. 2004. 221–231.

Gordon, Carol A. Methods for Measuring the Influence of Concept Mapping on Student Information Literacy. *School Library Media Research.* Volume. 5. 2002. www.ala.org/aasl/SLMR.

Guild, Sandy L. Modeling Recursion in Research Process Instruction. In *Curriculum Connections through the Library,* edited by Barbara K. Stripling and Sandra Hughes-Hassell. Libraries Unlimited. 2003. 141–155.

Harada, Violet H. Empowered Learning: Fostering Thinking across the Curriculum. In *Curriculum Connections through the Library,* edited by Barbara Stripling and Sandra Hughes-Hassell. Libraries Unlimited. 2003. 41–64.

Harada, Violet H. and Joan M. Yoshina. *Inquiry Learning through Librarian-Teacher Partnerships.* Linworth Publishing. 2004.

Harris, Frances Jacobson. There was a Great Collision in the Stock Market: Middle School Students, Online Primary Sources, and Historical Sense Making. *School Library Media Research.* Volume 5. 2002. www.ala .org/aasl/SLMR

Harvey, Stephanie and Anne Goudvis. *Think Nonfiction.* 30 minute video tape with study guide. Stenhouse Publishers. 2003.

Harvey, Stephanie and Anne Goudvis. *Strategies that Work: Teaching Comprehension to Enhance Understanding.* Stenhouse Publishers. 2000.

Inquiry and the National Science Education Standards: A Guide for Teaching and Learning. National Academy of Sciences, National Research Council, and the Center for Science, Mathematics, and Engineering Education. Washington, D.C. 2000.

Marchionini, Gary. Educating Responsible Citizens in the Information Society. *Educational Technology.* 39:2. 1999. 17–26.

Stripling, Barbara. Inquiry-Based Learning. In *Curriculum Connections through the Library,* edited by Barbara Stripling and Sandra Hughes-Hassell. Libraries Unlimited. 2003. 3–40.

Graphic Inquiry for All Learners

Annette Lamb and Daniel Callison

Daniel Callison and Annette Lamb introduced the concept of graphic inquiry in 2007. They proposed graphic inquiry as the process for extracting information and presenting information in visual formats such as political cartoons, diagrams, maps, photos, charts, infographics, and multimedia. Through a recursive process, employing the basic elements of inquiry (questioning, exploration, assimilation, inference, and reflection), students mature as information scientists and address their personal, academic, and even workplace information needs. Through the process of graphic inquiry learners of all ages can add visual dimensions to their abilities to make convincing arguments, evaluate information, solve problems, and make informed decisions.

VISUAL COMMUNICATION

A position paper distributed by the Hewlett-Packard Development Company reports the following:

> Visual communication is everywhere today, from electronic media like Web pages and television screens to environmental contexts such as road signs and retail displays. As the National Education Association has pointed out, Western civilization has become more dependent than ever on visual culture, visual artifacts, and visual communication as a mode of discourse and a means of developing a social and cultural identity. There is evidence to suggest that people not only communicate visually more than ever, they also communicate better when they communicate visually. (2004)

In their widely used college text, *Writing Arguments,* John D. Ramage of Arizona State University and his colleagues John C. Bean and June Johnson of Seattle University provide many examples for substantiating arguments with the use of convincing visuals. In today's visually oriented culture, arguments increasingly are supported with photographs, tables, and graphics to help text generate a more persuasive effect. Ramage and his colleagues conclude, "Using visuals in arguments also poses challenges. It places on arguers an even greater burden to understand their audience, to think through the effect visuals will have on the audience, and to make sure that the verbal and visual parts of an argument work together" (2010, 165).

"Graphic Inquiry for All Learners," by Annette Lamb and Daniel Callison, was published in *School Library Monthly* 28, no. 3 (December 2011): 18–22.

Graphic inquiry, the processes of creating, producing, and distributing material incorporating words and images to convey data, concepts, and emotions, encompasses graphic communication. Charts, diagrams, tables, graphs, and other visual interpretations of material bring together the visual and the verbal to add another dimension to inquiry and create an entirely new path toward unique meaning and broader understanding. The student and those with whom he shares the results of his inquiry "see" a deeper meaning than simply what is conveyed only verbally. As renowned visual researcher Edward R. Tufte has observed, "To envision information—and what bright and splendid visions can result—is to work at the intersection of image, word, number, and art" (1990).

Callison and Lamb contend that authentic learning is reached when the inquiry process not only combines verbal and visual literacy, but when academic, personal, and workplace learning needs become seamless (2004). Inquiry occurs in both formal and informal learning situations. The inquiry is learned through stages of controlled, guided, modeled, and free or open applications through which the student matures in his/her abilities to apply inquiry in order to address various learning challenges (Callison 2009).

A review of the impact of graphic organizers on learning was released by Inspiration Software in 2003. Conclusions reached in this review indicated that visual learning strategies improve student performance in the following areas:

- Use of graphic organizers is effective in improving students' reading comprehension.
- Students using graphic organizers show achievement benefits across content areas and grade levels. Achievement benefits are also seen with students with learning disabilities.
- The process of developing and using a graphic organizer enhances skills such as developing and organizing ideas, seeing relationships, and categorizing concepts.
- The use of graphic organizers supports implementation of cognitive learning theories: dual coding theory, schema theory, and cognitive load theory (IARE 2003).

BASIC INFORMATION INQUIRY ELEMENTS
RELATED TO GRAPHIC INQUIRY

Graphic inquiry can be woven throughout the information inquiry process. See Figure 1.

Questioning

Humans have a natural curiosity that drives the learning processes from birth. Through practice, modeling, and reflection, the ability to focus questions on specific issues and to link questions to refine the exploration for meaningful and relevant inference or conclusion are the intellectual abilities that set humans apart from the rest of the animal kingdom.

Benjamin Franklin, America's first self-taught scientist, described in his autobiography how the Socratic Method helped him pose critical questions. Both practical and theoretical, Franklin exemplifies how one learns through inquiry. Many other historical figures have found similar value in the ability to question wisely. The following quotations illustrate the idea that learners who lead and influence others also have a vision:

"The important thing is to never stop questioning."—Albert Einstein
"The fool wonders, the wise man asks."—Benjamin Disraeli
"You can tell whether a man is clever by his answers. You can tell whether a man is wise by his questions."—Naguib Mahfouz
"The soul never thinks without a mental image."—Aristotle

Figure 1. The Recursive Information Inquiry Cycle with Interactive Elements. (Callison 2003)

Typical questions that may help to analyze visual elements or arguments in the application of graphic inquiry include:

- What does the creator of the visual intend its effects to be?
- What effect does the choice of medium have on the message of the visual text? How would the message be altered if different media were used?
- What cultural values, emotions, or ideals does the visual evoke or suggest?
- Is anything in the visual repeated, intensified, or exaggerated?
- In what manner does the visual confirm or counter prior assumptions or knowledge? What does the visual text assume about its viewers, and about what they know and agree with? (Lunsford, Ruszkiewicz, and Walters, 2007).

Exploration

Closely tied to questioning, exploration is the action taken to seek answers to a question. There is, therefore, a continuous interaction between questioning and exploration as they inform and refine each other. In many cases, no specific questions are on the agenda, but the drive to satisfy curiosity moves the learner to read, view, listen, and search information. Exploration provides the opportunity for the learner to experience an expanding pool of information possibilities. The more open and wide ranging the exploration, the more likely it is that the exploration will provide a context for issues and help to refine questions that are truly meaningful and possible to answer.

Exploration of the expanding visual and textual information universe serves to help the learner become a more critical consumer. This exploration involves both the message and the medium. And it involves exploration of how messages may change from one medium to another, from one issue to another, and from one audience to another. Graphic inquiry is more powerful for the learner when there is also a growing knowledge of visual vocabulary, design techniques used to create images, and an understanding of how to identify the characteristics of an image that give it meaning.

One does not become visually literate by simply looking at images, but by comparing and contrasting many images as well as practicing a critical analysis of what various images contribute to the personal knowledge base. Exploration helps the critical learner gather a mental library of ideas to test for assimilation. The skills of analysis and synthesis are eventually interwoven and bring focus to the exploration, thus identifying specific issues as most relevant to the information need or problem.

Assimilation

The assimilation component of inquiry involves the actions to absorb and fit information to what is already known, believed, or assumed by the learner. In some cases, assimilation means reinforcing or confirming what is known. In other cases, assimilation involves an altering of what has been previously accepted as knowledge by the individual learner or group of learners.

In still other situations, new information may be rejected simply because it does not match current assumptions or beliefs of the learner. In such situations, the learner's behavior may be to select only from those data, images, arguments, or opinions that "confirm" what the learner believed to be true from the beginning of the inquiry process. Such "belief persistence" should not be mistaken as "holding to core ideals or principles" (Fitzgerald 1999). Belief persistence based on selective "cherry-picking" of only evidence that supports a pre-concluded notion or desired goal is counter to the values of inquiry. Truth and reason are destinations where the evidence takes the learner rather than where the learner wants to take the evidence. Such is not always simply "rejection of authority," but more often a refinement of authority that is based on critical analysis of what is reasonable evidence to justify or infer appropriate conclusions.

New information can result in frustrations for the learner, especially if new information is counter to what was previously assumed. New information may also cause frustration if it is not "age-appropriate," in other words, the learner does not have the background or maturity to comprehend the meaning of the new evidence. Such frustrations call for "learning and teaching moments" when teachers or other mentors can guide and explain the meaning, value, and relevance of this new information.

Inquiry, properly applied, turns learning into more than a gathering of facts. Assimilation through inquiry leads to consideration of a wider range of perceptions and options rather than simply those assumed by the learner. As the inquirer matures, assimilation evolves to linking diverse and multiple channels of new information to what is previously known personally. Assimilation involves accumulation of knowledge, alteration of accepted knowledge, and constant consideration of alternatives.

Assimilation encompasses not only the actions of reading and listening, but also the interactive processes of critical analysis, debate, as well as comparing and contrasting facts and ideas. New information assimilated with previously held information becomes new knowledge for the learner.

Inference

This component involves the actions or processes for deriving a conclusion from facts and premises. Inference may also involve personal choice and actions taken based on conclusions that seem most relevant and meaningful for the situation. This type of inference is usually the first step for a learner.

On a personal basis, inference is usually an internal message to the self, and not always conveyed in a formal manner to others. Inference may or may not involve presentation of findings to another audience. However, interpretation of inferences for presentation can be an excellent way to focus on clarification or conclusions, and present meaningful evidence for a specific audience. Assimilation and inference are constantly interacting as a decision process to accept or reject new information.

Graphic inquiry involves learning environments in which the student may experiment with a variety of media to present a set of inferences (conclusions or recommendations). Formats include not only written papers and oral presentations, but also comics, interactive media, and multimedia. An emphasis on graphic inquiry can lead to visuals that can increase the number of concepts learned, condense the amount of time to present, and compare multiple facts, concepts and conclusions, as well as increase the length of time those concepts are remembered.

A sharing of the conclusions may lead to further assimilation of increased information for both the presenter and the audience. Presentation of inferences often results in refining the meaning of the conclusions and can be used to both inform and persuade an audience. In nearly all cases, inference raises new questions for exploration, part of the recursive learning cycle of inquiry.

Reflection

The reflection element raises the questions designed to bring the interactions of other elements full circle. "Have I been successful in answering my question?" "Is this the best information or visual evidence to address this question?" "Was the table of data too cluttered and would a chart provide better clarity?" "Would the visual evidence be stronger if the images were in motion, rather than stills?" "What new questions have come from the consideration of the evidence I have gathered?"

Reflection involves evaluation and assessment at formative and summative levels. Each time new information is encountered, reflection should be placed in the information inquiry cycle. Each time a project, plan, or elaborated argument is completed, reflection is needed.

Evaluation levels can include self-reflection, peer feedback, measures of audience response based on argument acceptance or change in positions, and expert evaluation. At the expert level a teacher or mentor who has mastered the inquiry process provides guidance on how to revise and improve the inquiry processes for future application.

As the learner matures in his or her ability, reflection can be used more and more within each new information encounter. Reflections to assess exploration, assimilation, and inference are formative in that the leaner is aware of the consequences of actions in one element on the limitations or opportunities in other elements.

The learner who masters self-reflection becomes more likely to be not only a true independent learner, but also one who can help others master the information and graphic inquiry interactions. The teacher who masters both formative and summative assessment processes will provide more clarity to their guidance and feedback in evaluations of learner actions.

Evaluation is the highest critical thinking skill set. The learner who matures to the level of understanding the value and methods for continuous evaluation is reaching the most demanding aspects for meaningful graphic inquiry.

TEACHING, LEARNING, AND GRAPHIC INQUIRY

Inquiry is an important 21st century skill. Graphic inquiry fits within the 21st Century definition of information literacy offered by the American Association of School Librarians (AASL), "Information literacy has progressed from the simple definition of using reference resources to find information. [Today] multiple literacies, including digital, visual, textual, and technological, have now joined information literacy as crucial skills for this century" (AASL 2007). Placed within a formal educational environment, the graphic inquiry process can serve to meet the first, basic AASL skill standard, "Follow an inquiry-based process in seeking knowledge in

Teaching, Learning, and Graphic Inquiry

From historical novels and archival video footage to maps, photographs, and comics, consider the many ways that graphic inquiry can enhance learning. Students use graphic representations as they watch, wonder, web, wiggle, weave, wrap, wave, and wish through this recursive inquiry process. Guide students through this process of questioning, exploration, assimilation, inference, and reflection by providing quality pathfinders, scaffolds for thinking, and choice in learning.

Figure 2. Teaching, learning, and graphic inquiry
(Adapted from the book *Graphic Inquiry* by Annette Lamb and Daniel Callison).

curricular subjects, and make the real-world connection for using this process in [the student's] own life" (2007).

Young people need many experiences, both formal and informal, when working their way through the inquiry process. Whether learning about tessellations in mathematics or tracing the movement of animals during migration, graphic representations are useful throughout the inquiry process. Such a graphic representation using the dustbowl as the focus can be seen in Figure 2.

GRAPHIC INQUIRY AND THE SCHOOL LIBRARIAN

School librarians play an essential role in helping young people use graphic representations effectively. Whether helping children unlock clues in historical photographs or guiding them in the creation of infographics, librarians must address the needs of 21st century learners. The next graphic from the book, *Graphic Inquiry* by Annette Lamb and Daniel Callison, provides seven key ideas for building these visually-rich environments for inquiry. See Figure 3.

REFERENCES

American Association of School Librarians. *Standards for the 21st Century Learner*. American Library Association, 2007. (Downloadable for free at: www.ala.org/aasl/standards).

Callison, Daniel. *Keywords, Concepts and Methods for Information Age Instruction*. Baltimore, MD: LMS Associates, 2003.

Callison, Daniel. "Information Inquiry: Concepts and Elements." In *The Blue Book on Information Age Inquiry, Instruction and Literacy* by Daniel Callison and Leslie Preddy. Libraries Unlimited, 2006.

Callison, Daniel. "Inquiry." *School Library Media Activities Monthly* 15, no. 6 (February, 1999): 38–42.

Callison, Daniel, and Annette Lamb. "Authentic Learning." *School Library Media Activities Monthly* 21, no. 4 (December, 2004): 34–30.

Callison, Daniel and Annette Lamb. "Graphic Inquiry: Standards and Resources, Part I." *School Library Media Activities Monthly* 24, no. 1 (September, 2007): 39–43.

Callison, Daniel and Annette Lamb. "Graphic Inquiry: Skills and Strategies, Part II." *School Library Media Activities Monthly* 24, no. 2 (October, 2007): 38–42.

Fitzgerald, M.A. "Evaluating Information: An Information Literacy Challenge." *School Library Media Research* 2 (1999). http://www.ala.org/ala/mgrps/divs/aasl/aaslpubsandjournals/slmrb/slmrcontents/volume21999/vol2fitzgerald.cfm (accessed September 12, 2011).

Hewlett-Packard Development Company. "Communicating Effectively in the Visual Age." 2004. www.hp.com/go/printingandimaging (accessed September 12, 2011).

The Institute for the Advancement of Research in Education (IARE). "Graphic Organizers: A Review of Scientifically Based Research." 2003. http://cf.inspiration.com/download/pdf/SBR_summary.pdf (accessed September 12, 2011).

Kuhlthau, Carol C., Leslie K. Maniotes, and Ann K. Caspari. *Guided Inquiry: Learning in the 21st Century*. Libraries Unlimited, 2007.

Lamb, Annette and Danny Callison. *Graphic Inquiry*. Libraries Unlimited, Forthcoming 2012.

Lunsford, Andrea A., John J. Ruszkiewicz, and Keith Walters. *Everything's an Argument*. 4th edition. Bedford/St. Martin's, 2007.

Ramage, John D., John C. Bean, and June Johnson. *Writing Arguments: A Rhetoric with Readings*. 5th edition. Longman, 2010.

Tufte, Edward R. *Envisioning Information*. Graphics Press, 1990.

Graphic Inquiry and 21st Century Learning

As school librarians plan inquiry-based environments that address the needs of 21st century learners, consider how graphics can enhance the experience.

Graphic Inquiry by Annette Lamb and Daniel Callison explores seven key ideas for creating these learning environments.

❶ Graphic Literacy, Fluency, Inquiry, and Life Long Learning

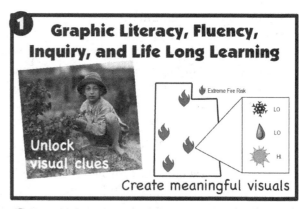

Unlock visual clues

Create meaningful visuals

❷ Types of Graphics

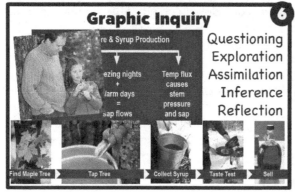

Charts
Diagrams
Illustrations
Maps
Organizers
Images
Symbols

❸ SCORE IT!
Standards and Deep Thinking

Storytelling
Communication
Organization
Representation
Evidence
Inference
Teaching

❹ Skills and Strategies

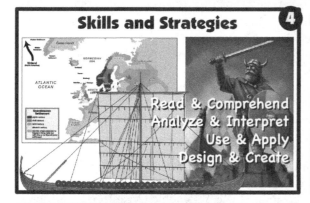

Read & Comprehend
Analyze & Interpret
Use & Apply
Design & Create

❺ Interdisciplinary Approaches and Individual Differences

Primary Sources
Data Collections
Photographs
Maps
Infographics
Comics
Literature

❻ Graphic Inquiry

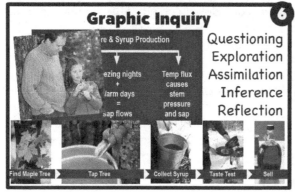

Questioning
Exploration
Assimilation
Inference
Reflection

❼ Learning through Graphic Inquiry

Object-based
Place-based
Collaboration
Innovation
Issues

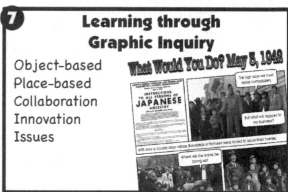

Figure 3. Graphic inquiry and 21st century learning
(Adapted from the book *Graphic Inquiry* by Annette Lamb and Daniel Callison).

Section III

Information Inquiry
across the Curriculum

<h1 style="text-align:center">Chapter 6</h1>

<h1 style="text-align:center">Inquiry in Science and Math</h1>

Part I: Multiple Shades of Inquiry Found in Science Education

Multiple Shades of Inquiry Found in Science Education

Daniel Callison

Several definitions for inquiry have emerged in the science education literature over the past few years. These definitions vary based on project demands and student achievement expectations. While the framework for the scientific method has remained the same, inquiry has advanced along a continuum. Today, inquiry-based learning can be identified through teacher controlled activities and projects that encourage greater responsibilities for the student. The learner matures to reach higher levels as he or she masters self-learning skills.

Some educators refer to this maturation as a progressive cognitive apprenticeship. Most school librarians describe it in terms of maturing in abilities to reach successful life-long learning. The shift has been driven by evolution in learning theory from behaviorist, to constructivist, to humanist. Application of these theories determines the depth of engagement with both scientific thought and application of actions that the learner can make to improve his or her society and environment.

Increased student initiative has improved dramatically in the processes of question generation, literature review and analysis, and student presentation of arguments to defend or reject a hypothesis. While not all students have the ability to reach independent learning status at the open or free inquiry levels, most have, with teacher guidance, the ability to work through a process to critically evaluate scientific reports. Equally important, even if students do not always fully engage in complete science research projects, most can gain an understanding and appreciation for the scientific method and its limitations as well as its potential to contribute to human knowledge.

STEPS IN THE SCIENTIFIC METHOD

The typical description of the systematic process for gaining knowledge based on controlled experimentation includes these steps:

"Multiple Shades of Inquiry Found in Science Education," by Daniel Callison, was published in *School Library Monthly* 30, no. 5 (February 2014): 20–22.

Ask a Question > Do Background Research > Construct a Hypothesis > Test with an Experiment > If the procedure is working, analyze data and draw conclusions; if not, troubleshoot the procedure. > Communicate the Results as the new data will become background research for future projects.

Recent science education reformers have argued that it is important to recognize that modern inquiry learning theory is much broader than the lock-step scientific method. When students come to learn about science as a process of inquiry they are to learn how scientists go about constructing explanations of natural phenomena and come to recognize that these methods are appropriate for questions posed in their own lives (Abrams, Southerland, and Silva 2008).

CRITICAL SCIENTIFIC THINKING

The Foundation for Critical Thinking has described five attributes of the mature or well-cultivated scientific thinker:

- raises vital scientific questions and problems, formulating them clearly and precisely;
- gathers and assesses relevant scientific data and information, using abstract ideas to interpret them effectively;
- comes to well-reasoned scientific conclusions and solutions, testing them against relevant criteria and standards;
- thinks with an open mind within convergent systems of scientific thought, recognizing and assessing scientific assumptions, implications, and practical consequences; and
- communicates effectively with others in proposing solutions to complex scientific problems (Paul and Elder 2006).

SCIENCE EDUCATION AND THE COMMON CORE STATE STANDARDS

While the Common Core State Standards (CCSS) recognizes the need for students to learn and practice common scientific experiment methods, emphasis in these standards is focused on student abilities to read and interpret scientific literature. This can be seen in selected standards for the senior high school level:

- Cite specific textual evidence to support analysis of science and technical texts, attending to important distinctions the author makes and to any gaps or inconsistencies in the account.
- Determine the central ideas or conclusions of a text; summarize complex concepts, processes, or information presented in a text by paraphrasing them in simpler but still accurate terms.
- Integrate and evaluate multiple sources of information presented in diverse formats and media (e.g., quantitative data, video, multimedia) in order to address a question or solve a problem.
- Evaluate the hypotheses, data, analysis, and conclusions in a science or technical text, verifying the data when possible and corroborating or challenging conclusions with other sources of information.
- Synthesize information from a range of sources (e.g., texts, experiments, simulations) into a coherent understanding of a process, phenomenon, or concept, resolving conflicting information when possible.

By graduation from high school, the senior is partially prepared for college and a career because of his or her proven ability to demonstrate independently, self-directed abilities based on free inquiry to read and comprehend science/technical texts proficiently.

GROWTH IN THE IMPORTANCE OF BACKGROUND READING AND LITERATURE REVIEW

There has been a great emphasis on the student's role in the stages of the information search process at Rutgers University. Carol Collier Kuhlthau has not only defined the student's behaviors and emotions at each stage, but she has expanded the concept of guided inquiry (1985, 2010). Her work is based on constructivist learning theory. She clarifies the teacher and school librarian roles and provides interventions that guide the student forward—in some situations even placing the student on an investigator level. She bridges inquiry from the traditional teacher-dominated process toward the more independent, life-long learner status. Her learners are guided toward independence.

Kuhlthau's graduate students have contributed to greater justification of the literature review in scientific inquiry. Mary Jane McNally and Kuhlthau documented the enhancements to student research projects that resulted from greater open reading and background exploration as well as literature reviews that helped students focus on their science projects (1994). More recently, an ethnographic study of selected senior high school students demonstrated their abilities to handle science journals and other technical documents. A modified approach to scientific literature review (SLR) resulted in greater efficiency and coverage of more relevant documentation even within a world of ever expanding scientific information (Schmidt, Kowalski, and Nevins 2010). Both studies found teacher and media specialist collaboration enhanced the depth of student research.

THE INQUIRY CONTINUUM

Ronald J. Bonnstetter, the University of Nebraska, Lincoln, and one of his students, Mark Lyke, organized a continuum to show the evolutionary processes of scientific inquiry (1998). Greater or lesser teacher control of the inquiry process was categorized across basic learning tasks. Callison has expanded and reclassified this continuum to illustrate a richer understanding of the various shades of inquiry now based on three modern teaching theories. See table 1.

Table 1. Progression toward student-centered learning.
Callison's Modification of Bonnstetter's Inquiry Level Continuum* to Reflect
the Progression toward Student-Centered Learning

Inquiry Levels & Modes Moving toward Greater Student Responsibilities & Less Teacher Control ———————→						
	Traditional Controlled	**Structured**	**Guided**	**Modeled Apprentice**	**Student Directed**	**Open or Free**
Inquiry Learning Tasks:						
Background Reading & Exploration	T(B) T(C) Not (H)	T(B) T>S(C) T&S(H)	T>S(B) T&S(C) S&T(H)	T&S(B) T=S(C) S=T(H)	Not (B) S>T(C) S(H)	Not (B) S or T(C) S or T(H)
Topic Selection	T(B) T(C) Not (H)	T(B) T>S(C) T&S(H)	T>S(B) S&T(C) S&T(H)	T&S(B) T=S(C) S=T(H)	Not (B) S>T(C) S(H)	Not (B) S or T(C) S or T(H)

(*continued*)

Table 1. Progression toward student-centered learning (*Continued*)

Question Development	T(B) T(C) Not (H)	T(B) T>S(C) T&S(H)	T>S(B) S&T(C) S&T(H)	T&S(B) T=S(C) S=T(H)	Not (B) S>T(C) S(H)	Not (B) S or T(C) S or T(H)
Materials Access & Formative Evaluation	T(B) T(C) Not (H)	T(B) T>S(C) T&S(H)	T>S(B) S&T(C) S&T(H)	T&S(B) T=S(C) S=T(H)	Not (B) S>T(C) S(H)	Not (B) S or T(C) S or T(H)
Literature Review, Assimilation & Focus	T(B) T(C) Not (H)	T(B) T>S(C) T&S(H)	T>S(B) S&T(C) S&T(H)	T&S(B) T=S(C) S=T(H)	Not (B) S>T(C) S(H)	Not (B) S or T(C) S or T(H)
Procedures Design/Method	T(B) T(C) Not (H)	T(B) T>S(C) T&S(H)	T>S(B) S&T(C) S&T(H)	T&S(B) T=S(C) S=T(H)	Not (B) S>T(C) S(H)	Not (B) S or T(C) S or T(H)
Results Analysis	T(B) T(C) Not (H)	T&S(B) T>S(C) T&S(H)	T>S(B) S&T(C) S&T(H)	T&S(B) T=S(C) S=T(H)	Not (B) S>T(C) S(H)	Not (B) S or T(C) S or T(H)
Inference Conclusions	T(B) T(C) Not (H)	T>S(B) T>S(C) T&S(H)	T>S(B) S&T(C) S&T(H)	T&S(B) T=S(C) S=T(H)	Not (B) S>T(C) S(H)	Not (B) S or T(H) S or T(H)
Presentation Mode & Preparation	T(B) T(C) Not (H)	T(B) T(C) T&S(H)	T>S(B) T&S(C) T&S(H)	T&S(B) T=S(C) S=T(H)	Not (B) S>T(C) S(H)	Not (B) S or T(C) S or T(H)
Summative Evaluation, Reflection	T(B) T(C) Not (H)	T(B) T>S(C) T&S(H)	T(B) T>S(C) T&S(H)	T(B) T=S(C) S=T(H)	Not (B) S>T(C) S(H)	Not (B) S or T(C) S or T(H)

T—Teacher Led or S—Student Led. Defined by Learning Theories and Perspectives on Teaching as summarized below:

(B)—Behaviorist (Breaks material into small units; Teaches each unit; Tests for mastery at each stage; Offers help to reach mastery if necessary; Does not let learners proceed to the next lesson if they have not mastered preceding ones.)

(C)—Cognitive or Constructivist (Knowledge construction is based on assimilation and accommodation; Emphasizes the active role of the learner; Views teacher as catalyst, facilitator, or guide who sets the stage for learning to occur; De-emphasizes lecture mode and transmission of information; Emphasizes learning through self-discovery; Creates situations in which learners can experiment with new material without previous instruction; Creates opportunities for interacting with the material that are unstructured enough to allow for self-exploration, but that have specific goals so that learners can have a feeling of accomplishment; Allows learners to try things out and see what will happen, including posing own questions and seeking own answers.)

(H)—Humanist (Learner-centered teaching); Self-directed/regulated learning; Allows learners to participate in evaluation of own work; Provides learners with self-paced, self-correcting exercises, so that learners can determine when they have accomplished the designated task; Encourages people to learn more about themselves and how they relate to others in order to prepare for their role in society; Asks learners to think for themselves and to make their own final decisions.)

*Adapted from Bonnstetter and Lyke (1998), and modified based on Callison (1999), Grassian and Kaplowitz (2009), Kuhlthau (1985, 2010)

While various classification blocks are open to debate and refinement, the cells illustrate the notion that the teacher and student roles change depending on the purpose of the inquiry, the expectations for student performance, and the philosophy, which allows for greater student initiatives. Cells illustrate, in some cases, complete teacher control with students absent in any decision-making opportunity. The last row of cells, at the most independent range, includes both students and teachers who engage in personal and professional development based on self-evaluation (Dana, Thomas, and Boynton 2011). See table 1.

REFERENCES

Abrams, Eleanor, Sherry A. Southerland, and Peggy Silva. *Inquiry in the Classroom.* Information Age Publishing, 2008.

Bonnstetter, Ronald J. and Mark Lyke. "Inquiry: Learning from the Past with an Eye on the Future." *Electronic Journal of Science Education* 3, no. 1 (1998). http://wolfweb.unr.edu/homepage/jcannon/ejse /bonnstetter.html (accessed November 4, 2013).

Callison, Daniel. "Inquiry—Key Instructional Term." *School Library Media Activities Monthly* 15, no. 6 (February 1999): 38–42.

Common Core State Standards Initiative. 2010. *Common Core State Standards for English Language Arts & Literacy in History/Social Studies, Science, and Technical Subjects.* http://corestandards.org/assets/CCSSI _ELA%20Standards.pdf (accessed August 2, 2012).

Grassian, Esther S. and Joan R. Kaplowitz. *Information Literacy Instruction Theory and Practice.* 2nd ed. Neal-Schuman Publishers, 2009.

Kuhlthau, Carol Collier. *Teaching the Library Research Process.* Center for Applied Research in Education, 1985.

Kuhlthau, Carol Collier. "Guided Inquiry." *School Libraries Worldwide* 16, no. 1 (January 2010): 1–12.

McNally, Mary Jane and Carol Collier Kuhlthau. "Information Search Process in Science Education." *Reference Librarian* 44 (1994): 53–60.

Paul, Richard and Linda Elder. *A Miniature Guide to Scientific Thinking.* The Foundation for Critical Thinking, 2006.

Schmidt, Randell K., Virginia Kowalski, and Lorraine Nevins. "Guiding the Inquiry Using the Modified Science Literature Review." *School Libraries Worldwide* 16, no. 1 (January 2010): 13–32.

Part II: Science Fairs and Inquiry Conferences

Science Fairs and Inquiry

Daniel Callison

Education literature for science fairs and science education based on the inquiry method seldom include the value of school library collections and services. Mirah J. Dow, professor at the School of Library and Information Management at Emporia State University, recently outlined the power of collaboration between science educators and school media professionals in the promotion of the Science, Technology, Engineering, and Mathematics (STEM) education standards. This support includes an active role for the school librarian in Science Fair project development—an active role that can expand across nearly the entire curriculum.

"Science Fairs and Inquiry," by Daniel Callison, was published in *School Library Monthly* 31, no. 2 (November 2014): 21–23.

WHO AND WHAT

Dow defines the traditional steps of the scientific method and sorts these between two overall collaborative stages involving three populations: students, STEM educators, and the librarian.

- The Preparation Stage > Literature Context Research involving topic, observation, question(s) and hypothesis.
- The Experimental Stage > Data Context Research involving design, conduct of experiment, analysis of data, conclusions, and communication (or presentation of findings in written and oral formats) (18, 2011).

The Literature Context stage has grown in depth and importance in Science Fair project development over the past five years. Many fair guidelines and help sites now include expectations for students to be critical reviewers of previous studies and to draw from those a context for the methods, general state of the field and the key leading names associated with the area of study relevant to the project's topic. Science Buddies, for example, lists these reasons for establishing a background research plan:

- Learn the history of similar experiments or inventions.
- Define important words and concepts that describe your experiment.
- Help answer your background search questions.
- Identify and understand mathematical formulas, if any, needed to present results.
- Establish a network of experts who [through the literature and possible interview] will help you think about and plan your project (http://www.sciencebuddies.org/science-fair-projects/project_background_research_plan.shtml).

MEANING AND CREDIBILITY IN THE BACKGROUND LITERATURE

Dow extends background literature compilation by adding resources and methods for wider information search and review processes. Any of these methods can greatly enhance the literature review and help to support the student's growth in using more complex text resources. The result can be more depth in answering additional questions and a better educated student scientist who is knowledgeable in the discourse and vocabulary of the scientific field he has selected.

Shannon Brown and Jim Hilburt were graduate students in my online section of the Drexel University iSchool course, "The Instructional Role of Information Specialists" (Summer Term 2013). Their task was to develop an instructional plan that would further engage the school librarian in development and presentation of high school science fairs. This project culminated in their document, "Team E: Senior High Scientific Method." A portion of what they developed included application of Delia Neuman's I-LEARN process to the literature review (2011). The purpose was to draw out what the science fair student actually learned from the literature, not just the few items they may have located solely for the project. A new assessment instrument resulted, and they established a rubric to test for the student's ability to apply knowledge from the literature:

- Information sources are credible, reliant, and timely.
- Information is corroborated from at least two credible sources.
- A thorough explanation demonstrating source credibility is provided.
- A thorough explanation either supporting proof or disproving the hypothesis is provided (Brown and Hilburt 2013).

Achieve Texas, a new initiative for college and health career education, has established clear steps for a practical and meaningful scientific literature review (http://www.achievetexas .org/). Such an exercise is important because the student has the opportunity to:

- determine the extent of the theory and research that have been developed in the field of study.
- identify the definition of concepts, and variables which have already been established in the literature and examine the research designs, methods, instruments, measures, and techniques of data analysis.
- discover what is known and what remains to be learned in the field. Many times a study can be identified that can be replicated or whose findings might be compared or contrasted with the proposed research study.
- become aware of difficulties experienced by others which may save time, money, and reduce chances for error or identify new ethical issues.
- find a well-written article to use as a guide in writing his/her new research paper.

EXTENDING THE SCIENTIFIC CULTURE THROUGH CONFERENCES

While these literature review experiences are important, opportunities for students to experience additional environments can help create a scientific climate for the entire school. This increases the possibility at all grade levels that students gain a greater understanding of what scientists do and how the student's own project relates to the projects and ideas of other students (Callison 2005).

Establishing these additional environments, either prior to or after science fair events, can lead to greater engagement of the school library staff, resources, and facilities. The coordinating and facilitating roles for the school library professional can result in events that gain the approval of both administrators and parents. The library becomes a learning lab for science in its many forms. It is not so much just for test tubes, but for testing resource content, understanding of intended message from practice student presentations, gathering data from interviews or guest speakers, and surveying for opinions. Scientists read, converse, think, and formulate ideas that are expressed at multiple levels of development, and these ideas are often revised through various interactions with others—informal and formal.

ELEMENTARY: THE KID'S INQUIRY CONFERENCE

Wendy Saul and her colleagues have initiated many field experiences in elementary schools in order to promote quality science books and science inquiry (2005). During her years as professor of education at the University of Maryland, Baltimore County, she worked with area teachers to bring into action the concept "Kid's Inquiry Conference." The purpose was to create events constructed around student science projects that would allow elementary and middle school students the opportunity to present their projects to peers, parents, and other audiences. Ultimately, the events have made science projects visible and valued. Guest speakers, often local scientists, lead discussions about their profession—everyday issues and not isolated work in dark laboratories.

Saul has an extensive documented history of being a promoter of read-alouds and think-alouds as a means to generate questions. Sparking this questioning process is an essential role of teachers and librarians. Priming inquiry ranges from picture books at kindergarten (Mantzicopoulos and Patrick 2011) to introductions of juvenile literature (Bircher 2009): What if? Do you think this is possible? How would you solve this problem? Other such questions are constantly raised during interactions while nonfiction texts are read aloud. Questions that raise self-reflection, persistence, and determination are important, too: Did he find his answers with one experiment? Did others work on similar problems and did they share early discoveries that lead to later and greater ones? What does it mean to be ethical in the study of animals?

Saul's colleagues give numerous examples of how various children's books can lead to discussions of "what scientists do." Familiar titles are *A Snake Scientist, Elephant Woman,* and *How to be a Nature Detective.* Kent State Professor Carolyn Brodie, a regular contributor to *School Library Monthly* with curricular connections to books for children, introduced the work of arachnologist Sam Marshall, a scientist who studies spiders and their eight-legged relatives (2005). According to Brodie, Dr. Marshall specializes in the study of tarantulas, and while he may take expeditions to other countries, student scientists can envision science exploration in their own school yard (with proper safety precautions as Dr. Marshall would expect as well). Exploration locally can be as much an adventure as exploration globally. The point Saul and others emphasize is that science is much more than the final presentation.

An example of a Kid's Inquiry Conference can be found on the Internet at the Pine Crest Lower School website. Photographs illustrate the typical event during which local scientists were invited to speak and to attend student presentations. Parents and siblings also came to hear and participate in science topic discussions. Paula Magee and Ryan Flessner from Indianapolis have managed several inquiry conferences for kids and have learned that conferences provide a noncompetitive environment where students gain a greater appreciation for the work ethic of local scientists (2011). Such a broader study of scientific methods and inquiry is in direct support of the National Science Education Standards (1996). International studies have shown that the Science Fair format, however, often falls prey to just meeting basic rules and mechanics of routine experiments. There is danger in a mismatch between the intended Science Fair inquiry curriculum and what the student actually experiences (Hume and Coll 2010).

SECONDARY: THE CULTURAL CONFERENCE

Science projects can obviously be used as the content for presentations and interactions on the high school level as well. The school library can often provide a variety of spaces for large and small group presentations, as well as a setting for display and examination of resource holdings ready to support student projects. Infographic posters, for example, designed by students to summarize major findings from their projects, can be displayed in the library and hallways. The tie between scholarship and supporting resources and services can become very tangible.

Mike Printz is familiar to many school librarians because of the young adult literature award that carries his name. As a school library media director at Topeka, Kansas, in the 1960s through 1990s, he was a curricular innovator and leader in inquiry learning long before the concept became fashionable. His programs serve here as an example of how the concept inquiry conference can be much more than an alternative to science fairs.

Printz, in collaboration with dozens of his teachers, would create cultural celebrations based on student projects ranging from local oral histories to poetry and drama, sculptures and paintings, historic artifact displays, video and film productions, and biographical sketches of local leaders from various ethnic groups. Library forums and a Speaker's Bureau organized by the library staff, provided guest speakers on rotating topics relevant to the culture being explored for the given term: Native Americans, African Americans, Jewish Americans, Mexican Americans, Chinese Americans, and others. It was a multi-disciplinary response to the expectation that public schools in Topeka should celebrate diversity. And celebrate they did at Topeka West High School—usually for a full week of presentations during each school day and evenings, centered in the school library and touching all study disciplines (Miller, Steinlage, Printz 1994).

Good, complex literature can generate inquiry. Just as the previous examples from the elementary level, Printz, at the secondary level, would spark the teacher and student projects based on a common core of literature that would be read and discussed by *everyone*—including principals and assistant principals. Whole Language is what some called it then, with a five-day conference experience that was recorded and shared widely with other schools over several semesters. Inquiry is what it is called now. No matter what it is called, students are given the opportunity and resources to investigate issues and topics of interest to them and others and a way to share them with others in a nonthreatening manner.

REFERENCES

Achieve Texas. http://www.achievetexas.org/ (accessed July 10, 2014).

Bircher, L. S. "Reading Aloud: A Springboard to Inquiry." *Science Teacher* 76, No. 5 (July 2009): 29–33.

Brodie, C. S. "Connect the Book: *The Tarantula Scientist.*" *School Library Media Activities Monthly* 22, no. 2 (October 2005): 53–55.

Brown, S. and J. Hilburt. "Team E: Senior High Scientific Method." Drexel University iSchool Summer Term, 2013.

Dow, M. J. "School Librarians and Science Fair Competition." *School Library Monthly* 28, no. 2 (November 2011): 17–20.

Hume, A. and R. Coll. "Authentic Student Inquiry: The Mismatch between the Intended Curriculum and the Student-Experiences Curriculum." *Research in Science and Technological Education* 28, no. 1 (April 2010): 43–62.

Magee, P. A. and R. Flessner. "Have a Kids Inquiry Conference!" *Science and Children* 48, no. 8 (April 2011): 63–67.

Mantzicopoulos, P. and H. Patrick. "Reading Picture Books and Learning Science: Engaging Young Children with Informational Text." *Theory into Practice* 50 (2011): 269–276.

Miller, L., T. Steinlage, and M. Printz. *Cultural Cobblestones: Teaching Cultural Diversity.* Scarecrow, 1994.

National Research Council. *National Science Education Standards.* NRC, 1996.

Neuman, D. "Constructing Knowledge in the Twenty-First Century: I-LEARN and Using Information as a Tool for Learning." *School Library Research* 14 (2011). http://www.ala.org/aasl/sites/ala.org.aasl/files/content/aaslpubsandjournals/slr/vol14/SLR_ConstructingKnowledge_V14.pdf (accessed January 21, 2014).

Pine Crest Lower School Holds First Annual Kids' Inquiry Conference. https://www.pinecrest.edu/podium/default.aspx?t=204&tn=Pine+Crest+Lower+School+Holds+First+Annual+Kids+Inquiry+Conference+&nid=659291&ptid=52302&sdb=0&mode=0&vcm=0 (accessed January 21, 2014).

Saul, W., et.al. *Beyond the Science Fair: Creating a Kids' Inquiry Conference.* Heinemann, 2005.

Science Buddies. http://www.sciencebuddies.org/science-fair-projects/project_background_research_plan.shtml (accessed January 21, 2014).

Part III: Common Core and Inquiry for Mathematics

Common Core and Inquiry for Mathematics

Daniel Callison

The *Common Core State Standards for Mathematics* (CCSM) was published in June 2010. Of the full array of standards reviewed and published as a "common core," those pertaining to math skills have become the most widely adopted. More than forty-seven states have adopted a portion or all of the math related recommendations.

That same month a joint public statement of the National Council of Teachers of Mathematics (NCTM), the National Council of Supervisors of Mathematics (NCSM), the Association

"Common Core for Mathematics," by Daniel Callison, was published in *School Library Monthly* 29, no. 5 (February 2013): 21–24.

of State Supervisors of Mathematics (ASSM), and the Association of Mathematics Teacher Educators (AMTE) gave support to the following principles:

- All students need to develop mathematical practices such as solving problems, making connections, understanding multiple representations of mathematical ideas, communicating their thought processes, and justifying their reasoning.
- All students need both conceptual and procedural knowledge related to a mathematical topic, and they need to understand how the two types of knowledge are connected.
- Curriculum documents should organize learning expectations in ways that reflect research on how children learn mathematics.
- All students need opportunities for reasoning and sense making across the mathematics curriculum—and they need to believe that mathematics is sensible, worthwhile, and doable (2010).

DATA DRIVE INQUIRY

Making a solid tie between the knowledge base for mathematics and the learning skills most relevant to the school library program has always proven difficult. The new national Common Core for State Standards (CCSS) in mathematics illustrates this challenge again. However, one key approach to knowledge construction may be the most central tie not only between school library and math, but also across all disciplines.

Within the CCSS curricular approach one clearly finds a promotion of a basic component of inquiry. Knowledge is to be constructed on open and fair assimilation of new information with that held by the student and teacher. Learners go where the numbers or data takes them. Learning is not driven by "cherry picking" statistics that might best support what one already believes. Inquiry is not a blind confirmation. Inquiry is an investigation that not only corrects held beliefs, but, at times, confirms those beliefs.

How one selects statistical approaches to generate potential data is a high level decision task that ranks with the ability to select the most authoritative sources and studies. Wise users of numbers understand that statistics have limitations, can be twisted to support nearly any conclusion, and are of merit only when validated across several sources and over time.

This article will provide a brief overview of the CCSS in mathematics, relevance to information inquiry programs in school libraries, and recommendations of some useful resources in the implementation of these standards. The reader will find additional articles in other issues of *SLM* that provide discussion of the other CCSS in history, writing, listening, argumentation, reading, and language arts.

LYING WITH STATISTICS

Darrell Huff's 1954 classic publication *How to Lie with Statistics* should be required reading for students, teachers and school librarians prior to dealing in any manner with the core curriculum in mathematics. Among several basic examples, Huff reminds the reader how numbers can be used to mislead:

- Which average (mean, median, or mode) should be used to report the results of an experiment or survey?
- It is essential that data come from a random sample of the population.
- A favorite source of statistical errors is selection bias, which can generally be categorized as a sample being unrepresentative of the population because some units are much more likely than others to be represented, with the more likely units differing from the unlikely units in some important way.

- The easiest form of lying with statistics is simply to make up a number, and place the responsibility on others to prove you wrong.
- A common error, whether accidental or intentional, is to compare raw numbers without adjusting for expected baseline differences.
- "Statistically significant" does not necessarily mean "important" and certainly is not a conclusive proof.
- A weak positive or negative correlation means very little, if anything, and a strong positive or negative correlation does not mean cause and effect, only that something may be happening and much more evidence is needed before drawing a conclusion.
- "The research data prove" is a sign of a novice. "Research data suggest and more study is needed" is a sign of a mature and experienced inquirer (1954).

ADDING UP THE COMMON CORE

The CCSS includes several statements that underscore how students at all grade levels should be expected to expand their knowledge and ideas through the use of information gained from illustrations (e.g., maps, photographs). Students should be expected to both interpret and present data and other information visually, orally, or quantitatively (e.g., charts, graphs, diagrams, timelines, animations, or interactive elements on Web pages) and explain how the information contributes to an understanding of the text in which it appears or is associated.

Expressly encouraging great use of complex and higher level materials for reading and study beyond the textbook, the CCSS authors note that "texts of high complexity tend to have similarly complex graphics, whose interpretation is essential to understanding the text, and graphics that provide an independent source of information within a text" (CCSS for English Language Arts, Appendix A).

MATHEMATICS AND THE AASL STANDARDS

The Crosswalk for linking the American Association of School Librarians' (AASL) *Standards for 21st Century Learning* to the CCSS Mathematics measures reflects a gallant effort, but is clearly filled with gaps. Perhaps condensing the standards for a more focused selection of where these important standard sets touch and support each other would show that there are important relationships. See Table 2 for examples of focused correlations between the two sets of standards.

GRAPHIC INQUIRY

In their new book, *Graphic Inquiry*, Annette Lamb and Daniel Callison, Indiana University educators, state,

> Students consume thousands of words, orally and visually, and they need a variety of communication methods to summarize their own sharing of information and knowledge. Illustrations serve to aid the student researcher who wants to grow and mature in communication skills through the use of graphics that enhance, condense, quicken, direct, heighten, or inspire the message (2012, ix).

They present graphic inquiry as the processes of extracting information from visuals as well as presenting knowledge through media that most effectively communicate the message to the intended audience.

Table 2. Correlating AASL Standards and Common Core State Standards for Math.

*AASL Standards for 21st Century Learning	**Common Core for State Standards for Math
3.1.4	F-IF.7.a. Graph functions expressed symbolically and show key features of the graph, by hand in simple cases and using technology for more complicated cases: Graph linear and quadratic functions and show intercepts, maxima, and minima.
2.1.1	S-MD.4. (+) Develop a probability distribution for a random variable defined for a sample space in which probabilities are assigned empirically; find the expected value. For example, find a current data distribution on the number of TV sets per household in the United States, and calculate the expected number of sets per household. How many TV sets would you expect to find in 100 randomly selected households?
2.1.2	1.MD.4. Organize, represent, and interpret data with up to three categories; ask and answer questions about the total number of data points, how many in each category, and how many more or less are in one category than in another.
2.1.3	6.NS.8. Solve real-world and mathematical problems by graphing points in all four quadrants of the coordinate plane. Include use of coordinates and absolute value to find distances between points with the same first coordinate or the same second coordinate.
1.1.1	S-IC.1. Understand statistics as a process for making inferences about population parameters based on a random sample from that population.
1.1.4	S-IC.3. Recognize the purposes of and differences among sample surveys, experiments, and observational studies; explain how randomization relates to each.
2.1.3	S-IC.4. Use data from a sample survey to estimate a population mean or proportion; develop a margin of error through the use of simulation models for random sampling.

*Excerpted from *Standards for the 21st-Century Learner* by the American Association of School Librarians, a division of the American Library Association, ©2007 American Library Association. Available for download at www.ala.org /aasl/standards.

**Selected Standards from the *Common Core State Standards for Mathematics* (CCSM). Available for download at http://www.corestandards.org/assets/CCSSI_Math%20Standards.pdf.

Through a compilation of over 300 graphic examples related to dozens of representative standards for student learning, Lamb and Callison make a case for moving typical student reports from print only into the multimedia realm and pushing beyond simple power-point lists to the rich and complex texts of charts, tables, photographs, maps, even cartoons and more.

Their examples of graphics and diagrams which can result in adding a sense of precision to student reports include:

Cosmograph—uses images to show parts of wholes
Pie Chart—depicts how parts are related to the whole
Scatter Graph—visualizes patterns using data points
Sparkline—shows trends and variations
Area Graph—compares changes over time

Graphical Projection—shows an imaginary 3-dimensional object
Flowchart—shows processes and relationships
Schematic—represents the elements of a system
Decision Tree—shows options in decision-making (Lamb and Callison 2012).

Edward Tufte has compiled the classic works that guide the principles of excellence in statistical graphics design and presentation. He argues that graphic displays should:

- Show the data;
- Induce the reviewer to think about the substance;
- Avoid distorting what the data have to say;
- Make large data sets coherent;
- Encourage the eye to compare different pieces of data;
- Reveal the data at several levels of detail;
- Serve a reasonably clear purpose;
- Be closely integrated with the relevant statistical and verbal descriptions (Tufte 2001).

Just as there is need for learning exercises where students and teachers raise questions concerning the validity of information found in printed text, so too should there be constant challenge to the graphically presented information found in the media. Critical reading of visuals should include at least these six components:

- Authority: What expertise does the author of the visual have in the area represented by the graphic? What resources did the author use to draw the conclusions reflected in the graphic?
- Sources: How was the graphic distributed? What individuals or groups support the communication of this information?
- Context: In what setting is this graphic presented? Is it shown with other data representing a particular viewpoint or context? Are particular social, economic, or political agendas associated with the information?
- Currency: Is the information in the graphic timely? When was the data collected?
- Methodology: How was the data for the visual collected? Was a reasonable approach used to limit bias, limit skewing of the data, and control for undue influence of participants?
- Assumptions: What are possible hidden assumptions and unstated facts about the content of the graphic? Does the visualization of the data clarify the message or result in making the message even more misleading? What else needs to be determined before a reasonable conclusion can be reached? ((Lamb and Callison 2012).

MATHEMATICS RESOURCES

The National Council of Teachers of Mathematics (NCTM) has developed a guide to current resources that will support mathematics teachers as they implement the core standards (http://www.nctm.org/standards/content.aspx?id=16909). In addition, Inside Mathematics, which features classroom examples of innovative teaching methods and insights into student learning, is currently working to align its resources with the core (http://insidemathematics.org).

To help educators understand the language of the core and to connect context to standards, McREL has hyperlinked the CCSS to its online compendium (http://www.mcrel.org/standards-benchmarks). Benchmarks within the compendium are organized around knowledge and skill statements, and associated concept vocabulary is provided with released assessment items and activities that teachers should find helpful (Kendall 2011).

REFERENCES

American Association of School Librarians. *Standards for the 21st-Century Learner.* American Library Association, 2007. (Downloadable for free at: http://www.ala.org/aasl/standards).

Common Core State Standards Initiative (CCSS). CCSS for Mathematics. 2010. http://www.corestandards.org/assets/CCSSI_Math%20Standards.pdf.

Common Core State Standards Initiative (CCSS). *Common Core State Standards for English Language Arts.* Appendix A. http://www.corestandards.org/assets/Appendix_A.pdf (accessed November 1, 2012).

Huff, Darrell. *How to Lie with Statistics.* W. W. Horton, 1954.

Kendall, John. *Understanding Common Core State Standards.* ASCD, 2011.

Lamb, Annette and Daniel Callison. *Graphic Inquiry.* Libraries Unlimited, 2012.

National Council of Teachers of Mathematics (NCTM), the National Council of Supervisors of Mathematics (NCSM), and the Association of State Supervisors of Mathematics (ASSM), and the Association of Mathematics Teacher Educators (AMTE). "Mathematics Education Organizations Unit to Support Implementation of Common Core State Standards." June 2, 2010. http://www.corestandards.org/assets/k12_statements/National-Mathematics-Education-Organizations-Statement-of-Support.pdf (accessed November 1, 2012).

Tufte, Edward R. *The Visual Display of Quantitative Information.* 2nd edition. Graphics Press, 2001.

ADDITIONAL RESOURCES

American Association of School Librarians. *Crosswalk of the Common Core Standards and the Standards for the 21st Century Learner.* http://www.ala.org/aasl/guidelinesandstandards/commoncorecrosswalk (accessed November 1, 2012).

Common Core State Standards Initiative (CCSS). 2010. http://www.corestandards.org/the-standards (accessed November 1, 2012).

Chapter 7

Inquiry in Language Arts

Part I: Reflective Practices for Inquiry in Language Arts

Reflective Practices for Common Core K–5 Informational Nonfiction

Daniel Callison

THE VALUE OF NONFICTION

A decade prior to the issuance of the new Common Core State Standards (CCSS), a young assistant professor at the University of Pittsburgh published a common sense guide to *Using Informational Books in the Classroom*. Now a professor for literacy and technology at Michigan State University, Douglas Hartman summarized the reasons for giving emphasis to nonfiction in elementary schools:

- Satisfy and broaden curiosity,
- Provide breadth and depth of information,
- Offer accurate information,
- Provide models for informational writing,
- Challenge readers to read critically,
- Help present familiar things in new ways,
- Promote [inquiry and] exploration,
- Stimulate direct experience [authentic learning],
- Connect readers and reading to the real world [preparatory for college, careers and lifelong learning] (Hartman 2002, 1).

Professor Hartman concluded that "students can learn facts from a textbook, but they learn to read passionately and critically with nonfiction trade books" (3). Authors of CCSS seem to agree because increased use of nonfiction serves as the foundation for standards designed to prepare students for learning through complex reading and writing.

Thirteen years ago this author published an overview in this magazine of practices in favor of increasing nonfiction reading K–12 (Callison 2000). Revisiting this topic under CCSS has

"Reflective Practices for Common Core K–5 Informational Nonfiction," by Daniel Callison, was published in *School Library Monthly* 29, no. 8 (May/June 2013): 20–23.

reinforced in his mind the importance of early reflective practice with nonfiction in order to lay the groundwork for more meaningful inquiry projects across the curriculum and eventually at college level study in secondary education.

ANCHOR STANDARDS FOR K–5 READING AND WRITING

Three of the ten anchor standards for reading in the Common Core K–5 reading emphasize the integration of knowledge and ideas. These three illustrate how closely the standard curriculum matches expectations of student information selection and use performance through inquiry learning:

- Integrate and evaluate content presented in diverse media and formats, including visually and quantitatively, as well as in words.
- Delineate and evaluate the argument and specific claims in a text, including the validity of the reasoning as well as the relevance and sufficiency of the evidence.
- Analyze how two or more texts address similar themes or topics in order to build knowledge or to compare the approaches the authors take (CCSS 2010, 10).

Similarly, the anchor standards for writing include three that are specifically relevant to inquiry learning through the practice of student research in order to build and present knowledge:

- Conduct short as well as more sustained research projects based on focused questions, demonstrating understanding of the subject under investigation.
- Gather relevant information from multiple print and digital sources, assess the credibility and accuracy of each source, and integrate the information while avoiding plagiarism.
- Draw evidence from literary or informational texts to support analysis, reflection, and research (CCSS 2010, 18).

APPLYING THE ALBERTA INQUIRY MODEL

Mary D'Eliso, an elementary school librarian in Bloomington, Indiana, shared her views in an email message to the author on December 10, 2012. She has found several practices from the Alberta Inquiry Model (Alberta Learning 2004) to be helpful in guiding student inquiry, especially in management of the Common Core State Standards for language arts and expanding nonfiction in reading and writing. See Figure 1.

D'Eliso finds the opportunities for reflection across all inquiry steps, as recommended in the Alberta approach, to be beneficial to students and teachers. If the school librarian is fully involved, reflection is also an important tool to help gain indications of resource needs as well as work with potential frustrations students face in the research process.

Students enjoy engaging with resources and exploring freely to get a taste of possibilities. D'Eliso finds, however, that after initial information engagements, it is time for students to journal or vocally share what they are experiencing. She establishes the primary reflective opportunities with questions such as:

- Before I began researching my topic, here's what I expected to find:
- Here are some surprises I have already found and examples of some that have changed my thinking:
- At this point in my research, I think it's important to focus on. . . .
- And at future steps, what continues to be a challenge to you in finding information and focus? (email message to author, December 10, 2012)

Inquiry Model

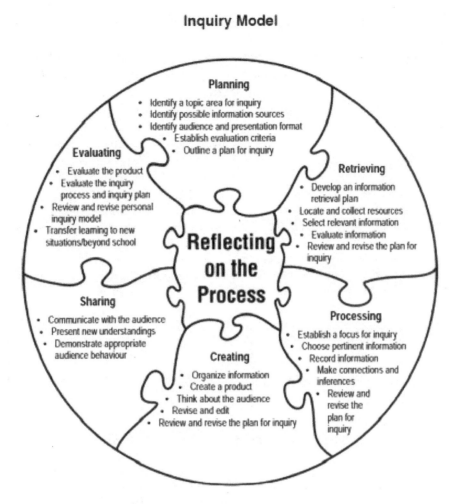

Fig. 1. The Alberta Inquiry Model (copyright 2004, Alberta Learning).
© Alberta Education. Focus on Inquiry; A Teacher's guide to Implementing Inquiry-based Learning.
2004. http://education.alberta.ca/media/313361/focusoninquiry.pdf (March 2013).

D'Eliso finds that as students express responses in writing and aloud, the reflective process keeps everyone hopeful, moving forward without becoming overwhelmed. Sharing findings and frustrations along the way with classmates also provides an interchange that helps stimulate ideas along with assuring some students that their challenges are common and to be expected.

Nothing within the Alberta Model differs greatly from other standard student inquiry models that have been established over the past twenty years, except the unique feature of placing reflection as the core of the process, touching each step repeatedly.

The purpose is to assure that students will be involved in their own learning by developing their metacognitive skills—thinking about what they are thinking and how they feel about it. Reflection touches each phase because it is key to the success of interlacing each step. The goal is for students to adopt and practice reflection as a natural process for all aspects of learning.

Application of the Alberta Inquiry Model is based on the expectation that "the inquiry process is an active interchange between students and teachers of ideas, information, learning experiences, activities and feelings, through which meaning is constructed" (Alberta Learning 2004, 41).

The interchange is "supportive, discursive, adaptive, interactive and reflective. Teachers suggest how students can move forward, see things from new perspectives, make connections between previous and new knowledge, and see the patterns of their learning" (Alberta Learning, 2004, 41).

The Alberta Learning guide, *Focus on Inquiry,* summarizes the basic interactions for stimulating the reflective process when the student is engaged with nonfiction texts for inquiry across all elementary grades:

- Submit their journals/logs on an ongoing basis and at the end of the inquiry process.
- Write/talk about new learning as a result of reflecting on the process.
- Give examples of other situations where the inquiry process could be or is used.
- Compare and contrast their learning process with that of others in class.
- Write/talk about strategies that they can use to cope with the frustrations of doing inquiry.
- Write/talk about their own inquiry process and compare it with the process of others in class.
- Write/talk about the strategies that they can use to support their learning in each of the phases of the inquiry process (2004, 41).

Reflection has become defined in today's standard research literature as "the process of thinking over ideas about which you have read or events you have experienced in order to analyze, re-evaluate, and perhaps readjust your views based on the content or events" (McMillan and Weyers 2013, 180).

TEACHING NONFICTION DIMENSIONS

Techniques for deeper learning through nonfiction have accelerated recently as teachers and school librarians team to harness student natural curiosity and to go beyond fact-gathering to meet or even exceed CCSS expectations (Fontichiaro 2012). Strategies introduced by Professor Gail Tompkins of California State University at Fresno, for example, have for many years placed K–5 students in exercises which explore dimensions of nonfiction (2001). Teachers and school librarians can use these techniques to stimulate pre-writing projects at all grade levels. Each student is expected to express and eventually elaborate on nonfiction topics within these aspects:

- Describe—talk about the topic in terms of color, shapes, size, and senses.
- Compare—what is the topic similar to and different from?
- Associate—what does this topic make you think about? What comes to mind immediately and what people, places, and other things do you relate to the topic?
- Analyze—what are the parts of this topic and how are the parts related to make the bigger picture of this topic? Use your imagination!
- Apply—what are examples from this topic of things you can use for fun or to solve problems or to learn more?
- Argue—can you take a stand for or against some aspect of this topic and can you make a list of reasons to support your arguments?

TEXT SETS

Elementary teachers and school librarians are finding themselves now extending nonfiction collections as never before. Text sets are being expanded to encompass a range of nonfiction types including:

- Concept books
- Nonfiction picture storybooks
- Photographic essays
- Identification books
- Life-cycle books
- Experiment and activity books
- Historical documents
- Journals
- Survey books
- Specialized books
- Craft and how-to books

Introduced as Instructional Resource Plans for multi-disciplinary lesson planning, "text sets" have become formalized today to provide a range of reading possibilities on a given topic supported by a wide variety of media (Callison 2001). A text set collection focuses on one concept or topic and can include multiple genres such as books, charts and maps, informational pamphlets, poetry and songs, photographs, nonfiction books, almanacs or encyclopedias, and much more (Goodman n.d.). A core title for all to read as a common reference may be fiction or nonfiction.

Mary Ann Cappiello and Erika Thulin Dawes have developed multiple approaches to teaching with text sets (2012). Cappiello is an associate professor at Lesley University who has promoted transitions to CCSS through the use of primary and other nonfiction resources especially in elementary social studies and language arts. She concentrates on processes to demystify nonfiction. Students learn that nonfiction has guiding features such as subheadings, sidebars, and insets, and that additional graphic devices are often triggers to uncover more details not found within the written text itself. Teachers and school librarians help students uncover content through diagrams, graphs, tables, timelines, maps, and more (Cappiello 2013).

REFLECTION AND GRAPHIC INQUIRY

Reflection in graphic inquiry calls the inquirer to review his or her selection of graphics for extraction and presentation of information (Lamb and Callison 2012). Annette Lamb describes this reflection experience as the "wishing stage" to assess and evaluate the graphic inquiry process and product (1997). Was the project a success? What will I do next?

Applying the skills of a student information scientist, the inquirer assesses his use of graphic resources and strives to reflect on questions such as:

- What visual evidence do I still need to gather?
- What has changed since my last cycle of questioning, exploring, assimilating, and inferring?
- Have I visualized the evidence in many different ways using a variety of media?
- What pieces of information still need to be connected? What's not obvious?
- Are there alternatives I haven't considered? Are there opinions I should seek?
- What are the risks and benefits of each approach?
- What generalizations can I draw based on the evidence I have so far? Are these initial conclusions meaningful?
- How do I most effectively present arguments?
- How can graphics be used to better understand the topic, to draw conclusions, and to communicate those thoughts to others? (Lamb and Callison 2012, 192)
- The Common Core Information Text Standards Related to Graphic Inquiry

The CCSS include many key ideas and details to support graphic inquiry and the process for students to both draw information from and to present information with graphics. Following are examples from grade level information in the CCSS:

Kindergarten
- With promoting and support, describe the relationship between illustrations and the text in which they appear (e.g., what person, place, thing, or idea in the text an illustration depicts) (13).

Grade One
- Use the illustrations and details in a text to describe its key ideas (13).

Grade Two
- Explain how specific images (e.g., a diagram showing how a machine works) contribute and clarify the text (13).

Grade Three
- Explain how specific aspects of a text's illustrations contribute to what is conveyed by the words in a story (e.g., create mood, emphasize aspects of a character or setting) (12).
- Use information gained from illustrations (e.g., maps, photographs) and the words in a text to demonstrate understanding of the text (e.g., where, when, why, and how key events occur) (14).

Grade Four
- Interpret information presented visually, orally, or quantitatively (e.g., in charts, graphs, diagrams, time lines, animations, or interactive elements on Web pages) and explain how the information contributes to an understanding of the text in which it appears (14).

Grade Five
- Draw on information from multiple print or digital sources, demonstrating the ability to locate an answer to a question quickly or to solve a problem efficiently (14).

REFERENCES

Alberta Learning. *Focus on Inquiry: A Teacher's Guide to Implementing Inquiry-based Learning.* Alberta Learning. 2004. http://education.alberta.ca/media/313361/focusoninquiry.pdf (accessed February 26, 2013).

Callison, Daniel. "Lesson Plan." *School Library Media Activities Monthly* 18, no. 1 (September 2001): 35–41.

Callison, Daniel. "Nonfiction." *School Library Media Activities Monthly* 26, no. 10 (June 2000): 29–32, 35. Reprinted in *The Blue Book on Information Age Inquiry, Instruction and Literacy* by Daniel Callison and Leslie Preddy, 442–449. Libraries Unlimited, 2006.

Cappiello, Mary Ann and Erika Thulin Dawes. *Teaching with Text Sets.* Shell Education, 2012.

Common Core State Standards Initiative (CCSS). 2010. http://www.corestandards.org/the-standards (accessed February 19, 2013).

Fontichiaro, Kristin, ed. *Navigating the Information Tsunami.* Cherry Lake Publishing, 2012.

Goodman, Janie Riddle. "Text Sets: Providing Possibilities for Adolescent Readers." n.d. www.ed.sc.edu/raisse/pdf/handouts/iraGoodman.pdf (accessed February 19, 2013).

Hartman, Douglas K. *Using Informational Books in the Classroom: Letting the Facts and Research Speak for Themselves.* Red Brick Learning, 2002. http://www.capstonepub.com/CAP/downloads/misc/LNCB_HartmanPaper.pdf (accessed February 19, 2013).

Lamb, Annette. "Wondering, Wiggling, and Weaving: A New Model for Project and Community Based learning on the Web." *Learning and Leading with Technology* 24, no. 7 (1997): 6–13.

Lamb, Annette and Daniel Callison. *Graphic Inquiry.* Libraries Unlimited, 2012.

McMillan, Kathleen and Jonathan Weyers. *How to Cite, Reference and Avoid Plagiarism at University.* Pearson, 2013.

Tompkins, Gail E. *Language Arts: Content and Teaching Strategies.* Prentice Hall, 2001.

ADDITIONAL READING

Pappas, Marjorie. "Reflection as Self-Assessment." *School Library Media Activities Monthly* 27, no. 3 (December 2010): 5–8.

Preddy, Leslie. "Student Inquiry in the Research Process, Part 5: Inquiry Research Conclusion and Reflection." *School Library Media Activities Monthly* 19, no. 7 (March 2003): 24–27, 51.

Trinkle, Catherine. "Teaching the Use of Informational Text _IS_ Information Literacy." *School Library Media Activities Monthly* 24, no. 3 (November 2007): 37–40.

Part II: Common Core for Secondary Level English Language Arts and Literacy

Inquiry Curricular Concepts: CCSS for Secondary Level English Language Arts and Literacy

Daniel Callison

The recently released Common Core State Standards (CCSS) Initiative has been described by some leading educators as an effort unprecedented in the history of United States educational reforms (Kendall 2011). In 2009, the National Governors Association and the Council of Chief State School Officers gathered representatives from nearly all states to develop a set of shared national standards. The premise was to develop standards that will help to assure higher academic performance across all student groups in the United States, prepare students for college and careers, and restore American student performance to rank with the most successful student populations around the globe.

Input was gathered from such influential groups as the College Board, the State Higher Education Executive Officers, ACT, and Achieve. Eventually, selected representatives from leading teacher organizations such as the National Council of Teachers of Mathematics and the National Council of Teachers of English were invited to review drafts. (Many educational groups, including the American Association for School Librarians (AASL), were not engaged in major interactions for review of the final product released in 2011).

The potential influence of the CCSS on school curricular design and implementation across the country is tremendous. Now adopted by all but four states, these standards will likely serve through the coming decade as the central core that will determine the content for teaching students across all grade levels and disciplines, not just language arts and math.

This brief overview focuses on the relationship of the CCSS in secondary level language arts to the AASL *Standards for the 21st Century Learner* and to basic principles of the process for teaching and learning through inquiry. Key projections regarding the impact of the CCSS on school library services and inquiry-based programs will be included. Examination of primary level language arts standards, writing, listening, argumentation, science and mathematics standards will appear in later issues of *School Library Monthly*.

THE AASL CROSSWALK

The AASL Common Core Task Force, chaired by Marcia Mardis of Florida State, compiled a "Crosswalk of the Common Core Standards and the Standards for the 21st-Century Learner" in 2011. Standards were sorted and paired with some showing a more direct relationship than others. Examples from the Common Core History/Social Studies, Science & Technical Subjects Crosswalk illustrate a reasonable fit and are as follows:

"Inquiry Curricular Concepts: CCSS for Secondary Level English Language Arts and Literacy," by Daniel Callison, was published in *School Library Monthly* 29, no. 4 (January 2013): 16–19.

*Common Core Standard Grades 11 & 12	**AASL Standards for 21st Century Learner
CC11-12/WH/SS/S/TS 1b: Develop claim(s) and counterclaims fairly and thoroughly, supplying the most relevant data and evidence for each while pointing out the strengths and limitations of both claims(s) and counterclaims in a discipline-appropriate form that anticipates the audience's knowledge level, concerns, values, and possible biases.	1.1.5
CC11-12WH/SS/S/TS2a: Introduce a topic and organize complex ideas, concepts, and information so that each new element builds on that which precedes it to create a unified whole; include formatting (e.g., headings), graphics (e.g. figures, tables), and multimedia when useful to aiding comprehension.	2.1.2 2.1.6 3.1.4
CC11-12WH/SS/S/TS5: Develop and strengthen writing as needed by planning, revising, editing, rewriting, or trying a new approach, focusing on addressing what is most significant for a specific purpose and audience.	1.2.5
CC11-12WH/SS/S/TS7: Conduct short as well as more sustained research projects to answer a question (including a self-generated question) or solve a problem; narrow or broaden the inquiry when appropriate; synthesize multiple sources on the subject, demonstrating understanding of the subject under investigation.	2.1.1

*American Association of School Librarians. *Crosswalk of the Common Core Standards and the Standards for the 21st-Century Learner.* http://www.ala.org/aasl/guidelinesandstandards/commoncorecrosswalk.

**American Association of School Librarians. *Standards for the 21st-Century Learner.* American Library Association, 2007. (Downloadable for free at www.ala.org/aasl/standards).

ADVANCED INFORMATION ENGAGEMENT

The CCSS refers just once to online search techniques and that example is rather basic. With the expectation that teachers and students should read progressively more complex texts found in documents relevant to demanding problems and issues, understanding how to delve deeply and target searches with precision is essential. Building a search vocabulary that both expands possibilities as well as focuses in on new searching tracks becomes an important stage for conversations among students, teachers, and school librarians.

Too often school librarians provide limited guidance with most discussions centered on only the need to locate a useful document online, and the school librarian leaving the conversation when such documents have been located. Deep text explorations will require the school librarians to guide evaluation of the located documents and continue the conversation to answer such questions as "Who is the authority?" "What is the social or historic context for this information?" "What new names and events found here lead to additional relevant documents?" Google's Search Education Lesson Plans provide specific strategies related to the CCSS. Teaching students and teachers to become "information scientists" who can compare and contrast the value of documents and sources will grow in importance under CCSS (Callison 2005).

Over the past two decades about a dozen models for guiding students through the information search process have been developed and marketed. Each of these models offers an efficient process for the information search, assimilation of new facts, and presentation of findings. Recently Delia Neuman, professor at Drexel and a longtime leader in school library program standards, published her I-LEARN model (2011). She stresses the elements that require students to demonstrate what they have learned through the access, evaluation, and use or presentation processes. Successful acceptance or rejection of evidence and integration of new knowledge with existing knowledge are the measures of student learning in the CCSS as well. Neuman's fresh steps into the Information Age are worth a study along with the multitude of other models that remain valuable guide posts for school librarians in their instructional role.

TEXT COMPLEXITY

In a recent publication from the International Reading Association, text complexity is defined as three interrelated components. These are paraphrased below:

1. Qualitative dimensions—aspects of the text measured by attentive readers for levels of meaning and purpose.
2. Quantitative dimensions—factors related to word and sentence length, text cohesion, measured by formula through the application of computer software.
3. Reader and task considerations—determined by the teacher's professional judgment to meet student needs and coverage of a topic under study (Frey, Lapp and Fisher 2012).

In the CCSS these components are applied increasingly through the grade levels with the goal of generating more reading for critical review of the narrative and less reading for pleasure that is tied to the curriculum. Promotion of good literature and popular reading should be continued and students should be encouraged to become independent readers, but the core of reading for knowledge is gauged by the complexity of the texts. Remedial texts may help to meet some student needs, but are to be removed from the student learning progress in favor of texts at the student's grade level and higher.

NONFICTION DOMINANCE

Clearly, the push from the CCSS is for the expansion of nonfiction resources in schools. While remedial texts may still serve the need to engage some students, the goal is to move all students toward more demanding text documents. This especially includes primary sources as well as scholarly journal articles. CCSS implementation could result in school library collections that house 70% or more nonfiction materials, current and of technical merit.

The CCSS Revised Publisher's Criteria includes this encouraging statement, "Additional materials aim to increase regular independent reading of texts that appeal to students' interests while developing both their knowledge base and joy in reading. These materials should ensure that all students have daily opportunities to read texts of their choice on their own during and outside of the school day. Students need access to a wide range of materials on a variety of topics and genres both in their classrooms and in their school libraries . . ." (2012, 4).

Access to current journal publications is expected for social and pure science. If the school library is to be a vital part of CCSS it must house nonfiction materials with publication dates in the past decade. The demands of CCSS are rigorous, and will generate the need and expansion of cooperative agreements for scholarly journal access through academic and public libraries.

E-TEXTBOOK EVOLUTION

Are students and teachers facing the demise of textbooks? This is probably not likely. Textbooks formatted as they have been for the past half century, however, will fade away. Gone will be the compilations that reduce historical events to a brief description without space for relevant discussions or in-depth reading (Callison 2006). Provision of quality nonfiction materials, especially in science, has a declining track record in most school libraries over the past two decades. Nonfiction collections are often out of date and key areas in the sciences often lacking because school librarians lack the expertise and therefore the interest in building new collections composed of current high text reading value (Mardis 2009).

New e-textbook options are likely to have some of the same characteristics of the e-text program currently in experimental development at Indiana University. Just as in college, future high school e-texts will include features such as:

- On-demand printing to save resources and dollars
- Links to selected primary documents for detailed analysis directly from the e-text to the Internet
- Links to relevant documents and studies that provide a variety of viewpoints purposefully selected to stimulate critical analysis and debate
- Functions for lecture notes shared by instructor to all students, and vice versa
- Links to relevant multimedia, including video presentations from teachers and professors from other schools for enhancement of the text
- Various options for different text levels that may serve to accelerate some students to more advanced discussions or provide explanations for those who are trailing behind

While there may be a new demand for quality historical nonfiction and updated collections in science in order to meet CCSS, instructional products that take the student to relevant documents for critical review are more likely to be offered as a part of that product, not as additional resources in the school library. An example is the Persistent Issues in History Network where students engage in review of historic events and issues by exploring the details of the happening through access to relevant primary documents. Students become engaged with texts in order to debate and recommend resolutions to problems.

These exercises present a new challenge to the school library's collection as the school librarian will need to work with teachers in order to expand inquiry from the multimedia product into the multi-resource library world. The age-old challenge to tie the textbook and the classroom to inquiry learning and the library is likely to become even more complex with the adoption of CCSS.

REFERENCES

American Association of School Librarians. *Crosswalk of the Common Core Standards and the Standards for the 21st-Century Learner.* http://www.ala.org/aasl/guidelinesandstandards/commoncorecrosswalk (accessed September 4, 2012).

American Association of School Librarians. *Standards for the 21st Century Learner.* American Library Association, 2007. (Downloadable for free at: www.ala.org/aasl/standards).

Callison, Daniel. "Student Information Scientist." *School Library Media Quarterly* 22, no. 2 (October 2005): 39–44.

Callison, Daniel. "Textbook." In *The Blue Book on Information Age Inquiry, Instruction and Literacy* by Daniel Callison and Leslie Preddy, 563–570. Libraries Unlimited, 2006.

Common Core State Standards Initiative (CCSS). 2010. http://www.corestandards.org/the-standards (accessed September 27, 2012).

Common Core State Standards Initiative (CCSS). CCSS Revised Publisher' Criteria in English Language Arts. Revised April 4, 2012. http://www.sde.ct.gov/sde/lib/sde/pdf/ccss/latest_news/publishers _criteria_for_literacy_for_grades_3_12.pdf (accessed September 25, 2012).

eTexts at IU. http://etexts.iu.edu (accessed September 4, 2012).

Frey, Nancy, Diane Lapp, and Douglas Fisher. *Text Complexity: Raising Rigor in Reading.* IRA, 2012.

Google Search Education Lesson Plans. http://www.google.com/insidesearch/searcheducation/lessons.html. (accessed September 4, 2012).

Kendall, John. *Understanding Common Core State Standards.* ASCD, 2011.

Mardis, Marcia. "You've Got the Hook: Droppin' Science on School Libraries and the Future of Learning." *Library Media Connection* (November/December 2009): 10–14.

Neuman, Delia. "Constructing Knowledge in the Twenty-First Century: I-LEARN and Using Information as a Tool for Learning." *School Library Research* 14 (2011). www.ala.org/aasl/slr (accessed September 25, 2012).

Persistent Issues in History Network. http://pihnet.org/ (accessed September 25, 2012).

Part III: The Unknown Power of Deep Revision

The Unknown Power of Deep Revision

Daniel Callison

According to Wendy Bishop, former Kellogg Hunt Professor at Florida State University, "Improving your attitude toward revision can revolutionize your writing and your enjoyment of it. With a positive attitude toward revision, you will listen to feedback with an open ear and not get so quickly offended when a reader tries to help" (2004, 1).

REVISION = PUNISHMENT?

In extensive studies conducted in the 1970s and 1980s, researchers discovered that high school and college writers in general do not know how to revise effectively (Faigley et al. 1985). Janet Emig's pioneering research observations of the writing processes practiced by high school students described resistance to revision (1971). Her research indicated that most seniors in high school saw revision as punishment. Attitudes have not changed, although modern computerized word processing has eased the revision drudgery. Negative attitudes persist as students usually do not welcome the revision process and specifically do not see it as an opportunity to improve their communication.

Revision seems to be a more acceptable action, however, if the potential audience is broadened beyond the student's classroom teacher. Peer review seems to stimulate a slightly higher investment in revision provided all peers are engaged in such activities (Harris and Graham 1996). Emig observed that students will reformulate "self-sponsored" writing, but will not volunteer to revise "school-sponsored" writing (1971). Successful writers who matured in varied writing experiences through college, tended to employ deeper revision strategies more frequently than those not as successful in formal education (Beach 1976).

REVISION AND INQUIRY

Revision is an inquiry stage seldom implemented to its most effective learning levels. Within most of the current models for student-centered inquiry, only two levels of revision are usually identified and encouraged:

"The Unknown Power of Deep Revision," by Daniel Callison, was published in *School Library Monthly* 30, no. 7 (April 2014): 19–21.

1. Assimilation of new information. The process of encountering new information and determining if it is to be accepted and how it is to be added to the construction of the overall growing knowledge base. Major assimilation may even revise the focus or hypothesis of the report. Consistent resistance to assimilation may be an indication of information bias and failure to be open to alternative findings (Fitzgerald 1999).
2. Proof reading. These mechanical steps clean the style and grammar, and are usually employed as a final step before submitting the written project. While this is an important part of the formal inquiry process and serves to improve communication under a standard style, deep revision is much more than this formative corrective procedure (Bishop 2004).

To suggest that a deep revision should take place is to raise flags of frustration for most teachers and school librarians who have guided the student through a complex maze in order to complete the student's first attempts at an elaborated inquiry project. Satisfaction of concluding accomplishment is noted in the elated emotions experienced by many successful students (Kuhlthau 1985).

Deep revision possibilities should not negate this stage of gratification, but deep revision possibilities can be retained for future engagements with the next inquiry project that extends beyond the initial experience. This is very important if the planned curriculum actually supports the Common Core State Standards' (CCSS) recommendation that students should experience short, but meaningful, research projects across their academic career. Yes, this progression of experiences can be very different, but a coordinated portfolio record can also show growth and maturation in the information literacy of students if some of the projects reflect meaningful revisits to topics throughout the student's academic career.

THE OPPORTUNITIES FOR REVISION

The opportunity for deep revision can take place in the following situations:

a. Changing the audience for the inquiry presentation. Major revisions may be needed in order to increase the effectiveness of the presentation of the report depending on the audience. Selection of evidence that may be more relevant from one audience to another, greater use of charts and other visuals, or greater use of story and analogies over hard data may involve substantial revisions. Varying examples to give focus and clarity may change, although final conclusions may remain the same. Different audiences in addition to the teacher may involve peers, older or younger students, parents and other adult groups. Authentic community service presentations to seek social actions beyond an academic exercise can bring new meaning to revision (Callison and Lamb 2006).
b. Changing the presentation mode or medium. A large percentage of student inquiry projects remain solely paper-based. Shifting the written report to a multimedia presentation will involve revisions that will generate visual content as well as options for media presentations that stand alone, or media presentations that are created to enhance oral reports (virtual inquiry and website). Shifts in the use of graphics may introduce new insights that influence changes in emphasis on some findings and even introduce the need for more supportive evidence in order to clarify findings in a visual manner. Science Fairs or Inquiry Fairs can provide a new environment in which the student modifies the presentation to meet changes in media, time limitations, and variable audiences (Saul et al. 2005).
c. Abstracting studies. Changes in the student's report to show elaboration or more extensive discussion for various groups can also pose a need for revision. Synthesis or abstracting findings to condense the message so that the student's report fits within space or timeframes with other students who have completed similar projects can also lead to a more refined focus.
d. Portfolio. Compilation of inquiry across disciplines and the student's academic career holds high potential, but requires coordination and maintenance by the local educational institution. Samples of various inquiry projects completed by the student can be gathered in a portfolio. Technology today allows for virtual collections along with assessments that can show how the student

has matured in topic selection, information management, evidence selection, and argument or conclusion presentations. Portfolios that include examples across disciplines can reveal students who hold multiple talents. Tracking student work on a similar topic allows for documentation of student growth in sophistication of information searching and evidence selection (Callison 1993). Modern technologies make storage, retrieval, sharing, and comparison of portfolio documents more manageable today than ever before (Beach et al. 2010).

e. Assimilation of complex texts. Also documented can be examples of the student's oral presentations. Community action projects may appear in the middle school stages. More complex debates on social issues may be more appropriate for senior high school levels. Specific examples of how the student has met local standards for information literacy can be charted in rubrics or other assessment instruments. Student research or inquiry journals, kept over time, may show growth in vocabulary to help the student master more complex texts as the years go by. Student maturation in how to handle more complex data as he or she enters higher levels of cognition can also display student changes in assimilation of findings earlier rejected, not understood, and not appreciated.

Meredith Sue Willis summarizes the value of seeking additional information that may result in elaboration and clarification through deep revision:

> After the first burst of inspiration, you usually need to add more. The purpose of adding to a piece is not merely to make it longer, nor is it merely to flesh out an idea or (perish the thought!) pad it. The real reason to add is to get further insight, to find new directions, to get a clearer understanding of your materials. If all you ever do in writing a draft is correct your spelling and punctuation, and make a fair copy, you are at risk of merely hovering over the surface of your material. When I think of going deeper, I always think of mining: you tunnel in, dig out the ore, and eventually smelt it to separate out the metal (1993, 63).

CCSS KEY POINTS IN LANGUAGE ARTS

The Common Core State Standards (CCSS) initiative emphasizes the expectation that each student should learn to deal with a variety of audiences and contend with different evidence modes:

> Students adapt their communication in relation to audience, task, purpose, and discipline. They set and adjust purpose for reading, writing, speaking, listening, and language use as warranted by the task. They appreciate nuances, such as how the composition of an audience should affect tone when speaking and how the connotations of words affect meaning. They also know that different disciplines call for different types of evidence (e.g., documentary evidence in history, experimental evidence in science).

Several key points from the CCSS in language arts lend credence to assessment practices for the purpose of documenting student progress in inquiry through revision:

- Reading—The standards require the progressive development of reading comprehension so that students advancing through the grades are able to gain more from whatever they read. Through reading a diverse array of classic and contemporary literature as well as challenging informational texts in a range of subjects, students are expected to build knowledge, gain insights, explore possibilities, and broaden their perspective.
- Writing—The ability to write logical arguments based on substantive claims, sound reasoning, and relevant evidence is a cornerstone of the writing standards. Research—both short, focused projects and longer term in-depth research—is emphasized throughout the standards, but most prominently in the writing strand since a written analysis and presentation of findings are so often critical.
- Speaking and Listening—The standards require that students gain, evaluate, and present increasingly complex information, ideas, and evidence through listening and speaking as well as through media.

- Language—The standards expect that students will grow their vocabularies through a mix of conversations, direct instruction, and reading.
- Media and Technology—Just as media and technology are integrated in school and life in the twenty-first century, skills related to media use (both critical analysis and production of media) are integrated throughout the standards.

Specifically (CCSS Writing Grades 9–10), the student is expected to mature in communication skills so that documentation can be made of his or her growth in sophistication to:

- Conduct short as well as more sustained research projects [more and more independently];
- Narrow or broaden the inquiry when appropriate;
- Synthesize multiple sources on the subject;
- Gather relevant information from multiple authoritative print and digital sources;
- Assess the usefulness of each source in answering the research question;
- Integrate information into the text selectively to maintain the flow of ideas;
- Write routinely over extended time frames (time for research, reflection, and revision);
- Develop and strengthen writing as needed by planning, revising, editing, rewriting, or trying a new approach, focusing on addressing what is most significant for a specific purpose and audience;
- Use technology, including the Internet, to produce, publish, and update individual or shared writing products, taking advantage of technology's capacity to link to other information and to display information flexibly and dynamically;
- Produce clear and coherent writing in which the development, organization, and style are appropriate to task, purpose, and audience.

REFERENCES

Beach, Richard. "Self-evaluation Strategies of Extensive Revisers and Non-revisers." *College Composition and Communication* 27 no. 2 (1976): 160–164.

Beach, Richard, et al. *Literacy Tools in the Classroom.* The National Writing Project, 2010.

Bishop, Wendy. *Acts of Revision.* Heinemann, 2004.

Callison, Daniel. "The Potential for Portfolio Assessment." In *School Library Media Annual.* Libraries Unlimited, 1993. http://www.ala.org/aasl/aaslpubsandjournals/slmrb/editorschoiceb/infopower/selctcallison87 (accessed December 27, 2013).

Callison, Daniel and Annette Lamb. "Audience Analysis." In *The Blue Book on Information Age Inquiry, Instruction, and Literacy,* 285–291. Libraries Unlimited, 2006.

Common Core State Standards Initiative. "Key Points in English Language Arts." http://www.corestandards.org/resources/key-points-in-english-language-arts (accessed December 27, 2013).

Common Core State Standards Initiative. "Writing Grades 9–10." http://www.corestandards.org/ELA-Literacy/W/9-10 (accessed December 27, 2013)

Emig, Janet. *The Composing Processes of Twelfth Graders.* National Council of Teachers of English, 1971.

Fitzgerald, Mary Ann. "Evaluating Information." *School Library Media Research* 2 (1999). http://www.ala.org/aasl/aaslpubsandjournals/slmrb/slmrcontents/volume21999/vol2fitzgerald (accessed December 27, 2013).

Faigley, Lester et al. *Assessing Writers' Knowledge and Processes of Composing.* Ablex, 1985.

Harris, Karen R. and Steven Graham. *Making the Writing Process Work.* Brookline, 1996.

Kuhlthau, Carol Collier. *Teaching the Library Research Process.* Center for Applied Research in Education, 1985.

Saul, Wendy, et al. *Beyond the Science Fair: Creating a Kids' Inquiry Conference.* Heinemann, 2005.

Willis, Meredith Sue. *Deep Revision.* Teachers and Writers Collaborative, 1993.

Chapter 8

Inquiry in History

Part I: Primary Sources and the Common Core for Secondary Level History

CCSS: Primary Sources for Secondary Social Studies

Daniel Callison

The study of history is very similar to other disciplines covered by the new Common Core Standards (CCSS). The emphasis is on more complex and demanding reading materials, especially the decoding of full-text primary documents. Students are encouraged to learn to read in the way professional historians read using context and resources that allow for exploration based on self-generated inquiry questions. The study of history when it is enhanced by access to original documents, digitized for student manipulation, means that the past is not just dates and isolated events from the textbook.

WIDER ACCESS

The availability of original documents through the Internet continues to increase, meaning greater access for students. School librarians face increased demands to broaden their definition of collection development so that they can include not only more complex, contemporary historical nonfiction and biographical books, but also original documents, photographs, and illustrations of artifacts online.

Electronic access, including both public domain and subscription options, make collection development a professional role that goes beyond simple acquisition of only books and periodicals that meet standard criteria for school library collections. Grappling with the historical issues of our democracy through digitized raw data can lead to interesting intellectual freedom challenges (Friese 2008).

"CCSS: Primary Sources for Secondary Social Studies," by Daniel Callison, was published in *School Library Monthly* 30, no. 2 (November 2013): 18–21.

THE AASL CROSSWALK WITH HISTORY

The following selected examples from the crosswalk curriculum map developed by the American Association of School Librarians (AASL) illustrates the close fit between the Common Core secondary level standards in history and AASL *Standards for the 21st Century Learner.*

*Common Core Standards	**AASL Standards for the 21st Century Learner
CC11-12WH/SS/S/TS2 Write informative/ explanatory texts, including the narration of historical events, scientific procedures/ experiments, or technical processes.	2.2.4 Demonstrate personal productivity . . . 3.3.4 Create products that apply to authentic . . .
CC11-12WH/SS/S/TS2b Develop the topic thoroughly by selecting the most significant and relevant facts, extended definitions, concrete details, quotations, or other information and examples appropriate to the audience's knowledge of the topic.	1.1.5 Evaluate information . . . 1.1.7 Make sense of information . . .
CC11-12WH/SS/S/TS7 Conduct short as well as more sustained research projects to answer a question (including a self-generated question) or solve a problem; narrow or broaden the inquiry when appropriate; synthesize multiple sources on the subject, demonstrating understanding of the subject under investigation.	1.4.1 Monitor own information-seeking . . . 2.1.1 Continue an inquiry-based research process . . .
CC9-10WH/SS/S/TS2f Provide a concluding statement or section that follows from and supports the information or explanation presented (e.g., articulating implications or the significance of the topic).	4.2.3 Maintain openness to new ideas . . . 4.4.4 Interpret new information . . .

*American Association of School Librarians. *Crosswalk of the Common Core Standards and the Standards for the 21st-Century Learner.* http://www.ala.org/aasl/guidelinesandstandards/commoncorecrosswalk.

**American Association of School Librarians. *Standards for the 21st-Century Learner.* American Library Association, 2007. (Downloadable for free at www.ala.org/aasl/standards).

A FOCUS ON PRIMARY SOURCES

Format does not necessarily determine that a source is primary. Recordings, films, and photos can all be secondary if they are a later interpretation of an event or a series of events. Secondary sources also include analyses of primary sources and other secondary sources. Tertiary sources are compilations over time; encyclopedias and even some textbooks are often regarded as third level interpretations. The *Yale University Primary Sources Collection* defines "primary source" as follows:

> Primary sources provide first-hand testimony or direct evidence concerning a topic under investigation. They are characterized by their content, regardless of their format. They are created by witnesses or recorders who experienced the events or conditions being documented. Often these sources are created at the time when the events or conditions are occurring, but primary sources can also include autobiographies, memoirs, and oral histories recorded later. Primary sources are characterized by their content, regardless of whether they are available in original format, in microfilm/microfiche, or digital format, or in published format (2008).

Specifically, the Common Core reading standards for literacy in history and social studies in grades six through eight focus on ideas, structure, and knowledge integrated from primary sources. Selected examples include:

- Cite specific textual evidence to support analysis of primary and secondary sources.
- Determine the central ideas or information of a primary or secondary source; provide an accurate summary of the source distinct from prior knowledge or opinions.
- Evaluate authors' differing points of view on the same historical event or issue by assessing the authors' claims, reasoning, and evidence.
- Integrate visual information (e.g. in charts, graphs, photographs, videos, maps) with other information in print and digital texts.
- Distinguish among fact, opinion, and reasoned judgment in a text.
- Analyze the relationship between a primary and secondary source on the same topic.
- Integrate information from diverse sources, both primary and secondary, into a coherent understanding of an idea or event, noting discrepancies among sources. (*Common Core State Standards Initiative, English Language Arts Standards, History/Social Studies, Grades 6–8*).

Are these information literacy skills? Yes. Cleary important here is that these standards place the teacher and student in the role of historian or information scientist (Callison 2005a). Critical evaluation of evidence is the key portion of the information search process and inquiry learning, not just the exercise of narrowing a topic or finding enough information to complete the assignment. The expectation is that critical review of artifacts can result in new insights for the student.

Making critical judgments on the quality and relevance of information found in documents, not simply the process of writing a descriptive narrative can mean teacher guidance is needed each time students engage in examining information. The expectation is that secondary school students determine the value of accessed information from various source levels, determine the quality of that information within its context and the context of the problem being researched (Callison 2005b). It means conflicting judgments will arise based on the analysis of the information in order to determine the extent of its assimilation to the student's prior knowledge (Kuhlthau 2004).

It means true historical information inquiry processes can be difficult, frustrating, and, at times, impossible. This realization may be one of the most important information literacy lessons.

RESEARCH ABOUT USING DIGITIZED PRIMARY DOCUMENTS

Key challenges to the implementation of using primary sources include access to documents, variance in the interpretation of primary sources as true original artifacts, and the degree of teacher understanding of the potential for new learning experiences. Early experimentation with digital primary resource collections raised obvious obstacles.

Adam M. Friedman at the University of North Carolina, Charlotte, found that world history teachers needed extensive training and practice in the use of technology before accepting digital primary materials as more than simple additions to lessons (2006). Teachers placed little value in primary documents if the means for access were not clear and if the document contents did not match previously established learning objectives. Teaching strategies changed very little even when the depth of online collections was illustrated.

As the head librarian at the University of Illinois Laboratory High School, Frances Jacobson Harris has frequently taken a leading role in the development and implementation of new instructional methods engaging untested resources (2002). She reported the results of an early use of digitized primary resources from the Great Depression by middle school students.

While she found that, with instruction, teachers and students were able to navigate the on-line archive and enjoyed creative writing options assigned for the lesson, the students tended to view the artifacts from the vantage point of their personal experiences and contemporary time frame. A great deal more modeling or coaching was needed to help students read and synthesize the documents within their historical context.

The Common Core curriculum calls for more critical analysis of documents than the creative writing experiences these students favored in this early study. The authors of the Common Core, however, favor informative, argumentative writing over personal narratives.

More recent studies have shown signs of greater acceptance and use of digitized primary sources as the collections have grown, become better organized with associated lesson plans, and teachers have matured in technological applications. Student application of critical analysis has also moved to the frontline.

Susan De La Paz from the University of Maryland and her colleagues have recently demonstrated how digital evidence serves to help create historical, argumentative discourse for adolescents (2012). Better writers used strategies based on facts and evidence from documents. Better writers also demonstrated the capacity to contextualize and corroborate evidence in their arguments.

READING CLOSELY AND OTHER UNNATURAL ACTS

Sam Wineburg's award-winning publication, *Historical Thinking and Other Unnatural Acts*, chronicles his series of field research projects in which he documents the limited visions students and teachers hold for the personalities and events found in American History. He found frequent acceptance of stereotypes and lack of enthusiasm for meaningful storytelling (2001). Classroom discussions seldom generated useful argumentation on key issues. History became stagnant in the hands of teachers limited to textbook content. Challenging politically correct and often simplistic conclusions found in most history curricula requires passion and open debate. Over a decade ago, Wineburg concluded:

> Discussions in such [interactive] classrooms will inevitably boil over into contentious issues of judgment, conflict, and tension that characterize a free society. This is what Dewey meant when he wrote that schools are not training grounds for democracy but the places where democracy is enacted. Either the classroom becomes a site where we learn to talk to one another, or we will suffer the enduring consequences of never having learned to do so. (2001, 230)

Wineburg is now Director of the Stanford University History Education Group. In cooperation with the George Mason University's Center for History and New Media, critical methods that model how historians think and demonstrate why history matters have emerged. Inquiry questioning into the meaning of primary sources are driven by the following techniques summarized on the website, *Why Historical Thinking Matters*:

> Sourcing—Considering a document's author and its creation.
> Contextualizing—Situating the document and its events in place and time.
> Close Reading—Reading carefully to consider what a source says and the language used to say it.
> Corroborating—Checking important details across multiple sources to determine points of agreement and disagreement (http://historicalthinkingmatters.org/why/).

BEST WEB SITES FOR PRIMARY SOURCE CORROBORATION

While the strategies to help students and teachers read like historians are becoming refined with practice, so, too, have the online collections of primary sources greatly improved in depth, organization, and curricular relevance. Some of the websites recommended by Thomas Daccord in his book, *The Best of History Web Sites,* are as follows:

> History Matters. http://historymatters.gmu.edu
>> From the George Mason University Center mentioned above, history lessons and syllabi for primary sources are abundant.
>
> Digital History: Resource Guides. http://www.digitalhistory.uh.edu/
>> The site's Ask the HyperHistorian feature allows users to pose questions to a professional historian. High quality resources are managed through the University of Houston.
>
> The History Lab. http://hlab.tielab.org
>> Free access is granted to all k–12 teachers. Bernie Dodge of WebQuest fame is a leading advisor for this site.
>
> The Library of Congress. http://www.loc.gov/index.html
>> This is the ultimate treasure of resources, many of which are organized to meet the Common Core curriculum. Viewers should examine the opportunities through the LC Teaching with Primary Sources Program and resources linked from the *Teaching with Primary Sources Journal.* Gail Petri, Education Resource Specialist, provides a regular topical update on primary resources in "The LOC Connection" published in the online periodical *The School Librarian's Workshop.*
>
> National Archives and Records Administration. http://www.nara.gov/
>> The Digital Classroom includes the growing section on Teaching with Documents. The Weighting the Evidence tools help students apply critical skills. This is promoted by the National Council for the Social Studies.
>
> Internet History Sourcebooks. http://www.fordham.edu/halsall/
>> A collection of public domain resources, the site is managed through Fordham University.
>
> American Rhetoric. http://www.americanrhetoric.com
>> This site is rich in multimedia presentations broadly structured for debate of today's political issues as well as those from the past.
>
> Best of History Websites. http://www.besthistorysites.net/
>> This portal created by EdTech Teacher Inc. updates Daccord's collection and provides over 1200 valuable links, many coordinated to meet the expectations found in the Common Core (Daccord 2007).

REFERENCES

American Association of School Librarians. *Crosswalk of the Common Core Standards and the Standards for the 21st-Century Learner.* http://www.ala.org/aasl/guidelinesandstandards/commoncorecrosswalk (accessed July 19, 2013).

American Association of School Librarians. *Standards for the 21st Century Learner.* American Library Association, 2007. (Downloadable for free at: www.ala.org/aasl/standards).

Callison, Daniel. "The Student Information Scientist Part I." *School Library Monthly* 22, no. 2 (October 2005a): 39–44.

Callison, Daniel. "The Student Information Scientist Part II." *School Library Monthly* 22, no. 3 (November 2005b): 37–41.

Common Core State Standards Initiative. http://www.corestandards.org (accessed July 1, 2013).

Common Core State Standards Initiative, English Language Arts Standards, History/Social Studies, Grades 6–8. http://www.corestandards.org/ELA-Literacy/RH/6-8 (accessed July 14, 2013).

Daccord, Thomas. *The Best of History Web Sites.* Neal-Schuman Publishers, Inc. 2007.

De La Paz, Susan, and others. "Adolescents' Disciplinary Use of Evidence, Argumentative Strategies, and Organizational Structure in Writing about Historical Controversies." *Written Communication* 29, no. 4 (October 2012): 412–454.

Friedman, Adam M. "World History Teachers' Use of Digital Primary Sources: The Effect of Training." *Theory and Research in Social Education* 34, no. 1 (2006): 124–141.

Friese, Elizabeth E. G. "Inquiry Learning: Is Your Selection Policy Ready?" *Library Media Connection* 37, no. 3 (November/December 2008): 14–16.

Harris, Frances Jacobson. "There Was a Great Collision in the Stock Market: Middle School Students, Online Primary Sources, and Historical Sense Making." *School Library Media Research* 5 (2002). http://www.ala.org/aasl/aaslpubsandjournals/slmrb/slmrcontents/volume52002/harris (accessed July 14, 2013).

Kuhlthau, Carol Collier. *Seeking Meaning.* Libraries Unlimited. 2004.

Why Historical Thinking Matters. A Project of the Roy Rosenzweig Center for History and New Media, George Mason University, and the School of Education at Stanford University. http://historicalthinkingmatters.org/why/ (accessed July 13, 2013).

Wineburg, Sam. *Historical Thinking and Other Unnatural Acts: Charting the Future of Teaching the Past.* Temple University Press, 2001.

Yale University Primary Sources Collection. 2008. http://www.yale.edu/collections_collaborative/primary sources/index.html (accessed July 14, 2013).

Part II: Expanding Exemplary Secondary Information Sources for Historical Inquiry

Expanding Exemplary Information Sources for the High School History Curriculum

Daniel Callison

Collection development in school libraries has usually been a process driven by the curriculum. The classic concepts in collection mapping (Loertscher and Wimberley 2009), examination of actual source citation or use (Mancall 1983), and statistical methods for circulation analysis (Doll 2002) continue to have relevance as the Common Core State Standards (CCSS) emerge across the country. Each of these collection development methods have come under extensive revisions over the past decade as application of greater holistic resource use approaches have come into favor in order to support inquiry learning (Hughes-Hassell and Mancall 2005).

SECONDARY SOURCES NEEDED

The CCSS brings additional issues, challenges, and expenses to the compilation of a quality collection. CCSS requires accessing primary artifacts and greater student access of online resources. Secondary resources, written from primary, scholarly research, also need to expand greatly, especially in high schools, to meet the complex text expectations of the CCSS.

While specific titles are given as "exemplars" in *Appendix B of the Common Core State Standards*, the composite list leaves many gaps. Expectations of the CCSS clearly indicate that the amount of nonfiction reading from elementary school on through graduation increases substantially. This increase could be as high as 70% of the reading content across the curriculum for senior high school students.

Add to this a strong push in the CCSS for students to analyze complex resources in order to make informed arguments while considering a broad spectrum of opinions and data. The process of acquiring the best resources to support these new curriculum foci can be overwhelming.

This [article] will focus on several methods that can add to the depth and quality of the process for selection of secondary nonfiction resources at the high school level. While specifically tailored to address expanding the exemplar list in high school American history,

"Expanding Exemplary Information Sources for the High School History Curriculum," by Daniel Callison, was published in *School Library Monthly* 30, no. 4 (January 2014): 23–26.

similar methods might be applied to the elementary school and middle school levels. These methods could also be applied to other disciplines including nonfiction for science and world history.

Collection building to meet CCSS is driven by quality, not popularity. Frequent circulation may not be a valid selection tool where the expectation is to build a collection that is academically demanding.

CRITERIA FOR SELECTING TEXT EXEMPLARS

Appendix B of the CCSS makes it clear that the text samples "serve to exemplify the level of complexity and quality that the Standards require [for] all students in a given grade. . . . Additionally, they are suggestive of the breadth of texts that students should encounter in the text types required by the Standards. The choices should serve as useful guideposts in helping educators select texts of similar complexity, quality, and range for their own classrooms. They expressly do not represent a partial or complete reading list" (CCSS, 2).

A selection of texts should be available that reflect the differing abilities of the students. For example, not everyone is expected to read David McCullough's *1776*. However, similar modern, popular historical scholarship should be on the agenda for all students seeking college level experiences. There is a plethora of such historical nonfiction suitable for any modern high school library. Good professional relations should easily lead to additional choices held by local public and college libraries. These works can be easily shared through interlibrary loan.

The CCSS lists only eleven titles for informational texts in history. Although there is no quantitative standard given, a high school of 1,000 students should have three to five titles per student in the historical nonfiction print and electronic book collection. This number would provide a rich pool for in-depth reading.

The selection process for the exemplary examples was guided by three criteria:

- Complexity. . . . based on qualitative and quantitative indices of inherent text difficulty balanced with educators' professional judgment in matching readers and texts in light of particular tasks.
- Quality. . . . classic or historically significant texts as well as contemporary works of comparable literary merit, cultural significance, and rich content.
- Range. . . . as broad a range of sufficiently complex, high-quality texts as possible. Among the factors considered were initial publication date, authorship, and subject matter (CCSS, 2).

Further, the Revised Publishers' Criteria for the CCSS details the expectation that "student read increasingly complex texts with growing independence as they progress toward career and college readiness" (Coleman and Pimental 2012, 14). These criteria give more substance to understanding the range and quality of nonfiction texts:

- Curricula provide texts that are valuable sources of information. Informational texts in science, history, and technical subjects may or may not exhibit literary craft, but may be worth reading as valuable sources of information to gain important knowledge. It is essential that the scientific and historical texts chosen for careful study be focused on such significant topics that they are worth the instructional time for students to examine them deliberately to develop a full understanding. . . . Students should also be required to assimilate larger volumes of content-area text to demonstrate college and career readiness (Coleman and Pimental 2012, 15).

Translation of these criteria into practical selection processes can present a challenging agenda among teachers who have history certification and expertise. Perhaps the most difficult aspect in building a collection of the scholarly, classic, and yet engaging stature necessary to meet the CCSS goals is that history teachers must be more than general educators. They should hold valid historian credentials and act accordingly.

School librarians should also hold academic credentials, which show they have professional skills in application of review guides and recommendations based on unbiased, authoritative standards. The challenge is for local professional educators to establish, practice, and defend their own selection criteria.

GUIDANCE FROM AND BEYOND HISTORY TEXTBOOKS

In his 1995 award-winning book, *Lies My Teacher Told Me*, University of Vermont sociology professor James W. Loewen points out that most textbook editors start their careers in publishing as sales representatives, not as historians. They don't know how to interpret history, but they know how to reach their market. These editors often include whatever is likely to be of concern to textbook selecting stakeholders. Everything gets mentioned, but seldom does anything receive depth and relevance to present-day issues.

Skirting controversy and displaying simplistic solutions to complex issues, Loewen asserts that history textbooks not only are misleading on events, but misleading in how democracy works and does not work (1995). American history textbooks have been the political football of classroom content for at least the past 150 years (Moreau 2008). There are a few exceptions, however, of breaking away from the simplistic and boring textbook outline approach which result in senior high school students actually debating the issues in American history linked to our continuing struggle to find solutions through democratic discourse (Kintisch and Cordero 2006; Williams 2008; Lesh 2011).

Leading history textbooks today provide nearly everything possible in graphically impressive appendices except for recommended reading lists of quality, secondary historical publications that provide the depth of scholarship to meet the demands of the common core standards. Atlases, glossaries, Presidential bio-sketches, Supreme Court decisions, key primary documents are all useful, but provision of recommended scholarly secondary book publications that illuminate the greater debate of the social and economic issues of building America are usually missing.

CONTROVERSIAL RESOURCES FOR DEEP DISCUSSION

Perhaps the most controversial and yet most widely used American History text across the past two decades has been Howard Zinn's *A People's History of the United States* (1995). Written in chapters that center on issues at the heart of what divides America today, Zinn never waters down the arguments. The prolific author has been criticized from the right and the left for his biased narratives, and yet few have questioned his selection of issues as unrepresentative of the greater democratic discussion (Murrow and Cohen 2013).

Hundreds of progressive American History teachers each year find that they set the stage for meaningful debate using a Zinn chapter as a springboard. Zinn's writings naturally invite debate and inquiry. His scholarship is documented with secondary source bibliographies, which can greatly enhance the pool for rebuilding high school American history book collections. Unfortunately, many of his secondary references are out of print, but some have new editions and all are potential candidates for comparisons to contemporary nonfiction on similar topics. The following examples are drawn from over 300 given by Zinn:

The Other Civil War
Cochran, Thomas and William Miller. *The Age of Enterprise.*
Dawley, Alan. *Class and Community: The Industrial Revolution in Lynn.*

Hofstadter, Richard and Michael Wallace. *American Violence.*
Horwitz, Morton. *Transformation of American Law.*
Myers, Gustavus. *History of the Great American Fortunes.*
Wertheimer, Barbara. *We Were There: The Story of Working Women in America.*

The Socialist Challenge
Aptheker, Herbert. *A Documentary History of the Negro People in the United States.*
Flexnfer, Eleanor. *A Century of Struggle.*
Kolko, Gabriel. *The Triumph of Conservatism.*
Lerner, Gerda. *The Female Experience: An American Documentary.*

Carter-Reagan-Bush: The Bipartisan Consensus
Piven, Frances Fox and Richard Cloward. *Regulating the Poor.*
Savage, David. *Turning Right: The Making of the Rehnquist Supreme Court.*
Rosenberg, Gerald N. *The Hollow Hope.*
Croteau, David and William Hoynes. *By Invitation Only: How the Media Limit the Political Debate.*
Kozol, Jonathan. *Savage Inequalities: Children in America's Schools* (1995, 635–653).

AMERICAN HISTORY BY INVENTION

In 2003, W.W. Norton & Company introduced a new approach to the American history textbook content. *Inventing America* by Maier, Smith, Keyssar, and Kevles reflects this approach (2003). Chronological, emphasis was moved away from military conflicts toward the great American ability to invent. Social, economic and even political issues are addressed with the genius of American ingenuity.

This textbook moves across transportation and communication, from inventiveness in social life that revolutionizes farming to new cities and skyscrapers, and on to *the* great inventive experiment itself—democracy. Included are secondary scholarly books listed as suggested readings. To reach the attributes of "student as historian" implied through the common core, students should have access to as many of these titles as possible at their school library media center. Here are a few to compare to Zinn:

A House Dividing
Bruce, Robert V. *The Launching of Modern American Science.*
Denny, Robert. E. *Civil War Medicine.*
Foner, Eric. *Free Soil, Free Labor, Free Men: The Ideology of the Republican Party before the Civil War.*
Hosley, William. *Colt: The Making of an American Legend.*

Prosperity and the Metropolis
Cott, Nancy F. *The Grounding of Modern Feminism.*
Cowan, Ruth Schwartz. *More Work for Mother: The Ironies of Household Technology from the Open Hearth to the Microwave.*
Grossman, James. *Land of Hope: Chicago, Black Southerners, and the Great Migration.*
Higham, John. *Strangers in the Land: Patterns of American Nativism, 1860–1925.*

The Reagan Revolution
Barkan, Robert Elliott. *And Still They Came: Immigrants and American Society.*
Faludi, Susan. *Backlash: The Undeclared War against American Women.*
Phillips, Kevin. *The Politics of Rich and Poor: Wealth and the American Electorate in the Reagan Aftermath.*
Wilson, William Julius. *The Truly Disadvantaged: The Inner City, the Underclass, and Public Policy.*

AMERICAN HISTORY ISSUES DEBATED ONLINE

ABC-CLIO Solutions has developed an online approach that introduces the student to key questions (a set of dilemmas) in American history. It follows an exploration format allowing the student to learn from various scholarly viewpoints on selected issues. Online access to websites by relevant resource institutions such as museums provides illustrated background information.

A major advantage of online access is that the supporting secondary scholarly resources can be updated regularly. While this allows for more recent historical nonfiction to be added, the educators who have designed this resource also retain a listing of tested and accepted classic titles.

Fifteen online curriculum programs have been developed; several have been recognized with national awards. Following is a sample of how ABC-CLIO Solutions can add to the richness of a scholarly secondary source collection for American History in high schools:

What was the primary reason for the Confederate defeat in the Civil War?
Foote, Shelby. *The Civil War: A Narrative.* Random House, 1958–1974.
Levine, Bruce. *Confederate Emancipation: Southern Plans to Free and Arm Slaves during the Civil War.* Oxford University Press, 2006.
How did Congressional legislation affect the economy during the Civil War?
Ekelund, Robert B., Jr. and Mark Thornton. *Tariffs, Blockages, and Inflation: The Economics of the Civil War.* SR Books, 2004.
Gresham, Otto. *The Greenbacks or the Money that Won the Civil War.* Kessinger Publishing, 2008.
Richardson, Heather Cox. *The Greatest Nation on the Earth: Republican Economic Policies during the Civil War.* Harvard University Press, 1997.

Was Ronald Reagan responsible for the collapse of the Soviet Union and the end of the Cold War?
Blum, William. *Rogue State: A Guide to the World's Only Superpower.* Common Courage Press, 2005.
Brzezinski, Zbigniew K. *The Grand Failure: The Birth and Death of Communism in the Twentieth Century.* Macmillan, 1989.
Kowalski, Ronald. *European Communism.* Macmillan, 2006
Lafeber, Walter. *America, Russia, and the Cold War.* McGraw Hill, 2006.

REFERENCES

ABC-Solutions. www.abc-clio.com (accessed August 25, 2013).
Coleman, David and Susan Pimentel. Revised Publishers' Criteria for the Common Core Standards: History/Social Studies, Science, and Technical Subjects Literacy Curricula, Grades 6–12. Revised April 12, 2012. http://www.sde.ct.gov/sde/lib/sde/pdf/ccss/latest_news/publishers_criteria_for_literacy_for_grades_3_12.pdf (accessed October 4, 2013).
Common Core State Standards (CCSS). Common Core State Standards for English Language Arts Literacy, History/Social Studies, Science, and Technical Subjects: Appendix B: Text Exemplars and Sample Performance Tasks. http://www.corestandards.org/assets/Appendix_B.pdf (accessed October 4, 2013).
https://www.commondreams.org/view/2013/08/07-3 (accessed October 5, 2013).
Doll, Carol Ann. *Managing and Analyzing Your Collection: A Practical Guide for Small Libraries and School Media Centers.* American Library Association, 2002.
Hughes-Hassell, Sandra and Jacqueline Mancall. *Collection Management for Youth: Responding to the Needs of Learners.* American Library Association, 2005.
Kintisch, Shelly and Wilma Cordero. *Breaking Away from the Textbook: A Creative Approach to Teaching American History.* R and L Education, 2008.
Lesh, Bruce. *Why Won't You Just Tell Us the Answer?* Stenhouse, 2011.

Loertscher, David V. and Laura H. Wimberley. *Collection Development Using the Collection Mapping Technique: A Guide for Librarians*. Hi Willow, 2009.

Loewen, J. W. *Lies My Teacher Told Me: Everything Your American History Textbook Got Wrong*. Simon & Schuster Touchstone, 1995.

Maier, Pauline, Merritt Roe Smith, Alexander Keyssar, and Daniel J. Kevles. *Inventing America*. W. W. Norton & Company, 2003

Mancall, Jacqueline. *Measuring Student Information Use: A Guide for School Library Media Specialists*. Libraries Unlimited, 1983.

Moreau, Joseph. *School Book Nation: Conflicts Over American History Textbooks from the Civil War to the Present*. University of Michigan Press, 2008.

Murrow, Sonia and Robert Cohen. "Who's Afraid of Zinn?" *The Nation* (August 7, 2013).

Williams, Yohuru R. *Teaching U. S. History Beyond the Textbook: Six Investigative Strategies*. Corwin, 2008.

Zinn, Howard. *A People's History of the United States*. Harper Perennial, 1995.

Chapter 9

Inquiry and the Argument Curriculum

Part I: Argument Terms and Processes

Inquiry and Common Core: Argument Processes, Part 1

Daniel Callison

The cornerstone skills for writing found in the new Common Core State Standards (CCSS) are based on argumentation and debate. Information inquiry, the process of investigative information review, is the keystone for the archway connecting information evaluation to the argumentative writing skills of the secondary level common core writing standards.

Basic terms and related processes for information and evidence search processes will be outlined in this [article]. [The next article] will explore the discourse for arguments through dialogue and debate which allow for testing claims and evidence.

DEFINING ARGUMENT

Argument is the content necessary for the inquiry process to function. Inquiry is investigative. It is the reason for the information search processes that move teachers and students through data and resources for the most meaningful, relevant, current, and valid evidence so that convincing conclusions can be reached. Using this process effectively means that one understands not only the process, but also trusted authoritative resources. The results are mature information scientists with lifelong critical thinking skills.

The CCSS states,

> Arguments are used for many purposes—to change the reader's point of view, to bring about some action on the reader's part, or to ask the reader to accept the writer's explanation or evaluation of a concept, issue, or problem. An argument is a reasoned, logical way of demonstrating that the writer's position, belief, or conclusion is valid (2010, 23).

The CCSS identifies the role of argument across the curriculum:

"Inquiry and Common Core: Argument Processes, Part 1," by Daniel Callison, was published in *School Library Monthly* 29, no. 6 (March 2013): 20–22.

- In English language arts, students make claims about the worth or meaning of a literary work or works. They defend their interpretations or judgments with evidence from the text(s) about which they are writing.
- In history/social studies, students analyze evidence from multiple primary and secondary sources to advance a claim that is best supported by the evidence, and they argue for a historically or empirically situated interpretation.
- In science, students make claims in the form of statements or conclusions that answer questions or address problems. Using data in a scientifically acceptable form, students marshal evidence and draw on their understanding of scientific concepts to argue in support of their claims (2010, 23).

While CCSS lacks a full discussion of oral argumentation skills, a clear division between informational and explanatory writing skills is provided. Narrative and creative writing formats are left to teacher discretion. Such is not because of their lack of importance, but because of the attention that must be given to expanding and raising the level for argumentative communication across the curriculum and across all student, teacher and parent populations. CCSS puts particularly high emphasis on the student's ability to "write sound arguments on substantive topics and issues, as this ability is critical to college and career readiness" (2010, 24).

TEACHING ARGUMENT BASED ON TOULMIN

Most methods for teaching argumentative communication are based on the elements of argument as defined by British philosopher, Stephen Toulmin. George Hillocks, professor emeritus at the University of Chicago, has provided a recent application of these elements as they relate to teaching argumentative writing in grades 6–12 (2011). The Toulmin method states the following:

- Claim—A statement or proposal that you are asking others to accept. This information includes information you are asking others to accept as true.
- Grounds—Data, especially hard facts, along with reasoning behind the justification for accepting your claim. Proof of the expertise behind the data as well as comparison to other data that may be faulty should be considered.
- Warrant—A warrant links data and other grounds to a claim, legitimizing the claim by showing the grounds to be relevant. It attempts to answer why the data mean your claim is true (best, most likely to address a problem).
- Backing—Additional associated data and logic that add to the support of the key claim.
- Qualifier—Indication of the strength of the association between the data and the claim. May indicate the degree of the association between the claim and evidence in that the conclusion is usually or sometimes true.
- Rebuttal—Despite the careful construction of the argument, there may still be counter-arguments usually based on a counter set of data and/or varying interpretations of the same data. A rebuttal can include opposition to one piece of evidence or be a counter proposal with a different set of needs and conclusions from the claim you have offered (Toulmin 2003).

FOCUS FOR SCHOOL LIBRARIANS

The ability to define a claim, support the argument with warrants based on valid evidence, located through systematic literature reviews, parallels established information search methods. What school librarians need to add are:

- Methods for student generation of original data, and
- Exercises that truly test the value and validity of information as meaningful evidence.

STRATEGIES TO MANAGE INFORMATION, TIME, AND TOPIC CHOICE

In 2012, Carol C. Kuhlthau and her colleagues constructed a framework for guiding inquiry based on the steps of her Information Search Process (IPS) (Kuhlthau 1994). Inquiry, under their enhanced framework, is a collaborative, social process driven by immersion into the literature and sharing of information findings that lead to meaning through personal journals and a variety of group discussion sessions designed to document the conversations about and the greater understanding of knowledge discovered (Kuhlthau, Maniotes, and Caspari 2012). Their exercises help to build the information use skills needed for dealing with the massive amount of resources now facing any researcher—student or professional. This form of guided inquiry is valuable, but additional attention should be given to evaluating information as evidence if it is to fit into the CCSS argument skill set.

Kuhlthau's ISP is topic-driven. Learning success is measured by increased student understanding and completion of the assignment by utilizing a meaningful topic. While the process works well in the general search, selection, and assimilation of information, additional actions would need to be taken to establish an argument based on claims supported or rejected by relevance and quality of evidence. Therefore, the information search should go beyond the library and electronic resources as the student applies methods to gather original data.

Basic research skills that engage proper methods for observation, interviewing, surveying, and experimentation should be exercised so that the inquiry can be based not only on a search for established information, but also on new information relevant to key arguments. Student generation, application, and defense of original data are the skills related to argumentative writing that form the basis for success on the job and in college in the 21st century (Lunsford, Ruszkiewicz, and Walters 2007).

Because of the emphasis on the time demands and the emotional impact on the student to find a focus that can be managed successfully given usual school library resource limitations, Kuhlthau's interventions for guiding inquiry best meet these common core skills found across secondary grade levels:

CC6-8WH/SS/S/TS5—With some guidance and support from peers and adults, develop and strengthen writing as needed by planning, revising, editing, rewriting, or trying a new approach, focusing on how well purpose and audience have been addressed (2010).
CC9-10WH/SS/S/TS2b—Develop the topic with well-chosen, relevant, and sufficient facts, extended definitions, concrete details, quotations, or other information and examples appropriate to the audience's knowledge of the topic (2010).

STRATEGIES TO PLAN ARGUMENTATIVE LESSONS

The Stripling Inquiry Model is lesson-driven. Success is measured by lessons that meet teacher goals as well as the needs of the widest portion of the student population. Barbara Stripling of Syracuse University provides a collaborative blueprint for teachers and school librarians to work together in order to bring common multiple source assignments designed to engage students in the questioning processes for inquiry. When the lessons are based on exploration of controversial issues, Stripling's widely adopted lesson planning processes serve to support much of the CCSS (Stripling and Harada, 2012). The two most applicable skills are as follows:

CC9-10WH/SS/S/T8—Gather relevant information from multiple authoritative print and digital sources, using advanced searches effectively; assess the usefulness of each source in answering the research question; integrate information into the text selectively to maintain the flow of ideas, avoiding plagiarism and following a standard format for citation (2010).

CC9-10WH/SS/S/T7—Conduct short as well as more sustained research projects to answer a question (including self-generated questions) or solve a problem; narrow or broaden the inquiry when appropriate; synthesize multiple sources on the subject, demonstrating understanding of the subject under investigation (2010).

INFORMATION INQUIRY FOR TESTING EVIDENCE

Information inquiry is evidence-driven (Callison and Preddy 2006). Success is measured by growth in student abilities to assimilate or reject information as evidence. It is a continuous cycle that is powered by raising questions and exploring evidence to select the needed information. The student may be successful in this process by showing the inadequacies of evidence available and the problems in addressing certain issues or questions because the methods and means for establishing credible evidence are not possible.

Acting as "student information scientists," the data [that] students locate and generate in response to initial questions create new questions (Callison 2005). The authority and relevance of the evidence are constantly challenged. There is interaction between assimilating new information with held beliefs and testing new warrants for change. Inference of conclusions or problem-solving is triggered when new evidence is found to be relevant and valid.

The student operates as an information scientist by reflecting on the success or shortcomings of the search process as well as the quality or limitations of the evidence obtained. Further, the student as information scientist establishes a knowledge of the authoritativeness of various resources so that he/she can quickly counter arguments when necessary based on quality of data obtained. The inquiry is driven by the data—expanding, countering or narrowing as the evidence determines. Information Inquiry addresses these CCSS skills:

CC6-8WH/SS/S/TS9—Draw evidence from informational texts to support analysis, reflection, and research (2010).

CC9-10WH/SS/S/TS1a—Introduce precise claims(s), distinguish the claim(s) from alternate or opposing claims, and create an organization that establishes clear relationships among the claim(s), counterclaims, reasons, and evidence (2010).

CC6-8WH/SS/S/TS1c—Use words, phrases, and clauses to create cohesion and clarify the relationships among claim(s), counterclaims, reasons, and evidence (2010).

CC11-12WH/SS/S/TS2a—Introduce a topic and organize complex ideas, concepts, and information so that each new element builds on that which precedes it to create a unified whole; include formatting (e.g., headings), graphics (e.g., figures, tables), and multimedia when useful to aiding comprehension (2010).

A MULTITUDE OF POSSIBLE PROCESSES

Many information research models or processes are effective in helping to improve how students seek, manage, and present information. Each has strengths and an accepting audience.

In the hands of good instructional school librarians, nearly any of the models will provide an adequate learning agenda (Wolf, Brush, and Saye 2003).

For the CCSS argument skills, however, there is a need for more attention, time, and practice to be given to raising a claim, counterclaims, reasons, and linking evidence. Students need the time and learning environment within the library as a learning lab to experiment with arguments, counter arguments, validity of evidence found, and identification of additional evidence needed (Callison 2000). Conference rooms within the school library, when managed as an information learning lab, can provide the space for peer interactions and teacher guidance that lead to selection and use of the best evidence possible. It is also in the laboratory environment that students draft plans for surveys, observations, and interviews that will lead to original data.

REFERENCES

Callison, Daniel. "Inquiry, Literacy and the Learning Laboratory." In *New Millennium, New Horizons*, edited by Lyn Hay, Kylie Hanson, and James Henri, 55–64. Centre for Studies in Teacher Librarianship, 2000.

Callison, Daniel. "Student Information Scientist, Part I." *School Library Media Activities Monthly* 22, no. 2 (October 2005): 39–44.

Callison, Daniel and Leslie Preddy. *The Blue Book on Information Age Inquiry, Instruction, and Literacy.* Libraries Unlimited, 2006.

Common Core State Standards Initiative (CCSS). Common Core State Standards for English Arts & Literacy in History/Social Studies, Science, and Technical Subjects, Appendix A: Research supporting key elements of the standards. 2010. www.corestandards.org/assets/Appendix_A.pdf (accessed December 7, 2012).

Hillocks, George, Jr. *Teaching Argument Writing, Grades 6–12.* Heinemann, 2011.

Kuhlthau, Carol C. *Teaching the Library Research Process.* 2nd ed. The Center for Applied Research in Education. Scarecrow Press, 1994.

Kuhlthau, Carol C., Leslie K. Maniotes, and Ann K. Caspari. *Guided Inquiry Design.* Libraries Unlimited, 2012.

Lunsford, Andrea A., John J. Ruszkiewicz, and Keith Walters. *Everything's an Argument.* St. Martin's, 2007.

Stripling, Barbara K and Violet H. Harada. "Designing Learning Experiences for Deeper Understanding." *School Library Monthly* 29, no. 3 (December 2012): 5–12.

Toulmin, Stephen Edelston. *The Uses of Argument.* Updated edition. Cambridge University Press, 2003.

Wolf, S., T. Brush, and J. Saye. "The Big Six Information Skills as a Metacognitive Scaffold." *School Library Media Research* 6 (2003). http://www.ala.org/aasl/aaslpubsandjournals/slmrb/slmrcontents/volume62003/bigsixinformation (accessed December 7, 2012).

Part II: Discourse for Dialogue and Debate

Inquiry and Common Core: Argument Discourse for Dialogue and Debate, Part 2

Daniel Callison

The relationship of the Common Core State Standards (CCSS) in secondary level argumentation to basic principles for teaching and learning through inquiry is the focus of this two part series on Inquiry and the Common Core. Specifically, Part Two will explore discourse through dialogue and debate as techniques for students and teachers to test information as evidence when applied to the inquiry processes.

The following article, "Inquiry and Common Core: Argument Discourse for Dialogue and Debate, Part 2," by Daniel Callison, was published in *School Library Monthly* 29, no. 7 (April 2013): 21–23.

What is the impact, and what are the key challenges of the CCSS on school library services and inquiry-based programs? The terms were defined and multiple information search processes school librarians can employ in the support of argumentative writing were discussed in "Inquiry and Common Core: Argument Processes, Part 1" (See *SLM*, March 2013, 20–22, [**preceding article**].)

CCSS gives emphasis to argument over persuasion. "A logical argument . . . convinces the audience because of the perceived merit and reasonableness of the claims and proofs offered rather than either the emotions the writing evokes in the audience or the character or credentials of the writer." (CCSS, 2010, 24) This is at the core of Information Inquiry (Callison and Preddy 2006).

The level of participation by school librarians in collaborative planning and teaching of argumentative skills has yet to be fully explored. This two part summary, "Inquiry and Common Core," offers a start. The Utah Educational Network has organized an excellent set of resources on inquiry and argumentative writing that is helpful (see Additional Resources).

THE ARGUMENT CURRICULUM

Deanna Kuhn, professor of psychology and education at the Teachers College of Columbia University, has summarized her critical observations of student "inquiry" practice in public schools and makes a justification for moving the typical student research report to higher levels where reason, evidence, and inferences are challenged through debate practice (2005). Student presentations, Kuhn observes, are usually limited to uninformed opinion, evaluated on organization and neatness more than content, and seldom address issues that make much difference in the student's learning or life (2005).

Across the curriculum, not just in science courses, students should be challenged to practice logic and reason through an argument curriculum that is centered on a layer of skills and tied to curriculum topics. The basic exercises of generating reasons, elaborating on reasons, supporting reasons with evidence, developing reasons into arguments, examining and countering evidence, generating rebuttals, and making an informed conclusion all hold merit in all curricular areas.

Kuhn's definition of inquiry for national standards associated with science education has the following components:

- Identify questions that can be answered through scientific investigations.
- Design and conduct a scientific investigation.
- Use appropriate tools and techniques to gather, analyze, and interpret data.
- Develop descriptions, explanations, predictions, and models using evidence.
- Think critically and logically to make the relationships between evidence and explanations (2005, 40).

LIMITS OF INQUIRY

Information inquiry is driven by authentic learning (Callison and Lamb 2004). Students need to seek data and generate original data that is directly relevant to original questions. While questions might be modified for clarity and depth, there may be limitations to acquiring data and, therefore, many questions cannot be answered directly. Evidence has limitations. Whenever possible, investigative or inquiry projects should meet authentic learning standards and not be modified when information is sparse.

Learning the restrictions, limits, as well as the merits and depth of data is key to the argument curriculum. Students should journal, discuss, and document the weaknesses of data and evidence. They should identify faulty evidence, as well as the best, most relevant, and most useful or convincing. The goal is to learn both the merits and the limitations of data gathering methods. Inquiry will frequently not lead to complete answers.

THE BIAS CHALLENGE

Perhaps the biggest challenge in introducing argument skills is that human nature tends to reject new information that is counter to held beliefs. The argument process fails to generate learning unless students and teachers do not believe all that they read. Further, mature inquirers should read and view beyond what they already believe. Bias based on prior knowledge and a determination to find only evidence that justifies held beliefs is the strongest barrier to application of information inquiry.

Bias is the application of existing mental constructs to new information in such a way that the resulting judgment contains flawed reasoning (Fitzgerald 1999). While prior knowledge can provide positive elements that strengthen background understanding, widen the potential for new questions, and move the inquirer along to new areas of discovery, reasoning and critical thinking are hampered when open and free inquiry is not encouraged.

Fitzgerald's recommendations for engaging students in discussions and debates centered on issues, claims, and evidence can result in moving beyond standard argumentative compositions that explore only surface issues (1999). The following exercises can take place in the classroom or in the library learning laboratory with mature peers providing guidance along with teachers and school librarians. Students can,

- be taught to respond to signals and doubts that occur as they read. Examples of specific situations that often involve misinformation, such as fake Web sites, can be provided.
- find problems such as inconsistency or exaggeration in a short piece of curriculum-relevant text. These exercises should represent well-structured problems at first and progress to ill-structured problems as students become more skillful. School librarians can extend these classroom exercises when student are engaged in inquiry.
- practice formal argumentation, which involves the evaluation of information as potential evidence. They should also switch sides and argue opposite positions. Debates, mock trials, and mock or genuine editorials present excellent opportunities to apply argument skills.

Belief perseverance is a person's refusal or inability to relinquish a belief despite new information discrediting it. Confirmatory bias is often associated with belief perseverance. This occurs when an individual seeks information to support his or her held beliefs while ignoring information supporting opposing beliefs.

TYPES OF EVIDENCE

Not all evidence is of equal value or reliability. It is, therefore, necessary to understand authority, age, and context of data. These considerations can make a great difference for acceptance and application (Callison and Lamb 2006). Variances in evidence include, but are not limited to the following:

- Conventional Wisdom—is this a commonly held assumption, but may need verification, especially when such has been greatly influenced by political correctness?
- Corroborative—does this new evidence confirm or conform to previous evidence derived from similar cases or situations, and therefore strengthen the claim?

- Contextual or textual evidence—does this evidence fit into the situation being examined and have links to evidence found in multiple texts?
- Circumstantial—although not direct and tangible proof, does this evidence offer observations that help to give credence to the claim?
- Chained or Connected—does this evidence link to other pieces of evidence to help develop a case or a full warrant in support of the claim?
- Credible—is the evidence from an authoritative source, and how widely accepted is that authority? Is it believable evidence? Is it logical?
- Counter—is this evidence in direct opposition to previously gained evidence (or evidence held by the opposing side) and to what degree does it offer a new claim that is reasonable to consider?
- Consensus—does this evidence help to bridge various arguments so that common ground can be identified and a resolution agreed on by most parties involved?
- Convincing—is this information understandable and likely to be recognized as valuable by the audience being addressed?
- Critical—is this the "smoking gun" or the essential piece of evidence to make the argument conclusive?
- Cherry-picked—is this factual or information, usually an opinion, selected because it fits in the support of an argument, but has questionable validity or little relevance? (Callison and Lamb 2006, pages 373–376)

DISCOURSE FOR TESTING EVIDENCE

Students should test arguments, including claims, evidence, and inferences. Argument discourse can be organized within two processes that allow for an informal and formal engagement among students and teachers. Dialogue can provide a basis for initial discussions on a wide range of claims and potential merits and needs of selected evidence. Debates provide more structure centered on a specific proposition. Debate will also narrow the argument to a set of needs, a specific plan for change, and the resulting advantages or disadvantages from that change (Callison and Preddy 2006).

Initial exploration and discussion of issues may best be organized under dialogue with students free to express a wide range of questions, observations, and potential conclusions. Debate allows for a focused comparison of specific proposals and plans. The following compilation illustrates several selected differences between discourse management managed as dialogue or debate forums. Depending on the level and complexity of the assignment, these conference sessions enrich the argumentative writing process. See Table 1.

Table 1. Dialogue and Debate

Dialogue	Debate
Dialogue is collaborative; two or more sides work together toward common understanding.	Debate is oppositional: two sides oppose each other and attempt to prove each other wrong.
In dialogues, finding common ground is the goal.	In debate, winning is the goal.
In dialogue, one listens to the other side(s) in order to understand, find meaning, and find agreement.	In debate, one listens to the other side in order to find flaws and to counter its arguments.
Dialogue enlarges and possibly changes a participant's point-of-view.	Debate affirms a participant's own point-of-view.

(*continued*)

Table 1. Dialogue and Debate (*continued*)

Dialogue opens the possibility of reaching a better solution than any of the original solutions.	Debate defends one's own positions as the best solution and excludes other solutions.
An open-minded attitude; openness to change and to admit when one is wrong.	A closed-minded attitude; dogmatic determination to be right.
Treats communication as a relationship; in dialogue, one searches for basic agreement.	Treats communication as a transaction; in debate, one searches for glaring differences.
In dialogue, it is acceptable to change one's position.	In debate, it is a sign of weakness and defeat to change one's position.
Dialogue assumes that many people have pieces of the answer, and that together they can put them into a workable answer.	Debate assumes there is a right answer and that someone has it.
Dialogue complicates positions and issues.	Debate simplifies positions and issues.

Adapted from "Dialogue vs Debate" by Barry Winbolt, 2010 (http://www.barrywinbolt.com/wp-content/uploads /Dialogue-Handout.pdf) and also posted on the Common Tables Blog on July 26, 2008, "Dialogue vs Debate" adapted from a paper by Shelley Berman (http://www.nald.ca/library/learning/study/scdvd.htm).

REFERENCES

Callison, Daniel and Annette Lamb. "Authentic Learning." *School Library Media Activities Monthly* 21, no. 4 (December 2004): 34–39.

Callison, Daniel and Annette Lamb. "Evidence." In *The Blue Book on Information Age Inquiry, Instruction and Literacy,* edited by Daniel Callison and Leslie Preddy. Libraries Unlimited, 2006.

Callison, Daniel and Annette Lamb. "Table Part 3.2 The Capital Cs to Challenge Evidence." In *The Blue Book on Information Age Inquiry, Instruction and Literacy,* edited by Daniel Callison and Leslie Preddy. Libraries Unlimited, 2006.

Callison, Daniel and Leslie Preddy, eds. *The Blue Book on Information Age Inquiry, Instruction, and Literacy.* Libraries Unlimited, 2006.

Common Core State Standards Initiative (CCSS). Common Core State Standards for English Arts & Literacy in History/Social Studies, Science, and Technical Subjects, Appendix A: Research supporting key elements of the standards. 2010. www.corestandards.org/assets/Appendix_A.pdf (accessed January 15, 2013).

Common Tables Blog. http://commontablesblog.blogspot.com/2008/02/dialogue-vs-debate.html (accessed January 30, 2013).

Fitzgerald, Mary Ann. "Evaluating Information: An Information Literacy Challenge." *School Library [Media] Research* 2 (1999). http://www.ala.org/aasl/aaslpubsandjournals/slmrb/slmrcontents/volume21999 /vol2fitzgerald (accessed January 30, 2013).

Kuhn, Deanna. *Education for Thinking.* Harvard University Press, 2005.

Winbolt, Barry. "Dialogue vs Debate." 2010. http://www.barrywinbolt.com/2010/03/handout-dialogue -vs-debate (accessed January 15, 2013).

ADDITIONAL RESOURCE

Utah Education Network. Argumentative Writing. http://www.uen.org/core/languagearts/writing/argu ments.shtml http://www.uen.org/core/languagearts/writing/argumentative.shtml.

Chapter 10

Inquiry and Communication

Part I: Roles for Student Talk

Inquiry Roles for "Student Talk" in the Social Curriculum and the CCSS

Daniel Callison

"Student Talk" can be defined as a "social curriculum" in which the student is placed in a variety of problem-solving situations and must express him or herself in order to gain needed information and share information. In the social curriculum, students are evaluated on their interactive and interpersonal performances. In an information inquiry setting, students may also be judged on their abilities to place degrees of value on information. Their abilities to negotiate, speculate, and debate verbally and constructively are seen as primary skills (Callison 2006). In the social curriculum, "student talk" is honored as least as much as adult talk.

POWER OF CONVERSATION

Adults tend to use talk to think aloud, to tentatively explore the beginning of an idea, to hitchhike on what others have said, to clarify and modify their personal knowledge base, to affirm thoughts to others, and to acknowledge how they might continue to seek answers. However, as David Booth and Carol Thornley-Hall suggest in *Classroom Talk*, children traditionally have been rewarded for using talk in a much more structured, formal way, and only in a question-and-answer pattern directed by the teacher where hesitation and ambiguous responses are not valued (1991). And yet, knowledge development through personal questioning, uncertainty, and formative reflection are at the heart of inquiry discourse.

The common culminating standards in communication courses that measure speaking and writing abilities are the term paper, public address, and often an extended formal debate. Within these complex measures are expectations for the student to demonstrate skills in information gathering, analysis, synthesis, and use in order to make a convincing set of arguments to address a meaningful issue, solve a problem, and identify knowledge new to the student. The focus here, however, is on how information skills and critical inquiry are taught through roles students

"Inquiry Roles for 'Student Talk' in the Social Curriculum and the CCSS," by Daniel Callison, was published in *School Library Monthly* 30, no. 9 (May/June 2014): 17–20.

can play in social conversations. From these experiences they can move toward mastering the "smaller" talk through which they can practice and gain confidence in using their inquiring voice.

Writing provides a more lasting documentation of communication, while speaking is the immediate expression on emerging tasks and new information. Those early stages can be modeled and molded so that conversations can result in voicing needs and defining actions. While a final formal presentation can serve to present the student's inquiry findings, initial oral skills can be those that get the foundation laid and ambiguities addressed. The test at this level is "can the student play a constructive role to get things accomplished?" More responsibility given to students for engaging in conversations increases the possibilities of success at the higher levels of formal speaking.

THE SMALLER TALK STANDARDS FOR CONVERSATION

Studies and government reports foundational to the 2014 Common Core State Standards emphasize the value employers and academic instructors place on the social interactive skills students should master for future college and career success (NCES 1995). Academic evaluators from higher education tend to rank the ability to be a critical reviewer of arguments and information much higher than representatives from the business world do. All evaluating groups have given high marks to communication skills that help students succeed in group settings. Examples of highly rated skills include:

- Begin and end a conversation in an appropriate manner.
- Sustain topics and discussion and offer follow-up comments.
- Use humor when appropriate.
- Give and receive compliments gracefully.
- Possess confidence to approach and engage in conversation.
- Adapt to changes in audience characteristics.
- Deliver an impromptu or extemporaneous talk.
- Prepare and adapt communication style to the context and situation.
- Compose and deliver an informative speech.
- Allow others to express different views.
- Detect and evaluate bias and prejudice.
- Evaluate the relevance, adequacy, and appropriateness of evidence.
- Analyze assumptions, evidence, and conclusions of an argument.
- Choose appropriate and effective organizing methods for the message.
- Support arguments with relevant and adequate evidence.
- Manage conflict.
- Identify and use appropriate statistics to support the message.

Many of these more favored skills suggest the need for practicing a discourse etiquette that serves to support the speaker as he either delivers a formal presentation or deals with the interactions within a small group setting. Clearly, there are likely to be even more demands on the student who is expected to chair the small group discussion, as well as many meaningful roles to be played.

Common Core State Standards (CCSS) reflect many expectations for constructive communication and the behaviors students are expected to practice. Beginning at early grade levels, oral communication is a primary tool for establishing comprehension and collaboration. The elementary language arts standards are associated with the general goal that students will prepare for and participate effectively in a range of conversations and collaborations with diverse partners, building on others' ideas and expressing their own clearly and persuasively. Specifically:

CCSS.1.SL.1b Build on others' talk in conversations by responding to the comments of others through multiple exchanges.

CCSS.3.SL.1c Ask questions to check understanding of information presented, stay on topic, and link comments to the remarks of others.

Foundational to secondary school levels, students gain understanding of communication rules and roles and gain confidence as they take greater personal responsibility for constructive discourse:

- CCSS.ELA.Literacy.SL.6.1 Engage effectively in a range of collaborative discussions (one-on-one, in groups, and teacher-led) with diverse partners.
- CCSS.ELA.6.1b Follow rules for collegial discussions, set specific goals and deadlines, and define individual roles as needed.
- CCSS.ELA.6.1c Pose and respond to specific questions with elaboration and detail by making comments that contribute to the topic, text, or issue under discussion.
- CCSS.ELA.6.1d Review the key ideas expressed and demonstrate understanding of multiple perspectives through reflection and paraphrasing (CCSS 2010).

PRIMARY ROLES FOR COLLABORATION AND CONVERSATION

In her seminal book, *Seeking Meaning*, Carol Kuhlthau defined the roles of instructors, librarians, and students in various information seeking and instructional situations. Two key strategies she recommends for engaging students more deeply in their initial information search projects are for students to collaborate [work jointly with others] and to converse [talk about ideas for clarity and further questions] (2004).

Merging these two strategies, along with others, into the framework for guided inquiry, specific roles begin to emerge for students. "Collaboration enables students to try out ideas, raise questions, and hear other perspectives at various stages of the inquiry process" (Kuhlthau, Maniotes and Caspari 2007, 137). Furthermore, "Conversation enables students to articulate their thoughts, identify gaps, and clarify inconsistencies in the inquiry process" (Kuhlthau, Maniotes and Caspari 2007, 138).

Extracting from her dissertation findings, Leslie Maniotes describes the power of literature circles to provide a structure for students to engage in collaboration and conversation (2005). Roles emerge to help sustain student active participation. Such roles, best employed in small groups, can be shared and exchanged from day to day, depending on the needs of the inquiry projects. Functioning in "jobs" within the inquiry circle, students have a more concrete charge and greater understanding as to what they may contribute to the discussions:

Word Hunter: finds key words and definitions.
Evaluator: evaluates the source.
Messenger: summarizes big ideas and main points.
Quiz Kid: raises questions.
Connector: makes connections between self, texts, and the world.
Note Taker: takes specific notes on content.
Image Maker: creates a visual scheme of the ideas (flow charts, graphic organizer, drawings).
Interpreter: asks, "what does this mean?" and "why is this important?" (Kuhlthau, Maniotes and Caspari 2007, 43).

While the teacher and school librarian team may initiate the discussions and model the jobs, students should increase their responsibilities as they grow in their job experiences.

SECONDARY LEVEL ROLES FOR SMALL GROUP DISCUSSIONS

While the jobs Maniotes has created can be transferred to secondary school students, such tasks have been identified by John K. Brilhart in his classic text on *Effective Group Discussion* (1997). Summarized by James Payne (2001), educator and administrator at the Blue Valley Schools, Overland Park, KS, several of these overlap Maniotes, but also provide new responsibilities. Small groups will find that students will need to take on two or three of these roles. Teachers may play one or more of these roles as well, but, again, as students mature in their responsibilities, teachers should release the tasks and move to facilitate assessment of observed student performance. Secondary level students should also have input in the final assessment of group members and their degree of participation.

Payne lists the following ten discussion group task roles and their influence on group dynamics:

- Initiator: proposes new ideas, new goals, procedures, methods, solutions.
- Information Seeker: asks for facts, clarification, or information from other members; suggests that more information is needed before making a decision.
- Information Giver: offers facts and information, personal experiences, and evidence; the information must be relevant and accurate.
- Opinion Seeker: states own belief or opinion; expresses a judgment.
- Clarifier: elaborates on ideas expressed by another, often by giving an example, explanation, or illustration.
- Coordinator: clarifies relationships among facts, ideas, and suggestions; poses an integration of ideas and activities of two or more group members.
- Orienter: makes sure the group is focused on purpose or goal; defines position of the group, summarizes or suggests the direction of the discussion.
- Energizer: prods the group to greater activity or to a decision; stimulates activity; warns the group to act while there is still time.
- Procedure Developer: Offers suggestions for accomplishing ideas of others, or handles such tasks as seating arrangements, setting up the computers, handing out papers, making copies.
- Recorder: keeps written record on paper, word processing and database, chart or blackboard; serves as the group's "memory" (2001, 219).

To these roles another important inquiry role can be added: Information Scientist. Here students make higher level judgments as to

- the adequacy of information;
- patterns in information encountered and accepted or rejected; and
- identification of key experts relevant to the topics of discussion so that fellow students may explore more recourses focused through information searches tied to those experts.
- The students role playing as Information Scientists may also identify the central or core documents that all group members should read to provide a common basis for further discussions (Callison 2005).

Observing teachers, with performance checklists and rubrics, can score or rate student role playing and oral participation. Narrative assessments from those teachers for use in student records and journals might be similar to the following examples:

> *Katherine seemed open to many opinions and often vocally summarized how those different perspectives could be supporting as well as contradictory.*
> *Frank often asks for clarification on evidence presented and on several occasions described how the documentation found on the Internet was weak and unreliable.*

HIGHEST LEVEL ROLES

Brookfield and Preskill define discussion roles at the height of maturity, where democratic discourse can take place for compromise and moving forward on issues. Oral communication skills honed at this level feed speeches that can be not only informative, but, at times, inspirational. While students can aspire to these levels, these roles are intended for teachers who wish to apply critical inquiry methods to their teaching practices and profession:

- Appreciator: makes comments indicating how he/she found another's ideas interesting or useful.
- Active Listener: tries to paraphrase others' contributions to the conversation; "So what I hear you saying is . . . ," "If I understand you correctly you're suggesting that . . . ".
- Connector: attempts to show how participants' contributions are connected to each other.
- Devil's Advocate: listens carefully for any emerging consensus, then formulates and expresses a contrary view to broaden the discussion and bring in unconsidered perspectives.
- Evidence Assessor: listens for comments that generalize or make unsupported assertions, then asks for the evidence that supports the assertions being made; may place a value on various sources of evidence as to their level of relevance, authority, thoroughness, and currency.
- Speculator: introduces new ideas, new interpretations, and possible new lines of inquiry.
- Umpire: listens for judgmental comments that sound offensive, insulting, and demeaning.
- Underscorer: emphasizes the relevance, accuracy, or resonance of another person's comments, and underscores why those comments are so pertinent (Brookfield and Preskill 2005, 111).

REFERENCES

Booth, D. and C. Thornley-Hall. *Classroom Talk.* Heinemann, 1991.

Brilhart, J. K. *Effective Group Discussion.* 9th ed. William C. Brown, 1997.

Brookfield, S. D. and S. Preskill. *Discussion as a Way of Teaching.* Jossey-Bass, 2005.

Callison, D. "Student as Information Scientist." *School Library Monthly* 22, no. 2 (October 2005): 39–44.

Callison, D. "Student Talk." In *The Blue Book on Information Age Inquiry, Instruction, and Literacy,* 539–542. Libraries Unlimited, 2006.

Common Core State Standards Initiative. English Language Arts Standards >> Speaking & Listening >> Introduction. http://www.corestandards.org/ELA-Literacy/SL/introduction (accessed January 21, 2014).

Kuhlthau, C. C. *Seeking Meaning.* 2nd ed. Libraries Unlimited, 2004.

Maniotes, L. "The Transformative Power of Literary Third Space." Ph.D. dissertation. University of Colorado, Boulder, 2005.

National Center for Education Statistics (NCES). *National Assessment of College Student Learning: Identifying College Graduates' Essential Skills in Writing, Speech and Listening, and Critical Thinking.* U.S. Department of Education, Office of Educational Research and Improvement, 1995.

Payne, J. *Applications Communication for Personal and Professional Contexts.* Clark, 2001.

Part II: Controlled Critical Listening Skills from the CCSS

Controlled Critical Listening Skills from the CCSS

Daniel Callison

The United States Department of Education, led by Jones, et al., conducted a national study in 1995 to identify the skills college educators and leading employers most valued. Results of

"Controlled Critical Listening Skills from the CCSS," by Daniel Callison, was published in *School Library Monthly* 30, no. 6 (March 2014): 19–21.

this study were among the resources used to compile the recent Common Core State Standards (CCSS). Not surprisingly, abilities to critically analyze information, both presented and received, were among those most valued for college and career entry.

> Listening is an active process where the receiver of the messages selects various portions to seriously attend to or act upon. Since listening is a skill, it can be learned or improved upon in the educational process. Listening also requires individuals to concentrate or understand, and effectively evaluate messages. In order to make judgments about messages, listeners need to use their critical thinking abilities to reach decisions. Effective listeners search for main ideas and critical supporting points, develop a sense of empathy and an awareness of biases both on the part of the speaker and listener, and decide which parts of the message to concentrate on and retain as well as which to discard (U.S. Department of Education 1995,109).

The way a person listens to another will affect the type of relationship that will develop between the listener and the speaker (Egan 1970). An individual who listens in a superficial, closed, or solely critical way will develop a very different relationship than a person who listens closely with an open mind and is attentive and supportive to the speaker (Larson et al. 1978).

CCSS AND CONTROLLED CRITICAL LISTENING

Students mature in their listening skills similar to their growth in reading and selecting information critically from print and visual documents. Listening, however, has more complex responsibilities for students engaging with others (teachers, parents, and peers) in the exchange of information. Listening reaches its most effective levels when there is interaction among those involved in the communication exchange. Skills that take the learner beyond the reactive and active listening levels are reflected in the high school CCSS. Interaction means that good listeners not only comprehend, but also collaborate. Examples from the *Common Core Standards for English Language Arts* (CCSS ELA) for grades 11–12 include the following (and are similar across other grade levels):

- CCSS ELA—Literacy SL. 11-12.1 Initiate and participate effectively in a range of collaborative discussions (one-on-one, in groups, and teacher-led) with diverse partners on grades 11–12 topics, texts, and issues, building on others' ideas and expressing their own clearly and persuasively.
  - a. Come to discussions prepared, having read and researched material under study; explicitly draw on that preparation by referring to evidence from texts and other research on the topics or issues to stimulate a thoughtful, well-reasoned exchange of ideas.
  - b. Work with peers to promote civil, democratic discussions and decision-making; set clear goals and deadlines, and establish individual roles as needed.
  - c. Propel conversations by posing and responding to questions that probe reasoning and evidence; ensure a hearing for a full range of positions on a topic or issue; clarify, verify, or challenge ideas and conclusions; and promote divergent and creative perspectives.
  - d. Respond thoughtfully to diverse perspectives; synthesize comments, claims, and evidence made on all sides of an issue; resolve contradictions when possible; and determine what additional information or research is required to deepen the investigation or complete the task.
- CCSS ELA—Literacy SL. 11-12.2 Integrate multiple sources of information presented in diverse formats and media (e.g., visually, quantitatively, orally) in order to make informed decisions and solve problems, evaluating the credibility and accuracy of each source and noting any discrepancies among the data.
- CCSS ELA—Literacy SL. 11-12.3 Evaluate a speaker's point of view, reasoning, and use of evidence and rhetoric, assessing the stance, premises, links among ideas, word choice, points of emphasis, and tone used. (CCSS 2010).

MATURING TOWARD STUDENT LED DISCUSSIONS

The assumption in the standards is that students will mature in their critical listening skills beyond simply taking directions toward higher levels of communication for reaching compromise and collaboration with not only peers but with various groups. Reaching higher levels of listening requires developing patience as well as acute decision-making. It requires opportunities for students to lead critical discussions and not be limited to teacher-led review alone.

The mature information literate student can apply skills from the critical information search process through effective interview and cross examination of oral resources. Practicing these skills enhances the maturing student's ability to select information with a focused purpose. These are high level skills, challenging even for the best teachers to master, demonstrate, and fairly evaluate. While leaders in higher education value interactive listening skills, they tend to agree that mastering such are life-long endeavors, but introduction to these skills should be made in K–12 settings and repeat on through college (Jones et al. 1995).

Practice, observation, and evaluation of these skills should take place not only in the classroom, but also actively and frequently in the learning laboratory areas (group discussion) of the school library. Modern school information commons labs also encourage active communication in the experimental preparation and presentation of student produced media. The school librarian who manages a virtual learning commons may seek out content experts for students to listen to and interview (Loertscher et al. 2012).

Some local topics may draw in point-counterpoint debates for students to hear and ask follow-up questions. The role of the school librarian includes not only pulling together the speakers and making the media connections, but also working with the teachers to prepare students for listening to the debates and how to formulate meaningful questions. Controlling the interviews by being sure the students are prepared and have practiced listening, note taking, and questioning skills leads to more efficient time management and better results for gaining desired information (Callison and Preddy 2006).

BAD LISTENING, GOOD LISTENING

A popular guide to preparing students for the "real world" identifies the following bad listening habits:

- Pseudo-listening—pretending to listen
- Stage-hogging—talking more than listening
- Selective listening—listening to what interests us only
- Insulated listening—avoiding the unpleasant
- Defensive listening—taking offense at what's said
- Ambushing—exposing the speaker's weaknesses
- Insensitive listening—giving inappropriate responses (Hartel, et al. 1994, 197).

A recent text for managing organizational behavior provides a useful list of tips for practicing good listening, many of which can be identified and modeled within group discussion situations:

- Focus and commit to overcoming bad habits. Much of poor listening can be solved with understanding the benefits of good listening habits.
- Look at the person talking. This can confirm your interest. Staring, however, can cause tension.
- Control random thoughts. Daydreaming and preoccupation with other thoughts are common barriers to communication.

- Make supportive comments. Especially during informal communication, positive reactions such as "that's an important point" or "that's interesting, please give me details" can encourage more constructive exchanges.
- Find something being said in which you can take interest. This can lead to mutual understanding.
- Put yourself in the speaker's shoes. There's nothing like empathy to enhance listening.
- Sift and sort to stay on focus with the main ideas. Constantly look for key ideas. Active listening means that you will summarize such insights for confirmation from the speaker.
- Rephrase what you're hearing. Especially in larger group situations this can provide a "reality check" and confirm if everyone is "on the same page."
- Conquer your fear of silence. This can especially be a challenge for teachers as the need to talk and explain is irresistible, and may come just when the student is on the verge of attempting to explain his or her view.
- Don't judge prematurely. Give the speaker a chance to establish an argument and have the benefit of the doubt before digging deeper into the issue.
- Ask questions. Not only those you bring to the conversation, but practice follow-up questions that test understanding on the part of all parties involved.
- Seek details leading to consensus whenever possible. Sharp disagreements probably call for more formal debate between speakers who have the expertise to handle such verbal conflicts based on a controlled agenda and specific propositions (Baldwin et al. 2008).

One more element that can be added to this list is that talking less does not mean keeping absolutely silent, but simply listening more carefully, giving time for reflection and being open for others to speak (Callison 2006).

ELEMENTS FOR A LISTENING ASSESSMENT RUBRIC

Two educators from the University of Texas at Dallas, Dennis Kratz, dean of undergraduate studies and Abby Robinson Kratz, librarian, co-authored the guide, *Effective Listening Skills*. Their checklists for self-assessment and listening skills maintenance identify over twenty useful actions. Several are helpful for construction of assessment rubrics in situations where evaluation of the student's listening behavior should be more detailed than simply indicating if they paid attention or not. Paraphrased examples include:

- The student is able to adapt listening skills to fit different requirements of a listening situation.
- The student takes active steps to use feedback effectively in order to elicit honest and direct communication from others.
- The student is able to recognize and eliminate inner distractions to better focus on speakers.
- The student tends to listen for important content, rather than simply style.
- The student in listening situations that require decision-making strives for and maintains a balanced attitude in the use of critical thinking to assess the situation.
- The student asks open questions to speakers in order to draw on their knowledge and experience.
- The student asks more specific questions to gain details or to question validity of information presented.
- The student adopts a "ready to learn" attitude when listening to others.
- The student practices a concise and reliable system for note-taking.
- The student is a controlled critical listener, able to discern assertions from facts.
- The student listens empathically, enabling others to express their emotions in a nonthreatening, controlled atmosphere.
- The student participates in consensus building that helps enable discussion participants to move from feelings to positive action by helping them set and meet goals (Kratz and Kratz 1995).

REFERENCES

Baldwin, Timothy T. et al. *Managing Organizational Behavior.* McGraw-Hill, 2008.

Callison, Daniel. "Student-Talk." In *The Blue Book on Information Age Inquiry, Instruction, and Literacy* by Daniel Callison and Leslie Preddy, 530–542. Libraries Unlimited, 2006.

Common Core State Standards Initiative (CCSS). *Common Core State Standards for English Language Arts.* 2010. http://www.corestandards.org/ELA-Literacy/SL/11-12 (accessed November 3, 2013).

Egan, Gerard. *Encounter: Group Process for Interpersonal Growth.* Brooks and Cole, 1970.

Hartel, William C. et al. *Ready for the Real World.* Wadsworth, 1994.

Kratz, Dennis M. and Abby Robinson Kratz. *Effective Listening Skills.* McGraw Hill, 1995.

Larson, Carl, et al. *Assessing Functional Communication.* Speech Communication Association, 1978.

Loertscher, David, et al. *The Virtual Learning Commons.* Hi Willow, 2012.

U.S. Department of Education. Office of Educational Research and Improvement and National Center for Education Statistics. *National Assessment of College Student Learning* by Elizabeth A. Jones, et al. 1995.

Section IV

Additional Research Reviews

Chapter 11

Challenges and Opportunities for Collaboration, Expanded Roles, and Future Facilities

In 1983 the United States Department of Education published *A Nation at Risk*. In an immediate response published the next year, *Realities: Educational Reform in a Learning Society*, the American Library Association (1984) stated, in part:

- Good schools enable students to acquire and use knowledge, to experience and enjoy discovery and learning, to understand themselves and other people, to develop lifelong learning skills, and to function productively in a democratic society. Libraries are essential to each of these tasks.
- Librarians are teachers, and they serve both students and teachers.
- School libraries serve as learner-oriented laboratories which support, extend, and individualize the school's curriculum.

Prior to publication of *A Nation at Risk* and the ALA response, David V. Loertscher (1982) had defined a concrete model for the instructional role of the school library media specialist, describing a series of stages that lead to extensive interaction with teachers, administrators, and curriculum. Not only was this role presented as exciting and rewarding, but Loertscher warned that the positive acceptance and perception of the school media specialist by fellow teachers and administrators is crucial to the future existence of the school librarian as a professional. This new role involving higher levels of instruction was a revolution for future school library media programs.

That educational role, Callison contended (1986), centered on inquiry-based learning. Borrowing from popular science education literature (Victor 1974), Callison raised the following inquiry characteristics and elements (some recently modified) for a potentially successful library program immersed in inquiry project learning:

- Lessons are carefully and extensively planned by teaching teams, including the school librarian. As a teacher, the school media specialist should participate in student assessment.
- Efforts to establish inquiry should be focused so they are of depth and quality to encourage more teachers to engage in the process.
- Inquiry will likely involve individualized objectives for students within the same class, and students, as well as teachers and school librarians, should take part in the evaluation of student performance to reach those objectives.
- The processes of inquiry should be measured and valued.
- Teaching and learning are question-oriented, so both teachers and learners should engage in that activity.

- The teacher is a director or facilitator of learning and as a coach provides steps (scaffolding) for students to progress in their learning, including independent projects when the student is ready.
- Inquiry projects should not be regimented by time restrictions, but allowed to flow as much as possible to meet instructional needs. Some projects may run across the full semester.
- Students learn from each other by presenting results and peer reflection. Team or group interactions can be very powerful.
- End products should be shared with a variety of audiences, and the inquiry process should be reflected on and explained in such presentations.
- Inquiry can involve topics for individual students to explore across their academic career and may raise the complexity each year. Documenting and measuring success in inquiry, and the student's maturation in using information resources, can be an important part of the student's academic record and evidence of self-regulation of learning.

COLLABORATION: ARE WE ANY CLOSER?

Of all the needs raised in the national standards for school library media programs over the past three decades, collaboration has received the most attention, with the term appearing dozens of times in some standards (Callison 1999). Levels of collaboration have been suggested, but acceptance and practice of the highest roles, including collaborative teaching and student evaluation by librarians along with teachers, have consistently been welcomed more by administrators and classroom teachers than by school librarians themselves (Church 2010).

However, collaboration with teachers is a frequent topic in courses for certification of school media specialists, yet the topic of collaboration of teachers with school librarians is seldom discussed in teacher or school administrator certification courses (Latham et al. 2013). There are various definitions of collaboration in instruction, and until its full potential is made clear across educational roles, it will continue to lack effective implementation for a rich impact on inquiry-based learning.

Gary Hartzell (2012), a former principal and now retired from higher education at the University of Nebraska, Omaha, has argued for many years that studies that tend to support a collaborative teaching role for school librarians are unseen by school administrators. Publication of such studies in the journals that school administrators and board members read has never been frequent. Study results are usually presented at school librarian state and national meetings, without funding provided in the study budgets to have results presented at professional gatherings for administrators.

REEDUCATING PRINCIPALS ONLINE

When immersed in the online study of school library media programs, practicing and future principals tend to see the value of the teaching role of the school library media specialist, and most even begin to project how they will improve their support of school library programs (Levitov 2009). "In terms of responsibilities of the library media specialist, the administrators ranked the following as highly important: developing and maintaining a library media collection aligned to the curriculum, working collaboratively with teachers to meet learning objectives, and exhibiting strong people skills" (132).

Each of the online course participants in Levitov's study established a plan for future media center development. Among the changes many planned were the following:

- Develop Web sites to correlate information literacy, technology, core curriculum standards, and resources.
- Seek solutions to scheduling through discussions with the library media specialists and teachers.

- Launch new technology by placing it in the limelight of the library media center and in the hands of the library media specialist.
- Encourage the library media specialist to make presentations at staff meetings and become a staff developer for colleagues.
- Encourage as well as empower the library media specialist to become a member of leadership teams in the building and district (e.g., school improvement, technology, department committees, leadership teams, etc.).
- Emphasize the connection of the library to the overall academic plan of the school (2009, 128–129).

TIME ON TASK STUDIES

While at St. John's University, Nancy Everhart (2000) compiled a comprehensive review of studies that measured the time typical school library media specialists spent weekly on various tasks. Across these studies from 1978 to 1999, high school librarians typically reported spending 3.74 hours on instructional planning per week, and elementary school librarians averaged over one hour less, at 2.64 hours. Factors that tended to reduce the amount of time invested in instruction at elementary school levels included job assignments that required the school librarian to travel to two or more schools and schedules that brought classes into the media center on a fixed rather than a flexible schedule associated with learning activities. Everhart studied the impact of new technologies in automation and found that such advances did not seem to result in more school librarian time being invested in instructional development. Principals and school media specialists expressed the desire to give more time to instruction, but consistently, actual practice involved less than 8 percent of professional time being invested in such activities.

Over the fifteen years since Everhart completed her meta-review, several studies have been conducted in various states to seek evidence of the impact of the school librarian and school library program on student achievement. One factor measured from several perspectives has been the time school librarians devote to instruction. While examining these studies, Callison (2007a) posed the following questions:

- If we assume that library media centers work (Scholastic Research Foundation 2008), can we also assume that library media specialists work?
- Work at the right tasks?
- Work consistently and extensively on a professional basis?
- Work in the most effective and efficient ways to increase the quality of the learning and teaching environment?
- Work willingly in an effective instructional role?
- Or, are there many cases when the barrier to more time and attention for the instructional role rests with the resistance, unwillingness, and inability of the library media specialist, rather than with the reluctance of administrators to grant time, encouragement, and funding?

FINDINGS FROM STATEWIDE STUDIES

The statewide study completed in Illinois (Lance, Rodney, and Hamilton-Pennell 2005) compared the highest and lowest achieving schools surveyed in that state. Findings showed that in the highest student achieving schools, the professional (certified) library media personnel invested the following time associated with instruction:

- 50 percent more time identifying materials for teachers.
- 240 percent more time planning with teachers.
- 347 percent more time teaching with other teachers.

- 42 percent more time teaching information literacy to students.
- 115 percent more time providing in-service training to teachers.
- 65 percent more time motivating students to read.
- 90 percent more time serving on school academic committees.

Although it was not possible for the Illinois study to document the quality and effectiveness of the instructional time invested by library media specialists, these numbers strongly suggest that in learning environments, where many factors support higher student achievement, library media specialists are expected to, and frequently do, perform their instructional role.

Simply serving on an academic committee does not tell us the specific role, but further studies have shown school librarians as information technology leaders shaping information literacy curriculum. Based on the Illinois study, as well as numerous other state studies (Scholastic Research Foundation 2008), following are the key characteristics of a library media specialist who is active in instruction:

- A school leader who meets regularly with the principal.
- A program administrator who oversees a competent staff.
- An information navigator who selects and guides effective and efficient use of both print and nonprint resources.
- A technology facilitator who guides selection and use of online resources and other technologies.
- A collaborative teacher and learner in the planning and delivery of instruction.

A Wisconsin study (Smith 2006) reported that the typical library media specialist spent more time on tasks related to basic management of the library media center than on teaching and learning activities. Planning instructional units with other teachers was typically less than 3 percent of the weekly time investment, and teaching cooperatively with teachers was typically less than 7 percent. This pattern seemed to be consistent with all grade levels, although library media specialists in higher achieving secondary schools reported a much greater time investment in instructional roles than did those in lower achieving secondary schools.

The Wisconsin study concluded that along with other factors, the amount of library media specialist interaction with teachers and students has a positive correlation with skill performance at all grade levels. Actions of library media specialists who influenced instruction in a positive manner in the Wisconsin schools included

- regular meetings with the principal and other district administrators,
- service on building or district curriculum planning and management committees,
- attendance at faculty and staff meetings and professional development in-services, and
- regular meetings with library media colleagues in the district.

The most recent statewide study, as of this writing, is the Pennsylvania School Library Study, completed in 2011. Data gathered from nearly three hundred administrators clearly demonstrated that they placed their highest value on librarians who serve on key school committees, partner with teachers to design and teach units, offer professional development for teachers, and provide flexible access to the library (Biagini 2014).

ENGAGING STAKEHOLDERS, ADMINISTRATORS, AND COMMUNICATING RESULTS

The most impressive result of this study, however, may be not so much the findings that confirmed previous support of collaborative teaching efforts, but rather the management of the project so that the Pennsylvania State Legislature was involved in the funding and final reporting (Kachel 2014). Perhaps this outreach effort will break the communication barrier that has resulted in many conclusions and recommendations that support quality school library media programs not reaching important stakeholder groups. Meaningful progress here may lie more in improving communication to promote quality school library programs and correcting previous shortcomings to present understandable data to principals, superintendents, and members of school boards.

Successful advocacy for improvement of school library media services requires a greater understanding among stakeholders of the true possibilities when school library programs operate at their highest levels (Everhart and Mardis 2014; Levitov 2012).

DEFINING COLLABORATION AS A PROFESSIONAL DEVELOPMENT ROLE

Bob Grover, when at Emporia State University, was the editor of a pamphlet defining collaboration for the American Association of School Librarians (AASL) in 1996. The definitions developed by his committee hold true today:

> Cooperation is informal, with no commonly defined goals or planning effort: information is shared as needed. A library media specialist and teacher in a cooperative relationship work loosely together. Each works independently, but they come together briefly for mutual benefit. Coordination suggests a more formal working relationship and the understanding of missions. Some planning is required and more communication channels are established. In a library media program, the teacher and the library media specialist make arrangements to plan and teach a lesson or unit, and a closer relationship is therefore required. Collaboration is a much more prolonged and interdependent effort. Collaboration is a working relationship over a relatively long period of time. Collaboration requires shared goals, derived during the partnership. Roles are carefully defined, and more comprehensive planning is required.

The progression of moving librarians into more active, curricular roles through professional development has shown some promise (Montiel-Overall and Hernandez 2012), but retaining such teaching status among school librarians over time is extremely difficult. Librarians are faced with the demands of other duties that take them away from the teaching role, and many resist attending lesson planning and larger curriculum development opportunities unless they are invited for specific duties. Expectations that they will service more than one school and limited support staff are also reasons noted for lack of real instructional engagements.

THE PROGRESSION AS EDUCATOR

There is a long history of attempts to promote the school library media specialist as an effective educator. Following are some examples:

- Kay Vandergrift (1979): "The primary teaching role of the school media specialist is, by definition, that of a teacher of media. . . . Media specialists should take it as their special prerogative to see that students develop critical skills in the access, evaluation, selection, and use of all materials" (16).
- Lillian Wehmeyer (1984) identified extensive roles for library media specialists across all grade levels and in managing curriculum development at a districtwide level as well.
- Phillip Turner (1993), with Ann Marlow Rieding (Turner and Rieding 2003), developed instructional design and evaluation processes to support classroom teachers and to enhance the use of media to enrich student learning.

- Daniel Callison (1994) proposed expanding the teaching role to include implementation of a critical thinking curriculum, and school library media specialists taking a more active role in evaluating student work. If library media specialists do not take on such a role, students are less likely to view them as serious teaching participants. In 2006 Callison proposed that the role of instructional media specialist is one all educators should play, including classroom teachers as evaluators of information literacy, teamed with school librarians. Leadership roles can be performed by technology managers, media center managers, and/or district curriculum directors. Certification content is not as important as ability, creativity, and persistence.
- Barbara Stripling (2008) focused on the role of supporting inquiry-based teaching so that such methods are employed across all disciplines of the curriculum and justify their adoption in state-level and national curriculum plans.
- Blanche Woolls (2008) is a longtime advocate for library media specialists who manage resources and also manage education in collaboration with administrators.
- Marla McGhee and Barbara Jansen (2010) state: "Inherent to an effective library media program is a library media specialist who functions first and foremost as a partner in the planning for and teaching of national, state, and local curriculum standards" (41).
- Allison Zmuda and Vi Harada (2008b) reframed the library media specialist as a learning specialist. A portion of their proposed new job description follows:
  o In assessment and instruction (with students)
    - Provide instruction for individuals or small groups.
    - Work on short-term basis with targeted students.
    - Provide strategies for classroom teachers.
    - Provide instruction, using research-supported programs.
  o Curriculum, Assessment, and Instruction (with staff)
    - Serve on curriculum committees.
    - Assist in development of assessment instruments.
    - Hold collaborative planning sessions to develop lessons and strategies.
    - Participate in observation (teacher peer observations) for professional growth.
  o Program Development, Leadership, and Management
    - Work with teachers in conducting professional development.
    - Serve as a mentor to new teachers.
    - Work with special educators and serve on instructional support teams.
    - Lead study groups in review of professional publications.
    - Serve as a resource to allied professionals, parents, other community members (44).

More recent coplanning publications may help create a greater role for certified library media specialists as educators (Harada and Yoshina 2004, 2010; Abilock, Fontichiaro, and Harada 2012). These new books provide specific examples and cases in which media specialist roles are illustrated in terms of leaders who educate fellow teachers. They are team leaders, not just committee attenders, in professional development. They actively seek engagement in shaping student performance through shared assessment responsibilities.

Collaboration that is truly meaningful requires long-term commitment and resources many schools have yet to provide, or they have drawn back on these in recent years of budget decline. Progress has been difficult and frustrating.

TANGIBLE OPTIONS FOR COLLABORATION

Sometimes school librarians fail to understand that an extensive collaborative role does not have to be established with all teachers and at all times. To move to the levels of coplanning, coteaching, and even coassessment of student performance, school librarians may be focused on collaboration with selected teachers who share the same teaching credentials and academic discipline interests. Nonprint collection development seems to result in opportunities for stronger collaboration between school librarians and science teachers, and Michigan school librarians who supported stronger science achievement standards also tended to engage in collaborative instruction and professional development (Mardis 2007).

COLLABORATION CAN BE CHAOTIC

Certainly school librarians want to serve all areas of their schools' curricula, but the "chemistry" and interaction, or what Paula Montgomery (1991) identified as compatible cognitive style that may spark long-term projects, may only occur with a few active teaching colleagues who have a shared commitment to inquiry and literacy. Collaboration can be chaotic (Kimmel 2012), time-consuming, and frustrating, but professional relationships bonded through major inquiry presentations can be extremely rewarding in viewing the value of the school library program and in support of high student achievement.

Bush and Jones (2010) found through a Delphi Study of a small group of leading school library media practitioners that their highest ranked professional dispositions include collaborative teaching responsibilities that serve to promote critical and creative thinking.

MULTIDISCIPLINARY TEAMS

Kuhlthau (2010) has recommended instructional teams of three to guide inquiry at the levels that truly engage students. She describes the team composition as including a subject teacher, a school librarian, and a teacher from a special field such as art, reading, music, or drama. Callison (2006) has recommended that collaborative teams be led by instructional media specialists who have full teaching credentials and advanced technology skills. They should hold full certification in order to participate in student assessment in a meaningful way, and their evaluation should become part of the student's academic record. Teacher-certified school library media specialists should be qualified to manage independent inquiry projects and should seek that role frequently. They should coordinate student research portfolios and presentations of student inquiry projects in the community.

Mike Printz (Miller, Steinlage, and Printz 1994) developed collaborative teams including teaching members from various disciplines in order to initiate multidisciplinary curricular projects as early as the 1970s. More recent publications concerning the application of information literacy to cultural heritage draw on the expertise of teachers, historians, librarians, museum educators, and archivists working together to create inquiry environments beyond the schools (Baker 2013).

BECOME MORE AGGRESSIVE TO BE PROGRESSIVE

Carol Kearney (2000), an experienced supervisor of school media programs, has highlighted actions the progressive school media specialist needs to take for collaborative actions to begin. Among her recommendations are the following:

- Develop an understanding of the teacher's role: classroom teachers experience the same type of challenges that we do. Instead of complaining about the lack of understanding from your teachers, we should gain a better appreciation for the breadth of their daily responsibilities and provide them with service at the level where they are presently—at their point of need.
- Share ideas with teachers or provide informal staff development; these are important steps in the creation of rapport as well as a validation of your competence.

- Be proactive—do not wait for teachers to come to you. Extend yourself through a variety of approaches, including personal interactions and written communication. Target a group of teachers, a team, a grade level on which to concentrate the program. Provide information and resources for both their professional and their personal interests.
- Develop an understanding about how critical it is that students become information literate and why these standards should be integrated into the context of their instructional program.
- Broaden your base of support. Join school committees and sponsor after-school activities. Let people see you outside the library media center (76–77).

PLAY THE TECHNOLOGY CARD

Technology integration represents one of the strong skill sets held by many professional school librarians, and yet they fall short in transferring these abilities to leadership situations across the school, the district, and the community. Along with instructional development, the leading graduate program in school media education at Florida State University and its Center for Partnerships Advancing Library Media have concluded that the following three key areas need more emphasis and will lead to effective collaboration and leadership (Everhart, Mardis, and Johnston 2011, 15):

- Participating in technology-based assessment and services to enhance opportunities for all learners, especially those with special needs.
- Developing processes to systematically collect, manage, and assess the effectiveness of digital resources.
- Sharing their knowledge and advocating for technology with the profession and in the community.

An extensively funded study on enhancing collaboration, conducted through the University of Arizona, included the following statement in its conclusion (Montiel-Overall and Hernandez 2012, 17):

> Lastly, school library professionals should not overlook the fact that, despite years of teachers and librarian collaboration being promoted within the profession, some school librarians still have little experience collaborating with teachers or have not yet initiated or participated in any collaborative instruction with teachers. This situation should be a major cause for concern if the role of librarians as instructional partner is to be fully implemented, and efforts should be undertaken to ensure more uniformity in how teacher/librarian cooperation is carried out. Furthermore, school library professionals must recognize that they alone cannot implement collaborative endeavors without teachers. School librarians' colleagues in education must know about and, more importantly, agree to work with librarians as instructional partners if teacher/librarian cooperation is to be successful.

THE PROFESSIONAL LIBRARIAN IS IMPORTANT
REGARDLESS OF COUNTRY

In the most comprehensive review of studies concerning the impact of school libraries on learning, Dorothy Williams (2013) and her colleagues at Robert Gordon University in Aberdeen, Scotland, have drawn from over sixty state, national, and international studies from the past two decades to support the school library media specialist as an essential element in provision of a successful information literacy program. These findings include evidence of librarian impact on higher student performance across the curriculum and higher quality student work on information projects. Specifically, the full-time school librarian who is proactive and a leading manager can increase the quality of the inquiry learning program. The most successful school library programs include a professional school librarian who engages in services that include

- the availability of support staff to undertake routine tasks, enabling the librarian to initiate instructional, collaborative, and promotional activities as well as professional duties to support collection development;
- a library that supports physical and virtual access to resources in the library, classrooms, and at home, during school hours and beyond;
- an adequate physical and virtual collection that is current and diverse and supports the curriculum as well as appealing to students' leisure needs;
- networked technology to support information access and use, as well as knowledge building and dissemination;
- instruction that supports individual and curriculum needs of students and teachers, encompassing subject content, information literacy, and voluntary reading interests; and
- collaboration with teaching colleagues, senior management, librarian colleagues, and outside agencies, including central school library services, to ensure the most appropriate services are delivered in support of learning.

SCHOOL LIBRARIAN ATTITUDES

Of major importance are attributes and practices of the professional school librarian that will bring about meaningful information literacy and inquiry programming. In addition to content knowledge and technological savvy, a study of school library media specialists in New Jersey (Todd, Gordon, and Lu 2011) indicated that the following attitudes were common among the more successful school librarians:

- Being resilient.
- Being nonjudgmental with students and teachers.
- Building an atmosphere of open communication.
- Being willing to go the extra mile to be supportive of teaching and learning.
- Building a profile of the school library as an active learning center.
- Having high visibility as a teacher.
- Being sociable and accessible, inclusive and welcoming.
- Loving to learn and being a lifelong learner who wants to share and model learning.
- Being a leader and instructional innovator who is not afraid to take risks, be creative, and do what best serves learners of all ages.

HAVE WE MADE PROGRESS?

A little over four decades after Loertscher published his taxonomy, he continues to collaborate with others (Loertscher and Lewis 2013, 17) through the AASL to promote the teaching role of the school librarian. Many characteristics of this role now reflect the potential of teaching inquiry techniques that have been fortified through research. Following are selected examples from a list that school educators should examine in its entirety:

The school librarian fully certified to teach:

- Co-creates short research projects with classroom teachers that require students to use an inquiry process in both classroom and library learning commons to answer compelling questions.
- Provides students opportunities to share their research work with their peers and teachers using online collaborative media.

- Provides and uses the best information sources, primary sources, multimedia, and other resources that can be used with every learner no matter his or her literacy level, language competence, or learning style.
- Promotes the use of real learning experiences that engage learners in topics they can be passionate about during inquiry.
- Emphasizes the use of quality information and a sense of healthy skepticism as students encounter information sources, both in print and across the Internet.
- Stresses digital citizenship as an essential skill in the world of information and technology.
- Embeds the ideas of intellectual freedom as students encounter a wide range of opinions, cultural groups, organizations, and individuals during inquiry.
- Helps students consider a variety of ways their research can be shared with others.
- Helps students evaluate their own research by providing multiple self-assessment opportunities at various stages in the research process.
- Joins teachers and students in reflecting about inquiry projects so the group becomes more sophisticated over time (Loertscher and Lewis 2013, 17).

SOCIAL TECHNOLOGY, FLEXIBLE SPACES, AND INFORMATION COMMONS SHAPE THE FUTURE ROLE (RIGHT NOW)

Perhaps the most exciting aspect of the future collaborative teaching role of school library media specialists is that much of that role is being shaped by reinventing the school library media spaces and nonspaces in the digital age. Loertscher has provided forums and publications (Loertscher et al. 2011) that provide descriptions of tangible examples for the emerging new Learning Commons. This technology-driven facility format has been in place for over a decade in many academic library settings.

Functioning with movable furniture, compact technologies, and large spaces that can be reconfigured quickly to address learning needs, the Learning Commons is the new space that allows technology and learning to merge, along with strategic interventions from library information technology specialists and other teachers who accept the tech-savvy role (Loertscher et al. 2012).

The opportunities for further evolution in inquiry-based learning are tremendous. New collaborative learning associations can be constructed, both physically at school and virtually across unlimited environments, 24/7. The Open Commons is the experimental learning center of the school. Multiple learning functions can take place in this center (Horan 2014) at the same time, with changes in group composition and learning objects moving in sync with flexible schedules (Loertscher et al. 2011).

THE ICENTRE

Much of the current discussion about reinventing the school library media center comes from Australia (Lee and Finger 2010). Recent presentations by Lyn Hay from the education faculty of Charles Sturt University have served to convey and further define her concepts of the iCentre:

The iCentre is a high-end multimedia production facility which acts as the information-technology learning hub for a school. While it is the technology engine of a networked school connecting classrooms, specialist learning spaces, offices, corridors, homes and mobile devices to the wider networked world, it also provides the school community with a large, flexible learning space based on fluid design principles to support collaboration, performance, creativity, interactivity and exploration, both online and offline (Schibsted 2005). One would expect the layout of an iCentre to look different on a daily basis depending on the range of individual, small group, class-based, or whole year–or discipline-based activities it accommodates at any given time, that is, the form it takes reflects the function. (Hay 2010)

According to Hay (2010) the function and core business of an effective iCentre involve the following:

- A qualified team of information technology and learning experts whose knowledge, skills, and motivation support twenty-first-century learners with relevant, flexible, 24/7, customized information technology and learning services—in school, at home, and via mobile devices.
- Pedagogical fusion—bringing information, technology, people, and pedagogy together to support student learning, where pedagogy is central to all decision making, policy, and practice.
- The support of inquiry learning and immersive learning experiences utilizing a range of information and resources, without privileging one format over another, where inquiry is not an add-on to the curriculum—students learn content, skills, and values within the curriculum through inquiry based on the work of Kuhlthau, Caspari, and Maniotes (2007).
- The design of curricula that move students beyond information literacy to transliteracy, developing students as independent, informed digital citizens (Hamilton 2010).
- Supporting teachers to take risks as learning and technology innovators, where "nuts and bolts" technical support and learning design supports change in pedagogical practice.
- The provision of customized "i" support for students, teachers, school administrators, and parents (face-to-face and online support for all information, technology, and learning needs).
- The management of a research agenda within the school in which evidence-based practice, action research, and data-driven policy inform a substantial program of improved student learning outcomes, pedagogical growth, learning innovation, and continuous improvement (Todd 2009).

Hay and Todd (2010) coordinated online discussions involving leading educators and their vision of future school libraries. Their futuristic responses included the following:

- A facility that features fluid library design that allows for the customization and personalization of learning, in which space is iterative, agile, transitional, transformational, evolving, and shifting based on the needs of individuals, small groups, and whole classes.
- A blended learning environment that harnesses the potential of physical learning spaces and digital learning spaces to best meet the needs of students, teachers, and parents, in school, at home, or by mobile connectivity. Collaborations among students, teachers, teacher librarians, and specialist teachers are transformed beyond the confines of the school precinct and the traditional hours of operation.
- A learning center whose primary focus is on building capacity for critical engagement, giving emphasis to thinking creatively, critically, and reflectively with information in the process of building knowledge and understanding. It centers on asking meaningful questions that lead to substantive engagement with the inquiry in real-world problems; evaluating the quality of ideas in information sources; constructing and refining one's own ideas; examining claims and evidence, arguments, points of view, and perspectives; and interpreting and synthesizing ideas and representing them in appropriate ways using oral, written, and nonverbal communication, including multiple media and technologies.
- As a unique learning space, the school library is not just a center for information access and knowledge production, but also a center of learning innovation where teachers and teacher librarians are involved in creatively designing learning experiences by way of testing and experimenting with information and tools to bring about the best knowledge outcomes for students.

NEW BEHAVIORS DETERMINE NEW FACILITIES

In 2000 Callison participated in the Charles Sturt University online conference, "New Millennium, New Horizons." One of the papers (Callison 2000) was a proposal on the school library for the future as a learning laboratory for inquiry. Among other elements, Callison's descriptions included the most necessary teacher and student behaviors for the future virtual information literacy inquiry environment to become a reality:

- Actions of instructional media specialists and other teachers:
  - Model and engage in research with students, selecting questions they will explore along with the rest of the class.
  - Value and reinforce the processes of research over the product, as everyone needs time and support to explore.
  - Provide access to a wide variety of resources at various levels of sophistication and authority so that students grapple with determining value levels.
  - Listen to, observe, and reflect on student information needs, performance, and revisions to improve inquiry engagements and environments.
  - Intervene and discuss alternatives at point of need to help students hypothesize and test their assumptions.
  - Give time to inquiry process tasks and issues as well as to products and presentations.
- Actions of students:
  - Work in and be rewarded for team and cooperative efforts, but ultimately display individual initiative to continue similar investigations beyond that given as the academic exercise.
  - Plan and demonstrate ways to verify, extend, organize, and/or discard ideas, information, and resources.
  - Express ideas in a variety of ways, including personal journals, talking or reporting out, drawing, graphing, and charting.
  - Link information to evidence and share information and leads to information with classmates; express appreciation to those who help and acknowledge them in final products.
  - Communicate their level of understanding of concepts that they have developed to date.
  - Ask questions that lead to investigations, generating and redefining further questions and ideas.
  - Observe carefully and make connections to previously held ideas.
  - Accept, create, and use quality indicators to assess their work.
  - Reflect on their work with peers and teacher-mentors.
  - Predict search strategies and resources that are most likely to be relevant in other information need situations.
- Displays, bulletin boards, classroom and hallway wall charts, Web sites
  - are maintained by students who display individual and group work on the information search and use processes;
  - show student products and describe the actions taken to produce them, including information selection, contacts with experts, and scripting the final presentation;
  - are archived for future student researchers to examine and thus provide a jump start on ideas and directions;
  - display student work in the library media center, across the curriculum, and in spaces provided in hallways and classrooms to illustrate student research projects;
  - are readily available to parents at any time, but clearly on display at parent visitations and school open house events;
  - are viewed and examined by many instructional media specialists and peer teachers for ideas and information literacy lesson sharing; and
  - are part of the annual review process for evaluation of school library media services and instructional library media specialist performance.

- Furniture, space, computers, and other tools:
  - o There is space so inquirers may spread out resources, paper materials, and plans for outlines or storyboards as well as having access to terminals networked to a variety of design tools and information databases.
  - o Connections are provided to databases and resources beyond those held by the school.
  - o Connection to human resources is facilitated through telecommunications and a resource guide maintained by instructional media center staff.
  - o Portals are created so students may view and critique peer work on drafts and test sites and can share information leads or specific evidence.
  - o Quick electronic cut and paste can be used to experiment with a variety of ways to display information and data, but is used less and less often to copy materials as the inquirers mature in their process skills.
  - o There are production and presentation areas so students can experiment across all stages of the information search and use processes.
  - o Various audiences have access to student projects at process and product levels.

BACK TO THE FUTURE: THE FOUNDATION OF THE EVOLUTION

In 1972 I was a first-year senior high school library media specialist. As an experienced teacher, I was certified in speech, history, and English. Seeking the opportunity to work with teachers, I often proposed ways that the school library program could be a leader in multidisciplinary curriculum development if we had the adequate space and technology.

This was prior to any computer being introduced into my school. We had received some national attention because of our experimental program in film production with art and English teachers. We found that parents appreciated the finished student film productions much more when they learned of the vast decision making behind each short production: storyboarding, costuming, scripting, staging, rehearsing, editing, and re-editing based on peer feedback. In other words, we found that parents appreciated the student product much more when they understood the process.

Facilities for media production associated with the school library media center were rare. As an aspiring school media specialist, I admired futuristic ideas I found in publications for emerging school library media associations. Kenneth Taylor from Wisconsin published his article on creative inquiry in 1972. His ideas then helped me dream of possibilities. Today his ideas take us back to the future and help us reflect on possibilities, mostly on ideas in the technologies of inquiry-based learning now becoming reality. Following are selected comments from Taylor's article, published in the first issue of *School Media Quarterly*:

Under what conditions or in what situations does creative inquiry occur? It is proposed that at least four are needed by students for success in this process. The first condition is opportunity for mastery of established knowledge and traditional procedures for discovering new knowledge. . . . A second condition for creative inquiry is independence, with opportunity for elected solitude when required. On occasion, an individual student may wish to use the community as his laboratory to explore problems of contemporary interest or may find it necessary, in the school, to be alone to relate experiences of others to his own ideas and experience. . . . A third condition for creative inquiry is the sharing of one's ideas with his peers, a condition closely related to the need for independence. . . . The fourth condition for creative inquiry is individualized consultation with and assistance from one or more experts who are knowledgeable about and have had experience with the problem under investigation. (21–22)

The four conditions for creative inquiry require four kinds of facilities in which media are used for differing purposes: (1) facilities for large group instruction, including classrooms

Table 1. A Rubric for Places of Inquiry, Exploration, Conversation, and Discovery

Basic 0 – 1 – 2 – 3	Progressive 4 – 5 – 6 – 7	Exemplary 8 – 9 - 10
Questioning: Students are encouraged to raise questions in school.	Relevant student questions are captured and displayed in written assignments, posters, bulletin boards, Web sites, and other school and library media center locations. Space is provided in the school and community to display the processes and products of student and teacher inquiry.	Space and time, in classrooms and media center facilities, are given for student and teacher discussions and debate concerning the most relevant questions for authentic learning matched to the needs and interests of the learners and teachers involved.
Exploration: Students have access to current and relevant resources in school.	Student and teacher access to current and relevant resources extends beyond the school to a community of experts and guided, informed, and open access to electronic documents.	The school library media center functions as an information network hub and facilitates links to community agencies, museums, archives, other libraries, human experts, and electronic discussions both locally and worldwide.
Assimilation: A school library media center is accepted and operated as a core location for relevant resources.	The concept of considering the merits of ideas and information is central to learning in all functional areas of the school, with multiple resources and technologies readily available in the classroom as well as the school library.	Students and teachers openly display acceptance or rejection of information resulting from the exploration of resources through open critical literacy discussion groups, school and public posters and displays, Web sites, and audio/video-casts.
Inference: Investments in the school library media center are viewed as investments in quality learning and teaching.	The access and open use of information is accepted as a concept across the school more so than in a specific place.	Multiple locations are provided in the school and community in which learners may apply, in a consultative manner, information addressing personal needs, academic and workplace needs, and social action.
Reflection: Revision, renovation, and evaluation of the school media center facility and collection are serious and regular activities in which key stakeholders participate extensively.	Teachers and learners judge the educational environment in terms of quality of information access and support for information examination to select the best information possible.	Information access and use are evaluated in terms of how they lead to improving the common good for the local educational learning environment and local community.

and laboratories, in which mastery of established knowledge and traditional procedures are gained; (2) facilities for independent activities in which students explore media, generate personal ideas, and plan communications in settings free from distraction; (3) facilities for conference and committee interaction for expert assistance and peer assessment of ideas and original media; and (4) facilities for producing original communications via any desired form of media. It is implicit that facilities for all conditions be found in and outside the Instructional Media Center core. (24)

EVALUATION CRITERIA IN A RUBRIC FOR PLANNING PLACES FOR INQUIRY

Now consider future school library media centers, some already emerging with wireless capabilities and growing multimedia production spaces. These may be technology-based work centers, along with team-project spaces, spreading into square footage left vacant by shelves formerly needed for print resources. These new centers have been weeded deeply and selectively. Many future media center collections will provide electronic access to a wider array of nonfiction resources in support of national standards emphasizing complex reading practices.

In 2006 Callison and Preddy offered the rubric in table 1 as a means to measure the progression toward learning spaces that support inquiry. It was reprinted in 2007 (Callison 2007b) and is offered here again as a foundation on which futuristic planners can construct new visions for school library media centers as Virtual-I-tech-no-plexes, or whatever titles best suit environments for Taylor's creative inquiry. This rubric is based on the five common elements found in information inquiry (Callison and Tilley 2006).

A RUBRIC FOR EVALUATING THE TEACHER OF INQUIRY

The rubric for evaluation of the professional educator acting as instructional media specialist and teacher of inquiry shown in table 2 is based on Loertscher's (1982) taxonomy of school library media programs, moving from reactive service to higher levels of interaction and leadership.

Table 2. The Professional as Instructional Media Specialist and Teacher of Inquiry

Basic 0 – 1 – 2 – 3	Progressive 4 – 5 – 6 – 7	Exemplary 8 – 9 – 10
Questioning: Reacts to student questions by locating relevant resources.	Proactive to extend and elaborate on student questions and helps cluster them by relationships of importance to need and task.	Interactive, listening and responding to others to model and guide through extending and grouping of questions for focused inquiry leading to a meaningful investigation.
Exploration: Reacts to information needs through locally owned resources.	Proactive to extend and elaborate on the search for relevant information in various media in and out of the school.	Interactive, learning and sharing with others to examine closely the merits of resources and evidence discovered.

(continued)

Table 2. The Professional as Instructional Media Specialist and Teacher of Inquiry (*continued*)

Assimilation: Reacts to supporting curriculum as designed by others.	Proactive to experiment within the standard curriculum and capitalize on local relevant resources.	Interactive, testing and experimenting to accept or reject teaching methods and techniques that change the curriculum in order to address diverse student needs.
Inference: Reacts to application of information for learning within established curriculum.	Proactive to enrich the standard curriculum with access to many new and relevant resources.	Interactive, proposing and defending to establish new curriculum that will best allow for effective use of technologies and resources.
Reflection: Reacts to review and evaluation of routine curriculum led by others.	Proactive to revise routine curriculum to fit needs of local learners.	Interactive, visible and responsive as a respected leader and educator, to provide evidence of successful student and teacher achievements. Promotes curriculum constructed to help students and educators practice effective and ethical use of information.

REFERENCES

Abilock, D., K. Fontichiaro, and V. H. Harada. 2012. *Growing Schools: Librarians and Professional Developers.* Santa Barbara, CA: Libraries Unlimited.

American Library Association, Task Force on Excellence in Education. 1984. *Realities: Educational Reform in a Learning Society.* Chicago: ALA.

Baker, K. 2013. *Information Literacy and Cultural Heritage: Developing a Model for Lifelong Learning.* Oxford: Chandos.

Biagini, M. K. 2014. "The Pennsylvania Story: Lessons Learned." *School Library Monthly* 30, no. 5 (February): 5–7.

Bush, G., and J. L. Jones. 2010. "Exploration to Identify Professional Dispositions of School Librarians." *School Library Research* 13. http://www.ala.org/aasl/sites/ala.org.aasl/files/content/aaslpubsandjourn als/slr/vol13/SLR_ExplorationtoIdentify.pdf (accessed March 1, 2014).

Callison, D. 1986. "School Library Media Programs & Free Inquiry Learning." *School Library Journal* 32, no. 6 (February): 20–24. Reprinted in *School Library Journal's Best,* compiled by M. L. Miller and T. W. Downen and edited by L. N. Gerhardt. New York: Neal-Schuman, 1997.

Callison, D. 1994. "Expanding the Evaluation Role in the Critical-Thinking Curriculum." In *Assessment and the School Library Media Center,* edited by C. C. Kuhlthau, 43–58. Englewood, CO: Libraries Unlimited.

Callison, D. 1999. "Collaboration." *School Library Monthly* 15, no.5 (January): 38–40.

Callison, D. 2000. "Inquiry, Literacy and the Learning Laboratory." In *New Millennium and New Horizons: Information Services in Schools,* edited by L. Hay, K. Hanson, and J. Henri, 55–64. New South Wales, Victoria, Australia: Online Conference Proceedings for the Centre for Studies in Teacher Librarianship, Charles Sturt University.

Callison, D. 2006. "The Instructional Media Specialist: A Role for All Inquiry Educators." In *The Blue Book on Information Age Inquiry, Instruction and Literacy,* by D. Callison and L. Preddy, 146–169. Westport, CT: Libraries Unlimited.

Callison, D. 2007a. "Data on the Instructional Role of the Library Media Specialist—Are Schools Getting Their Money's Worth?" *School Library Monthly* 23, no. 10 (June): 55–58.

Callison, D. 2007b. "Evaluation Criteria for the Places of Learning." *Knowledge Quest* 35, no. 2 (January/February): 4–9.

Callison, D., and L. Preddy. 2006. *The Blue Book on Information Age Inquiry, Instruction and Literacy*. Westport, CT: Libraries Unlimited.

Callison, D., and C. L. Tilley. 2006. "Information Literacy, Media Literacy, and Information Fluency." In *The Blue Book on Information Age Inquiry, Instruction and Literacy*, by D. Callison and L. Preddy, 69–84. Westport, CT: Libraries Unlimited.

Church, A. P. 2010. "Secondary School Principals' Perception of the School Librarian's Instructional Role." *School Library Research* 13. http://www.ala.org/aasl/sites/ala.org.aasl/files/content/aaslpubs andjournals/slr/vol13/SLR_SecondarySchool_V13.pdf (accessed February 9, 2014).

Everhart, N. L. 2000. "School Library Media Specialists' Use of Time: A Review of the Research." *School Libraries Worldwide* 6, no. 1: 53–65.

Everhart, N., and M. A. Mardis. 2014. "What Do Stakeholders Know about School Library Programs? Results of a Focus Group Evaluation." *School Library Research* 17. http://www.ala.org/aasl/slr/vol.ume17 /everhart-mardis (accessed June 16, 2014).

Everhart, N., M. A. Mardis, and M. Johnston. 2011. "National Board Certified School Librarians' Leadership in Technology Integration: Results of a National Survey." *School Library Research* 14. http://www .ala.org/aasl/sites/ala.org.aasl/files/content/aaslpubsandjournals/slr/vol14/SLR_NationalBoard Certified_V14.pdf (accessed March 11, 2014).

Everhart, N. L., and F. J. Harris. 2002. "Using Primary Sources and Creative Writing to Teach Middle School History." *Knowledge Quest* 31, no. 2 (November/December): 52–54.

Grover, R. 1996. *Collaboration*. Lessons Learned Series. Chicago: American Association of School Librarians.

Hamilton, B. J. 2010. "Reading and Writing the World: School Libraries as Sponsors of Transliteracy." Paper presented at Information Fluency Literacy for Life, Conference for Computers in Libraries, Arlington, VA, April 12–14.

Harada, V., and J. M. Yoshina. 2004. *Inquiry Learning through Librarian-Teacher Partnerships*. Worthington, OH: Linworth.

Harada, V., and J. M. Yoshina. 2010. *Assessing for Learning: Librarians and Teachers as Partners*. Westport, CT: Libraries Unlimited.

Hartzell, G. 2012. "Why Doesn't School Library Impact Research Have More Influence on School Leaders?" *Library Media Connection* (October). http://www.librarymediaconnection.com/pdf/lmc/reviews _and_articles/featured_articles/Hartzell_October2012.pdf (accessed March 4, 2014).

Hay, L. 2010. "Shift Happens: It's Time to Rethink, Rebuild, and Rebrand." *Access* 24, no. 4. http://www .asla.org.au/publications/access/access-commentaries/shift-happens.aspx (accessed March 29, 2014).

Hay, L., and R. J. Todd. 2010. "A Report of the School Libraries 21C Online Discussion." NSW Department of Education and Training. http://theunquietlibrarian.wordpress.com/2010/04/12/reading -and-writing-the-world-school-libraries-as-sponsors-of-transliteracy-cil-2010/ (accessed March 24, 2014).

Horan, T. 2014. "How to Start Your School Library Writing Center." *School Library Monthly* 31, no. 1 (September-October): 8-10. Kachel, D. E. 2014. "Communicating with Legislators." *School Library Monthly* 30, no. 5 (February): 8–10 (accessed March 1, 2014).

Kearney, C. A. 2000. *Curriculum Partner: Redefining the Role of the Library Media Specialist*. Westport, CT: Greenwood.

Kimmel, S. C. 2012. "Collaboration as School Reform: Are There Patterns in the Chaos of Planning with Teachers?" *School Library Research* 15. http://www.ala.org/aasl/sites/ala.org.aasl/files/content/aasl pubsandjournals/slr/vol15/SLR_Collaboration_as_School_Reform_V15.pdf (accessed February 28, 2014).

Kuhlthau, C. C. 2010. "Guided Inquiry: School Libraries in the 21st Century." *School Libraries Worldwide* 16, no. 1: 17–28. https://comminfo.rutgers.edu/~kuhlthau/docs/GI-School-Librarians-in-the-21-Century .pdf (accessed February 28, 2014).

Kuhlthau, C. C., A. K. Caspari, and L. K. Maniotes. 2007. *Guided Inquiry: Learning in the 21st Century*. Libraries Unlimited.

Lance, K. C., M. J. Rodney, and C. Hamilton-Pennell. 2005. *Powerful Libraries Make Powerful Librarians: The Illinois Study.* Canton: Illinois School Library Media Association.

Latham, D., et al. 2013. "Preparing Teachers and Librarians to Collaborate to Teach 21st Century Skills: Views of LIS and Education Faculty." *School Library Research* 16. http://www.ala.org/aasl/sites/ala.org .aasl/files/content/aaslpubsandjournals/slr/vol16/SLR_PreparingTeachersLibrarianstoCollaborate _V16.pdf (accessed March 6, 2013).

Lee, M., and G. Finger, eds. 2010. *Developing a Networked School Community: A Guide to Realizing the Vision.* Victoria, Australia: ACER.

Levitov, D. D. 2009. "Perspectives of School Administrators related to School Library Media Programs after Participating in an Online Course, 'School Library Advocacy for Administrators'." PhD diss., University of Missouri, Columbia.

Levitov, D. D. 2012. *Activism and the School Librarian: Tools for Advocacy and Survival.* Santa Barbara, CA: Libraries Unlimited.

Loertscher, D. V. 1982. "The Second Revolution: A Taxonomy for the 1980s." *Wilson Library Bulletin* 56 (February): 415–421.

Loertscher, D. V., and K. R. Lewis. 2013. "Implementing the Common Core State Standards." AASL and Achieve Project. http://www.achieve.org/files/CCSSLibrariansBrief-FINAL.pdf (accessed March 29, 2014).

Loertscher, D. V., et al. 2011. *The New Learning Commons: Where Learners Win from Reinventing School Libraries and Computer Labs.* Salt Lake City, UT: Hi Willow Research and Publishing.

Loertscher, D. V., et al. 2012. *The Virtual Learning Commons.* Salt Lake City, UT: Hi Willow Research and Publishing.

Mardis, M. 2007. "Collection and Collaboration: Science in Michigan Middle School Media Centers." *School Library Research* 10. http://www.ala.org/aasl/aaslpubsandjournals/slmrb/slmrcontents /volume10/mardis_collectionandcollaboration (accessed February 28, 2014).

McGhee, M. W., and B. A. Jansen. 2010. *The Principal's Guide to a Powerful Library Media Program.* Worthington, OH: Linworth.

Miller, L., T. Steinlage, and M. Printz. 1994. *Cultural Cobblestones: Teaching Cultural Diversity.* Metuchen, NJ: Scarecrow.

Montgomery, P. K. 1991. "Cognitive Style and the Level of Cooperation between the Library Media Specialist and Classroom Teacher." *School Library Media Quarterly* 19, no. 3 (Spring). http://www.ala.org /aasl/aaslpubsandjournals/slmrb/editorschoiceb/infopower/slctmontgomery (accessed February 28, 2014).

Montiel-Overall, P., and A. C. R. Herandez. 2012. "The Effect of Professional Development on Teacher and Librarian Collaboration." *School Library Research* 15. http://www.ala.org/aasl/sites/ala.org.aasl /files/content/aaslpubsandjournals/slr/vol15/SLR_EffectofPDonCollaboration_V15.pdf (accessed March 21, 2014).

National Commission on Excellence in Education. 1983. *A Nation at Risk: The Imperative for Educational Reform.* Washington, DC: United States Department of Education.

Pennsylvania State Board of Education. 2011. "Pennsylvania School Library Study." Ad Hoc Committee on School Libraries, M. Phillips, Chair. http://www.psla.org/assets/Documents/Publications/Board-of -Ed-Report/School-Library-Study-FINAL.pdf (accessed March 1, 2014).

Pitts, J. M. 1994. "Personal Understandings and Mental Models of Information: A Qualitative Study of Factors Associated with the Information Seeking and Use of Adolescents." PhD diss., Florida State University.

Schibsted, E. 2005. "Way beyond the Fuddy-Duddy: Good Things Happen When the Library Is a Place Kids Want to Be." *Edutopia Magazine* (October). http://www.edutopia.org/design (accessed February 19, 2015).

Scholastic Research Foundation. 2008. *School Libraries Work.* 3rd ed. http://www.scholastic.com/content /collateral_resources/pdf/s/slw3_2008.pdf (accessed March 1, 2014).

Shannon, D. 2002. "The Education and Competencies of School Library Media Specialists." *School Library Research* 5 (2002). http://www.ala.org/aasl/aaslpubsandjournals/slmrb/slmrcontents/volume52002 /shannon (accessed March 2, 2014).

Smith, E. G. 2006. *Student Learning through Wisconsin School Library Media Centers.* Madison: Wisconsin Department of Public Instruction.

Stripling, B. K. 2008. "Inquiry-based Teaching and Learning: The Role of the Library Media Specialist." *School Library Monthly* 25, no. 1 (September): 2.

Taylor, K. I. 1972. "Creative Inquiry and Instructional Media." *School Media Quarterly* (Fall): 18–26.

Todd, R. J. 2009. "School Librarianship and Evidence Based Practice: Progress, Perspectives, and Challenges." *Evidence Based Library and Information Practice.* 4, no. 2. https://ejournals.library.ualberta.ca/index.php/EBLIP/article/view/4637 (accessed March 29, 2014).

Todd, R. J., C. A. Gordon, and Y. Lu. 2011. *One Common Goal: Student Learning; Report of Findings and Recommendations of the New Jersey Survey Phase 2.* New Brunswick, NJ: CISSL.

Turner, P. 1993. *Helping Teachers Teach: A School Library Media Specialist's Role.* Englewood, CO: Libraries Unlimited.

Turner, P., and A. M. Rieding. 2003. *Helping Teachers Teach: A School Library Media Specialist's Role.* Westport, CT: Libraries Unlimited.

Vandergrift, K. E. 1979. *The Teaching Role of the School Media Specialist.* Chicago: American Association of School Librarians.

Victor, E. 1974. "The Inquiry Approach to Teaching and Learning." *Science and Children* (October): 23–26.

Wehmeyer, L. B. 1984. *The School Librarian as Educator.* Littleton, CO: Libraries Unlimited.

Williams, D., et al. 2013. "Impact of School Libraries on Learning: Critical Review of Published Evidence to Inform the Scottish Education Community." Robert Gordon University. http://www.scottishlibraries.org/storage/sectors/schools/SLIC_RGU_Impact_of_School_Libraries_2013.pdf (accessed June 14, 2014).

Woolls, B. 2008. *The School Library Media Manager.* 4th ed. Westport, CT: Libraries Unlimited.

Zmuda, A., and V. H. Harada. 2008a. *Librarians as Learning Specialists.* Westport, CT: Libraries Unlimited.

Zmuda, A., and V. H. Harada. 2008b. "Reframing the Library Media Specialist as a Learning Specialist." *School Library Monthly* 24, no. 8 (April): 42–46.

Chapter 12

Research on Inquiry Learning and Teaching Techniques

Research on the effectiveness of inquiry-based learning has been mixed. Negative evaluations of such methods as discovery learning prior to the 1990s often came from failures to fully plan, understand, and support projects designed to encourage greater student responsibilities. Expectations for student performance were also often too high without the necessary scaffolds, resources, and teacher modeling in place. Inquiry projects frequently did not include investment of adequate time for students to learn how to question, how to explore a wide variety of resources, or to how to engage peers in sharing and evaluating information.

Forty years ago the range of inquiry practice, from encyclopedic fact-gathering up to critical examination of new and perhaps alienating information, was stuck at the basic worksheet level. Topics were usually not argumentative-based, but in journalistic reporting style. Students were expected to answer "who, what, where" questions, but seldom expected to reflect on "how and why." Controversial topics were usually drawn from mainstream issues (capital punishment, abortion, civil rights) and tended to be sanitized through literature selected for the library collection. Few ventured beyond the boundaries of pro and con arguments approved through the school's materials selection process. Investigative projects that had some degree of inquiry were usually science projects. However, there has been a progression in research to support teaching techniques and methods associated with inquiry learning.

Harriet Selverstone (2007) published the following justification for encouraging and supporting student inquiry through researching controversial issues:

Controversial issues become controversial when the ideas inherent in the content are questioned or challenged by adults in a community, by religious groups, by community leaders or elected officials, by organized national groups, by political activists, by board of education members, or by school administrators. In a democratic society, and in a public school setting, students are entitled to be exposed to a myriad of topics, and to viewpoints of others that may differ from their own or those of their families. A public school environment provides a safe place where ideas may be explored, where discussions are open, viewpoints of others respected and tolerated, and where new discoveries are made. A public school environment provides for enrichment of knowledge and the engagement of students in the pursuit of this knowledge. Controversy is natural; controversy should be encouraged, not stifled in a school community. This adds to the intellectual growth of the child and should nurture the curiosities inherent in growing up to be a responsible citizen. (xv)

Controversial issues associated with the Common Core standards that support inquiry in the "argument curriculum" are discussed at greater length in chapters 9 and 10 of this book. The research review presented here touches on some disagreements among science education researchers about the true value of inquiry learning. Some studies provide indications of effective teaching strategies when it comes to managing discussions on controversial subjects. These techniques, of course, serve to engage student discussion and broaden topic selection for inquiry studies, controversial or not.

THE CASE AGAINST INQUIRY IN SCIENCE EDUCATION

Three highly regarded educational psychologists have recently called for an end to soft instructional strategies that come under such terms as discovery learning, constructivist, problem-based instruction, and inquiry-based teaching (Kirschner, Sweller, and Clark 2006; Clark, Kirschner, and Sweller 2012). Strategies that follow a minimal amount of guided instruction result in lower student achievement, they assert, and mislead students, who confront problem-solving assignments that are falsely described as authentic.

While they agree that constructivist theory correctly accounts for progress in student learning influenced by previous experiences added to long-term memory, they argue that having novice students carry out experiments involving new concepts, new principles, and new information is time-consuming and results in high frustration for students who do not receive adequate teacher direction.

THE DEFENSE OF INQUIRY

Three other highly regarded educational psychologists (Hmelo-Silver, Duncan, and Chinn 2007) defend inquiry learning:

> Kirschner and colleagues have indiscriminately lumped together several distinct pedagogical approaches–constructivist, discovery, problem-based, experiential, and inquiry-based–under the category of minimally guided instruction. . . . [S]ome of these approaches, in particular, problem-based learning and inquiry learning, are not minimally guided instructional approaches, but rather provide extensive scaffolding and guidance to facilitate student learning. . . . [E]vidence suggests that these approaches can foster deep and meaningful learning as well as significant gains in student achievement on standardized tests. . . . Scaffolded inquiry and problem-based environments present learners with opportunities to engage in complex tasks that would otherwise be beyond their current abilities. . . . [S]caffolding [is] a key element of cognitive apprenticeship, whereby students become increasingly accomplished problem-solvers given structure and guidance from mentors who scaffold students through coaching, task structuring, and hints, without explicitly giving students final answers. (99–100)

These techniques, infused throughout inquiry-based science instruction in the Detroit Public Schools, as one example, resulted in greater performance on standardized tests and more students passing the statewide exams. Specifically, urban African American males who engaged in inquiry-based science curricula closed the academic performance gap and demonstrated that standards-based inquiry science curriculum can lead to standardized achievement test gains among historically underserved urban students (Geier et al. 2007).

The most recent meta-analysis of research on inquiry-based lessons (Lazonder 2014, 454) provides these observations:

- Accumulating evidence confirms the effectiveness of inquiry learning if there is strong learner support, and as such even discovery learning can show favorable learner outcomes when compared to traditional methods (Alfieri et al. 2011).
- Well-guided inquiry learning is more effective than hypermedia learning and observational learning. Of particular interest is the superiority of guided inquiry learning to observational learning when students merely observed experts rather than becoming engaged in inquiry with hands-on practice and mentor direction (Eysink et al. 2009).

TESTING INQUIRY TEACHING STRATEGIES

During the past two decades, more focus has been placed on the teaching strategies associated with inquiry-based learning. Are there specific steps teachers can take, many in collaboration with school library media specialists, to create a learning environment that is fertile for student exploration of self-generated questions and critical use of multiple resources?

Teachers (and school library media specialists as co-inquiry instructors) can be powerful models of the techniques to discover meaning from new information that students encounter in their inquiry projects. They can model in at least four ways (Alfassi 2004):

- Generating questions: Ask internally and externally those questions that, when answered, help to promote understanding of the text.
- Summarizing: Find the main idea for manageable notes and future documentation as well as gaining a flow for an eventual hypothesis or central message.
- Clarifying: Determine the meaning of new words through sounding text or seeking other resources.
- Predicting: Ask "what's next" questions to help students visualize issues and possible solutions. What resources might be best for helping to address these problems?

Strategies that enhance reading comprehension and help students from upper elementary school through college generate meaningful, focused, and actionable questions have been documented through many studies (Rosenshine, Meister, and Chapman 1996). Such exercises in language arts, history, and science inquiry provide the foundational key words and first questions that lead to working hypothesis development and, eventually, a menu of topics to explore further. In addition to the teacher's modeling the process to address example problems by thinking through the resolutions aloud, practice is guided in reciprocal questioning techniques:

- First a question is generated, which the students answer.
- The generated question serves as a model for the students in generating their own questions.
- The students then generate a question, which the teacher answers.
- Extensive student practice of question generation is provided.
- Students may practice individually or in pairs, both with guidance.
- Students' ability to ask questions throughout the lesson is assessed.
- The students are asked to summarize the passage upon the completion of the reading.
- The students' ability to ask questions is assessed at the end of the learning unit, along with their comprehension of the subject matter.

Studies have also shown positive growth in reading comprehension when students are expected to demonstrate how to identify the most important information relative to questions raised and experiment in linking such information together into formative ideas (Davey and McBride 1986). These practices could be of value if carried over to the later assessment stages on student inquiry products and presentations. Can students identify the most important resources and the key experts associated with their final topic of study? Does the student gain expertise in both content and resource selection? Do these resource skills transfer to later inquiry projects?

ORGANIZERS, ARGUMENTS, AND TEAMS

Graphic organizers have been shown to help set an agenda for learning by illustrating where the lesson is intended to progress. Student-generated graphic organizers can help students summarize their own reflections on the topics being explored, and student-developed graphic organizers following lessons can help with knowledge retention (Griffin and Tulbert 1995). Such organizers have been found to be very helpful for students to sort and associate ideas as they proceed with an inquiry project.

At higher levels of discourse, secondary school students and young adults have shown gains in comprehension of science principles when they take an active role in supporting or rejecting notions and evidence through argumentation. Such debate seems to increase long-term change in student understanding of those concepts (Guzzetti 2000). In information inquiry terms, is assimilation of new information or rejection of that information determined through argumentation a viable exercise that leads to learning, as suggested in the Common Core State Standards Initiative (Callison 2013)?

As part of their compilation and review of thousands of publications on effective instruction, educators at the Institute for Evidence-Based Decision-Making in Education (Friedman, Harwell and Schnepel 2006) analyzed 383 studies on peer teamwork. They concluded that achievement of learning objectives is enhanced when students (at elementary or secondary grade levels, or college) are taught to perform complementary tasks as a team in pursuit of the learning objectives. Characteristics of effective group investigations include the following:

- The teacher presents a broad problem or issue to the entire class.
- Students meet in groups to determine the subtopics to be investigated.
- Once the subtopics are determined, the students form groups according to the subtopic in which they are interested.
- The students in each group plan what and how they will study.
- Each group plans the division of labor.
- Students within the groups gather information, analyze data, and reach conclusions, with every group member contributing to the group effort.
- Students exchange, discuss, clarify, and synthesize ideas.
- Group members plan what they will report and how they will present their findings to the whole class.
- Teachers and students collaborate in evaluating student learning.

INQUIRY AND THE GENDER CHALLENGE IN READING

The tendency of adolescent males to not read as much as girls is well known. Boys also tend to seek out nonfiction more than fiction. New emphasis on nonfiction in the Common Core State Standards may encourage additional reading incentive efforts that draw males to read more and to adopt frequent reading habits after high school graduation and into college (Uecker, Kelly, and Napierala 2014). Inquiry, modeling, and choice served as motiving factors in a recent study reported by the International Reading Association (Fisher and Frey 2012).

Teachers modeled reading through reading aloud, sharing experiences with other books they had read, and raising questions for their own consideration from the texts. Questions became the evidence of inquiry, as they were posted as part of each student's learning record (on the school walls as well as in student journals). Choice in additional reading was supported through access to additional titles, but voluntary decisions were made by students. The result for boys was a dramatic increase in the number of books read, equal to or more than the girls. These same strategies also have power in the development of inquiry-based projects (Wilhelm 2007, 2008).

REFERENCES

Alfassi, M. 2004. "Reading to Learn: Effects of Combined Strategy Instructions on High School Students." *Journal of Educational Research* 97, no. 4: 171–184.

Alfieri, L., et al. 2011. "Does Discovery-based Instruction Enhance Learning? *Journal of Educational Psychology* 103: 1–18.

Callison, D. 2013. "Inquiry and Common Core: Argument Discourse for Dialogue and Debate." *School Library Monthly* 29, no. 7: 20–23.

Clark, R. E., P. A. Kirschner, and J. Sweller. 2012. "Putting Students on the Path to Learning: The Case for Fully Guided Instruction." *American Educator* (Spring): 7–11. http://www.aft.org/pdfs/americaneduca tor/spring2012/Clark.pdf (accessed February 6, 2014).

Common Core State Standards Initiative. n.d. http://www.corestandards.org/ (accessed February 3, 2010).

Davey, B., and S. McBride. 1986. "Effects of Question-Generation on Reading Comprehension." *Journal of Educational Psychology* 78: 256–262.

Eysink, T. H. S., et al. 2009. "Learner Performance in Multimedia Learning Arrangements: An Analysis across Instructional Approaches." *American Educational Research Journal* 46: 1107–1149.

Fisher, D., and N. Frey. 2012. "Motivating Boys to Read: Inquiry, Modeling, and Choice Matter." *Journal of Adolescent & Adult Literacy* 55, no. 7 (April): 587–596.

Friedman, M. I., D. H. Harwell, and K. C. Schnepel, eds. 2006. *Effective Instruction: A Handbook of Evidence-based Strategies.* Columbia, SC : Institute for Evidence-Based Decision-Making in Education.

Geier, R., et al. 2007. "Standardized Test Outcomes for Students Engaged in Inquiry-Based Science Curricula in the Context of Urban Reform. *Journal of Research in Science Teaching* 45, no. 8: 922–929.

Griffin, C. C., and B. L Tulbert. 1995. "The Effect of Graphic Organizers on Students' Comprehension and Recall of Expository Text: A Review of the Research and Implications for Practice." *Reading & Writing Quarterly* 11: 73–89.

Guzzetti, B. J. 2000. "Learning Counter Intuitive Science Concepts: What Have We Learned from over a Decade of Research?" *Reading and Writing Quarterly* 16: 89–96.

Hmelo-Silver, C. E., R. G. Duncan, and C. A. Chinn. 2007. "Scaffolding and Achievement in Problem-Based and Inquiry Learning: A Response to Kirschner, Sweller, and Clark." *Educational Psychologist* 42, no. 2: 99–107.

Kirschner, P. A., J. Sweller, and R. E. Clark. 2006. "Why Minimal Guidance during Instruction Does Not Work: An Analysis of the Failure of Constructivist, Discovery, Problem-based, Experiential, and Inquiry-based Teaching." *Educational Psychologist* 41, no. 2: 75–86.

Lazonder, A. W. 2014. "Inquiry Learning." In *Handbook of Research on Educational Communications and Technology*, edited by J. M. Spector et al., 453–464. New York: Springer.

Rosenshine, B., C. Meister, and S. Chapman. 1996. "Teaching Students to Generate Questions: A Review of the Intervention Studies." *Review of Educational Research* 66, no. 2: 181–221.

Selverstone, H. S. 2007. *Encouraging and Supporting Student Inquiry: Researching Controversial Issues.* Westport, CT: Libraries Unlimited.

Uecker, R., S. Kelly, and M. Napierala. 2014. "Implementing the Common Core State Standards." *Knowledge Quest* 42, no. 3 (January/February): 48–51.

Wilhelm, J. 2007. *Engaging Readers and Writers with Inquiry: Promoting Deep Understandings in Language Arts and the Content Areas with Guiding Questions.* New York: Scholastic.

Wilhelm, J. 2008. *Improving Comprehension with Think-Aloud Strategies: Modeling What Good Readers Do.* New York: Scholastic.

Chapter 13

Research on Student Online Searching and Information Evaluation

CHALLENGES IN EVALUATING INFORMATION

With the expansion of information access primarily because of the Internet, greater skills in evidence selection and evaluation of data have come to the forefront. Mary Ann Fitzgerald (1999), from the University of Georgia's Department of Instructional Technology (IT), provided an extensive review and definitions of various behaviors that result in misjudging information needs and false application. Persistent bias and impatience, among other factors, result in selection of evidence that fails to move the student closer to true perspectives, especially in the information age. While such information-inefficient behaviors have always existed, Fitzgerald's thorough discussion of information assimilation is more and more relevant to K–12 student evaluation of information. Fitzgerald summarized her insights as follows:

> The ideas a person holds about the origin of knowledge may greatly affect the way in which that person approaches new information. A person who believes some knowledge to be unquestionable may neither criticize new information about that knowledge nor consider new information that contradicts it. On the other hand, the person who believes in the fluidity of all or most knowledge may be more likely to consider new information in an evaluative light and judge how it may change knowledge already in memory. There is tremendous space between these two extremes for people who hold varying amounts of certain and uncertain knowledge on different topics.

More than ever before, school library media specialists have become necessary as mentors and guides through the information maze, and as guides they not only direct, but also help students evaluate information as critically as possible (Todd and Gordon n.d.).

Fitzgerald made the following recommendations for practices that may help students deal with persistent information bias:

- When a skill is introduced, or when students seem to be having inordinate difficulty, teachers and school library media specialists can reduce cognitive load by breaking the skill down into smaller parts (Markman 1981) and by beginning new skills in familiar contexts (Flavell 1981). For example, in distinguishing between fact and opinion, students can first seek cue words like "I think . . ." and "I feel . . .".
- In a daily fifteen-minute exercise, children should find problems such as inconsistency or exaggeration in a short piece of curriculum-relevant text (Markman 1981). These exercises should represent well-structured problems at first and progress to ill-structured problems as students

become more skillful. School library media specialists can extend these classroom exercises when students perform research.

- Teachers should attempt to ensure that the cause of the potential bias is clear. Research shows that people evaluate more effectively if causes are revealed, where available (Anderson 1982).
- Students should practice formal argumentation, which involves the evaluation of evidence (Kuhn 1991). They should also switch sides and argue opposite positions. Debates (Paul 1992), mock trials, and mock or genuine editorials present excellent opportunities for this skill.
- There is no better way to practice evaluation than to perform research regularly and intensely. Research should stem from either an authentic problem affecting the student or personal interest, because only motivated students exercise their optimal capabilities.

PRACTICES OF YOUNG PEOPLE IN EVIDENCE SELECTION

Additional research on evidence selection and evaluation is found in the IT field (Lazonder 2014, 455):

> Children often hold strong prior beliefs about the topics they are investigating. Pupils in the age of 12–14 are able to state and investigate their own hypotheses; younger children often conduct experiments without explicit hypotheses (Tomkins and Tunnicliffe 2001). . . . During an inquiry, children are unable to induce implausible (but correct) hypotheses from data–a skill that is known to be problematic to older students too, in particular when data are anomalous. As a result, both children and adults are susceptible to confirmation bias (Tschirgi 1980) and prefer to state and verify "safe" or familiar hypotheses. Falsifying alternative hypotheses that contradict the student's initial beliefs occur significantly less often, but are the driving force behind the discovery of new ideas (Dunbar 1993). It thus seems that students of all ages use an investigation to demonstrate their knowledge of a domain rather than rigorously test thought-provoking [and controversial] hypotheses in search for new understanding.

Lazonder (2014, 456) concluded:

> It thus seems that people of all ages are rather reluctant to change their beliefs when confronted with anomalous data. . . . To conclude, evidence evaluation may be the most critical and difficult skills to develop. Across settings and ages, the observation and interpretation of data require additional support and guidance. Providing content support by offering background information or predefined hypotheses could be a powerful means to help domain novices to make more accurate observations. When students already have some understanding of the topic they are investigating, possible incorrect beliefs might impede observation and interpretation. Process support could help overcome this problem.

Application of the constructivist theory that students build knowledge on prior experiences should be done with some consideration of the legitimacy of those experiences. All learners can bring "baggage" to a learning situation. Searching for and accepting only information that supports beliefs held destroys the very essence of inquiry. The exploration should be substantial, but managed with the application of testing for information credibility.

THE CHALLENGE OF HAVING PRIOR BELIEFS OR NOT A CLUE

This challenge is substantial. Students entering an inquiry project without any knowledge of the issues may be overwhelmed and struggle to gain a handle on a basic focus for their investigation. Students entering an inquiry project with some background knowledge may hold to those beliefs no matter how invalid and resist new information that may be introduced in the exploration processes. Children often experience information-seeking failures, and usually this is because of problems found in the attitudes of students and the practices of librarians. Andrew Shenton (2007) of Northumbria University has explored the complexities of student search behavior on the Internet and notes these paradoxes, among others:

- Verification of information in sources is widely advocated, but strategies for implementing this process may be of questionable real value.
- Information skills models that take a linear rather than dynamic perspective often imply that sources are investigated once the need has been determined, but in real life, situations frequently emerge in which knowledge of content in sources triggers an information need.
- In order to access information in a source, the user must often apply knowledge that he or she does not yet possess.
- Despite the sophistication of today's information age, youngsters frequently follow a basic formula for action when finding and using information.
- Young people are often highly critical of particular information resources, yet continue to use them habitually.
- Library goers' reduced reliance on the information professional, which may result from effective programs of user education, may deprive such staff of key opportunities to learn more about the information needs of their patrons (13).

To say that successful instruction reduces the communication among student, teacher, and librarian concerning specific information needs, or new needs that grow from the process, again emphasizes the necessity for the library media specialist to be engaged in projects across their development and not just at a point of "library orientation." Understanding how newly encountered information may actually open a new line of valuable inquiry rather than simply suggesting an answer to an initial question requires conversations and time for reflection. It requires, most importantly, teacher and library media specialist engagement across all stages of the inquiry process. Student information needs and interpretations evolve and change across inquiry projects. True investigations "turn" on the student who is open to where the evidence will take him or her. Thus, new discoveries with new evidence warrant new reflections with guides or mentors.

THE COMPLEXITIES OF THE INFORMATION SEARCH

Shenton and Dixon (2005) have questioned the adequacy of research studies that simply observe student search behavior on a given topic or problem. The complexities of student information searching are immense and become even more difficult to track when personal information desires mix with academic information requirements. "It is inadequate to investigate youngsters' information needs purely in terms of the subjects of the desired information and the purposes for which the material is required. There is an increasing realization that an array of other factors must also be considered if a more multi-dimensional picture of information needs is to be gained" (Shenton and Dixon 2005, 26). Among the many variables they identify are

- the manner in which the need is initially represented,
- the specificity of the purpose for which the information is needed,
- the extent to which youngsters can define the totality of their need before seeking information,
- the degree to which the overall topic changes during the information-seeking process,
- the urgency with which information is required,

- whether highly up-to-date information is necessary,
- the degree of accuracy necessary within the information sought,
- the motivation of youngsters and the priority they attach to a particular need, and
- the contribution that the desired information makes to the end product (26).

A HISTORY OF THE PROBLEMS IN EFFECTIVE ONLINE SEARCHING

In 1987 I received permission from H. W. Wilson to field test their new online indexes. This included not only the database for the *Readers' Guide*, but access to all of Wilson's academic indexes as well. Our learning laboratory for this unique experience was at the highly respected Carmel High School, north of Indianapolis, a library media center held in high regard for its leadership in adoption of new learning technologies. Ironically, there was some opposition to the project from a few colleagues at Indiana University, as online searching was seen at that time as strictly a task for adult, professional librarians, not for young people.

Our experiences with a small group of high school students engaged in a traditional research term paper were documented through observations of student searches, student interviews, and examination of the student's final papers. We (Callison and Daniels 1988; Callison 1988) found the following:

- Typical high school students had few problems in searching databases by using keywords from their topics and keywords associated with articles they found of interest in preliminary searching. While there was understanding of controlled vocabulary, students really did not have to search extensively, as their topics were broad and the written assignment not exceptionally challenging.
- While academic journal articles were obtained through interlibrary loan, students seldom cited the journals in their final papers and needed additional interaction with teachers and librarians in order to draw out useful information. Most did not engage in such discussions, however. They were content with other information resources, including those found at home.
- Books identified through online searching were also obtained through interlibrary loan and were more likely to become key sources, cited often in student papers, especially those books obtained at local public libraries. This was obviously decades before the Internet.
- Students frequently had difficulties determining the potential value of a source identified from an online search and usually discarded sources that seemed to emphasize information that did not relate to the topic or thesis they were exploring. Any term or personality served to either confirm the item to be of value for further examination or immediately led to rejection of the article simply based on the abstract. (For example, "I don't care about whatever President Reagan had to say"; the student refused to use any document or abstract that gave the president's name.)

This first experimentation with the H. W. Wilson online databases with a high school population demonstrated that this age group could conduct constructive searches and could learn to refine their searches. The project highlighted for the researchers behaviors associated with information bias and quick rejection of information considered to be in opposition to the mindset of the student. The focus of most students was to find materials that supported their initial ideas and to do so as quickly as possible. Information inquiry at this level failed to lead to any substantial change in the student topics, although some original topics were salvaged because of a broader access to materials through local interlibrary loan. The new experience with open screen display, which allowed both the student and librarian to see student search results, tended to allow for more interaction in search options than do student searches in print indexes, which are often difficult to observe.

MORE RECENT OBSERVATIONS WITH THE INTERNET

The progression in examining student search behavior now, as would be expected, concentrates on the Internet. Search abilities have been monitored across all secondary grades. Access to and selection of information found on the Internet has also come under closer examination as teachers and students face the complexities of misleading and sensational information, which was usually not found in print-only collections, composed of different resources selected through a review process by the school librarian. Building the ability to evaluate information has become the most critical skill in the information inquiry teaching and learning processes. *The Handbook of Research on New Literacies* (Kuiper and Volman 2008) provides more recent insights:

- One may assume that assessing and evaluating Web sites proves difficult for anyone confronted with the abundance of information the Web offers. For several reasons, this applies to children in an even greater degree (Kuiper and Volman 2008, 257).
- Children often lack sufficient prior knowledge to which information found on the Web can be related. Prior knowledge of a specific subject makes it easier both to formulate suitable keywords and to evaluate the relevance and reliability of the information (Fidel et al. 1999).
- Students hardly assessed the reliability and authority of information. This tendency did not appear to improve with age. On the basis of a study involving a group of fifteen-year-old girls, Agosto (2002) constructed a theoretical model of the criteria young people use to evaluate Web sites. Students did evaluate sites on their content—the expected relevancy and reliability—but often used inappropriate criteria in the process, equating quantity with quality.
- Wallace et al. (2000) concluded that inquiries on the Web must be incorporated into a broader educational approach: "In many classrooms, and schools, students are accustomed to seeking correct answers and producing work that meets clear specifications, laid out in advance. Getting on the Web to 'do inquiry' is unlikely to cause a change in that orientation even in the short term" (100).
- In a project conducted by Hoffman et al. (2003), students used a specially designed interface, which structured and guided both their inquiry and their Web use. Students did not search freely on the Web, but their searches were mediated by the interface, which allowed access to a digital library that contained preselected, preapproved, and age-appropriate online resources. [Not unlike the resource carts school librarians have often provided with a gathering of in-house resources that support initial or background reading prior to beginning a research project.]
- Research conducted by Jones (2002), however, indicated that offering online support and preselected Web sites alone does not diminish students' tendency to look only for the right answer. In a less structured search environment, students were free to choose between searching freely on the Web or using the Project Web Page, similar to WebQuests (Lamb 2004). Contrary to expectations, the students who were allowed to search freely made little use of the opportunity. They simply expected that the sites selected by the teacher would provide the right answer and were afraid that they would use incorrect information in their papers if they searched for themselves.

In a study not included in the Kuiper and Volman review, secondary school teachers developed and validated the following Web site evaluation with their students (Karchmer 2008). Teacher and student experiences concluded that there can be greater trust placed in sites that contain

- an organization signature with address, telephone number, and e-mail contact;
- a link showing the credentials of the person responsible for the material on the site;
- citations from sources quoted or referenced;
- links to other reputable sites;
- awards and endorsements from independent organizations; and
- secondary sources that verify the information on the source page.

Kuiper and Volman (2008, 261) concluded:

> The Web invites students to demonstrate behavior that is the opposite of the behavior necessary for the development of valid and meaningful knowledge. The Web invites students to think that every answer can be found ready-made, given the abundance of information it offers. It also invites students to be more or less passive searchers, because of the speed with which information appears on the computer screen. In contrast, the development of valid and meaningful knowledge assumes that students are actively involved in the learning process, that they construct knowledge by connecting new information to already acquired knowledge, and that they reflect on this process and its results.

CONTROL FOR PRACTICE, MENTOR FOR INDEPENDENCE

Controlled inquiry that allows for practice and background knowledge can help set the stage for inquiry. It can help students form initial hypothesis statements and test feasibility. True inquiry, guided or independent, however, should involve the student in a wide array of information searching, access, and evaluation. Until students actually face similar sets of information and can identify various degrees of validity and value among those items, they have not experienced the evaluation demands of inquiry in the information age.

Lesley Farmer, professor at California State University, Long Beach, warns about the limitations to inquiry when teachers are not qualified digital citizens: "While technology may sometimes feel ubiquitous in today's society, its use is not ubiquitous in education. Even [though we have progressed] with well-maintained labs and a solid collection of digital resources, learners will not profit from technology-enhanced activities if educators do not provide such learning opportunities" (2013, 284). She concludes: "Assessment seems straightforward: how efficiently and effectively does one evaluate digital information? Ultimately, the most valid assessment consists of examining the use of the information in deriving the final solution. In the digital world, learners may find it very hard to discern the verity of information because it can be modified so easily and with so much sophistication. Furthermore, youth do not have the life experiences to compare statements with prior knowledge to the extent that adults can. . . . Educators need to teach explicit guidelines for evaluating the quality of digital information and its relevance—to check for learner understanding, and to engage them in active examination, debate, and self-reflection" (286).

PROBLEMS IN INITIATING TRUE INQUIRY

Pitts (1994), Gordon (1999), and Stripling (2011) have each reported problems in the limited abilities of students, teachers, and school librarians to fully grasp inquiry concepts, and thus to not be able to generate inquiry projects much beyond general information gathering and nominal presentations.

Pitts found middle school students unable to fully understand how to take an inquiry project to presentation levels that reflected more than simple facts. She observed students searching for information in a limited manner, without fully understanding the options to seek materials beyond the library catalog. Further, information resource support for teachers and librarians tended to stop at location of resources, without engaging students in reading and thinking through the content of resources obtained.

Gordon found that most so-called inquiry projects failed to challenge students to engage in critical or creative thinking. Their topics seldom sparked passion for the topic and tended to boil back down into factual reports at best.

Stripling found history teachers lacking in meaningful intellectual constructs that fully reflected appreciation or comprehension of the value of historic inquiry. If teachers don't "get it," how can we expect students to grasp any meaningful inquiry?

MOTIVATING STUDENTS FOR INQUIRY: BUILDING VALID CONFIDENCE

Karchmer (2008) reported on highly successful teacher-driven inquiry when there was heavy use of the Internet to support information searches, presentation of findings, and above all, sharing of student products with peers and parents. Motivation to complete projects seemed to be strongest in the elementary grade levels when students became aware that their work would appear on a school Web site. Secondary school students tended to be a little more careful in the information content they used when knowing others in addition to teachers would read their final work. While writing increased at all grade levels, the major factors were the high technical abilities of the teachers involved and their willingness to take a risk on new forms of teaching and learning and to use technology to drive the learning agenda.

Marilyn Arnone and Ruth Small, along with their colleagues at Syracuse University, have devoted three decades to the study of motivational techniques that might enhance instruction and draw in more students for deeper, closer, authentic experiences. The progression of recent findings shows that school librarians and other teachers can diagnose gaps in student confidence which, when addressed, can move the student closer to managing information-rich projects (Arnone, Small, and Reynolds 2010).

Confidence and therefore motivation to take on difficult multiple resource assignments tends to increase when students recognize their teacher and librarian as highly competent in the information search and use processes, especially in skilled application of technology (Arnone, Reynolds, and Marshall 2009). Students are more likely to be drawn to competent (perhaps inspiring) mentors. A talented, resourceful, and energetic school library media specialist may be the most important ingredient in making inquiry projects successful. Exemplary interpersonal communication skills, possible only from the human educator, not the computer, are also essential (Shannon 2002).

Among the abilities on the Syracuse Component Matrix (Arnone, Small, and Reynolds 2010, 57) are the following:

I am CONFIDENT in my ability to . . .
- Formulate smaller (more specific) questions that help me narrow down my big (broad) research paper.
- Choose the best sources of information for my particular research.
- Tell the difference between a primary and a secondary resource.
- Determine whether the information I find is appropriate for my information need.
- Use technology tools to help organize new information I find.
- Evaluate the truth of information I find in books, Web sites, magazines, and media.
- Recognize if information I find is biased or slanted toward a particular point of view.

These items represent about half of the statements on which students self-report and self-judge. The instrument, when used to survey student populations who are scheduled for large research or inquiry projects, can provide one snapshot to help librarians prepare to meet student needs. Limitations, of course, include students not understanding the statement and often judging themselves as more confident than they really are in the information search and evaluation processes.

Overly Confident Undergraduates

Such was the case in the studies conducted on undergraduates by Melissa Gross and Don Latham at Florida State University (2009). A series of measures with first-year community college students showed a larger than expected overconfidence in knowing how to find information, especially through the Internet. The population's general lack of knowledge about the holdings of the library, lack of knowledge about the library services available to help them access resources, and assumptions that librarians would be of little value to help guide information use were consistently evident across the groups surveyed. The overly confident profile in this case resulted in development of entry level, computer-based instruction modules that focused on the fundamentals of information search, keyword development, and peer interaction for analysis of information value: relevant, credible, and current (Gross and Latham 2011).

Student contact with reference librarians viewed more as resource experts also increased substantially. Not all undergraduates, however, established efficient information-seeking behaviors, and their persistent actions served to enforce how ingrained personal beliefs are in some who believe themselves to be technologically savvy and in need of no further assistance to search the Internet or evaluate findings (Gross and Latham 2013).

INCOMING COLLEGE FRESHMEN ARE NOT PREPARED

Another recent study, conducted in partnership with the Information School at the University of Washington (Head 2013), concluded that a majority of freshmen interviewed find it difficult to effectively search academic library portals. To a lesser extent, they struggle with reading and comprehending scholarly materials once they are able to find them and have trouble figuring out faculty expectations for course research assignments. The conclusions suggest that the "Google-centric" search skills that freshmen bring from high school only get them so far with finding and using trusted sources they need for fulfilling college research assignments.

Many freshmen appeared to be unfamiliar with how academic libraries—and the vast array of digital resources they provide—can best meet their needs. The study also noted that the recent decline in the number of teacher librarians in secondary schools may further increase the problem of graduating high school seniors who are not fully prepared for the information demands they will face in higher education and life in general.

THE MOST RECENT REVIEWS OF INTERNET CREDIBILITY AND STUDENT USE

Sponsored by the MacArthur Foundation, MIT Press recently published results of a national survey that measures digital media use by America's young people and their perspectives and practices on determining information credibility (Flanagin et al. 2010). Andrew Flanagin introduces the study with these remarks:

> Contemporary youth are a particularly intriguing and important group to consider with regard to credibility because of the tension between their technical and social immersion with digital media and their relatively limited development and experience compared to adults. Although those who have grown up in an environment saturated with networked digital media technologies may be highly skilled in their use of media, they are also inhibited by their [limited] cognitive and emotional development, personal experiences, and familiarity with the media apparatus. (Flanagin et al. 2010, ix)

Among other insightful findings, the executive summary included the following observations:

- Children believe that they are highly skilled Internet users. Even eleven-year-olds believe that their technical skill, search skill, and knowledge about Internet trends and features are higher than those of other Internet users.
- Young people are concerned about credibility on the Internet, yet they find online information to be reasonably credible, with 89 percent reporting that "some" to "a lot" of information online is believable. While the amount of information they find credible increases somewhat with age, their concern about credibility does not.
- Among several options, the Internet was rated as the most believable source of information for schoolwork, entertainment, and commercial information, as well as second most believable source for health information, and the most believable for news information. Notably, children report that the Internet is a more credible source of information for school papers or projects than books (xi–xiii).

Even net-savvy youth know they should be cautious (they have been told to think that way), but they trust the open system of the Internet to police itself and therefore make the Internet environment at least reasonability safe to travel. Credibility of information pertains more to the Internet resource's ability to address immediate needs and less to meeting any extensive evaluation criteria. Young people do, however, raise and apply evaluative judgments on topics and issues that are of great interest to them personally. Their expertise and judgments seem to increase in sophistication as they mature.

COMING OF AGE ON THE INTERNET

Frances Jacobson Harris (2008) provides further insights on young people and their online information-seeking behaviors and summarizes the key behavior challenges:

Older youths may not have the knowledge base to contextualize the digital information they encounter (Wineburg 1991). They often lack the analytical strategies, such as source corroboration, required to make meaningful assessments of conflicting information sources. To compensate for these deficits, young people tend to employ different evaluation criteria than adults (Fidel, et al. 1999). They are more likely to simplify Web site evaluation tasks and make credibility judgments that rely heavily on design and presentation features rather than content. . . . [Y]oung people evaluate content in a depth equal to their levels of motivation and ability. The more personally important the search task is, the more likely users are to employ a more systematic . . . evaluation of the information (Gross 2006).

Assignments for which students acquire greater ownership may provide the motivation needed to bring student evaluation of content to the necessary levels where students actually want to determine credibility. Student choice should be an important factor if the expectation is for students to apply a positive attitude to the information evaluation and selection processes. Factors that lead to mediocre student search performances may often be related to low feelings about the inquiry assignment. This in turn leads to acceptance of "anything" from the Internet that can at least complete the assignment. Donham (2014) concludes that student choice recognized and supported through peer interactions can be very powerful and provide a foundation for the persistence and passion that are necessary for anyone to pursue and complete complex multiresource assignments:

Peers may serve as listeners and responders if we create peer response groups for inquiry projects. Passion or interest increases when young researchers have the power to determine their own line of inquiry and own their questions, and when the questions are deep or complex enough to ignite genuine interest. Simply raising awareness of the importance of perseverance for deep and insightful inquiry is an important step. (11)

In the second edition of her ALA guide for public and school librarians for dealing with the demands of a youth population immersed in digital communication, Harris notes: "The complexities of selecting and evaluating information will only increase as information technologies continue to diversity and grow" (2011, 191). Therefore it seems that a plan to teach techniques for determining document content credibility should be flexible and grow with the times. The plan must be as situational-oriented (adjusted to meet issues and specific student needs) as the goals of learning itself.

PRACTICE IN WEB SITE EVALUATION

As the director of the University of Illinois lab school library, Harris has written widely, presented nationally, and taught extensively concerning information access and use by teens. Her thirty years of research and practice have led her to develop several progressive Internet evaluation methods. The major goal is to instill in her students (and their parents) and teachers dispositions that trigger caution and scrutiny, but do not employ evaluative processes that get in the way of learning.

The elements of Web site evaluation reviewed on the Illinois University Laboratory High School Library Web site include the standard criteria, but with links directly to examples on the Web so students can access the sites and make comparisons. The examples are linked from key questions and concerns that Harris has posed (http://www.library.illinois.edu/uni/computer lit/evaluation.html):

- Authority
  - What are the author's credentials? When do credentials matter?
  - Is the source known and respected? Is there a way to contact the source?
  - Are there "backdoor" ways of determining authority, like reviewer ratings? Can you trust these?
  - Does a high ranking on search engine results mean a source is authoritative?
- Accuracy
  - Can the information be corroborated? In other words, can you confirm the information in another source? (Harris says this is a very difficult concept for students to grasp and show.)
  - Does the information need to be current?
  - Is the information documented, either directly or indirectly?
  - Is the information presented with integrity (i.e., no copyright violations, fabrications, and other misuses of intellectual property)?
- Balanced Treatment
  - Is the site fair and objective?
  - Is it an advocacy site? Advocacy sites promote the interests of an organization, a cause, or a point of view, and are by definition biased.
  - Is there a conflict of interest? Does the Web site producer stand to benefit from the information being provided?
  - How important is balance? Is it required for your purposes? Do hobbyists' sites, "fun" sites, and advocacy sites need to be unbiased? Is bias necessarily a bad thing?
- Sample Persuasion Techniques
  - Calling on a higher authority (e.g., religion, the medical profession) to justify a position.

- o Using the "plain folks" technique ("We are just like everyone else") to elicit sympathy and understanding.
- o Employing pseudoscience: using scientific-sounding references or data to justify a position, make an argument, or sell a product.
- o "Co-opting" symbols and traditions to use in other contexts.
- o "Cloaking" identity: acting like something it is not. Know how to conduct a domain name search.

Students are expected to review these questions and examples of misleading Web sites with their parents. Harris provides a rotating set of challenging site examples on climate change, health issues, and historical events

Not all middle and high school students (or teachers) succeed, but Harris's exercises and her student interactions serve to provide a safe environment in which students can question Internet content validity. This is the best of what we can expect for inquiry-based learning situations: young people can explore information from various perspectives and learn how to compare and contrast content in order to identify what is not only satisfactory, but best for their needs. They are expected to share and discuss their experiences on the Internet with their parents. The goal is to develop informed students who grow in appreciation and respect for valid, credible documentation.

To provide this environment, students use the Internet and databases without filters. Harris collaborates closely with teachers across the curriculum to design introductory WebQuests for various assignments that will provide quick and efficient background readings. Not all Internet access is structured in this way, or students would miss opportunities to learn, through guided practice, important searching and evaluation skills. Therefore some assignment information needs to remain open for students to explore the Internet on their own. The extent of free and open inquiry depends on teacher expectations (Harris 2008).

Harris also fully employs direct contacts to the local public and university libraries for access to advanced resources, including online human library reference expertise. These channels serve to broaden extensively the resources linked from her high school library Web site (http://www.library.illinois.edu/uni). A greater pool of resources opens the doors for student inquiry. Frequent assignments that involve students in field studies, interviews, and oral histories all result in an active inquiry environment, often modeled by Harris as librarian, teacher, and researcher (Everhart and Harris 2002).

> Our response to life without filters has been to institute aggressive and long-term education efforts in the ethical and responsible use of information and communication technologies. We see it as a distinct advantage that our students' online experiences at school are not so different from their or their peers' online experiences outside of the school setting. Our choice has been to directly address issues related to the freedom they enjoy–issues ranging from intellectual property and cyberbullying to content evaluation. (Harris 2011, 39–30)

While Harris is a wonderful example of a senior high school librarian who has thought through the processes needed to help students gain some initial levels of mature online searching, other recent experiences (Pieper and Mentzer 2013) reflect student shortcomings if a professional information specialist (school librarian) is not involved. The following example of the lack of teacher guidance in Internet engagement was reported about a group of high school students who have advanced science and math skills, but clearly have had no information literacy education:

Data from this study suggested that students spend substantial amounts of time on the Internet with few information pieces accessed. Observations of student behavior by research administrators tended to suggest that students drifted from one website to another and accidently discovered information rather than purposefully searching for it. . . . Students rarely commented on the quality of the information source. . . . Information access has dramatically accelerated in recent years. Future pedagogical efforts may need to refine student information literacy skills to prepare students for applying available information in meaningful ways to the design problem at hand. Students in this study demonstrated frequent use of the Internet and made requests of the administrator for paper-based information. However, they spent a substantial amount of time searching for information with a relatively low yield. Information literacy skills and educational efforts focusing student attention on critical missing pieces of information may increase efficiency of student research work. (92)

TOOLS THAT HELP

While the intent of this chapter is to provide a review of recent research on student online search behaviors, a brief summary of important tools and techniques now in practice is worthwhile. Most of these demonstrate the need for school library media specialists, as they are about other resources, to be informed and stay ahead of the curve in emerging technologies and Internet content.

Joyce Kasman Valenza, recently appointed as an associate professor of practice at Rutgers University, served as a high school library media specialist who established a wide array of technological experiences for her students and faculty. Her high school home page is an example of the multitude of virtual options she managed in support of guided inquiry (http://springfield library.wikispaces.com).

In 2005 Valenza published a collection of interviews of school library media leaders who have special expertise in student online search experiences. The interviews were edited by Reva Basch. One question Valenza posed to her teaching colleague Sue Fox was: "You've been teaching this [online searching] for several years; what barriers do you encounter?" Fox responded:

I see several. The first involves our students. They have to experience success with proper searching methods, like using advanced search screens, brainstorming keywords, mining result lists for alternative language, examining the help or tips pages so that they might best exploit a tool's features. Students need to know that they shouldn't necessarily accept the first piece of information they find as the best piece of information they will find. (151)

Valenza then asked: "So how can we get students to recognize that the effort they spend on searching will improve their results?" Fox concluded:

It may not happen in their first searches; it may not happen in their first semester. We have to remind students about good search habits. We have to brainstorm together before we turn them loose. But, after seeing some success, students start to trust that these techniques will work for them and they will become habit, not just more work they're being asked to do. Another barrier to searching success is the teacher. I am sometimes guilty of this. I think the student has had enough guided practice searching, and I assume that they "get it" sooner than they actually do. The result is that suddenly—at least it seems that way to me—they are reverting to old search habits and becoming frustrated. Another barrier is that adults were never formally trained on using the Internet. They might not know about tools they could access. This is true of both teachers and parents. . . . I find that it helps if you have a project of your own—building a backyard play gym, teaching yourself how to knit—and pay attention to what you specifically want to find out and the questions you have when you are learning something new. That really helps you develop better projects for the kids. (152)

Ken Haycock, a leading voice over four decades in education and school media administration, coordinated a group of expert library media specialists to review hundreds of Web sites that included online search portals for various age groups. Although the guide was published in 2003, most of it remains valid for today's parents and teachers. The most valuable aspect of the guide is the documentation of how the evaluations were conducted. Haycock also provides useful and practical discussion on difficult issues such as Internet filtering and censorship and the alternatives for managing Internet use at various grade levels. This guide includes the top twenty recommended search engines for children, notable online tutors and homework help sites, and a gallery of recommended reference sites for kids. Especially in elementary and middle school settings, the resource is invaluable (Haycock, Dober, and Edwards 2003).

SEARCH SUPPORT TOOLS ACROSS AGE GROUPS

For elementary grade students, one of the most useful (and free) online search sites is KidsClick! (http://www.kidsclick.org). Maintained by the School of Library and Information Science at Kent State University, it is designed to allow simple (usually one- or two-keyword) searches that sort through a collection of sites identified at reading levels and often providing additional visuals and graphics. Site descriptions are annotated with children in mind. Alternative search modes allow for topic or category searching, alphabetical searching, searching digital media, and electronically browsing by Dewey Decimal numbers. Standards for the site's content are high, and any parent can feel comfortable allowing his or her child to fully explore the possibilities. It is designed for students in grades K–7, and Kent State maintains a very reasonable site selection policy that includes the following statements:

- Do not add commercial sites that only offer particular product/ordering information. In order to be cataloged, commercial sites must contain entertainment content or educational content.
- Do not catalog any site with unsafe privacy features.
- Do not catalog sites that celebrate evil, shock, or scare, or advocate violence, hatred of other groups of people, or illegal activities.
- Will catalog religious organization sites, even if many people disagree with the beliefs of that particular religion. As long as the web sites of these religious organizations don't conflict with any of the above criteria, they will not be excluded.
- Will catalog sites that offer objective treatments (or a combination of sites that taken together offer a balanced treatment) of major social issues including: homosexuality; child abuse; family violence; AIDS; abortion; alcoholism; drug abuse; etc. We recognize that these topics are often difficult for adults to discuss and agree on; however, we also believe that as issues in the public forum, children are exposed to news concerning these topics and should have access to any material that can explain them in understandable, non-partisan terms. We'd encourage the development of web sites that can present such topics in age-appropriate ways.

FOR MIDDLE GRADES AND HIGH SCHOOL

ProQuest Research Companion (http://www.proquest.com/libraries/schools) has a substantial Web presence associated with academic dissertations and journals. It also provides one of the more understandable overviews of the information research process. The modules are organized in a clear manner that serves to direct secondary school students away from the more complex graduate school tools. Online exercises help students gain some sophistication in evaluation of sources, refining search formulas, and working toward a research focus. ProQuest states that its approach supports the new Common Core State Standards Imitative (http://www.core standards.org/).

NOODLETOOLS

NoodleTools, Inc. is a California company cofounded in 1999 by mother and son team Debbie and Damon Abilock and incorporated in 2002. Based on many years as a professional school media specialist, technology coordinator, and curriculum developer, Debbie Abilock has wide experience with the K–12 virtual information processing world. She has served as the editor of *Knowledge Quest* in recent years and now presents widely around the country. According to the Web site (http://www.noodletools.com/about/), "NoodleTools has emerged as the leading integrated academic research platform on the Web, transforming the way that teachers provide differentiated instruction of literacy to students in upper elementary through university. A cornerstone in thousands of subscribing schools and universities, NoodleTools supports the research process with a platform of integrated tools for note-taking, outlining, citation, document archiving/annotation, and collaborative research and writing." Modules, live support staff, and online guidance services have grown and undergird a philosophy of collaborative inquiry across disciplines, academic ranks, and research maturation levels.

Perhaps the most impressive part of the NoodleTools Web site is the guide that helps searchers "Choose the Best Search" for their information needs (http://www.noodletools.com /debbie/literacies/information/5locate/adviceengine.html). A wide variety of information need possibilities are presented, each having a legitimate relationship to an inquiry project and each tied to a menu of online information services that can address it. It is the most comprehensive and yet straightforward matrix for information search platform selection yet devised. A portion of the information need grid raises these options, and a visit to the Web site will show the multiple platforms associated with the information need:

- I need to define my topic:
  - I need to understand the scope of my topic.
  - I need to see related topics.
  - I need to refine and narrow my topic.
  - I need to choose a controversial issue.
  - I need background on possible topics.
- I need to find quality results:
  - I need authoritative sites chosen by an expert researcher.
  - I need personal help from experts.
  - I need sites ranked or tagged as valuable or relevant.
  - I need primary sources.
  - I need peer-reviewed journal articles.
- I need to do research in a specific discipline:
  - I need official government information.
  - I need in-depth information about a country or unrepresented territory.
  - I need reputable health information.
  - I need legal documents, agencies, or news.
  - I need creative and performing arts sources.
- I need opinions and perspectives:
  - I want opinions on current issues.

   ○ I need news from other countries' perspectives.
   ○ I want multiple perspectives on hot social and political topics.
   ○ I want to compare news treatment.

NoodleTools also provides useful, authoritative discussions on twenty-first-century literacies that include visual literacy, spatial literacy, historical literacy, cultural literacy, political literacy, information literacy, scientific literacy, and mathematical literacy. NoodleTools drives the virtual information search process by knowledge and understanding of tool content in association with the learning process. Guided inquiry thus becomes an interaction between learning academic content and learning the range of tools available to both focus and expand the inquiry. This sets the stage not only to meet a given academic exercise, but also to feed lifelong learning.

JUDGING INFORMATION VALUE

The rubric in table 1 provides guidance in the evaluation of new information encountered at the high school, undergraduate, and graduate levels. It represents the two major components for judging information value: potential utility and established authority (Callison 2007).

Table 1. A Rubric for Judging Information Value (Web site, Book, Article) by Utility and Authority

Function	Lacking: Of Little or No Value	Sufficient: Of some Selective Value	Exemplary: Key to My Inquiry
UTILITY			
Term definitions	This resource provides no meaningful definitions relevant to the topic.	This resource gives some useful definition of terms, names, and events relevant to my topic.	An extensive set of historical and current terms, names, and events is included, including core and peripheral.
Links and references	Links or references to other resources are not provided.	Some links or references are given that appear to be worth tracing.	An extensive listing of core and associated links and citations is provided and referenced within the text to help determine specific additional tracings of high potential.
Clarity	The organization and content of this source are too simplistic, too complex, or too poorly structured to be understood.	Most of the content is understandable and holds potential for assimilation in association with my current thinking.	The content is challenging for me, but understandable, and offers meaningful information to help me advance my thinking on this topic.

(continued)

Table 1. A Rubric for Judging Information Value (Web site, Book, Article) by Utility and Authority (*continued*)

Idea confirmation and generation	Very little in the resource confirms or rejects ideas and concepts relevant to this topic.	Several standard, core ideas and concepts are covered, and they may serve to either confirm or counter my current thinking. Some questions new to me are generated.	Not only are the basic and common ideas and concepts relevant to this inquiry described extensively, many new perspectives are offered that I have not previously considered. Many intriguing new questions are generated.
Overall usefulness	Very low—reject	Moderate—acceptable if few other sources are available	Highly valuable—will be a key or core source for this inquiry; cited often and linking to other sources.
AUTHORITY			
Expertise	This resource seems to be compiled and written by a person or group with little or no expertise relevant to the topic.	This resource contains information and data from people or groups who have documented expertise relevant to the topic.	This resource is clearly composed and fully substantiated by a person or persons who have established credentials and expertise relevant to my inquiry.
Open perspectives	This resource is clearly biased, providing a narrow perspective by a person or group who hold a very personal agenda and low expertise relevant to the topic.	Most common perspectives related to the issues of this topic are presented in a fair and balanced manner with authorities identified when necessary.	A wide array of perspectives is covered and related in terms of mainstream, fringe, or radical stances, and leading experts are associated with these perceptions.
Current data	Data provided are not clear and tend to be out of date.	Most data seem to be understandable to me and my audience and tend to be fairly recent. Data along with other confirming data will help me infer conclusions.	Data presented are convincing and complete and seem to be the most recent available. Data are strong enough to infer conclusions.

(*continued*)

Table 1. A Rubric for Judging Information Value (Web site, Book, Article)
by Utility and Authority (*continued*)

Notoriety	Person or persons are of little notability and standing.	Written by a person or persons not widely known, but associated with a group or institution of accepted reputation relative to the topic, therefore giving merit to conclusions reported.	The person, persons, group, association, agency, or institution is widely accepted as the leading authority relative to the topic. Stature is such that opinions expressed are of high persuasive value.
Overall authority	Very low—reject	Reasonable—use to elaborate on issues	Impressive and adds value to the information and data in a convincing manner. A key figure, or expert, is frequently central to the full discussion and inquiry at hand.

REFERENCES

Agosto, D. E. 2002. "Bounded Rationality and Satisficing in Young People's Web-based Decision Making." *Journal of the American Society for Information Science and Technology* 53, no. 1: 16–27.

Anderson, C. A. 1982. "Inoculation and Counter Explanation: Debiasing Techniques in the Perseverance of Social Theories." *Social Cognition* 1: 126–139.

Arnone, M. P., R. Reynolds, and T. Marshall. 2009. "The Effect of Early Adolescents' Psychological Needs Satisfaction upon Their Perceived Competence in Information Skills and Intrinsic Motivation for Research." *School Libraries Worldwide* 15, no. 2: 115–134.

Arnone, M. P., R. V. Small, and R. Reynolds. 2010. "Supporting Inquiry by Identifying Gaps in Student Confidence." *School Libraries Worldwide* 16, no. 1: 47–60.

Baker, K. 2013. *Information Literacy and Cultural Heritage: Developing a Model for Lifelong Learning.* Oxford: Chandos.

Callison, D. 1988. "Methods for Measuring Student Use of Databases and Interlibrary Loan Materials: The WilSearch Project with Forty-one High School Juniors at Carmel, Indiana." *School Library Media Quarterly* 16 (Winter): 138–144.

Callison, D. 2007. "Higher Order Information Literacy Skills: Evaluation, Synthesis, and Critical Thinking." Keynote address at the Iowa Library Cooperative and the 4th Annual Information Literacy Forum hosted at the Des Moines Area Community College, Ankeny Campus, June.

Callison, D., and A. Daniels. 1988. "Introducing End-User Software for Enhancing Student Online Searching: The WilSearch Project at Carmel High School." *School Library Media Quarterly* 16 (Spring): 173–181.

Donham, J. 2014. "Inquiry." In *Inquiry and the Common Core*, edited by V. H. Harada and S. Coatney, 3–15. Santa Barbara, CA: Libraries Unlimited.

Dunbar, K. 1993. "Concept Discovery in a Scientific Domain." *Cognitive Science* 17: 397–434.

Everhart, N. L., and F. J. Harris. 2002. "Using Primary Sources and Creative Writing to Teach Middle School History." *Knowledge Quest* 31, no. 2 (November/December): 52–54.

Farmer, L. S. J. 2013. "Digital Citizenship Instruction in K–20 Education." In *Handbook of Research on Teaching and Learning in K–20 Education*, edited by V. C. X. Wang, 281–299. Hershey, PA: Information Science Reference.

Fidel, R., et al. 1999. "A Visit to the Information Mall: Web Searching Behavior of High School Students." *Journal of the American Society for Information Science* 50, no. 1: 24–37.

Fitzgerald, M. A. 1999. "Evaluating Information: An Information Literacy Challenge." *School Library Media Research* 2. http://www.ala.org/aasl/aaslpubsandjournals/slmrb/slmrcontents/volume21999/vol2fitzgerald (accessed February 8, 2014).

Flanagin, A. J., et al. 2010. *Kids and Credibility: An Empirical Examination of Youth, Digital Media Use, and Information Credibility.* Cambridge, MA: MIT Press.

Flavell, J. H. 1981. "Cognitive Monitoring." In *Children's Oral Communication Skills*, edited by W. P. Dickson, 35–60. New York: Academic Press.

Gordon, C. A. 1999. "Students as Authentic Researchers." *School Library Research* 2. http://www.ala.org/aasl/aaslpubsandjournals/slmrb/slmrcontents/volume21999/vol2gordon (accessed February 8, 2014).

Gross, M. 2006. *Studying Children's Questions: Imposed and Self-Generated Information Seeking at School.* Metuchen, NJ: Scarecrow.

Gross, M., and D. Latham. 2009. "Undergraduate Perceptions of Information Literacy: Defining, Attaining, and Self-Assessing Skills." *College & Research Libraries* 70: 336–350.

Gross, M., and D. Latham. 2011. *Information Skills: How to Find the Information You Need.* The Florida State University. http://attaininfolit.org/_assets/AILInstructorGuide.pdf (accessed March 1, 2014).

Gross, M., and D. Latham. 2013. "Addressing Below Proficient Information Literacy Skills: Evaluating the Efficacy of an Evidence-Based Educational Intervention." *Library & Information Science Research* 35, no. 3 (July): 181–190.

Harris, F. J. 2008. "Challenges to Teaching Credibility Assessment in Contemporary Schooling." In *Digital Media, Youth, and Credibility*, edited by M. J. Metzger and A. J. Flanagin, 155–179. Cambridge, MA: MIT Press.

Harris, F. J. 2011. *I Found It on the Internet: Coming of Age Online.* 2nd ed. Chicago: American Library Association.

Haycock, K., M. Dober, and B. Edwards. 2003. *Authoritative Guide to Kids' Search Engines, Subject Directories, and Portals.* New York: Neal-Schuman.

Head, A. J. 2013. "Learning the Ropes: How Freshmen Conduct Course Research Once They Enter College." Cengage Learning in partnership with the Information School at the University of Washington and in affiliation with the Berkman Center for Internet and Society at Harvard.

Hoffman, J. L., et al. 2003. "The nature of Middle School Learners' Science Content Understandings with the Use of On-line Resources." *Journal of Research in Science Teaching* 40, no. 3: 323–346.

Jones, B. D. 2002. "Recommendations for Implementing Internet Inquiry Projects." *Journal of Educational Technology Systems* 30, no. 3: 271–291.

Karchmer, R. A. 2008. "The Journal Ahead: Thirteen Teachers Report How the Internet Influences Literacy and Literacy Instruction in Their K–12 Classrooms." *Handbook of Research on New Literacies*, edited by J. Coiro et al., 1241–1280. New York: Lawrence Erlbaum.

KidsClick! The Freedom to Explore. School of Library and Information Science, Kent State University. http://www.slis.kent.edu (accessed March 31, 2014).

Kuhlthau, C. C. 1996. "The Concept of a Zone of Intervention for Identifying the Role of Intermediaries in the Information Search Process." Paper presented at Global Complexity: Information, Chaos and Control, American Society for Information Science (ASIS) Annual Meeting, October 22.

Kuhn, D. 1991. *The Skills of Argument.* Cambridge, UK: Cambridge University Press.

Kuiper, E., and M. Volman. 2008. "The Web as a Source of Information for Students in K–12 Education." In *Handbook of Research on New Literacies*, edited by J. Coiro et al., 241–266. Lawrence Erlbaum.

Lamb, A. 2004. "WebQuests." *School Library Monthly* 21, no. 2 (October): 38–40.

Lazonder, A. W. 2014. "Inquiry Learning." In *Handbook of Research on Educational Communications and Technology*, edited by J. M. Spector et al., 453–464. New York: Springer.

Markman, E. M. 1981. "Comprehension Monitoring." In *Children's Oral Communication Skills*, edited by W. P. Dickson, 61–84. New York: Academic.

NoodleTools. http://www.noodletools.com/index.php. (accessed March 30, 2014).

Paul, R. 1992. "Critical Thinking: What, Why, and How." In *Critical Thinking: Educational Imperative*, edited by C. A. Barnes, 3–24. San Francisco: Jossey-Bass.

Pitts, J. M. 1994. "Personal Understandings and Mental Models of Information: A Qualitative Study of Factors Associated with the Information Seeking and Use of Adolescents." PhD diss., Florida State University.

Pieper, J., and N. Mentzer. 2013. "High School Students' Use of Paper-Based and Internet-Based Information Sources in the Engineering Design Process." *Journal of Technology Education* 24, no. 2 (Spring): 78–95.

Shannon, D. 2002. "The Education and Competencies of School Library Media Specialists." *School Library Research* 5. http://www.ala.org/aasl/aaslpubsandjournals/slmrb/slmrcontents/volume52002/shannon (accessed March 2, 2014).

Shenton, A. K. 2007. "The Paradoxical World of Young People's Information Behavior." *School Libraries Worldwide* 13, no. 2 (July): 1–17.

Shenton, A. K., and P. Dixon. 2005. "Information Needs: Learning More about what Kids Want, Need, and Expect from Research." *Children & Libraries: The Journal of the Association for Library Service to Children* 3, no. 2: 20–28.

Stripling, B. K. 2011. "Teaching the Voices of History through Primary Sources and Historical Fiction." DPS diss., Syracuse University, iSchool Information Science and Technology.

Todd, R. J., and C. A. Gordon. n.d. "School Libraries, Now More Than Ever." Position paper for the Center for International Scholarship in School Libraries. http://www.nmm.net/storage/resources/The_Importance_of_School_Libraries.pdf (accessed March 2, 2014).

Tomkins, S. P., and S. D. Tunnicliffe. 2001. "Looking for Ideas: Observations, Interpretation and Hypothesis-Making by 12-Year-Old Pupils Undertaking Science Investigations." *International Journal of Science Education* 23: 791–813.

Tschirgi, J. E. 1980. "Sensible Reasoning: A Hypothesis about Hypotheses." *Child Development* 51: 1–10.

Valenza, J. K., and R. Basch, eds. 2005. *Super Searchers Go to School*. Medford, NJ: Information Today.

Vygotsky, L. 1978. *Mind in Society: The Development of Higher Psychological Processes*. Cambridge, UK: Cambridge University Press.

Wallace, R. M. et al. 2000. "Science on the Web: Students On-line in a Sixth-grade Classroom." *Journal of the Learning Sciences* 9, no. 1: 75–104.

Wineburg, S. S. 1991. "Historical Problem-Solving: A Study of the Cognitive Processes Used in the Evaluation of Documentary and Pictorial Evidence." *Journal of Educational Psychology* 83 (March): 73–87.

Chapter 14

A Time Line for the Progression through Information Literacy to Inquiry

This time line is based on a review of hundreds of documents that include learning standards, best practices reflecting the adoption of information literacy, and its progression as inquiry-based learning over the past five decades. The chronological listings represent various groups of educators and researchers who have identified the key components of information literacy and have come to apply inquiry-based strategies as a method to improve teacher and student learning in the information age.

Author clusters are based on professional relationships established through joint authorships and/or cooperative affiliation with institutions and professional associations that have sponsored the documents listed. Some affiliations have involved coauthoring across the past five decades and relationships that have molded national standards, especially in the American Association of School Librarians.

The progression, or evolution, of these notions shows a movement toward more attention to the student as an active participant in his or her own learning. There is also movement toward enhancing the role of school library media specialists and other teachers to be collaborating information specialists as they manage and mentor the learning processes associated with inquiry. And there are clear indications that the technologies of our time have a significant impact on the opportunities to make wider inquiry adoption and implementation possible.

Inquiry technologies include not only incredible social hardware and software advances, but also the techniques to harness effective methods of learning and teaching: systematic planning based on analysis of student needs and abilities. Techniques include organizing, scaffolding, mentoring, praising and rewarding the successful student inquirer, and sharing those accomplishments throughout the community.

Concepts are not necessarily based on empirical evidence, but usually are drawn from notions included in documents providing standards from various education associations and ideas from academic essays. Important exceptions are the conclusions drawn parallel to those of Carol Collier Kuhlthau and her associates, including those by Carol A. Gordon and Ross J. Todd at the Center for International Scholarship in School Libraries (CISSL), Rutgers University. Findings reported from CISSL, for the most part, have been derived from systematic studies. Ruth V. Small and Marilyn Arnone have also established an extensive research record over the past few decades at Syracuse University. Important field studies have been conducted by Judy Pitts, Barbara Stripling, Violet Harada, and Julie Tallman. Daniel Callison and Annette Lamb have drawn from these field studies along with the extensive research from instructional systems technology.

Portions of this time line were published previously in *School Library Monthly* (2014).

The team of Michael Eisenberg and Bob Berkowitz has probably been the most successful across the country with their practical six-skill approach.

Concepts and notions reported in this time line have been associated with successful educational practice and leading educational theories. The entire body of work, offered in chronological order, serves to document the corresponding list of concepts. All associated documents should be examined in full to gain the greater meaning behind the concepts given.

Documents have been placed in sections based on the affiliation of authors as cowriters and/or professional status with an educational association. In many cases the reader will find these notions come from several of the documents or Web sites listed. Readers are encouraged to explore all of the documents reported in association with related concepts in order to gain an understanding of the development, depth, and application of these notions derived from the cluster of literature cited.

Overall, this time line illustrates the progression from information literacy skills to the adoption of inquiry concepts in practice that are student-centered and can be managed through school library media programs with adequate professional staff. Many national educational associations now promote inquiry-based learning as a prominent set of instructional strategies for guiding a learning philosophy in twenty-first-century education.

A TIME LINE: KEY CONCEPTS AND ASSOCIATED LITERATURE FROM THE PROCESSES DESIGNED TO TEACH INFORMATION LITERACY THROUGH INQUIRY AND PROBLEM SOLVING: A PROGRESSION FROM 1960 TO 2014

1960: The School Library Is a Learning Laboratory for Inquiry and Independent Learning

Key Concepts

- The true concept of a school library program means instruction, service, and activity throughout the school rather than merely within the four walls of the library quarters. All phases of the school program are enriched by means of library materials and services. The degree to which teachers and pupils can and do depend on the services, materials, and staff of the library measures the extent to which the library program is successful.
- The library is a laboratory for research and study where students learn to work alone and in groups under the guidance of librarians and teachers. Thus it contributes to the growth and development of youth in independent thinking.
- The focus of the media program is on facilitating and improving the learning process in its new directions—with emphasis on the learner, on ideas and concepts rather than on isolated facts, and on inquiry rather than on rote memorization.
- It is important that every media specialist participate actively in shaping the learning environment and design of instruction. The media program is indispensable in the educational programs that now stress individualization, inquiry, and independent learning for students.
- Because there is no set sequence of steps in creative inquiry, a student should be able to move from one condition to another with ease, working in one momentarily and in another at greater length. His or her ultimate goal is the pleasurable discovery of what are, at least to the student, new ideas and, eventually, the development of original media in which he or she conveys his or her ideas to others.
- It is conceivable that the training of all students to create a variety of media for purposes of creative inquiry may become the most rapidly growing service of future media centers. The primary role of the school media specialist is, by definition, that of a teacher of media.

- The learner is at the center of instructional interests, and learning is the central outcome. Programs of media services are designed to help learners grow in their ability to find, generate, evaluate, and apply information that helps them function effectively as individuals and participate fully in society.
- The four conditions for creative inquiry require four kinds of facilities: large group instruction, independent activities, conference and committee interaction, and production of original media.

Associated Literature in Chronological Order

American Association of School Librarians. *Standards for School Library Programs.* Chicago: American Library Association, 1960.

American Library Association and the National Education Association. *Standards for School Media Programs.* Chicago: ALA, 1972.

Taylor, K. "Creative Inquiry and Instructional Media: A Revision of a Theory Underlying the Continuing Development of the School Instructional Media Center and Its Program." *School Library Quarterly* (Fall): 18–26, 1972.

1972: The International Baccalaureate Program Is an Early Adopter of Inquiry

Key Concepts

- Interpretation, implementation, and assessment of the inquiry program are guided by local educators.
- Students and teachers are knowledgeable. They explore concepts, ideas, and issues that have local and global significance.
- Together, teachers and students are thinkers who exercise initiative in applying thinking skills critically and creatively in order to recognize and approach complex problems and make reasoned, ethical decisions.
- All learners maintain an open mind to understand and appreciate their own cultures and personal histories as well as the opinions and cultures of others.

Associated Literature in Chronological Order

Peterson, A. D. *The International Baccalaureate: An Experiment in International Education.* London: Harrap and Company, 1972.

Mathews, J., and I. Hill. *Supertest: How the International Baccalaureate Can Strengthen Our Schools.* Chicago: Open Court, 2005.

Tilke, A. *The International Baccalaureate Diploma Program and the School Library.* Santa Barbara, CA: Libraries Unlimited, 2011.

1975: New AASL Standards Reflect Inquiry Learning and Teaching Students to Think

Key Concepts

- The library is an apprentice's workshop for thinking—a place where children actively construct their own understandings through interactions with human, physical, and symbolic worlds—a learning laboratory. School librarians must be proactive in leading educational change.
- Good schools enable students to acquire and use knowledge, to experience and enjoy discovery and learning, to understand themselves and other people, to develop lifelong learning skills, and to function productively in a democratic society.

- Librarians are teachers, and they serve both students and teachers. Collaboration among educators should strive to reach the highest levels of interaction for quality educational programs.
- School library media specialists must take visible action to demonstrate that they deserve the role of instructional specialist. The primary function performed by the school library media specialist or program can be viewed as a mediation function. From this perspective, the specialist plays the role of an intermediary between the incredibly complex and rapidly expanding information world and the client.
- Questions that drive inquiry should address real-world problems. Educators often define problems for students to solve, while in the everyday world, the first and often most difficult step is recognition that a problem exists. Engage students in activities that force them to think about their own thinking.
- Library media specialists need to realize that a major part of their time must be spent helping students develop the thinking skills that will equip them to not only locate but also evaluate and use information effectively and thereby become information literate; librarians will need to employ new assessment methods to judge student performance. Students can be taught to apply an evaluation process to selection of information, including from the Internet.
- If library media professionals are to assist other educators effectively in providing sound educational programs, they must become knowledgeable about the ways in which children and young adults actually process information. The library media program models and promotes collaborative planning and curriculum development. The mission of the library media program is to ensure that students, teachers, and staff are effective users of ideas and information.
- The school library program models an inquiry-based approach to learning and the information search process. The development of higher level intellectual and problem-solving skills can only be accomplished in an environment where they can be repeatedly applied and tested throughout the learner's school experience. The library media program is essential to learning and teaching and must be fully integrated into the curriculum to promote students' achievement of learning goals.
- Students realize they will find conflicting facts in different sources, and they determine the accuracy and relevance of information before taking notes. They determine the adequacy of information gathered according to the complexity of the topic, the research questions, and the product that is expected.
- Inquiry provides a framework for learning. To become independent learners, students must gain not only the skills but also the disposition to use those skills (curiosity, open-mindedness, perseverance), along with an understanding of their own responsibilities and self-assessment strategies. The library media program fosters individual and collaborative inquiry.
- Twenty-first-century learners reach maturation in the inquiry process when they pursue personal growth by gaining quality information ethically and efficiently and applying critical thinking to make informed decisions and share knowledge.
- To be an independent learner, especially in an online digital environment, one must also be information literate, appreciate literature, and strive for excellence in information seeking and knowledge generation.
- The driving force of the Common Core writing standards is student development and use of logical arguments based on claims, solid reasoning, and relevant evidence.
- Short, focused research projects, similar to the kind of projects students will face in their careers as well as long-term, in-depth research are another piece of the writing standards. This is because written analysis and the presentation of significant findings are critical to career and college readiness.

Associated Literature in Chronological Order

American Association of School Librarians. *Media Programs: District and School.* Chicago: ALA, 1975.
Chisholm, M. E., and D. P. Ely. *Instructional Design and the Library Media Specialist.* Chicago: ALA, 1979.
Vandergrift, K. E. *The Teaching Role of the School Media Specialist.* Chicago: AASL, 1979.

Cleaver, B. P., and W. D. Taylor. *Involving the School Library Media Specialist in Curriculum Development.* Chicago: ALA, 1983.

American Library Association Task Force on Excellence in Education. *Realities: Educational Reform in a Learning Society.* Chicago: ALA, 1984.

Flower, L. *Problem-Solving Strategies for Writing.* San Diego: Harcourty Brace Jovanovich, 1985.

Leisner, J. W. "Learning at Risk: School Library Media Programs in an Information World." *School Library Media Research* 14 (Fall 1985): 11–20.

Bertland, L. H. "An Overview of Research in Metacognition: Implications for Information Skills Instruction." *School Library Media Quarterly* 15 (Winter 1986): 96–99.

Craver, K. W. "The Changing Instructional Role of the High School Library Media Specialist, 1950–1984." *School Library Media Quarterly* 14, no. 4 (Summer 1986). http://www.ala.org/aasl/aaslpubsandjournals/slmrb/editorschoiceb/infopower/selctcraver.

Mancall, J. C., S. L. Aaron, and S. A. Walker. "Educating Students to Think." *School Library Media Quarterly* (Fall 1986): 18–27. http://www.ala.org/aasl/aaslpubsandjournals/slmrb/editorschoiceb/infopower/slctmancall.

Sheingold, K. "Keeping Children's Knowledge Alive through Inquiry." *School Library Media Quarterly* 15, no. 1 (1986): 80–85.

American Association of School Librarians (AASL) and Association for Educational Communications Technology (AECT). *Information Power: Guidelines for School Library Media Programs.* Chicago: ALA, 1988.

Kuhlthau, C. C., M. E. Goodin, and M. J. McNally, ed. *Assessment in the School Library Media Center.* Englewood, CO: Libraries Unlimited, 1994.

American Association of School Librarians (AASL) and Association for Educational Communications Technology (AECT). *Information Literacy Standards for Student Learning.* Chicago: ALA, 1998.

American Association of School Librarians (AASL) and Association for Educational Communications Technology (AECT). *Information Power: Building Partnerships for Learning.* Chicago: ALA, 1998.

Fitzgerald, M. A. "Critical Thinking 101: The Basics of Evaluating Information." *Knowledge Quest* 29, no. 2 (2000): 13–20.

Stripling, B. K., and S. Hughes-Hassel, eds. *Curriculum Connections Through the Library.* Westport, CT: Libraries Unlimited, 2003.

American Association of School Librarians. *Standards for the 21st-Century Learner.* Chicago: ALA, 2007. http://www.ala.org/aasl/standards-guidelines/learning-standards.

Vance, A. L., ed. *Assessing Student Learning in the School Library Media Center.* Chicago: AASL, 2007.

American Association of School Librarians. *Empowering Learners.* Chicago: ALA, 2009.

Harris, F. J. *I Found It on the Internet: Coming of Age Online.* 2nd ed. Chicago: ALA, 2011.

Loertscher, D. V., and K. R. Lewis. *Implementing the Common Core State Standards: The Role of the School Librarian.* Chicago: AASL, 2013. http://www.ala.org/aasl/sites/ala.org.aasl/files/content/externalrelations/CCSSLibrariansBrief_FINAL.pdf.

Common Core States Standards Initiative. 2014. http://www.corestandards.org/.

"AASL Learning Standards & Common Core Standards Crosswalk." http://www.ala.org/aasl/standards-guidelines/crosswalk.

Keeling, M. "An Exploration of the Inquiry Process." *Knowledge Quest* 43, no.2 (November/December 2014): 6–7.

1981: Early Information Curriculum Ideas Emerge from the United Kingdom

Key Concepts

- There are nine key questions students must address in projects based on an information use curriculum.
- Recognize instances in which more than one interpretation of materials is valid and necessary.

- Accept and give constructive criticism.
- Describe most valuable resources used.
- Establish a portfolio of products completed in the information curriculum.

Associated Literature in Chronological Order

Irving, Ann. *Instructional Materials for Developing Information Concepts and Information-Handling Skills in School Children.* Paris: UNISIST and the United Nations, 1981.

Marland, M. *Information Skills in the Secondary Curriculum: Recommendations of a Working Group Sponsored by the British Library.* London: Methueb Educational, 1981.

1981: Kuhlthau's Research Moves from Practice to Search Process to Guided Inquiry

Key Concepts

- Actions for teaching information literacy are constructed on tested intervention and enabling strategies that are valid across all age groups and a wide variety of learning environments.
- The emerging theory of library instruction is founded on principles of constructivist learning rather than the content of resource tools and library holdings alone. Various roles for librarians should serve to support student learning, not just access to resources. In attaining information literacy, students gain proficiency in inquiry as they learn to interpret and use information.
- Depending on the students' abilities and the task at hand, there are zones of intervention in which students are best guided and enabled to seek and learn from and understand new information.
- The information search process usually includes feelings of uncertainty, optimism, and frustration, all of which often require teacher guidance that enables students to achieve success through actions or enablers that result in management of information use tasks.
- Proven instructional intervention strategies encourage student exploration of resources with written and oral rephrasing and retelling along with keeping a journal and visually charting progress.
- Team planned, supervised guidance should be implemented by SLMS and teacher partners; they are both prepared to provide guidance at critical points in the information search and other inquiry stages or processes.
- Students learn by being actively engaged and reflecting on the experience.
- In attaining information literacy, students gain proficiency in inquiry as they are guided by teachers and librarians to learn to interpret and use information effectively.
- New insights are documented that emphasize addressing student emotional experiences, especially declines in confidence, as well as new knowledge assimilation for reaching a workable topic or focus and meaningful conclusion(s), resulting in deeper knowledge for the student.
- Students should be guided to information resources beyond the school: museums, the Internet, public and academic libraries, and subject experts both from the local community and from a distance.
- Maturing in the information search process includes understanding concepts such as browsing, monitoring, chaining, differentiating, and extracting.
- Evaluating sources should be based on expertise, currency, perspective, quality, and accuracy.
- Constructivist principles encourage student independence when possible, with the teacher and student cooperatively seeking a "third space merger" for acceptable learning experiences that meet academic requirements and personal interests and/or real-world issues.
- Summative and formative evaluations of process as well as product are documented with student-prepared charts and research experience journals.
- Guided Inquiry design requires that teams of teachers use backward design, beginning with the standards, such as the Common Core, to identify a theme, essential question, or big idea for study. Through this theme, students engage their own interests and understandings to come up with an aspect of learning or a question that particularly interests them within that topic.

- Inquiry learning shifts emphasis to student questioning, critical thinking, problem solving, engagement with diverse information sources, and development of deep knowledge and understanding.
- Five decades of research, experience, insights, and systematic measures support the transformative role of school libraries in the development of the student's personal, social, and cultural growth.
- School libraries and librarians are now, more than ever, crucial to the development of students in their teaching roles as intellectual agents. Schools without libraries minimize the opportunities for students to become discriminating users of a diverse information landscape and to develop the intellectual scaffolds for learning deeply through information. Schools without libraries are at risk of becoming irrelevant.
- The major shift in information literacy education is away from traditional research assignments to guided inquiry learning. Without adequate guidance, students commonly experience anxiety and frustration. Inquiry is learning-centered, not product-driven.
- Inquiry is driven by students' high level of questioning. Inquiry goes beyond low-level fact finding to deep understanding.

Associated Literature in Chronological Order

Kuhlthau, C. C. *School Librarians' Grade-by-Grade Activities Program: A Complete Sequential Skills Plan for Grades K–8*. West Nyack, NY: Center for Applied Research, 1981.

Kuhlthau, C.C. *Teaching the Library Research Process*. West Nyack, NY: Center for Applied Research in Education, 1985.

Kuhlthau, C. C. "Cognitive Development and Student's Research." *School Library Journal* 33, no. 11 (1987): 46.

Kuhlthau, C. C. "An Emerging Theory of Library Instruction." *School Library Media Quarterly* 16, no. 1 (1987): 23–28.

Kuhlthau, C. C. "The Information Search Process of High-, Middle-, and Low-Achieving High School Seniors." *School Library Media Quarterly* 28, no. 2 (1989): 224–228.

Todd, R. J. "Integrated Information Skills Instruction: Does It Make a Difference?" *School Library Media Quarterly* 23, no. 2 (1995): 133–139.

Kuhlthau, C. C. "Constructivist Theory for School Library Media Programs—Keynote Address." In *Instructional Interventions for Information Use*, edited by D. Callison, J. H. McGregor, and R. W. Small, 14–28. San Jose, CA: Hi Willow, 1998.

Todd, R. J. "Critical Literacies and Learning Outcomes." *Teacher Librarian* 26, no. 2 (1998): 16–21.

Donham, J., K. Bishop, C. C. Kuhlthau, and D. Oberg. *Inquiry-based Learning: Lessons from Library Power*. Worthington, OH: Linworth, 2001.

Kuhlthau, C. C. *Seeking Meaning*. 2nd ed. Westport, CT: Libraries Unlimited, 2004.

Harada, V. H. "Librarians and Teachers as Research Partners: Reshaping Practices Based on Assessment and Reflection." *School Libraries Worldwide* 11, no. 2 (2005): 49–72.

Kuhlthau, C. C., L. K. Maniotes, and A. K. Caspari. *Guided Inquiry: Learning in the 21st Century*. Westport, CT: Libraries Unlimited, 2007.

Gordon, C. A. "An Emerging Theory for Evidence Based Information Literacy Instruction, Part 1: Building a Foundation." *Evidence Based Library and Information Practice* 4, no. 2 (2009). http://Ejournals.library.ualberta.ca/index.php/EBLIP.

Gordon, C. A. "An Emerging Theory for Evidence Based Information Literacy Instruction in School Libraries, Part 2: Building a Culture of Inquiry." *Evidence Based Library and Information Practice* 4, no. 3 (2009). http://Ejournals.library.ualberta.ca/index.php/EBLIP.

Gordon, C. A. "The Culture of Inquiry." *School Librarians Worldwide* 16, no. 1 (2010): 73–88.

Kuhlthau, C. C. "Guided Inquiry: School Libraries in the 21st Century." *School Libraries Worldwide* 16, no. 1 (January 2010): 17–28. http://comminfo.rutgers.edu/~kuhlthau/docs/GI-School-Librarians-in-the-21-Century.pdf.

Thomas, N. P., S. R. Crow, and L. L. Franklin. *Information Literacy and Information Skills Instruction*. 3rd ed. Santa Barbara, CA: Libraries Unlimited, 2011.

Kuhlthau, C., L. K. Maniotes, and A. K. Caspari. *Guided Inquiry Design*. Santa Barbara, CA: Libraries Unlimited, 2012.

Maniotes, L. K. "Guided Inquiry Design and the Common Core." In *Inquiry and the Common Core*, edited by V. H. Harada and S. Coatney, 69–81. Santa Barbara, CA: Libraries Unlimited, 2014.

Todd, R. J., and C. A. Gordon. "School Libraries, Now More Than Ever." The Center for International Scholarship in School Libraries, 2010. http://www.nmm.net/storage/resources/The_Importance_of_School_Libraries.pdf.

Center for International Scholarship in School Libraries. http://cissl.rutgers.edu/.

Maniotes, L. K., and C. C. Kuhlthau. "Making the Shift from Traditional Research Assignments to Guided Inquiry Learning." *Knowledge Quest* 43, no.2 (November/December 2014): 9–15.

1985: Information Skills Should Be Placed Directly into the Curriculum, K–College

Key Concepts

- Resource-based education should address individual differences in learning and teaching styles.
- The research process (outlined in nine steps) is cross curricular and is an integral part of our everyday lives.
- Information skills are inherently present in all learning tasks.
- The student gains control of his or her future by learning how to handle information.

Associated Literature in Chronological Order

Irving, A. *Study and Information Skills across the Curriculum*. London: Heinemann, 1985.

Breivik, P. S. and E. G. Gee. *Information Literacy: Revolution in the Library*. New York: American Council on Education, 1989.

1985: Important Steps Toward Collaboration: Helping Teachers Teach

Key Concepts

- The school library media specialist is in a position to have a great positive impact on children and young adults in our schools. This impact can be made directly, through work with students, and indirectly, through helping teachers teach more effectively.
- Instructional consultation assessment involves needs assessment, instructional objectives, learner analysis, assessment of student performance, strategies and activities development, materials selection, implementation, and evaluation. These strategies are fundamental to course redesign in higher education as well as K–12 curriculum.
- Long-term course redesign requires putting together and sustaining a variety of human resources. An important task is to begin with a small number of participants and add additional faculty while maintaining the involvement of the pioneers.

Associated Literature in Chronological Order

Turner, P. M. *Helping Teachers Teach*. Englewood, CO: Libraries Unlimited, 1985.

Turner, P. M. *A Casebook for Helping Teachers Teach*. Englewood, CO: Libraries Unlimited, 1988.

Turner, P. M. and A. M. Riedling. *Helping Teachers Teach*. 3rd ed. Westport, CT: Libraries Unlimited, 2003.

Turner, P. M. and R. S. Carriveau. *Next Generation Course Design*. New York: Peter Lang, 2010.

1986: Free Inquiry Made Practical and Reenvisioned
for Graphic Information Inquiry

Key Concepts

- Meaningful, authentic learning is often found at the intersection of academic, personal, and likely workplace information needs. The school media center can serve as a learning laboratory to investigate and debate meaningful questions and issues.

- Information literacy, media literacy, critical thinking, and creative thinking are concepts enveloped within inquiry. Information fluency is the ability to apply the skills associated with information literacy, computer literacy, and critical thinking to address and solve information problems across disciplines, academic levels, and information format structures. Roles for assessment of student work and modeling of information use should be expanded to include the school librarian as a coinstructor with other teachers.

- Information inquiry is a repeating, cyclical process that triggers each time new information is encountered: questioning interacts with exploration, assimilation interacts with inference, and reflection is a summative process to determine the value of the information accepted or rejected.

- Inquiry can be found in both formal and informal learning environments and can be applied through at least four levels: controlled, guided, mentor/apprentice, and independent or free. The student matures in abilities to gather original data and conclude with original analyses of findings in a progression toward free inquiry.

- Inquiry does not stop at the gathering of information, but must include reasonable inference of findings as well as judgment about the quality of the information used. Inquiry encompasses critical and creative thinking and information and media literacy. Inquiry can become a critical learning process if students are allowed to explore a full range of information, including making judgments about those documents that are not authoritative or fully relevant.

- Students document the processes of learning as well as their products. These are shared with peers and parents as well as teachers. Projects may extend across a student's academic career.

- Ownership of learning begins with students developing their own researchable questions. This can be done as individual students, in small groups, or in an educator-led classroom discussion.

- The educator's roles for inquiry include appraiser, coach, guide, instructor, motivational speaker, and role model; he or she is a mentor for advanced inquiry. To be teachers, librarians need to expand their assessment role to include evaluation of student performance.

- Inquiry content is driven by questions raised by students and modified by teachers, less frequently as the student matures toward the level of master apprentice for independent free inquiry.

- The educator should provide students with an occasion every day for self-analysis. Giving students the opportunity to reflect personally on what they are doing, thinking, and still need to do is an invaluable use of instructional time. They may learn to address bias and be more open to assimilating information that is new and counter to held beliefs.

- Learning to critically evaluate information requires modeling on a regular basis by teachers and SLMS. Cognitive apprenticeship is the highest level of guiding students to become independent, critical thinkers. Librarians and teachers should be models of constructive inquiry.

- Students, as amateur information scientists, learn to gather data through exploring multimedia documents and primary sources, as well as conducting interviews and surveys.

- Information inquiry findings are debated among students to clarify the strength of authority and relevance, and end products are presented to a variety of groups, with media designed to meet specific audience needs and abilities. A goal of information inquiry is that the student learns the value of various information resources.

- All processes are recursive, from encountering new information to revision of formal writing and speaking, maintained in students' portfolios and journals over their academic careers.

- Critical evaluation of information becomes more substantial as the student matures in his or her scientific habits and learns to make convincing arguments.

- The ability to manage information assimilation and personal bias drive the maturation of the student researcher.

- A key component of information inquiry is the opportunity to present the research quest and final product to a peer group, who will evaluate the final product and provide honest, constructive, and critical feedback.
- Information literacy and media literacy have more common aspects than differences.
- In conjunction with the Common Core State Standards, students can extend and enhance inquiry through the examination of graphics and other visuals both to acquire and to present information. Employing arguments based on constructive evidence is a critical skill for all learners.
- The five core elements of information inquiry are found in each of the current models designed for teaching information literacy through inquiry. These elements impact student learning through a recursive cycle as students attempt to evaluate new information for assimilation or rejection and ultimately solving their information needs.
- Assessment methods need to be refined so that they more effectively measure student learning through inquiry experiences, both academic and authentic.

Associated Literature in Chronological Order

Callison, D. "School Library Media Programs and Free Inquiry Learning." *School Library Journal* 32, no. 6 (1986): 20–24.

Callison, D. "Expanding the Evaluation Role in the Critical-Thinking Curriculum." In *Assessment and the School Library Media Center*, edited by C. C. Kuhlthau, 43–57. Englewood, CO: Libraries Unlimited, 1994.

Callison, D., and C. L. Tilley. "Information and Media Literacies: Towards a Common Core." In *Instructional Interventions for Information Use*, edited by D. Callison, J. H. McGregor, and R. V. Small, 110–116. San Jose, CA: Hi Willow, 1998.

Tilley, C. L., and D. Callison. "The Cognitive Apprenticeship Model and Adolescent Information Use." In *Instructional Interventions for Information Use*, edited by D. Callison, J. H. McGregor, and R. V. Small, 245–254. San Jose, CA: Hi Willow, 1998.

Callison, D. "Inquiry [Four Levels Defined]."*School Library Media Activities Monthly* 15, no. 6 (February 1999): 38–42.

Fitzgerald, M. A. "Evaluating Information: An Information Literacy Challenge." *School Library Media Research* 2 (1999). http://www.ala.org/aasl/aaslpubsandjournals/slmrb/slmrcontents/volume21999/vol2fitzgerald.

Callison, D. "Inquiry, Literacy and the Learning Laboratory." In *New Millennium New Horizons in Information Services in Schools Centre for Studies*, edited by L. Hay, K. Hanson, and J. Henri, 55–63. Wagga Wagga, NSW, Australia: Centre for Studies in Teacher Librarianship, Charles Sturt University, 2001.

Tilley, C. L. "Cognitive Apprenticeship." *School Library Monthly* 18, no. 3 (November 2001): 37–38, 48.

Callison, D. "Critical Literacy and Inquiry." *Educators' Spotlight Digest* 1, no. 3 (Fall 2006). http://www.informationliteracy.org/users_data/admin/Volume1_Issue3_Guest_writer.pdf.

Callison, D. *Key Words, Concepts and Methods for Information Age Instruction: A Guide to Teaching Information Inquiry*. Baltimore, MD: LMS Associates, 2003.

Callison, D. "Questioning Revisited." *School Library Monthly* 22, no. 6 (February 2006): 40–43.

Callison, D., and A. Lamb. "Authentic Learning and Assessment." In *The Blue Book on Information Age Inquiry, Instruction, and Literacy*, 292–302. Westport, CT: Libraries Unlimited, 2006.

Callison, D. and L. Preddy. *The Blue Book on Information Age Inquiry, Instruction, and Literacy*. Westport, CT: Libraries Unlimited, 2006.

Callison, D. "Evaluation Criteria for the Places of Learning." *Knowledge Quest* 35, no. 3. (January–February 2007): 14–19.

Tilley, C. L., and D. Callison. "New Mentors for New Media: Harnessing the Instructional Potential of Cognitive Apprenticeships." *Knowledge Quest* 35, no. 5 (May–June 2007): 26–31.

Preddy, L. B. "Student Inquiry in the Research Process." Reprinted in *21st-Century Learning in School Libraries*, edited by K. Fontichiaro, 130–146. Santa Barbara, CA: Libraries Unlimited, 2009.

Lamb, A., and D. Callison. *Graphic Inquiry*. Santa Barbara, CA: ABC-CLIO, 2012.

Callison, D. "Inquiry and the Common Core: Argument Processes" [Parts I and II]. *School Library Monthly* 29, no. 6 (March 2013): 20–22; 29, no. 7 (April 2013): 21–23.

Callison, D., and K. Baker. "Elements of Information Inquiry, Evolution of Models, and Measured Reflection." *Knowledge Quest* 43, no. 2 (November/December 2014): 18–24.

Lamb, A., and D. Callison. "Information Age Inquiry." n.d. http://virtualinquiry.com/about/.

Preddy, L. "Student Inquiry in the Research Process." n.d. http://www.lesliepreddy.com/Inquiry/inquiry index.HTM.

1986: The Student Is the Center of the Writing and Research Processes

Key Concepts

- Through gaining understanding of personal interests, the topic for inquiry emerges to "find the student."
- First-person narratives encourage a wider range of students to engage in writing in order to communicate personal feelings and real-life observations.
- Students convey a personal reaction to the inquiry process through learning logs, in which they describe feelings and needs as they progress through the information gathering and writing processes, and receive guidance from SLMS and teachers, who read the logs on a regular basis.
- Community narratives tend to work best in this process, enhanced by interviews and oral histories.
- Student products are shared with parents in a celebration of learning.
- Examples of student products are published as models for future student inquiry.
- A great positive effect occurs when the directors or teachers of a writing group write and celebrate alongside the other members of the group.
- Throughout the I-Search unit, the teaching team, including the SLMS, demonstrates and explains research techniques and strategies, and they model the collection of data and drawing of conclusions and reflections.

Associated Literature in Chronological Order

Macrorie, K. *Telling Writing*. Upper Montclair, NJ: Boynton/Cook Publishers, 1985.

Macrorie, K. *The I-Search Paper*. Upper Montclair, NJ: Boynton/Cook Publishers, 1988.

Miller, L., T. Steinlage, and M. Printz. *Cultural Cobblestones: Teaching Cultural Diversity*. Metuchen, NJ: Scarecrow Press, 1994.

Joyce, M. Z., and J. I. Tallman. *Making the Writing and Research Connection with the I-Search Process*. New York: Neal-Schuman, 1997.

Tallman, J. I. "Effective Teaching and Learning Strategies Modeled through the I-Search: An Inquiry-based, Student-centered, Reading/Writing Process." In *Instructional Interventions for Information Use*, edited by D. Callison, J. H. McGregor, and R. V. Small, 232–244. San Jose, CA: Hi Willow, 1998.

Tallman, J. I., and M. Z. Joyce. *Making the Writing and Research Connection with the I-Search Process*. New York: Neal-Schuman, 2006.

1988: Moving School Libraries into the Center of Student Inquiry and Deeper Thinking

Key Concepts

- The Stripling and Pitts research process model connects ten steps with frequent reflection points that lead to greater use of information to focus on a meaningful research topic.
- Exercises are designed for students to demonstrate critical thinking, cognitive creativity, and metacognitive skills in the language arts and social studies student research paper.

- Students should be encouraged to move beyond who, what, and where to levels of how and why whenever possible, to the highest levels of the learning taxonomy.
- Students should be taught how to judge information on the basis of authority, significance, bias, currency, and relevance.
- Learning is centered on student engagement in a thoughtful learning cycle.
- Students, where ability levels allow, draw conclusions and conceptualize original solutions.
- Both experience and research tell us that students engaged in inquiry are more motivated to pursue learning on their own than students who are fed preorganized information that they are expected to remember.
- Teaching teams can effectively implement a framework for inquiry and thinking skills across the curriculum based on collaborative school library media specialist and teacher extensive planning, and setting goals for holistic learning and measured assessment.
- The Stripling Inquiry Model is a frame for learning that involves connecting to personal interests and a desire to know, asking questions that probe beyond simple fact gathering, investigating answers from multiple perspectives, constructing new understandings and conclusions, expressing the new ideas through a variety of formats, and reflecting on both the process and product of learning. The model can be an effective instrument to coplan lessons in a nonthreatening manner and has been a foundation for statewide curriculum development. To be meaningful, inquiry should be student directed and involve authentic information problems.
- Troubling aspects of the digital information environment include the double digital divides: first, between those who have access to the advanced technologies and those students who do not, and second, between those who are educated in information literacy and those students who are not as fluent and are therefore more likely to be falsely persuaded and mislead.

Associated Literature in Chronological Order

Stripling, B. K., and J. M. Pitts. *Brainstorms and Blueprints: Teaching Library Research as a Thinking Process.* Englewood, CO: Libraries Unlimited, 1988.

Stripling, B. "Learning-Centered Libraries: Implications from research." *School Library Media Quarterly* 27, no. 3 (Spring 1995): 163–170.

Harada, V. H. "Empowered Learning: Fostering Thinking across the Curriculum." In *Curriculum Connections through the Library: Principles and Practice*, edited by B. K. Stripling and S. Hughes-Hassell, 41–66. Westport, CT: Libraries Unlimited, 2003.

Stripling, B. "Inquiry-Based Learning." In *Curriculum Connections through the Library*, edited by B. K Stripling and S. Hughes-Hassell, 3–39. Westport, CT: Libraries Unlimited, 2003.

Stripling, B. "Inquiry: Inquiring Minds Want to Know." *School Library Monthly* 25, no. 1 (September 2008): 50–52.

Stripling, B. "Dispositions: Getting Beyond 'Whatever'." *School Library Media Activities Monthly* 25, no. 2 (October 2008): 47–50.

The New York City School Library System. "The Empire State Information Fluency Continuum: Benchmark Skills for Grades K–12, Assessments, and Common Core Alignment." 2012. http://schools.nyc .gov/Academics/LibraryServices/StandardsandCurriculum/default.htm.

Stripling, B., and V. H. Harada. "Designing Learning Experiences for Deeper Understanding." *School Library Monthly* 29, no. 3 (December 2012): 5–12.

Donham, J. "Inquiry." In *Inquiry and the Common Core*, edited by V. H. Harada and S. Coatney, 4–15. Santa Barbara, CA: Libraries Unlimited, 2014.

Fontichiaro, K. "Evolution, Not Revolution: The Nudging Toward an Inquiry Approach." In *Inquiry and the Common Core*, edited by V. H. Harada and S. Coatney, 109–132. Santa Barbara, CA: Libraries Unlimited, 2014.

Stripling, B. "Inquiry in the Digital Age." In *Inquiry and the Common Core*, edited by V. H. Harada and S. Coatney, 93–105. Santa Barbara, CA: Libraries Unlimited, 2014.

1988: Students Need to Be Given Time to Think, Reflect, and Apply Guidance

Key Concepts

- We want students to think, but we allow them almost no time to do so.
- Journals kept by students as they experience research provide a tangible communication channel if teachers and librarians read them and respond thoughtfully, providing more personalized service to all and not just the most assertive students. Students also tend to value journals as a task and time management device.
- Student research should begin with a presearch: the process helps them relate preliminary information to their prior knowledge of a topic. Then they can develop initial questions for a meaningful start or a plan for more in-depth searching.
- Note taking cannot be taught in a single session. It should be practiced as often as possible and in as many note-taking styles as are relevant every time the student is engaged in some level of research.
- The librarian has an important role at the information interpretation stage, one in which many librarians fail to engage, believing their job is over at location of information.
- Students too often do not perceive adults as helpers in library research, including the librarian, who is frequently seen as being too busy to help.
- Our goal is to create independent, self-directed students.

Associated Literature in Chronological Order

Rankin, V. "One Route to Critical Thinking." *School Library Journal* 34, no. 5 (January 1988): 28–31.

Rankin, V. "Pre-Search: Intellectual Access to Information." *School Library Journal* 38, no. 3 (March 1992): 168–170.

Rankin, V. "A Wonderful Idea for the Library Resource Center: Piagetian Theories Applied to Library Research." *Emergency Librarian* 20, no, 2 (1992): 28–32.

Rankin, V. *The Thoughtful Researcher: Teaching the Research Process to Middle School Students.* Englewood, CO: Libraries Unlimited, 1999.

1988: A Collaborative, Integrated Curriculum Model Results in Effective Problem Solving

Key Concepts

- The big six model follows straightforward steps based on Bloom's classic learning taxonomy and essential items from Irving's nine-step model.
- The big six model follows a systematic approach to integrated library and information skills instruction that is based on six broad skill areas necessary for successful information problem solving.
- Curriculum mapping provides a means to establish information use skill across disciplines.
- The model's focus is on information need or problems and helping the student understand how to address the task through analysis and synthesis of relevant information.
- The model is a user-friendly approach that adapts for younger learners to "Plan, Do, and Review" and expands to meet skills for those in higher education as well. Students and teachers alike often recite the Big6 steps by heart.
- Open brainstorming is encouraged among students, teachers, and school librarians in order to identify a wide range of possibilities, from solving problems to accessing a wide spectrum of resources, including digital and human ones.
- Instruction in library and information skills is a valuable and essential part of the school's education program. Emphasizing information processes and information skills instruction ensures the

viability of our field and the success of our students in the future. Our future is dependent upon having a broad view of information processing: it is not just a set of skills that we use in the library, but a way to live our lives. However, in implementing the integrated model effectively and gaining maximum benefits, both teachers and library media specialists face two problems: (1) how to select the best opportunities within the content curriculum scope and sequence with which to integrate; and (2) how to design instructional units that motivate students to learn and use information problem-solving skills effectively.

- Essential library and information skills encompass more than just location of and access to sources. The skills curriculum should emphasize general information problem solving and research processes. The value of an integrated approach to library and information skills instruction is undeniable. It promotes cooperative planning between teachers and library media specialists and commitment to joint goals and objectives. It is through the integrated instructional model that the content curriculum and library and information problem-solving skills are linked to provide meaningful information skills instruction.
- The Big6 provides a useful framework for students and teachers to visualize the scaffold or steps in information problem solving.
- Library and information skills should not be taught in isolation. The skills program must be fully integrated with the school's curriculum.
- Emphasis is placed on integrating computer literacy to enhance the possibilities for problem exploration and solution presentation, resulting in information literate students. The focus is on learning *with* technology, not just *about* technology.

Associated Literature in Chronological Order

Eisenberg, M. B., and R. E. Berkowitz. *Curriculum Initiative.* Norwood, NJ: Ablex, 1988.

Eisenberg, M. B., and R. B. Berkowitz. *Information Problem-Solving: The Big Six Skills Approach to Library and Information Skills Instruction.* Norwood, NJ: Ablex, 1990.

Eisenberg, M. B., and M. K. Brown. "Current Themes Regarding Library and Information Skills Instruction: Research Supporting and Research Lacking." *School Library Media Quarterly* 20, no. 2 (Winter 1992). http://archive.ala.org/aasl/SLMR/slmr_resources/slect_eisenberg.html.

Berkowitz, R. E. "From Indicators of Quantity to Measures of Effectiveness." In *Assessment and the School Library Media Center,* edited by C. C. Kuhlthau, 33–41. Englewood, CO: Libraries Unlimited, 1994.

Berkowitz, Robert E., et al. "Collaboration: Partnerships for Instructional Improvement." *School Library Media Activities Monthly* 10, no. 7 (March 1994): 32–35.

Dalbotten, M. S. "Inquiry in the National Content Standards." In *Instructional Interventions for Information Use,* edited by D. Callison, J. H. McGregor, and R. V. Small, 30–82. San Jose, CA: Hi Willow, 1998.

Eisenberg, M. B., and C. A. Lowe. "Keynote: The Big 6 Skills; Looking at the World through Information Problem-solving Glasses." In *Instructional Interventions for Information Use,* edited by D. Callison, J. H. McGregor, and R. V. Small, 23–28. San Jose, CA: Hi Willow, 1998.

Spizer, K. L., M. B. Eisenberg, and C. A. Lowe. *Information Literacy: Essential Skills for the Information Age.* Syracuse, NY: ERIC Clearinghouse on Information & Technology, 1998.

Eisenberg, M. B., R. E. Berkowitz, and B. A. Jansen. *Teaching Information and Technology Skills.* Worthington, OH: Linworth, 1999.

Grover, R., C. Fix, and J. M. Lakin. *The Handy Five: Planning and Assessing Integrated Information Skills Instruction.* Lanham, MD: Scarecrow, 2001.

Wolf, S., T. Brush, and J. Saye. "The Big Six Information Skills as a Metacognitive Scaffold." *School Library Media Research* 6 (2003). http://www.ala.org/aasl/aaslpubsandjournals/slmrb/slmrcontents/volume62003/bigsixinformation.

Eisenberg, M. B., D. Johnson, and R. B. Berkowitz. "Information, Communications, and Technology (ICT) Skills Curriculum Based on the Big6 Skills Approach to Information Problem-Solving." *Library Media Connection* (May/June 2010): 24–27.

1989: Information Literacy Is Multidisciplinary Academic Content for the Information Age

Key Concepts

- This approach affirms the fundamental definition of information literacy—the ability to recognize the need for information; formulate questions based on that need; and access, evaluate, and use information from a variety of sources—a new way of thinking for the information age in social, popular, and academic environments.
- In the last decade a variety of literacies have been proposed, including cultural, computer, scientific, technical, global, and mathematical. All of these literacies focus on a compartmentalized aspect of literacy. Information literacy is, in contrast, an inclusive term. Through information literacy, the other literacies can be achieved.
- The information literate person recognizes that accurate and complete information is the basis for intelligent decision making.
- The information literate person will integrate new information into an existing body of knowledge.
- The information literate person will use information in critical thinking and problem solving.

Associated Literature in Chronological Order

Breivik, P. S., and E. G. Gee. *Information Literacy.* New York: American Council on Education and Macmillan, 1989.

Doyle, C. S. *Outcomes Measures for Information Literacy within the National Education Goals of 1990.* ERIC Document ED351033. Washington, DC: ERIC, 1992.

Doyle, C. S. *Information Literacy in an Information Society: A Concept for the Information Age.* ERIC ED372763. Washington, DC: ERIC, 1994.

Bruce, C. *The Seven Faces of Information Literacy.* Adelaide, Australia: Auslib Press, 1997.

Breivik, P. S., and J. A. Senn. *Information Literacy: Educating Children for the 21st Century.* Washington, DC: National Education Association, 1998.

1993: Scientific Inquiry Has a Strong Relationship to the Elements of Information Literacy

Key Concepts

- Scientific inquiry reflects how scientists come to understand the natural world, and it is at the heart of how students learn.
- Students learn how to ask questions and use evidence to answer them. In the process of learning the strategies of scientific inquiry, students learn how to conduct an investigation and collect evidence from a variety of sources, develop an explanation from the data, and communicate and defend their conclusions.
- Teachers should implement approaches to teaching science that cause students to question and explore and to use those experiences to raise and answer questions about the natural world. The learning cycle approach is one of many effective strategies for bringing explorations and questioning into the classroom. Librarians can enhance this through resource support of science papers and fairs.
- There is no fixed sequence of steps that all scientific investigations follow. Different kinds of questions suggest different kinds of scientific investigations. Different sources may have more or less value in various situations, and students should make informed judgments in selecting the best documentation.

Associated Literature in Chronological Order

American Association for the Advancement of Science. *Benchmarks for Science Literacy.* Oxford: Oxford University Press, 1993.

National Research Council. *National Science Education Standards.* Washington, DC: National Academy, 1996.

National Research Council. *Inquiry and the National Science Education Standards.* Washington, DC: National Academy, 2000.

Reiff, R., W. S. Harwood, and T. Phillipson. "A Scientific Method Based upon Research Scientists' Conceptions of Scientific Inquiry." In *Proceedings of the 2002 Annual International Conference of the Association for the Education of Teachers of Science.* ERIC ED 465 602. Washington, DC: ERIC, 2002.

Callison, D. "The Student Information Scientist." *School Library Monthly* 22, no. 2 (October 2005): 39–44.

Abrams, E., and S. Southerland, eds. *Inquiry in the Classroom: Realities and Opportunities.* Charlotte, NC: Information Age, 2007.

Dow, M. J. "School Librarians and Science Fair Competition." *School Library Monthly* 28, no. 2 (November 2011): 17–20.

Grant, M. C., D. Fisher, and D. Lapp. *Teaching Students to Think Like Scientists.* Bloomington, IN: Solution Tree, 2014.

1994: Librarians Must Take on a New Role as Specialists of Literacy, Inquiry, and Learning

Key Concepts

- Teachers and teacher-librarians should move toward an instructional model in which they act more as coaches and facilitate students who become more and more self-directed.
- Teachers and teacher-librarians monitor and provide feedback as students apply criteria for evaluating and selecting or rejecting information using practice data in cooperative learning settings.
- Students should establish skills that lead to independent organization and synthesis of information.

Associated Literature in Chronological Order

Brock, K. T. "Developing Information Literacy through the Information Intermediary Process: A Model for Teacher-Librarians and Others." *Emergency Librarian* 22, no. 1 (September–October 1994): 21–25.

Callison, D. "Expanding the Evaluation Role in the Critical-Thinking Curriculum." In *Assessment and the School Library Media Center*, edited by C. C. Kuhlthau, 43–57. Englewood, CO: Libraries Unlimited, 1994.

Callison, D. "Information Inquiry." *School Library Media Activities Monthly* 18, no. 10 (June 2002): 35–39.

Zmuda, A., and V. H. Harada. *Librarians as Learning Specialists.* Westport, CT: Libraries Unlimited, 2008.

1995: Pathways to Knowledge Based on Multimedia and Appreciation of Literature

Key Concepts

- Inquiry activities are most productive in learning environments where there is strong appreciation for literature, the arts, and the use of information from a variety of formats, including multimedia, to spark the imagination.
- Information literacy models should reflect technology, media, and visual literacies as well.

- A presearch of the literature is helpful before defining final information needs and will likely include information sources beyond the library that come in a wide variety of formats.
- Information requires interpretation in order to become knowledge, and mature inquirers reflect deeply on the information gathered before constructing a final meaning.
- Presentation formats should match the audience and knowledge acquired in order to be most effective.
- Peer evaluation has value along with personal, parent, SLMS, and teacher evaluations.
- Evaluation of both the process and product are important.

Associated Literature in Chronological Order

Pappas, M. L., and A. E. Tepe. *The Follett Information Skills Model and Teaching Electronic Information Skills.* McHenry, IL: Follett Software Company, 1995.

Pappas, M. L., and A. E. Tepe. "Media, Visual, Technology and Information: A Comparison of Literacies." In *Instructional Intervention for Information Use,* edited by D. Callison, J. H. McGregor, and R. V. Small, 97–109. San Jose, CA: Hi Willow, 1998.

Pappas, M. L. "Managing the Inquiry Learning Environment." *School Library Monthly* 16, no. 7 (March 2000): 27–30, 36.

Pappas, M. L. and A. E. Tepe. *Pathways to Knowledge and Inquiry Learning.* Greenwood Village, CO: Libraries Unlimited, 2002.

Pappas, M. L. "Inquiry and 21st Century Learning." *School Library Monthly* 25, no. 9 (May 2009): 49–51.

Pappas, M. L. "Reflection as Self-Assessment." *School Library Monthly* 27, no. 3 (December 2010): 5–8.

1995: Students Learn Inquiry through an Authoring Cycle, Discourse, and Self-Reflection

Key Concepts

- Curriculum is not something teachers do to children, but rather it involves opportunities for learning built by teachers and students together.
- All children bring the language of their experiences and should be encouraged to recontextualize what they bring to the learning situation in order to make connections with others (voice for learning).
- Differences, not consensus, propel the learning process (tension in learning). Learners have nothing to learn by concentrating on what they already know. Focusing on the new, the anomaly, the surprise is more efficient. When the surprise makes sense, learning has occurred.
- Teacher collaboration through participation in inquiry groups serves to create opportunities for discovery: to encourage it, record it, and value it.
- Inquiry curriculum is problem posing and problem solving that is not limited by textbook content.
- Maturation in critical literacy leads to constructive levels of civic participation.
- Authoring is a metaphor and a method for the learner to gain personal and social understanding through inquiry.
- Electronic portfolios are effective tools for student self-reflection and documentation of maturation in the inquiry processes, including use of multimedia technologies for presentations.

Associated Literature in Chronological Order

Burke, C., J. Harste, and K. Short. *Creating Classrooms for Authors and Inquirers.* Portsmouth, NH: Heinemann, 1995.

Short, K. *Learning Together through Inquiry.* York, Maine: Stenhouse, 1996.

Beach, R., G. Campano, B. Edmiston, and M. Borgmann. *Literacy Tools in the Classroom: Teaching through Critical Inquiry.* New York: Teachers College Press, 2010.

1996: Historical Inquiry Moves the Student and Teacher into Primary Resources

Key Concepts

- Historical inquiry proceeds with the formulation of a problem or set of questions worth pursuing.
- Students should obtain historical data from a variety of sources, including library and museum collections, historic sites, historical photos, journals, diaries, eyewitness accounts, newspapers, documentary films, oral testimony, and other primary resources. A growing number of historical documents are available to students and teachers through the Internet and provide an unprecedented pool for extensive inquiry.
- Students learn to corroborate sources through triangulation of primary documents, secondary documents, and expert opinion, a growing amount of which is available through the Internet and social media.
- Historical inquiry shifts from a story well told in a textbook to an emphasis on sources well scrutinized from history and mass media.
- Investigative strategies include a continuous cycle through five phases: summarizing, contextualizing, inferring, monitoring, and corroborating.
- History is a way of organizing and explaining the past. One cannot come to know history by merely learning overviews.
- At advanced levels, students should be able to interrogate historical information by uncovering the social, political, and economic context in which it was created; testing the information source for its credibility, authority, authenticity, internal consistency, and completeness; and detecting and evaluating for bias, distortion, and propaganda.

Associated Literature in Chronological Order

Ankeney, K., ed. *Bring History Alive.* Los Angeles: National Center for History in the Schools, 1996.

Levstik, L. "Negotiating the History Landscape." *Social Education* 24 (1996): 393–397.

National Center for History in the Schools. "National Standards for History." UCLA, 1996. http://www.nchs.ucla.edu/history-standards.

Levstik, L., and K. Barton. *Doing History: Investigating with Children in Elementary and Middle Schools.* Mahwah, NJ: Erlbaum, 2001.

Wineburg, S. *Historical Thinking and Other Unnatural Acts.* Philadelphia: Temple University, 2001.

Anderson-Inmann, L., and P. Kessinger. "Promoting Historical Inquiry: GATHER Model." 2002. http://anza.uoregon.edu/TeachersWWW/GATHER_Intro.html.

Doolittle, P. E., and D. Hicks. "Constructivism as a Theoretical Foundation for the Use of Technology in Social Studies." *Theory and Research in Social Education* 31, no. 1 (2003): 72–104.

Bolick, C. "Digital Libraries: The Catalyst to Transform Teacher Education." *AACE Journal* 12, no. 2 (2004): 213–233.

Coatney, S., and R. Smalley. "Inquiry and Living History" [Parts I–III]. *School Library Monthly* 22, no. 4 (December 2005): 24–27; 22, no. 5 (January 2006): 28–31; 22, no. 9 (May 2006): 25–28.

Pappas, M. L. "Primary Sources and Inquiry Learning." *School Library Monthly* 27, no. 1 (September 2006): 23–26.

"Shape of the Australian Curriculum: History." May 2009. http://www.acara.edu.au/verve/_resources/Australian_Curriculum_-_History.pdf#search=inquiry.

Wineburg, S., and D. Martin. *Reading Like a Historian.* New York: Teachers College Press, 2012.

Lamb, A. "Primary Source Digital Documents: CCSS and Complexity of Text." *School Library Monthly* 30, no. 4 (January 2014): 5–8.

Monte-Sano, C., S. De La Paz, M. Felton. *Reading, Thinking, and Writing About History.* New York: Teachers College Press, 2014.

National Center for History in the Schools. http://www.nchs.ucla.edu/.

Historical Inquiry. http://www.historicalinquiry.com/.

1996: Levels of Higher Engagement Lead to Successful Inquiry and Technology Programs

Key Concepts

- Information literacy can be represented as a cycle of inquiry skills centered on student learning and responsibilities.
- To capitalize on the thoughtful use of resources and technology, students should be taught how to allocate time to different stages of the research process.
- Students need content knowledge before they can develop search terminology.
- Young people do not seem to develop sophisticated searching skills intuitively and often require a human interface, experienced in searching, to achieve success.
- The student is at the center of inquiry, and more emphasis should be given to students investing time in reading, thinking about, assimilating, and "consuming" the information they find.
- Various media attributes (sound, motion, color, audio, graphical representations) can and do accelerate learning and engage interest.
- Thinking can be enhanced by the use of concept maps of various kinds as learners encounter important ideas, and as they compare, contrast, judge, and test information found across sources.
- Students and teachers learn from reflection on inquiry projects and improve their performance on future projects because of critical self-assessment.
- Creative inquiry lessons move students away form fact-gathering worksheets and into projects that demand deep thinking and multiple resources.
- Learning facilities for school library media programs need to adapt to high tech concepts that include 24/7 services and wider access to materials in digital format.
- Students are tech natives ready to explore and learn in virtual environments that bring shared learning together.

Associated Literature in Chronological Order

Loertscher, D. V. "All That Glitters May Not Be Gold." *Emergency Librarian* 24, no. 2 (November–December 1996): 23–25.

Woolls, B. "Assessment Methods: On beyond Craver." In *Instructional Interventions for Information Use*, edited by D. Callison, J. H. McGregor, and R. V. Small. 256–286. San Jose, CA: Hi Willow Research, 1998.

Loertscher, D. V. *Taxonomies of the School Library Media Program.* 2nd ed. San Jose, CA: Hi Willow Research and Publishing, 2000.

Loertscher, D. V., and B. Woolls. *Information Literacy: A Review of the Research and a Guide for Practitioners and Researchers.* 2nd ed. San Jose, CA: Hi Willow Research, 2002.

Loertscher, D. V., C. Koechin, and S. Zwaan. *Beyond Bird Units: Models for Teaching and Learning in Information-rich and Technology-rich Environments.* San Jose, CA: Hi Willow Research and Publishing, 2007.

Loertscher, D. V., C. Koechin, and S. Zwaan. *The Big Think.* San Jose, CA: Hi Willow Research and Publishing, 2009.

Loertscher, D. V., C. Koechlin, and S. Zwaan. *The New Learning Commons: Reinventing School Libraries and Computer Labs.* San Jose, CA: Hi Willow Research and Publishing, 2011.

Woolls, B., and D. V. Loertscher. *The Whole School Library Handbook 2.* San Jose, CA: Hi Willow Research and Publishing, 2013.

1997: Students Can Think Globally in Order to Apply Inquiry to Local Needs

Key Concepts

- Students enhance their differences through expansion of their awareness of local and global issues.

- Students organize ideas and information as they cluster resources to connect ideas and their interests.
- Students formulate plans to address problems with solutions documented by their own analysis and synthesis of information.
- The final presentation of solutions includes authoritative audiences who are in positions to take action.

Associated Literature in Chronological Order

Lamb, A., L. Johnson, and N. Smith. "Surfin' the Web: Project Ideas from A to Z." *Learning and Leading with Technology* 24, no. 7 (1997): 6–13.
"Wondering, Wiggling, and Weaving: A New Model for Project- and Community-Based Learning on the Web." *Learning and Leading with Technology* 24, no. 7 (April 1997). http://eduscapes.com/instruction/articles/1997article.pdf.
Eduscapes. http://eduscapes.com/.

1997: Motivation Is Critical to the Success of Information Literacy and Technology Use

Key Concepts

- Effective library and information skills instruction programs not only help students acquire the skills they will need to solve their information problems, but also stimulate intellectual curiosity and encourage continued information seeking and exploration.
- Motivation includes strategies for arousing and sustaining curiosity; linking instruction to important learning needs and interests; supporting positive expectations; and providing reinforcement that is both extrinsic and intrinsic and appropriate to need, behavior, and maturity levels.
- Inquiry follows a continuum of learning experiences, from simply discovering a new idea or an answer to a question to following a complete inquiry process. Data can be gathered from student surveys and interviews to determine gaps in confidence as perceived by students individually and serve to guide school librarians in addressing those gaps to improve student performance in inquiry-based assignments.
- Technology, advanced planning, and creative intervention can all be important tools for strategic support of student learning, leading to success and greater confidence. Perceived student self-competence and school media specialist competence, especially in use of technology, can serve as strong motivational factors to engage students in meaningful inquiry.
- Students are a learning audience, and if they find learning to be enjoyable, the chances increase that they will be lifelong inquirers.

Associated Literature in Chronological Order

Small, R. V. "Motivational Aspects of Library and Information Skills Instruction." In *Instructional Intervention for Information Use*, edited by D. Callison, J. H. McGregor, and R. V. Small, 220–231. San Jose, CA: Hi Willow, 1998.
Small, R. V., and M. P. Arnone. *Turning Kids on to Research: The Power of Motivation.* Englewood, CO: Libraries Unlimited, 2000.
Small, R. V. *Designing Digital Literacy Programs with ImPact: Motivation, Purpose, Audience, Content, and Technique.* New York: Neal-Schuman, 2004.
Arnone, M. P., R. Reynolds, and T. Marshall. "The Effect of Early Adolescents' Psychological Needs Satisfaction upon Their Perceived Competence in Information Skills and Intrinsic Motivation for Research." *School Libraries Worldwide* 15, no. 2 (2009): 115–134.

Arnone, M. P., R. V. Small, and R. Reynolds. "Supporting Inquiry by Identifying Gaps in Student Confidence: Development of a Measure of Perceived Competence." *School Libraries Worldwide* 16, no. 1 (2010): 47–60.

Small, R. V., M. P. Arnone, B. K. Stripling, and P. Berger. *Teaching for Inquiry: Engaging the Learner Within.* New York: Neal-Schumann, 2011.

S.O.S. for Information Literacy. http://www.informationliteracy.org/.

Teaching for Inquiry. http://www.teachingforinquiry.net/.

Center for Digital Literacy. http://digital-literacy.syr.edu/.

1997: Managing Knowledge through Many Levels of Questioning

Key Concepts

- Learning activities are based on continuous question development and refinement by students and teachers.
- Students are placed in the role of information consumers and strive to demonstrate increasing independence and good judgment in selecting information.
- Students repeatedly recycle through the stages of research to enhance experiences in the gathering, sorting, synthesizing, and evaluation of questions and information.
- Inquiry is more than word moving and topic construction; it is a persistent cycle of finding pertinent and reliable information.

Associated Literature in Chronological Order

McKenzie, J. "The Research Cycle Revisited." *FromNowOn* 7, no. 2. (October 1997). http://questioning .org/Q6/research.html.

McKenzie, J. *Beyond Technology: Questioning, Research, and the Information Literate School.* Bellingham, WA: FNO Press, 2000. http://www.fno.org/index.html.

McKenzie, J. *Learning to Question, to Wonder, to Learn.* Bellingham, WA: Amazon Digital Services, 2005.

From Now On. http://www.fno.org/index.html.

The Question Mark. http://questioning.org.

1997: Inquiry Helps Address Language and Literacy Differences for School Improvement

Key Concepts

- The increasing diversity of our population demands that we acknowledge sources of information in all languages and recognize that students can and must be information literate in the language in which they communicate.
- Information literacy is inherent in a thinking, meaning-centered curriculum for all students.
- The curricular planning team that collaborates to guide students toward information literacy includes classroom teachers, library media specialists, bilingual/ESL specialists and aides, other specialists, and the students themselves.
- Students and teachers integrate information literacy skills into all areas of learning.
- Before constructing and assigning complex information literacy tasks to diverse learners, school librarians must unpack and teach different preskills to the entire range of learners.
- Teaching about information and technology is not enough. It is imperative to teach learners how to be responsible and ethical users of them. They need to be digital citizens.

- As coplanners in curriculum development and instructional design, educational librarians often teach classroom teachers information literacy skills and ways to impart that knowledge to students.
- As reflective practitioners, educational librarians are increasingly assessing the impact of the educational library program on student success and school-wide improvement.
- The educational community also needs to realize that learning *about* technology differs from learning *with* technology: the former views technology as an end in itself, while the latter views technology as a means.

Associated Literature in Chronological Order

California School Library Association. *From Library Skills to Information Literacy: A Handbook for the 21st Century.* San Jose, CA: Hi Willow, 1997.

Farmer, L. S. J. "Learner-Centered Assessment of Information Literacy." In *Educational Media and Technology Yearbook*, edited by M. Orey, V. J. McClendon, and R. M. Branch, 2. Westport, CT: Libraries Unlimited, 2007.

Farmer, L. S. J. and J. Henri. Information Literacy Assessment in K-12 Settings. Lanham, MD: Scarecrow, 2008.

Farmer, L., and A. M. Safer. "Developing California School Library Media Program Standards." *School Library Research* 13 (2010). http://www.ala.org/aasl/sites/ala.org.aasl/files/content/aaslpubsandjourn als/slr/vol13/SLR_DevelopingCalifornia_V13.pdf.

California State Board of Education. *Model School Library Standards for California Public Schools.* Sacramento: California Department of Education, 2011.

Farmer, L. S. J. *Instructional Design for Librarians and Information Professionals.* New York: Neal-Schuman, 2011.

Farmer, L. S. J. "Digital Citizenship Instruction in K–20 Education." In *Teaching and Learning in K–20 Education*, edited by V. C. X. Wang, 281–299. Hershey, PA: Information Science Reference, 2013.

Farmer, L. S. J. "K–20 Education in Relation to Library Science." In *Teaching and Learning in K–20 Education*, edited by V. C. X. Wang, 377–398. Hershey, PA: Information Science Reference, 2013.

1998: Statewide Resource- and Instruction-Sharing Programs to Advance Literacy

Key Concepts

- These programs transform teaching and learning by connecting educational resources with the power of information technology.
- These programs provide equitable access to quality resources across all schools in the state.
- DIALOGUE helps students gain a global perspective and deep comprehension.
- Students organize and synthesize information to show reasoning abilities.
- Inquiry and knowledge-building processes are demonstrated across the state to encourage participation by teachers, administrators, and parents.

Associated Literature in Chronological Order

Byerly, G., and C. S. Brodie. "INFOhio DIALOGUE Model for Information Literacy Skills." Ohio's PreK–12 Digital Library, 1998. http://learningcommons.infohio.org/index.php?option=com_content &view=article&id=298&Itemid=3.

Brodie, C. S., and G. Byerly. "Information Literacy Skills Models." In *Learning and Libraries in an Information Age: Principles and Practices*, edited by B. Stripling, 54–82. Englewood, CO: Libraries Unlimited, 1999.

INFOhio: Ohio's PreK–12 Digital Library. http://www.infohio.org/.

1998: Inquiry Can Build Local Communities of Learning

Key Concepts

- Educators from various levels can work together to create opportunities to engage students in active learning based on the students' questions.
- Good questions create an endless cycle of more questions, often resulting in community action.
- Active learning is hands on, tangible, and local, but tied to global thinking.
- Inquiry units and lesson plans are shared as models, mostly over the Internet, to trigger more activities among schools.
- The best education constantly reconstructs experience, relating it to both the past and contemporary life.
- Authentic contexts require that teachers, students, and community members become partners in inquiry, including inquiry into the world and inquiry into pedagogy.
- Inquiry-based learning is sometimes described as a philosophical and pedagogical response to the changing needs of the information age, but its roots are much deeper. It assumes that all learning begins with the learner. That is, what people know and what they want to learn are not just constraints on what can be taught; they are the very foundation for learning.
- Inquiry learning is not a method or an option to consider for teaching and learning; instead, it is what happens when people *do* learn.

Associated Literature in Chronological Order

Bruce, B. C. "The Inquiry Page." 1998. http://www.inquiry.uiuc.edu.

Bruce, B. C., and A. P. Bishop. "Using the Web to Support Inquiry-based Literacy Development." *Journal of Adolescent and Adult Literacy* 45, no. 8 (2002): 706–714.

Bruce, B. C., and A. P. Bishop. "New Literacies and Community Inquiry." In *Handbook of Research on New Literacies*, edited by J. Coiro et al., 699–744. New York: Lawrence Erlbaum, 2008.

1998: Analysis Skills Must Dominate Student Use of the Internet

Key Concepts

- Critical information use is focused on the Internet nearly exclusively through the five A process: asking, accessing, analyzing, applying, and assessing data.
- The learner becomes information savvy or fluent through continued practice, review, and assessment across various information technology platforms.
- Searchers should consider all authoritative sites that provide an alternative point of view.
- Students are digital natives mismatched with traditional information curriculum.

Associated Literature in Chronological Order

Jukes, I., A. Dosaj, and B. Mcdonald. *Net.Savvy: Building Information Literacy in the Classroom*. Thousand Oaks, CA: Corwin Press, 1998.

Jukes, I., T. McCain, L. Crockett, and M. Prensky. *Understanding the Digital Generation*. Thousand Oaks, CA: Corwin, 2010.

2001: Inquiry Includes Observing, Interviewing, Experimenting, and Sharing

Key Concepts

- Inquiry is not a method of doing science, history, or any other subject, in which the obligatory first stage is a fixed, linear sequence of students each formulating questions to investigate. Rather, it is an approach to the chosen themes and topics in which the posing of real questions is positively encouraged, whenever they occur and whoever asks them.
- All questions and tentative answers are taken seriously and are investigated rigorously as the circumstances permit.
- Inquiry study develops habits of mind that encourage learners to ask questions of evidence, viewpoint, supposition, and why such investigation matters.
- Technology is used in a purposeful manner that demonstrates an appreciation of new ways of thinking and doing; digital resources are essential to the project's success.
- Students gather information through fieldwork, observations, and interviews.
- Students observe and interact with adults who have relevant expertise.
- Students have extended opportunities to support, challenge, and respond to each other's ideas as they negotiate a collective understanding of relevant concepts.

Associated Literature in Chronological Order

Wells, G. *Action, Talk, and Text: Learning and Teaching through Inquiry.* New York: Teachers College Press, 2001.

Jardine, D. W., P. Clifford, and S. Friesen. *Back to the Basics of Teaching and Learning: Thinking the World Together.* Mahwah, NJ: Routledge, 2008.

Clifford, P., and S. J. Marinucci. "Voices Inside the Schools: Three Elements of Classroom Inquiry." *Harvard Educational Review* 78, no. 4 (2009): 675–688.

The Galileo Educational Network. http://galileo.org/.

2002: Peer Collaboration and Ethics Are Powerful in Application of Information Literacy

Key Concepts

- Students and faculty enrich their research and writing skills through a Web-based, individualized platform of integrated tools for note-taking, outlining, citation, and collaboration.
- Researchers should learn and practice proper and ethical citation etiquette, which in turn will illustrate the depth of their content knowledge understanding.
- Information literacy is a transformational process that takes practice, time, and refinement throughout an academic career; patience, honesty, and fairness are each more important than speed.
- Paraphrasing and referencing are powerful techniques to tie research findings together.
- Students learn and teach through interactive peer review.
- Information, regardless of format, can be tested by students for validity, authority, and level of acceptance in the broader academic environment.
- Promotion of meaningful inquiry and information literacy comes through professional development coordinated by professional school library media specialists.
- Through the creation of infographics, students can demonstrate visual, open-minded inquiry, especially through argument-based or persuasive, and experience editing skills for the best effects.

Associated Literature in Chronological Order

Abilock, D. "Ten Attributes of Collaborative Leaders." *Knowledge Quest* 31, no.2 (November/December 2002): 8–10.

[Abilock, D., and D. Abilock]. "NoodleTools: Smart Tools, Smart Research." [2002]. http://www.noodle tools.com/index.php.

Abilock, D. "Choosing Assessments That Matter." *Knowledge Quest* 35, no. 5 (May/June 2007): 8–12.

Abilock, D. "Visual Information Literacy: Reading a Documentary Photograph." *Knowledge Quest* 36, no. 3 (January/February 2008): 7–13.

Abilock, D. "Inquiry Evaluation." *Knowledge Quest* 38, no. 3 (January/February 2010): 34–45.

Abilock, D. "Building Blocks of Research: Overview of Design, Process and Outcomes" (n.d., accessed April 17, 2015). http://www.noodletools.com/debbie/literacies/information/1over/infolit1.html.

Abilock, D. "How Can Students Know Whether the Information They Find Online Is True—or Not?" *Educational Leadership* 69, no. 6 (2012): 70–74. http://www.noodletools.com/debbie/consult/articles/true_or_not.pdf.

Abilock, D., K. Fontichiaro, and V. H. Harada. *Growing Schools: Librarians as Professional Developers.* Santa Barbara, CA: Libraries Unlimited, 2012.

Abilock, D., and C. Williams. "Recipe for an Infographic." *Knowledge Quest* 43, no. 2 (November/December 2014): 46–55.

"Information Literacy: What Is Information Literacy?" Updated January 24, 2015. http://www.noodle tools.com/debbie/literacies/information/1over/infolit1.html.

2003: Online Information Searching by Young People Involves Complex Attitudes

Key Concepts

- Information literacy, research, and scientific inquiry are effectively underpinned by common axioms, and the teaching of these general principles can facilitate the development of skills and understanding in relation to all three areas.

- The model demonstrates the importance of the information professional's educative role, in terms of both delivering formal information literacy instruction and providing assistance at the point of need.

- It is inadequate to investigate young people's information needs purely in terms of the subjects of the desired information and the purposes for which the material is required. There is an increasing realization that an array of other factors must also be considered: the extent to which they can define the totality of their need before seeking information, the degree to which the overall topic changes during the information-seeking process, the precision of the subject on which information is desired, whether highly up-to-date information is necessary, and more.

- Information skills models that take a linear rather than dynamic perspective often imply that sources are investigated once the need has been determined, but in real life, situations frequently emerge in which knowledge from sources triggers an information need.

Associated Literature in Chronological Order

Shenton, A. K., and P. Dixon. "Models of Young People's Information Seeking." *Journal of Librarianship & Information Science* 35, no. 1 (March 2003): 5–22.

Shenton, A. K. and P. Dixon. "Information Needs: Learning More about What Kids Want, Need, and Expect from Research." *Children & Libraries: The Journal of the Association for Library Service to Children* 3, no. 2 (Summer/Fall 2005): 20–28.

Shenton, A. K. "The Paradoxical World of Young People's Information Behavior." *School Libraries Worldwide* 13, no. 2 (July 2007): 1–17.

Shenton, A. K. "Information Literacy and Scholarly Investigation: A British Perspective." *IFLA Journal* 35, no. 3 (2009): 226–231.

Shenton, A. K. "Modelling the Information-Seeking Behavior of Children and Young People." *Aslib Proceedings* 63, no. 1 (2011): 57–75.

Shenton, A. K. "Towards an Integrated Approach to Information Literacy Instruction in Schools." *Feliciter* 57, no. 1 (2011): 21–23.

2003: Project-Based Learning Creates Opportunities for Teaching Teams and Student Assessment

Key Concepts

- Project-based learning inspires proactive learning. Classroom activities shift away from isolated, short, teacher-centered lessons to emphasize lessons that are long term, interdisciplinary, student-centered, and integrated with real-world issues and practices.

- Move beyond questions of who, what, and where, to questions of why and what if.

- For an instructional plan to work, it must effectively engage students as proactive players in the learning process. However, a significant number of students (especially at the secondary level) appear to be reluctant learners.

- School library media specialists are educational partners who participate in the assessment of student performance through conferences, presentations, evidence folders, and portfolios.

- Students measure current work (both their own and that of their peers) based on a set of established criteria and articulate adjustments that would improve the quality of their work.

- Students routinely explain both to one another and to staff how they arrived at a conclusion and are curious about the process as a result.

- Project-based learning should capitalize on concerns and skills valued in the community.

- Student assessments should include reflections on their dispositions to learning: initiative, adaptability, resilience, openness, social responsibility, and collaboration.

Associated Literature in Chronological Order

Harada, V. H. "Empowered Learning." In *Curriculum Connections through the Library*, edited by B. Stripling and S. Hughs-Hassell, 41–64. Westport, CT: Libraries Unlimited, 2003.

Harada, V. H., and J. M. Yoshina. *Inquiry Learning through Librarian-Teacher Partnerships*. Worthington, OH: Linworth, 2004.

Harada, V. H. "Building Evidence Folders for Learning through Library Media Centers." *School Library Media Activities Monthly* 23, no. 3 (2006): 25–30.

Harada, V. H. "From Eyeballing to Evidence: Assessing for Learning in Hawaii School Libraries." *School Library Media Activities Monthly* 14, no. 3 (November 2006): 21–25.

Farmer, L. S. J., and J. Henri. *Information Literacy Assessment in K–12 Settings*. Lanham, MD: Scarecrow, 2008.

Zmuda, A., and V. H. Harada. *Librarians as Learning Specialists*. Libraries Unlimited, 2008.

K. Fontichiaro, K., ed. *21st Century Learning in School Libraries*. Libraries Unlimited, 2009.

Keeling, M. "A District's Journey to Inquiry." *Knowledge Quest* 38, no. 2 (November/December 2009): 32–37.

Harada, V. H. "Librarians as Learning Leaders: Cultivating Cultures of Inquiry." In *The Many Faces of School Library Leadership*, edited by S. Coatney, 13–28. Santa Barbara, CA: Libraries Unlimited, 2010.

Harada, V. H. "Self Assessment: Challenging Students to Take Charge of Learning." *School Library Monthly* 26, no. 10 (June 2010): 13–15.

Harada, V. H., and J. M. Yoshina. *Assessing for Learning: Librarians and Teachers as Partners*. Libraries Unlimited, 2010.

Harada, V. H., C. Kirio, S. Yamamoto, and E. Arellano. "Engaging Students through Project-Based Learning." *In Inquiry and the Common Core*, edited by V. Harada and S. Coatney, 84–92. Libraries Unlimited, 2014.

2003: Inquiry Can Provide a Framework for Meaningful Professional Development

Key Concepts

- Inquiry provides an effective way to differentiate instruction for every learner in the school district, adults and students alike. Four levels of inquiry defined by Callison provide a useful framework for application of inquiry.
- Creating a culture of collaboration unleashes learning potential and plays a vital role in Common Core implementation through inquiry.
- Effective Common Core implementation means abandoning a one-standard-at-a-time approach to teaching and instead looking for ways to seamlessly integrate multiple standards into a single rich task. Inquiry can help to make that goal a reality.

Associated Literature in Chronological Order

Callison, D. *Key Words, Concepts and Methods for Information Age Instruction: A Guide to Teaching Information Inquiry*. Baltimore, MD: LMS Associates, 2003.

Dana, N. F., C. Thomas, and S. Boynton. *Inquiry: A Districtwide Approach to Staff and Student Learning*. Thousand Oaks, CA: Corwin, 2011.

Abilock, D., K. Fontichiaro, and V. H. Harada. *Growing Schools: Librarians as Professional Developers*. Thousand Oaks, CA: Libraries Unlimited, 2012.

Dana, F. N., J. B. Burns, and R. Wolkenhauer. *Inquiring into the Common Core*. Corwin, 2013.

2003: A Primary Goal of Information Literacy Is Demonstration of What Students Learn

Key Concepts

- Information specialists must become expert not only in the content and scope of the information resources available, but also in their own personal pedagogical potential.
- The primary expectation is for students to use or apply information in order to demonstrate knowledge generated or gained.
- Important assessments concern documenting what the student knows because of the inquiry experience.
- Part of learning is to demonstrate credibility of sources used: How do you know what you know, and is your evidence to support such knowledge credible?
- Learning can be seen as factual, conceptual, procedural, and/or metacognitive.
- The contemporary understanding of learning is that it is the construction of personal meaning from the facts, concepts, rules, and procedures that comprise information.
- Information is the basic building block of learning: the "stuff" we access, evaluate, and use to make sense of our world.

Associated Literature in Chronological Order

Neuman, D. "Learning in an Information-Rich Environment." In *Measuring Student Achievement and Diversity in Learning*, edited by D. Callison, 39–51. San Jose, CA: Hi Willow, 2003.

Neuman, D. "The Library Media Center: Touchstone for Instructional Design and Technology in the Schools." In *Handbook of Research on Educational Communications and Technology*, edited by David H. Jonassen, 499–522. Mahwah, NJ: Lawrence Erlbaum Associates, 2004.

Neuman, D. "Constructing Knowledge in the Twenty-First Century: I-LEARN and Using Information as a Tool for Learning." *School Library Research* 14 (2011).

Neuman, D. *Learning in Information-Rich Environments.* New York: Springer, 2011.

http://www.ala.org/aasl/sites/ala.org.aasl/files/content/aaslpubsandjournals/slr/vol14/SLR _ConstructingKnowledge_V14.pdf.

2003: Reflection Is Important at Every Stage of the Information Literacy Inquiry Process

Key Concepts

- Reflection promotes establishing a culture of inquiry for students, teachers, and administrators, but carefully guided with strategic instructional interventions.
- Administrators in each school have a clearly articulated vision for inquiry.
- Inquiry is introduced in the form of authentic problems within the context of the curriculum and the community.
- Reflection or formative evaluation is expected at each inquiry stage, with time for full discussion.
- Students are expected to take ownership of learning through frequent interactions with teachers, but this is based on extensive support on the part of teachers and librarians in learning the inquiry-based processes.

Associated Literature in Chronological Order

Branch, J. L. "Inquiry-Based Learning: The Key to Student Success." *School Libraries in Canada* 22, no. 4 (2003): 6–12.

Branch, J. L. "Instructional Intervention Is the Key: Supporting Adolescent Information Seeking." *School Libraries Worldwide* 9, no. 2 (July 2003): 47–61.

Branch, J. L., and D. Oberg. "The British Models." *School Library Monthly* 19, no. 10 (June 2003): 17–19, 24.

Alberta Learning. *Focus on Inquiry: A Teacher's Guide to Implementing Inquiry-based Learning.* 2004.

http://www.teachingbooks.net/content/FocusOnInquiry.pdf.

2004: Information Literacy Is a Catalyst for Major Educational Change

- A national curriculum, such as that developed in Australia and New Zealand, can be framed around inquiry-based learning and skills for critical thinking.
- Information literacy is a natural extension of the concept of literacy in our information society, and information literacy education is the catalyst required to transform the information society of today into the learning society of tomorrow.
- There is a continuum across which inquiry progresses along with the maturation of the student. These stages include structured inquiry, guided inquiry, and open inquiry.

Associated Literature in Chronological Order

Bruce, C. "Information Literacy as a Catalyst for Educational Change." In *Proceedings—Lifelong Learning: Whose Responsibility and What Is Your Contribution?* The Third International Lifelong Learning Conference, Yeppoon, Queensland (2004): 8–19.

Lupton, M. J. *The Learning Connection: Information Literacy and the Student Experience.* Adelaide, Australia: Auslib Press, 2004.

Bruce, C., S. Edwards, and M. Lupton. "Six Frames for Information Literacy Education." *Innovation in Teaching and Learning in Information and Computer Sciences* 5, no. 1 (2006): 1–18.
Lupton, M. "Inquiry Pedagogy and the Australian Curriculum." *Primary and Middle Years Education* 11, no. 2 (2013): 23–29.
The Australian Curriculum. http://www.australiancurriculum.edu.au/.

2007: Traditional Inquiry Has Not Been Critical and Requires Greater Cultural Understanding

Key Concepts

- Traditional approaches to inquiry in the library media center have been problem based and process oriented, but have not necessarily been critical.
- Students need a substantial understanding of the literature and historical background of the social issue before framing initial questions.
- A critical perspective on inquiry (and literacy) presumes that knowledge is value-laden and that no information problem is neutral.
- The goal of critical inquiry is to help students develop creative ways to work toward social justice.
- Cultural inquiry is rooted in sociocultural notions of knowledge, which recognize learning as a communal act that is deeply intertwined with social, historical, and political forces.
- By itself, social constructivist theory does not fully help librarians understand how to tap into students' social and cultural environments as a place for them to develop personal meaning and tackle larger structural issues affecting their communities.

Associated Literature in Chronological Order

Kumasi-Johnson, K. "Critical Inquiry: Library Media Specialists as Change Agents." *School Library Monthly* 23, no. 9 (May 2007): 42–45.
Kumasi, K. "Cultural Inquiry: A Framework for Engaging Youth of Color in the Library." *Journal of Research on Libraries and Young Adults* 1 (November 2010). http://www.yalsa.ala.org/jrlya/2010/11/cultural-inquiry-a-frameworK–for-engaging-youth-of-color-in-the-library/.

Index

About the Author

Daniel Callison, EdD, is professor emeritus in school media and instructional systems technology and dean emeritus in continuing studies at Indiana University, Bloomington. He started his career as a history teacher and assistant debate coach. He managed a national demonstration library media center at Topeka High School in Kansas. Callison was founding editor of the first online refereed research journal in school media, *School Library [Media] Research*, under the sponsorship of AASL. His previous books include *The Blue Book on Information Age Inquiry, Instruction and Literacy* with Leslie Preddy and *Graphic Inquiry* with principal author Annette Lamb, PhD.

Upon Callison's retirement in 2008 from serving as *SLMR* founding editor, AASL released a statement, which read in part (Jones 2008):

> The peer-reviewed journal (*SLMR*) owes much of its success to the efforts and dedication of Daniel Callison. In 1997, AASL's research journal, *School Library Media Quarterly*, converted to digital format. The journal was later renamed *School Library Media Research* to better reflect the dynamic nature of its publication schedule. In 2004, *SLMR* was ranked 16th out of more than 70 journals in the library and information science field by the deans and directors of ALA-accredited MLS-degree programs in North America. *SLMR* was the top-ranked journal related to the school library media field and is the only online journal that ranked among the top twenty. Current *SLMR* co-editor Jean Donham said, "At the time Dr. Callison proposed going to an open-access online journal, there was some degree of skepticism in the scholarly world about the viability of online publication of scholarship. As a result of his vision, *SLMR* has been a leader among scholarly journals in this regard. Dr. Callison (2004) has set the standard for *SLMR* as a respected and rigorous peer-reviewed publication. As co-editor, I am committed to continuing his tradition."

Donham and coeditor Carol Tilley renamed the journal *School Library Research* and have taken it to new heights of respectability. Callison's publications were referenced multiple times in each edition of the national standards for school library programs issued by AASL from 1988 through 2009. The ALA Library Instruction Round Table (LIRT) has on three different occasions (Callison and Daniels 1988; Callison 1998, 1999) selected an article written by Callison as among the "Top Twenty" by scholars and practitioners of information literacy education. Callison's 1986 article introducing concepts of inquiry in *School Library Journal* was selected as one of the best articles published in *SLJ* (Gerhardt 1997). In 1995 LIRT gave the Silver Award to Callison on its fifteenth anniversary for his essay on expanding the evaluation role of the school librarian in the emerging critical thinking curriculum (Callison 1995).

Since retiring in 2012 from Indiana University, Callison has taught online graduate courses in school library media for Drexel University and Simmons College.

REFERENCES

Callison, D. 1986. "School Library Media Programs & Free Inquiry Learning." *School Library Journal* 32 (August): 20–24.

Callison, D. 1995. "Expanding the Evaluation Role in the Critical-Thinking Curriculum." In *Information for a New Age: Redefining the Librarian,* 153–169. Englewood, CO: Libraries Unlimited.

Callison, D. 1998. "Time on Task." *School Library Monthly* 14 (April): 32–34.

Callison, D. 1999. "Analysis: Evaluating Information." *School Library Monthly* 15 (April): 37–39.

Callison, D. 2004. "Establishing Research Rigor in *SLMR.*" *Knowledge Quest* 32, no. 5: 18–20.

Callison, D., and A. Daniels. 1988. "Introducing End-User Software for Enhancing Student Online Searching." *School Library Media Quarterly* 16 (Spring): 173–181.

Gerhardt, L. N., ed. 1997. *School Library Journal's Best.* New York: Neal-Schuman.

Jones, M. B. 2008. "AASL Honors the Retirement of SLMR Editor." http://www.ala.org/news/news/press releases2008/june2008/AASLcallison (accessed February 21, 2015).